The Politics of Human Rights
in Argentina

The Politics of
Human Rights
in Argentina

*Protest, Change, and
Democratization*

Alison Brysk

Stanford University Press
Stanford, California
1994

Stanford University Press
Stanford, California
© 1994 by the Board of Trustees of the
Leland Stanford Junior University
Printed in the United States of America

CIP data appear at the end of the book

Stanford University Press publications are
distributed exclusively by Stanford University Press
within the United States, Canada, and Mexico; they are
distributed exclusively by Cambridge University Press
throughout the rest of the world.

To my family—past, present, and future

Acknowledgments

I have received an extraordinary level of academic, financial, and personal support from a variety of sources. While I cannot possibly acknowledge the depth of my gratitude to the persons and institutions listed below, the reader should be aware that a large measure of whatever merits this study may have properly accrues to these sources. I alone bear full responsibility for any errors, problems, or misinterpretations.

Timely and generous financial support for various phases of this project was provided by Stanford University, the Mellon New Directions Fund, the Institute for the Study of World Politics, the Tinker Foundation, and the MacArthur Foundation. I would also like to thank Grant Barnes and Stanford University Press for their support and editorial skill.

While at Stanford, I benefited greatly from the guidance of my thesis committee: Professors Richard Fagen, Terry Karl, and David Abernethy. Richard Fagen, the chair of the dissertation committee, provided unfailing encouragement and wisdom. Terry Karl has been a source of inspiration, stimulation, and enlightenment for many years. Her patient and intensive efforts launched the project, and kept me going through the long haul. Colleagues at the University of New Mexico gave insight and support during the transition from dissertation to manuscript: Karen Remmer, Bill Stanley, and Miguel Korzeniewicz. Kathryn Sikkink and Martin Andersen provided close, helpful readings and shared their own expertise on the topic, as did Juan Mendez of Americas Watch.

From brainstorming the concept to proofing the bibliography, my husband Mark Freeman has played an essential academic as well as personal role. His keen and broad-ranging intellect, social concern, sharp editorial eye, creativity, and vision fundamentally and profoundly shaped this research. Another crucial academic contribution came from Allison Hyde, who worked generously and enthusiastically as a volunteer research assistant—both in Argentina and in the United States. Her efforts are reflected throughout the book, but especially in the Bibliography, notes, tables, and calculations. Dedicated and capable research assistance has also been provided by Erika Coventry of Pomona College.

While in Argentina, I was a Visiting Researcher at the Centro de Estudios del Estado y Sociedad (CEDES). Various scholars there provided helpful ideas and access to resources and interviews, especially Carlos Acuña, Mercedes Botto, and Marcelo Cavarozzi. I am grateful to CELS (Centro de Estudios Legales y Sociales) for the use of its extensive archives. Other researchers who assisted my efforts in Argentina include Samuel Amaral, Seth Maisel, Jorge Meyer, and the late Margaret Grammer.

My deepest debt is to the dozens of individuals I interviewed for this study. It is their insights and experiences that grant the project whatever power and authenticity it may possess. I would like to highlight my gratitude to the human rights organizations, which all contributed generously of their time, records, and sensibilities.

Finally, I am very grateful for the personal support of my friends and family. Mark Freeman must be singled out as a source of unstinting, unwavering assistance and encouragement. From footnotes to footrubs, his love, partnership, and wonderful cooking made my life possible and productive. His flexibility and resourcefulness in accompanying me to Argentina throughout the course of the fieldwork sustained me through a challenging experience. I would also like to thank my parents and grandparents for their emotional and financial support—and for their example.

In a profoundly appropriate way, my research has been nurtured by an extraordinary chain of women, the mothers of this project. Each entered my life and provided her special skills, resources, and support just when they were needed. They are my mother—Lucy Brysk, the late Mary Boyd, Terry Karl, Allison Hyde, Karen Remmer, Kathryn Sikkink, and my daughter, Miriam Brysk Freeman. Miri, who was created along with this book, taught me the kind of love that drives the struggle for human dignity.

A.B.

December 1992
Claremont, California

Contents

Tables and Figures

Tables

Figures

Preface

I wrote this book because I wanted to understand how powerless people could resist repression. I was drawn to Argentina by the drama and tragedy voiced by its human rights movement. I sought to transcribe and transmit a principled popular movement's triumph over adversity—but the drama unfolded differently. The more complicated and ambiguous story I found in Argentina led me to situate the movement's experience in the context of a larger politics of human rights: a set of relationships and struggles among the movement(s), state, society, and international system. This book has become an attempt to chronicle and interpret that larger experience in a way that can inform the struggles of the disempowered through triumph, adversity, and the many conditions in between.

My fieldwork in Argentina was conducted during July–August 1987 and throughout the 1988 calendar year. The initial fieldwork period immediately followed the adoption of the Obediencia Debida legislation limiting the trials of military officers accused of human rights violations. Most of the reforms in human rights policy had already been implemented by the time of my 1988 fieldwork. During 1988, I witnessed two military rebellions (the January 1988 Monte Caseros uprising and the December Villa Martelli rebellion), primaries, and campaigning for the first post-transition elections in 1989. I also attended dozens of human rights demonstrations, strikes, and political rallies, as well as a variety of conferences on military reform, the Church and democratization, the declaration of forced disappearance as a crime against humanity, educational reform and human rights, human rights and social rights, and FEDEFAM (international federation of families of the disappeared).

I did in-depth interviews with almost one hundred people: human rights movement activists, government officials, leaders of political parties, unions and other social organizations, academics, journalists, and military officers. Unless otherwise indicated, interviews were conducted in Buenos Aires and in Spanish (all translations are mine). I offered anonymity to everyone I interviewed, but none of the interviewees requested it. Some did ask that specific statements not be attributed to them by name. However, owing to political uncertainties in Argentina and the concerns of the Stanford University Human Subjects Committee (under whose auspices the research was conducted), I identify interviewees only if they are well-known public figures—and only when such identification contributes significantly to the value or interpretation of the statement cited. In all other cases, interview subjects are identified by relevant affiliation or position, and the date of the interview is provided.

My time in Argentina and the years of reflection, analysis, and comparison that have followed have taught me some important lessons about the politics of human rights and the process of social change. First, I was reminded that social movements are not made of heroes, and that a common experience of repression is not a sufficient basis for political identity. The Argentine human rights movement contains some incredibly brave, creative, intelligent, and dedicated people. But like anyone else, some activists can sometimes be petty, short-sighted, arrogant, or simply mistaken; I was initially surprised by the level of "politics as usual" within the movement and in its relationship with other forces. Furthermore, suffering does not necessarily ennoble or even mobilize—some victims do transform their pain into principled politics, but others become paralyzed, bitter, or even calculating in the face of overwhelming loss. This sad and sobering observation is unexpectedly empowering, because it shows that *ordinary* people can do extraordinary things. Social change does not require heroes; it requires some small group of limited human beings to behave courageously on some days—and simply to persist on others.

On a larger social level, I learned the many ways in which ideas matter. Tens of thousands of Argentines died because of ideas about populism, subversion, psychosexuality, and national identity. Hundreds of thousands of unarmed civilians confronted mutineers' tanks to defend ideas of democracy, the rule of law, and human dignity. Debates over fundamental policies reflected different readings of Argentine history, organic or pluralistic visions of political community, and different locations of moral accountability for violence. Politics is not a marketplace; struggles for identity, principle, and visions of power are the essence of the political process.

The central principle of this study—human rights—also assumed new meaning for me as a result of my research in Argentina. Argentina's descent was founded on a cynical, pragmatic devaluation of the cumbersome and absolutist guarantees of due process and civil liberties. When such guarantees protect despicable people and frustrate laudable social goals, we are often tempted to suspend or ignore them— in our own increasingly violent society, in new or weak nations struggling to transform themselves, in just or necessary wars. Argentina reminds us that dirty wars begin when we overlook small smudges on those who threaten us; not just "subversives," but also the terrorist, drug dealer, or counterrevolutionary. My criticisms of the Alfonsín administration were sometimes challenged on the argument of a pragmatic trade-off between absolute human rights ideals and the greater common good of democratic consolidation. It is precisely to preserve democracy that I hold the new democracy to its own highest claims. And I have come to believe that only this moral core of human rights can guide the process of democratization unfolding in so many troubled areas of the world.

Finally, this research renewed my appreciation of the importance of the state. The irony of higher levels of human rights abuse in more modern, developed societies is partially explained by the expansion of state power in those societies. But simply shrinking the state is no solution, since the state is also the ultimate guarantor of civil liberties. My time in Argentina was marked by a series of right-wing bombings, military mutinies, kidnappings, riots, and police abuses that required *more* state control, not less. To the extent that human rights movements like those in Argentina fall short of their goals, it is because they fail to capture and transform the state: military, police, judiciary, and Executive. Despite the historic role of citizen movements around the world in transitions to democracy, it is unlikely that they can bear this burden. We must search for other channels and strategies to institutionalize human rights. But we must also honor and preserve those who made the search possible.

The Politics of Human Rights
in Argentina

Introduction

Under Argentina's military dictatorship (1976–83), tens of thousands of people "disappeared"—abducted, tortured, and murdered by their own government.[1] Almost ten thousand more were held as political prisoners under extremely inhumane conditions—and they too were often tortured. Thousands of others were kidnapped and tortured but ultimately released. Pregnant women were detained and tortured until they gave birth; their children were then taken and illicitly adopted by friends and relatives of the torturers while the mothers were killed.

The only force that resisted this widespread state terror in a principled, consistent, and effective way was the human rights movement. This human rights movement brought together grieving families, civil libertarians, and concerned religious figures. The movement used a unique combination of public symbolic protest, information gathering, legal appeals, and international pressure to demand accountability from the state and to defend the victims of repression. After Argentina's 1984 transition to democracy, this social movement continued to work for accountability for past human rights violations through trials of former military officials. But under the democratic regime, activists have also asserted new claims, designed to institutionalize human rights safeguards and transform civil society. Their activities and demands have had broader, unforeseen consequences for democratization.

This study examines the achievements and limitations of this path-breaking social movement. In order to do so, it addresses the following questions: Why was a group of ordinary citizens able to resist and challenge an authoritarian state? How could activists drawn from and operating outside of mainstream political institutions reshape those institutions during the transition to democracy? What has been the ultimate impact of the human rights movement in establishing long-term norms and mechanisms for the protection of human rights?

At the most general level, this discussion illuminates the process of social change. How can a nontraditional social movement affect a basic structure of state power: the monopoly of violence against the citizen? How much change is possible in the context of a transition to democracy? Can state power and social norms be restructured to consolidate democracy in a dependent and historically authoritarian nation such as Argentina?

This book argues that the human rights movement was not destroyed under authoritarian rule precisely *because* it was composed of ordinary citizens: activists who were politically marginal—but economically secure and socially legitimate. The dynamics of repression mobilized new activists, drawn from outside of mainstream political institutions, who were protesting to defend traditional, legitimate values like the right to life, the rule of law, and the sanctity of the family. By necessity, these activists were forced to rely on expressive "powers of the weak" and symbolic strategies of collective action, using their only resource—legitimacy. Protesters who were powerless in their own state sought and gained protection from a new external reference group: the international "human rights regime." Symbolic protesters spearheaded a wider social movement that drew on a variety of reform strategies in a way that reinforced the effectiveness of both insiders and outsiders. Through the form as well as the content of protest, the human rights movement was able to produce unexpected social change under both authoritarian and democratic regimes by unleashing symbolic challenges to regime legitimacy.

Argentina's human rights movement reshaped the public political agenda, compiled, analyzed, and distributed critical information to government and international organizations, provided influential personnel to new governmental and social institutions, and served as a symbol and referent for collective memory and an advocate for the consolidation of democracy. Specific changes that the study will trace to the human rights movement include:

—international delegitimation of the authoritarian regime,

—post-transition establishment of a presidential investigatory commission on disappearances and the Subsecretariat of Human Rights,

—the trials of the former military rulers and attempt to try significant numbers of former military officers,

—new legislation to safeguard civil liberties and trace missing children, and

—the introduction of new social norms and institutions throughout civil society—especially in education, the media, and the union movement.

These changes, in turn, have shaped the construction of democracy in Argentina and provided an international model for protest organizations and human rights reform.

The boundaries of what the movement could achieve were determined by a context of economic crisis, an incomplete transition to democracy marked by continued military veto power and a government strategy of partial and preemptive reform. Within this bounded space for social change, the movement's strategies produced unexpected and unprecedented results: institutions and ideas assumed a life of their own, which subsequently extended the boundaries of political possibility. But the very nontraditional strategies that had enabled the movement to survive authoritarian rule, produce deep change in the political agenda, and diffuse new norms ultimately limited the movement's ability to institutionalize human rights and movement influence in the new democratic environment.

Argentina's human rights movement produced change at the level of norms and institutions through a logic of persuasion, not bargaining or disruption. Much of the movement's impact on the state was paralleled by a wider process of change in civil society. Thus, even as the movement's reforming role recedes, its influence on values endures and diffuses. Because of the importance of collective learning and the particular characteristics of human rights claims, a movement that failed to achieve its stated goals has had a profound and consequential influence on democratization.

The chapters that follow trace and evaluate the politics of human rights during the transition to democracy, with a focus on the Alfonsín administration (1983–89). Chapter 1 establishes the theoretical framework for the study of symbolic protest and the measurement of social change. The following chapters lay historical groundwork for the study: Chapter 2 sets the context of Argentine historical trends and repression under the military dictatorship, and Chapter 3 presents the emergence of the human rights movement and the transition to democracy. Chapters 4–9 discuss the impact of the human rights movement in terms of reforms in the state and society. Chapters 4 and 5 discuss human rights policy during the establishment of the new democratic regime, and Chapters 6 and 7 treat attempts to institutionalize human rights reform in state structures through the later years of the Alfonsín government. Parallel developments in civil society are covered in Chapters 8 and 9. Chapter 10, the concluding chapter, assesses the implications of the politics of human rights for democratization, in Argentina and elsewhere.

Chapter 1

Symbolic Protest
and Social Change

I have to cast my lot with those
Who age after age, perversely,
With no extraordinary power,
reconstitute the world.

Adrienne Rich

Human rights protest and reform in Argentina comprise an extraordinary chapter in the history of that country. This study seeks to chronicle that critical period, but also to frame the Argentine experience in a general model of social movements, symbolic politics, and social change.[1] A theoretical discussion of these issues is important to understanding seemingly anomalous features of the Argentine case, while theoretical treatment of this case can then contribute to the development of general approaches. What are the key elements of the pattern of the politics of human rights in Argentina? Social change can be analyzed in terms of the actor that is the source of change, the mechanism by which change is effected, the results of change, and the context that provides an opportunity for change.

First, change came from a social movement, not a political party, social class, or individual leader. Thus, the Argentine experience may be understood in terms of the nature and impact of social movement activity, and social movement theory may be enriched by consideration of symbolic human rights protest in Argentina. Social movement theory can help us to interpret what happened in Argentina because it shows how outsiders can challenge and change a political system—and also how they are ultimately limited if they remain outsiders. What happened in Argentina is important for social movement theory because it illustrates an emerging model of social movement *impact*; most discussions of social movements still focus on who they are or how they organize rather than on what they accomplish.

The next key element in the Argentine experience was the mechanism of change: symbolic politics. A discussion of legitimacy challenge and the politics of persuasion can shed light on how a weak but principled political force survived dictatorship and shaped democracy in Argentina. The use of symbolic politics in Argentina challenges economistic models of social change.

The results of the Argentine human rights movement challenge were multilevel and multidimensional, not captured by a narrow measurement of reform: a social movement engaged in symbolic politics changed society, the state, the regime, the international system, and its own members. This observation may serve to broaden our assessment of social change, which has traditionally focused narrowly on institutional reform.

Finally, the Argentine movement's success and limitations must be seen in the context of democratization. The Argentine human rights movement achieved both more and less than it intended—less human rights reform and more democratization. We can only understand this paradoxical impact by treating the human rights movement as both an agent and a subject of democratization. The regime change the movement helped bring about provided a space for human rights reform, but also created a legitimate state with multiple agendas, which ultimately limited that space. What happened in Argentina also shows the tension inherent among various procedural and substantive dimensions of democratization. Democratic rules and institutions, democratic empowerment of citizens, democratic uncertainty of outcomes, and democratic realization of human rights build, conflict, and evolve against each other. This evolution is the essence of the politics of human rights in Argentina.

Social Movements and Social Change

What does it mean to say that human rights activists in Argentina constituted a social movement, and what does it tell us about their prospects? A social movement is a group of people who mobilize to pursue principled goals.[2] They may belong to a specific organization, a set of organizations, or simply a community of values. Some members of this community usually engage in protest, but the protest wing of a social movement often works in tandem with others who exert pressure through institutional channels.[3] Whatever its form, the movement shares a sense of collective identity, a complex of common goals that challenge the existing social order, and some history of organizational contact.

The Argentine human rights movement mobilized to defend the

traditional "rights of the person": life, liberty, and personal security.[4] Its activities were centered in ten organizations, which shared these goals, some overlapping membership and leadership, and a declared and recognized identity as human rights activists. The movement included family-based groups such as the Madres de Plaza de Mayo, who concentrated on symbolic protest and catalyzed the movement as a whole. Civil libertarian groups such as the Asamblea Permanente por los Derechos Humanos (APDH) gathered, analyzed, and presented information—to the legal system, international fora, and the general public. A smaller sector of religiously oriented activists such as the Movimiento Ecuménico por los Derechos Humanos (MEDH) provided pastoral services to those affected by repression and linked other kinds of activism to religious communities and concepts.[5]

What does the literature on social movements tell us about why and how these organizations achieved social change in Argentina? The earliest approaches to social movements focused on patterns of social strain that created grievances and a sense of "relative deprivation," expressed in anomic, dysfunctional protest.[6] Informed by social psychology, this view told us that expressive protest served mainly to vent social tensions, although it occasionally mushroomed into revolutionary activity. This perspective continues to influence political actors' interpretations of social movements; volcano models are often used by elites to delegitimize protest. In Argentina, the military originally labeled Las Madres as Las Locas (The Madwomen): poor naive women undone by grief, not citizens demanding accountability from their government.

In reaction to the explanatory limits and status quo bias of traditional views, a wide range of American scholarship of the past generation has adopted economistic models of collective action.[7] Protesters are rational actors who calculate the marginal utility of protest in securing their political preferences.[8] The dominant contemporary American approach, resource mobilization theory, situates the rational individual in a context of group resources and a social structure that presents political constraints and opportunities.[9] The nature of political opportunities and the deployment of movement resources will then explain the impact of a social movement; standard variables include the opportunities of access to formal institutions, political alignments, and alliances with support groups, and the resources of centralization and bureaucratization of movement organization, leadership, and "form of group solidarity."[10] Many analysts within this framework stress that a social movement's ultimate resource is disruption, lending some importance to "strength in numbers."[11]

Economistic models can help to map the boundaries within which the Argentine human rights movement arose. For example, the family emerged as a new kind of political actor in Argentina because state terror victimized the family as a unit, and because all other social institutions were repressed or acquiescent (including the Catholic Church, unions, and political parties).[12] Mothers of the disappeared asked other relatives (especially fathers) not to go to the Plaza, since they felt that the police were least likely to attack unarmed middle-aged women, while the men might become drawn into conflict.[13] But resource mobilization theory cannot tell us how family-based human rights protest differed from a union-organized strike, nor the political implications of that difference. Resource mobilization can also identify a major limitation of human rights movement influence under the democratic regime: limited, preemptive reform separated the movement from domestic and international supporters.[14]

Although structural and material factors do become important in explaining the Argentine human rights movement's *limitations*, these constraints cannot adequately explain how a powerless movement could achieve social change in the first place. While economistic theory is often motivated by a desire to provide practical guidance to social movements, its implications are ironically disempowering. People seek social change precisely because they lack political access and material resources, but resource mobilization can only suggest that some of the powerless have hidden resources, and can organize to acquire more and deploy them more strategically. The truly powerless will have to do something else. More general analyses of powerless people show that the "powers of the weak" who lack material resources (including organization) lie in the normative and expressive realm slighted by economistic models.[15] Thus, some theorists within the economistic tradition are eventually forced to recognize this symbolic "something else"; they attach it to their model as a resource, a repertoire, or a dimension of disruption—but they cannot *explain* it.[16]

The "new social movement" school—a European-inspired Third Wave of social movement studies—*can* capture some of the sources and character of expressive protest by issue-based groups. New social movement theory points to the importance of consciousness-raising for the formation and representation of a collective identity, in contrast to the economistic focus on the organization of interests.[17] It highlights the value of unconventional, symbolic protest that challenges social boundaries rather than forms of mobilization based on bargaining or disruption.[18] And new social movement approaches claim that the existence and activities of new social movements have politically important effects beyond reform of state institutions. New social movements are said to promote personal empowerment, the autonomy of civil society, and democratic values—in short, the development of a new kind of public space and state-society relationship.[19]

While the new social movement perspective was developed to deal with phenomena such as ecological movements in postindustrial Western Europe, it has been adopted extensively to describe Latin American popular movements of the 1970s and 1980s.[20] Thus, much of the debate on new social movements has centered on the conditions that give rise to expressive protest in diverse historical and regional settings.[21] The nature of such movements makes it difficult to develop generalizable models of their emergence or effectiveness, but new social movements do seem linked to legitimacy crisis, lack of conventional political resources, issues that cross functional economic boundaries, and situations where information is highly salient. It is clear that the Argentine movement fits the new social movement profile, and that discussions of collective identity and symbolic protest are the best tools for understanding the movement's origins and activities. The new social movement emphasis on multidimensional social change also helps us to interpret the democratizing effect of the movement.[22]

Framing the Argentine movement as a new social movement also makes sense of some of the problems the movement experienced during the Alfonsín period. Movements whose identity is based on autonomy and "apolitical" independence from state power find it difficult to channel their demands effectively through the new state, and ties with parties (democracy's designated channel for popular participation) threaten to undercut the legitimacy of movements that are defined as "above politics."[23] Mobilization based on issues and identity is inherently somewhat ephemeral and is often overwhelmed by the emergence of new interests.[24] Even within the ranks of a new social movement, diverse sources of collective identity diverge over time—especially when external threat is removed.[25]

But the Argentine human rights movement is a "critical case" for social movement theory because it forces us to go further—to reexamine the *traditional* impact of nontraditional movements.[26] New social movement theory identifies issue-based movements using symbolic protest and highlights their contribution to political culture and discourse. This study argues that symbolic protest can also transform political behavior and institutions in a way related to the use of identity and expressive forms. The Argentine case argues that symbolic protest represents a distinct *logic* of collective action.

The Politics of Persuasion

How does symbolic protest produce social change? Symbolic protest is a part of the politics of persuasion, defined as "the use of strictly symbolic manipulation, without substantial rewards or punishments under the control of the movement."[27] Persuasion changes political behavior and institutions through changing norms and values. New media and messages change the political consciousness of activists, allies, and elements within institutions. This changed consciousness results in the formation of a collective identity for the movement, the transformation of social agendas, the reframing of narrative structures that link state and society, and a legitimacy challenge to state institutions.

Social change involves a transformation of norms (political culture), practices, and institutions.[28] *Norms* are sets of values and ideals that enter into a political actor's definition of its identity, interests, or political "rules of the game." "Political values are basic orientations which determine the way reality is comprehended. They are embodied in political discourse and in the style of doing politics."[29] *Institutions* are patterns of rule-governed collective behavior that are guided by norms or the preservation of rules, rather than by direct and immediate calculations of individual self-interest. Institutions are amenable to norm-driven social change in that they involve independent criteria of legitimacy and predictability and may be activated by information. *Practices* are political behavior, which is shaped by norms and institutions but sometimes takes on a "life of its own."[30] Most social movements combine pressure at each of these levels, but the Argentine human rights movement focused heavily on changing norms. Why was this so, and how did it work?

Argentine human rights activists turned necessity into a virtue in two senses. Symbolic protest was a necessity in Argentina because other channels were blocked. This necessity became a virtue because those spaces available for resistance were collective and normative. Grieving mothers and dissident priests did not calculate their personal utility function from protest.[31] The human rights movement was formed by people who were politically marginal but socially legitimate—initially they were somewhat sheltered by their perceived powerlessness. But their ultimate power came from the politicization of their social legitimacy as mothers, clergy, and jurists.[32]

Symbolic protest was also a necessity—and a virtue—because repression was normative as well as material, and initially rationalized by the wider political community. State terror had paralyzed political activity and reshaped political consciousness:

Terror has two dimensions, one behavioral and another ideological. On the one hand, it shapes political behavior to exact compliance with the directives of power holders. On the other hand, it molds attitudes so as to obtain voluntary obedience. It seeks to constitute new political subjects. Terror aims not only to control but also to change social actors. . . . Its main effect is the generation of an atmosphere of anxiety—a 'culture of fear.'[33]

This "culture of fear" isolated individuals, cutting them off from public life and a sense of political efficacy.[34] One of the few studies of social psychology done during the Argentine dictatorship shows the effects of the "culture of fear" as depoliticization and withdrawal, denial, privatization, "de-enlightenment" about authority figures, and the acceptance of "micro-despotism" in a variety of social environments.[35] An analyst of Argentina traces processes of resistance to a reversal of this culture and the development of a "culture of solidarity" with the opposite features, such as trust, representation, and moral autonomy.[36] The necessary virtue of a politics of persuasion was that it contested the dictatorship at its roots: the consciousness of its citizens.

Expressive Forms of Protest

Expressive modes of political action consist of the public projection of symbols, messages, and stories to change political consciousness. While political consciousness may derive from or defend material interests, the perception and assessment of interests is filtered through political symbols, stories, and scripts.[37] "While much attention is given to 'ideology' in the social sciences, virtually none as far as I know is given to the fact that people delineate their world, including its large as well as its micro-scale politics, in stories and story-like creations."[38]

The politics of persuasion can then be analyzed as a form of communication; its efficacy will depend on the speaker, message, narrative structure, and media.[39] The speakers—mothers, clergy, lawyers, and teachers—were legitimate, credible, and charismatic. The message (human rights) was morally coherent and internationally salient. The narrative structure and media rewrote history through political theater.

In Argentina, "the official story" was that of a nation rescued from chaos and subversion by warrior-heroes. The villains of the piece were hidden, anonymous, and guilty by definition; a common response to indications of disappearances was "they must have done something." One of the first expressive strategies used by the movement was to take out paid advertisements in newspapers. These notices always included names and/or photos personalizing the disappeared, and a demand for information and truth from the government. Most legal activity was quickly seen to be expressive rather than efficacious, but the filing of habeas corpus came to be a gesture of protest and a challenge to the residual fiction of a legal system. These symbolic protests tried to publicize and personalize the victims of the Dirty War from within the discourse and institutions dominated by the military regime.

But in order to rewrite history, human rights protesters had to enact a new story in a new space through the use of political theater. Political theater can introduce new actors onto the stage and enlarge the political agenda by linking new issues to old stories. The dramaturgical perspective on political action chronicles a universal (Western) repertoire of basic plots, which can be mapped onto a range of social situations. In dramaturgical terms, the Mothers presented a new script drawing on the universal plot of Search.[40] In an unconscious echo of this perspective, one scholar of Latin American social movements writes: "History, then, is the history of the transformation of the stage at the same time as an account of the entry of the actors on to that stage."[41]

The Mothers of the Disappeared chose as their stage the Plaza de Mayo, the most central and political public space in the country. The Plaza, fronting the Presidential Palace, has been the traditional site of the establishment and celebration of national independence, military parades, government speeches, Peronist populist rallies, and most previous protest. Within this space, Las Madres developed a formalized ritual of a silent vigil around the central monument that represents the nation. The marchers consciously emphasized their identification with motherhood and with the grieving Madonna, wearing white headscarves embroidered with the names of their children. Each mother carried a poster-sized photo of her disappeared child, definitively reclaiming the victims as "every mother's son." The centrality and effectiveness of this new expressive strategy of political theater meant that the Mothers' protest catalyzed and synthesized the wider human rights movement. The Mothers were later joined in the Plaza by representatives of other human rights groups.[42]

The tone of the Mothers' placards, later slogans, and finally speeches and statements was single-minded, tragic, and unrelenting; they served as a kind of political Greek chorus, constantly referring the unfolding national history back to the tragedy of their lost children. As the movement grew and the voices of other sectors joined the chorus, the collective and symbolic processing of tragedy linked it to universal values of truth, justice, and the integrity of the family. Civil libertarians provided patterned information to support the new history, while dissident clergy lent their own charismatic legitimacy to protest. The message, which began as a personal plea for human dignity, ended as a campaign for universal human rights.

The Message Matters

The ability to persuade is related to the content of the message as well as the identity and strategies of the messengers.[43] If social change is tied to the transformation of collective norms and values, it becomes important to examine the *content* of those values. The Argentine movement's human rights goals provided coherence, credibility, politicization, and protection.

The nonpartisan promotion of human dignity lent the human rights movement credibility and coherence. The concept of human rights as human dignity (rather than the rival concept of contractual protection from the state) resonated strongly in a Catholic Latin society.[44] The nonpartisan and principled character of human rights was especially important in Argentina, where populist Peronism had hegemonized the discourse of dissent—colored by violence, hierarchy, and a subordination of ideological coherence to political pragmatism.[45]

Human rights demands also politicized the movement, in the sense of directing demands against the state. Since the state holds the legitimate monopoly of force, security issues like human rights assume state responsibility (in contrast to the programs of other social movements, especially those that involve the market).[46] Human rights claims are demands for state *accountability*—and not, as is often assumed, for the mere limitation of state power. The demand for accountability for state power presents a particularly powerful challenge in an authoritarian context like the Argentine dictatorship, since authoritarian regimes lack a stable vision of community and are usually justified in terms of an instrumental and temporary political project.[47]

Finally, the human rights message helped to protect the movement by linking it to an international public.[48] As an issue, human rights have an inherently international dimension.[49] Argentine human rights protest mobilized a set of international allies through the international "human rights regime"; the movement's information was internationally relevant even before it was recognized domestically.[50] International recognition helped to shelter the movement from repression (although it did not save some human rights leaders from death or detention).[51] The international alliance cemented by human rights also reinforced the Argentine movement's logic of symbolic politics. The link between Argentine dissidents and First World supporters was often defined by transnational identities (for example, a shared identity as women, Church members, or civil libertarians). International allies and the wider set of international institutions labeled the "human rights regime" were activated precisely by the politics of persuasion, which produced the internationally salient resources of information and drama.

Voice had been reclaimed in Argentina: the human rights movement had formed a collective identity and projected a new message through expressive politics. This alone was important; the emergence of the movement began to raise consciousness and reframe conflict. But in order to achieve social change, the movement also had to use norms to change practices and institutions. This involved reshaping the social agenda and mounting a legitimacy challenge to state institutions.

Agenda Change

Agenda change is a critical step in linking changes in consciousness to changes in political behavior.[52] The first barrier to social change is the invisibility of issues and activists.[53] Agenda change begins with the recognition that a social circumstance is a public and political problem. Agenda change ultimately establishes a problem or claim as a permanent referent for political discourse and mobilization. The politics of persuasion and the Argentine movement's human rights claims were well suited to agenda-building.[54]

In Argentina, the translation of grievance into a political problem was sharpened by the incidence of human rights violations that were sudden, severe, invaded the home, and victimized members of the middle- and upper-class sectors of society to an unprecedented extent. Recognition of this problem as political involved a dual process of making the private public and establishing state responsibility for disappearances. The mere public presence of women identified by family roles—the archetypal hidden residents of the home—transformed activists and troubled observers.[55] One relative of a *desaparecido* explained why she chose to participate in the Mothers' movement, saying: "They had a public presence that I feel is very important. . . . The big change from the movement is in us, to leave the personal and come to protesting for other people's children."[56] The movement's emphasis on collecting testimonies documenting repression served a function beyond its legal or international value, in publicizing the "hidden state" and promoting a shared interpretation of hidden violence. One of the dictatorship's first directives had forbidden reporting of "subversive incidents, the appearance of bodies and the deaths of subversive elements and/or members of the armed forces and security forces, unless these are announced by a high official source. This includes kidnappings and disappearances."[57] Hannah Arendt, in her discussion of tyranny, stresses the use of subjectivity as a mode of domination and the empowering role of testimony:

Each time we talk about things that can be experienced only in privacy or intimacy, we bring them out into a sphere where they will assume a kind of reality which, their intensity notwithstanding, they never could have had before . . . Where nobody can any longer agree with anybody else, as is usually the case in tyrannies. . . . They are all imprisoned in the subjectivity of their own singular experience, which does not cease to be singular if the same experience is multiplied innumerable times.[58]

Testimonies also helped to establish a pattern of state responsibility, reinforcing the human rights claim for accountability. The establishment of state responsibility was especially critical since abuses followed a period of guerrilla conflict.[59]

The concept of human rights was established as a permanent referent for political discourse in Argentina. One of the most telling indicators of public recognition is the adoption of key concepts by groups outside of and even opposed to the movement. By 1980, the Argentine military felt the need to publish its own accounts of human rights in Argentina and adopted the slogan "Somos derechos y humanos" ("We are human and we are right"). Asked to assess the impact of activism for human rights in Argentina, Jacobo Timerman replied: "Now at least everybody knows what they are."[60]

Legitimacy Challenge

The Argentine human rights movement changed political institutions by using symbolic politics to link movement demands to the central legitimating principles of the regime in power and the norms of the specific institutions that emerged during the transition to democracy. Since institutions use orienting norms to foster legitimacy and predictability, the politically marginalized can sometimes use the politics of persuasion to tie their claims to institutional requisites. Similarly, institutions designed to process information can sometimes exhibit politically consequential bureaucratic autonomy when presented with challenging data, regardless of the source. The Argentine human rights movement had its greatest success in the judiciary in part because the judiciary is the most institutionalized branch of government—and because the central legitimating principle of equality before the law coincided with a key human rights movement demand ("No impunity!").[61]

The original demand of the movement, "We do not ask for anything more than the truth," was well within the claims of the military government.[62] The demand for the truth played a special role in delegitimating the exercise of state terror by showing that violence that might have been legitimate within the government's discourse of the "Dirty War" had been concealed and falsified.[63] The demand for truth continued after the transition, now directed at the legal system and investigatory commission—and followed up with a flood of formatted information. Luis Moreno Ocampo, the assistant prosecuting attorney at the trials of the military juntas, attributes substantial impact on the legal system to the movement's unleashing of the *fuerza de la verdad* (power of the truth).[64]

Under a democratic regime, the movement added demands for justice and restructuring—government accountability for the past and future.[65] The challenge to justice was again directed primarily at the legal system, which responded by assuming a surprisingly autonomous role in the establishment of a democratic regime. A broader and more problematic challenge was contained in the movement's slogan *¡Nunca más!* ("Never again!"). This challenge to consolidate a legitimate democracy meant full state control over the forces of coercion, so that the military could never again assume power, police could never again abuse suspects, and the state would serve as the guarantor of civil liberties. The institutionalization of human rights was most successful at the regime level, and to some extent with the police (an institution subsumed under the regime's democratic legitimacy).

The framework of legitimacy challenge also helps us to make sense of movement demands that did not transform institutions but nonetheless contributed to the politics of human rights in Argentina. It is only as a legitimacy challenge to democratic accountability that we can understand one sector of the movement's post-transition demand for *aparición con vida* ("Bring them back alive"). A representative of Las Abuelas explained, "It means that when you take someone away alive, the government has the responsibility to return them alive, explain what happened, and judge those responsible."[66]

The Impact of Protest

The preceding discussion of new social movements and symbolic politics gives us a framework within which to assess social change. Traditional studies focus on measuring change in state institutions and goal achievement: institutional reform and regime change.[67] But social movements never come to confront the state unless they emerge through prior stages of consciousness-raising and mobilization.[68] Once protest has emerged, social change is not limited to the state; movement impact develops in civil society and within the movement's membership. Social change must thus be assessed through a variety of phases and channels: formation and institutionalization of a social movement, impact on the state, and effect on society.[69]

The first level of social change is the emergence and survival of a new actor, the social movement (see Chapter 3). Collective action will only become a lasting social movement if its participants develop a collective identity, stable resources, and institutionalized social role.[70] Institutionalization is both internal and external. Resource mobilization theorists stress organizational durability and resource base, but the new social movement emphasis on diffusion of movement messages also mandates attention to activist circulation and institutional linkages to other areas of civil society. Indeed, the latter dimension seems stronger in the Argentine movement's development.

The movement's impact on society can be seen through social recognition of the movement, reform responses to the movement, and collective learning (see Chapters 8 and 9). Recognition of the protest group is the first issue in any social conflict.[71] Politically relevant social reforms will be those that affect the political consciousness of society: changes in the media, education, and social institutions that represent political demands to the state (parties, corporations). Collective learning, the social internalization of the movement's impact, will reinterpret a common history and its lessons, and apply movement values to diverse arenas.

Finally, the traditional treatment of movement impact on the state can be expanded beyond state recognition and reform (see Chapters 4, 5, 6, and 7). Reforms may be symbolic, redistributive, or structural. Policy reform may go beyond the substantive goals of the movement to create new rights of participation or veto for the movement.[72] The movement's relationship to the state may also expand to the point where it becomes an interlocutor to the state, with delegated power over its issue-area.[73]

If a social movement's impact develops to the point where it fundamentally changes any of these relationships with state, society, or membership, it ceases to be a social movement and becomes some other kind of social actor. We can refine our understanding of the nature of a social movement in terms of the parameters of its triple relationship with itself, its society, and its government. Once a movement becomes too institutionalized, its goals become organizational maintenance and thus constituency benefits rather than social change; the social move-

TABLE 1
Development of the Impact of a Social Movement

EMERGENCE

Consciousness
perception of injustice
perception as *political*

Mobilization
conquering fear
movement survival

. . . .

INTERNAL DEVELOPMENT	SOCIETY	STATE
Collective identity	*Recognition*	*Recognition*
common frameworks	group identity	group identity
relationships	political claim	state responsibility
other-identified		
Institutionalization	*Reform*	*Reform*
activist circulation	media	symbolic
social linkages	parties	redistributive
leadership succession	education	structural
survive change	corporations	participation rights
Stabilization	*Collective learning*	*Interlocutor*
stable mobilization	reinterpret history	manages issue for state
material base	value diffusion	
ongoing incentives	apply to new situations	

. . . .

Interest group	*Political party*	*Revolutionary movement*
changing purpose	contender for state power	antisystem violence

ment becomes an interest group. On the other hand, if a movement transforms society so much that a wide variety of actors enter the movement and seek state power to pursue movement goals, the social movement becomes a political party. And if the movement tries to become a state, a competitor for the state's monopoly of violence, it has taken the shape of a revolutionary force.

In order to bring together these various ways to measure the impact of a social movement, I have outlined a schematic depiction of them in Table 1 that incorporates the significant elements of each dimension of change: internal movement development, impact on the state, and impact on society. While some elements are necessary conditions for others (such as movement survival), the model is not strictly linear or sequential. Although levels of development among the areas are often linked, the model does not posit a determinate and universal set of relationships among internal development, social impact, and impact on the state. (For example, in the Argentine case it appears that the movement's impact on civil society ultimately exceeded its impact on the state; this may be generally true of new social movements.)

Finally, the model is explicitly dynamic rather than static. Not only do movements develop upward toward greater impact, but a movement may have a higher measurable impact in one historical moment than at subsequent stages. The Argentine movement emerged as a bearer of new norms, evolved into a brief experience of institutional reform, and has since resumed a role defending the norms introduced.

Human Rights and Democratization

Thus far, we have discussed the sources, character, and dimensions of social change in Argentina; change must now be situated in the context of democratization. Democratization was both a framework for and result of human rights activism.[74] In order to understand what happened in Argentina, we must trace the differences in social movement opportunities and logics under authoritarian, transitional, and consolidating democratic regimes. An account of the Argentine movement's contribution to democratization may, in turn, inform a growing body of theory on democratic transitions that systematically tends to slight the role of social movements and other noninstitutional mass actors.[75]

We have traced the emergence of a politics of persuasion and human rights claims under dictatorship. Under democracy, persuasion is more accessible and human rights claims allow for broader and deeper legitimacy challenges to emerging democratic institutions. However, as the system moves into a phase of attempted consolidation of democracy, social movements face new constraints. The Argentine movement fits the general observation that Latin American social movements are more likely to be marginalized under democracy if the transition has been sudden and the prior regime harsh.[76]

The limitations of social movements under new democracies are related to the character of the consolidating state as well as the character of the movement itself. State responsiveness to the Argentine human rights movement was hampered under democracy because the new system was in fact quasi-democratic: the rules of contestation applied to civilians like activists, but not to the privileged military corporation. After at least four major military uprisings and countless "incidents of indiscipline" (including what appears to have been an attempt to assassinate President Alfonsín), democracy still stops at the barracks door. "When military officers enter the president's office, you never know what will happen—and this level of suspicion reinforces the power of the military," a presidential advisor complained.[77] The Alfonsín administration therefore drew on many of the nonrepressive strategies democratic governments can use to deflect the demands of social movements: symbolic support, the creation of new government-sponsored organizations, limited anticipatory concessions, and simple postponement.[78]

The origins and nature of the movement—which had made it uniquely effective under authoritarian rule—limited its ability to respond to the new democratic environment.[79] The human rights movement arose in a political environment in which bargaining was impossible, but the new democratic environment rewarded the logic of bargaining more than persuasion.

To the extent they deal with the state, the demands are frequently symbolic and moral in nature, and non-negotiable. One of the paradoxes of these new social movements' work is that part of their political impact derives from this new "apolitical" way of doing politics. But this very aspect of their political impact is also linked to a very significant limitation and internal contradiction, for the "apolitical" means of doing politics may curtail their ability to transform political regimes.[80]

Moreover, because of organizational rigidities, an expressive tactic of persuasion may later limit bargaining.[81] Similarly, the human rights movement's emergence and persistence under authoritarian rule required determined, charismatic, and single-minded leadership, which often proved inappropriate to consolidation-era democratic politics.[82]

If democracy set a new agenda for the movement, the movement also set new terms for democracy. The nature of movement demands and the mode of movement participation catalyzed—and later challenged—democratization. Human rights demands for the ethical and predictable exercise of state power challenged the dictatorship's policy of state terror, and expanded into a demand for security and accountability that only democracy could satisfy. Raúl Alfonsín, Argentina's first president following military rule, explained that:

The process of transition to democracy . . . was basically a response to a state of social disintegration in which the fundamental links necessary for cooperation and solidarity among individuals had been destroyed. For years the country endured a state of generalized violence in which Argentina lost the set of guidelines that constitute public ethics, legality and even primary social relations. This loss generated fear, uncertainty, self-criticism and, above all, insecurity stemming from the impossibility of predicting the arbitrary exercise of public authority.[83]

In Argentina, people disappeared simply because their names appeared in a suspect's address book. Security is a "public good"—and human rights violations are a "public bad."[84] Insofar as security is a public good, it is indivisible; the state can compromise on a few clinics or more participation at the local level, but it is more difficult to dispense a little peace or a little safety. Security requires universal, legitimate norms embodied in a regularized legal system.[85] Only democracy could guarantee the rule of law in Argentina.

The emergence of a human rights movement in Argentina also promoted a democratic relationship between civil society and the state. A revival of social channels of representation *precedes* most transitions to a democratic regime. Participation in social movements creates a social base for democracy by encouraging participation, critical thinking, and other attributes of citizenship. This democratization of civil society is described as the "invisible transition" to democracy.[86] It is an important source of the political learning necessary to construct democracy in structurally limited environments.[87]

After the transition, the human rights movement challenged the consolidating system to provide accountability, representation, and substantive as well as procedural democracy. This deeper challenge and its results are traced below. The concluding chapter considers how the Argentine human rights experience illuminates the inherent tensions in democratization: process and content, stability and representation.

Democracy in Argentina has remained incomplete, as Argentina has been unable to fully institutionalize human rights—in the shape of ethical boundaries and state accountability for the exercise of coercive power. Like other new social movements, Argentine activists have been limited in moving from resistance to democratic participation. But within the constraints of consolidation, the Argentine human rights movement has played a key and unexpected role in rewriting history, providing an international model, and constructing democratic citizenship.

Conclusion

The Argentine human rights movement produced a far-reaching and unexpected impact on state and society through the transformation of norms, practices, and institutions. The movement itself experienced consciousness-raising, mobilization, formation of collective identity, and some internal institutionalization. Argentine activists achieved public and political recognition, as well as reform of both social institutions and state structures. Using expressive modes of collective action, they created a counterhegemonic "culture of resistance" to the privatization of state terror and linked both institutional and regime legitimacy to movement demands. Ultimately, both the particular nature of the human rights agenda and the movement's use of symbolic politics led to a kind of collective learning that has shaped the transition to democracy.

But neither the movement, the newly democratic regime, nor the "recovering authoritarian" society has been able to consolidate these changes. The state's ability to respond was limited by military veto power over contestation and the government's own "realist" strategy of limited, preemptive reform. Civil society was distracted by acute economic crisis and failed to develop appropriate alliance partners for a consolidating coalition with the movement. And the movement was crippled and divided by the very characteristics that derive from its origins and the exhaustion of the very strategies that were uniquely effective under authoritarian rule.

The following chapters detail the symbolic protest and social change brought about by the Argentine human rights movement. Through them, we shall come to understand the sources and parameters of the struggle to restructure state power: the politics of human rights. In the concluding section, I assess the implications of this struggle for the role of human rights and social movements in the consolidation of democracy.

Chapter 2

Historical Background

> There are two critical points in the life of power when habit
> does not suffice. The first is at its birth. . . . The other comes
> when the customary ways and limits of power are altered,
> when subjects are presented with new and disturbing uses
> of power and are asked to assume new burdens and accept
> new claims.   John Scharr, *Legitimacy in the Modern State*

Which features of the Argentine historical experience inform our
understanding of the emergence of the human rights movement
as a political actor?[1] The movement arose in response to an unprecedented level of repression and transformation of state and society: the
military dictatorship of the National Process of Reorganization, or Proceso (1976–83). But the authoritarian regime was rooted in long-standing social, political, and economic decline.

The key elements of this long-standing crisis, from the perspective
of human rights and resistance to authoritarian rule, were the following. First, Argentina's model of accumulation was unstable and contested by a series of highly mobilized social forces. Second, the military
was accepted as a legitimate political actor that regularly intervened in
Argentine society in tandem with civilian political forces. Third, the
tension between the norms and institutions of representative democracy and the exclusion or vetoing of majoritarian political forces created
a profound legitimacy crisis. And, finally, almost all political forces
engaged in and countenanced human rights violations and fostered
the growth of the repressive apparatus of the state.[2] Each of these
dynamics, in turn, contributed to the new form of authoritarianism that
arose during the 1970's, which provided the context for the emergence
of the Argentine human rights movement.

But none of the above factors alone can account for Argentina's decline, and the trajectory of that decline cannot fully predict the intense
repression of the Proceso period. Chronic and recurrent economic crises
had particular political consequences owing to the nature and evolution of Argentine political institutions. Strategic responses to the result-

ing systemic failures were filtered through actors' perceptions of threats and "rules of the game." And during the 1970's, each of these processes operated in a distinct regional and international context.

Historical Background

Argentine Exceptionalism

Argentina is often described as a paradox: a country with the geography, cultural models, and early prosperity of the "lands of recent settlement" (such as Canada and Australia) whose economic and political experience in the twentieth century has nonetheless assumed a Latin American profile of underdevelopment and repression. Widespread consciousness of this paradox has shaped Argentines' interpretations of, and policy projections from, their history.[3] In interpreting Argentina's experience of authoritarianism and human rights abuses, a further irony is that South America's most developed, modern society produced a dictatorship with the highest level of repression in the region.[4]

The most obvious resemblance to a "land of recent settlement" comes from geography, since Argentina is a temperate-zone agricultural producer with a surplus of arable land. But the resulting political economy was different, since the dominant form of land tenure was the large estate, not the owner-operated small farm characteristic of the "new countries."[5] Argentina was also similar to the "new countries" in its high level of European immigration and reduced influence of Indian culture.[6] However, because of the unusually high ratio of immigrants to creole settlers, because land ownership and political assimilation were not available to most of the immigrants, and because most immigrants did not come from the colonial mother country, Argentina experienced distinct problems of national integration.[7] Like Canada or Australia, Argentina quickly developed a large middle class; but Argentina's middle class was composed of bureaucrats and professionals rather than shopkeepers, and thus did not serve as a source of entrepreneurship or resistance to state power.[8]

Thus, despite its apparent exceptionalism, Argentina's ultimate development was shaped by a complex of traits more typical of Latin America. The relationship between agriculture and industry was distorted and untenable in relationship to the international system. Economic and political liberalism did not develop in tandem.[9] And the military dominated political life.[10]

A Political Economy of Stalemate

A highly mobilized struggle over shares in a shrinking economy has inspired cycles of authoritarianism and repression. At a general level, economic upswings have been associated with civilian constitutional government (in 1945, 1957, and 1963), while periods of economic instability and decline have coincided with military intervention.[11] According to Carlos Waisman, the basic destabilization mechanism (particularly since Perón, and peaking in 1976) has been that balance-of-payments problems lead to recessionary policies, which produce labor mobilization, which leads to inflation, which polarizes society and threatens the bourgeoisie and state, which leads to a coup to restore "order" through demobilization.[12] In shaping this pattern of political economy, "two great issues have faced the country since 1945, industrial development and the political role of the working class."[13]

Argentina suffers from a fundamentally unbalanced productive structure: an internationally competitive primary sector with a protected import-substituting industrial sector. This means that an exchange rate based on the agricultural sector does not permit sufficient imports of the intermediate and capital goods necessary for industry, leading to a bottleneck and chronic balance-of-payments problems.[14] It also holds the entire economy hostage to the international market for Argentina's primary exports, wheat and beef, which compete with exports of the regional hegemon, the United States.[15] A recognition of this dynamic led one human rights attorney to the unexpected comment that the most important reform possible to consolidate democracy in Argentina would be a tax on idle land (to increase exports and decrease the market veto power of the rural oligarchy).[16]

A highly protectionist, import-substituting model of industrialization intersected with the Argentine anomaly—a typically Latin American pattern of highly concentrated land ownership combined with a "new country" lack of labor reserve—to produce the unusual class configuration of a strong rural oligarchy *and* a strong urban working class.[17] The resulting structural stalemate, exacerbated by the labor movement's corporatist relationship to the state, led to drastic swings between populist and orthodox economic policies and intense politicization of economic decision making.[18] Attempts to relieve balance-of-payments pressures while maintaining full employment and keeping wheat and beef prices low for urban workers produced chronic inflation under populist regimes.[19] The orthodox policy, devaluation, redistributed income away from urban workers, which decreased output and government revenues—and ironically stimulated both inflation and

TABLE 2

Governments of Argentina, 1930–1990

President	Tenure	Form of ascension
Genl. José F. Uriburu	1930–32	Military coup
Genl. Agustín P. Justo	1932–38	Restricted elections
Roberto M. Ortiz	1938–42	Unfair elections
Ramón S. Castillo	1942–43	Resignation
Genl. Pedro Ramírez	1943–44	Military coup
Genl. Edelmiro Farrell	1944–46	Military designation
Genl. Juan D. Perón	1946–52	Free elections
Genl. Juan D. Perón	1952–55	Open elections
Genl. Eduardo Lonardi	1955	Military coup
Genl. Pedro Aramburu	1955–58	Military coup
Arturo Frondizi	1958–62	Restricted elections
José María Guido	1962–63	Military coup
Dr. Arturo Illia	1963–66	Restricted elections
Genl. Juan C. Onganía	1966–70	Military coup
Genl. Roberto Levingston	1970–71	Military coup
Genl. Alejandro Lanusse	1971–73	Military coup
Héctor Cámpora	1973	Restricted elections
Raúl Lastiri	1973	Brokered resignation
Genl. Juan D. Perón	1973–74	Special elections
Isabel Perón	1974–76	Death of predecessor
Genl. Jorge Videla	1976–81	Military coup
Genl. Roberto Viola	1981	Military designation
Genl. Leopoldo Galtieri	1981–82	Military coup
Genl. Reynaldo Bignone	1982–83	Military designation
Raúl Alfonsín	1983–89	Free elections
Carlos Saúl Menem	1989–	Free elections

labor militancy.[20] As the economic pie steadily shrank (after World War II), all of these cycles and policies also produced changes in *relative* income shares. State policies had differential effects, depending both on relationship to the means of production and on urban-rural cleavages, with concomitant political divisions.[21] Since Argentina maintained an extraordinary level of state control of ownership, wages, prices, and exchange rates under all types of regimes, politically organized sectors fared best, intensifying the level of mobilization and the attendant dynamics of "praetorian politics."[22]

The Routinization of Military Intervention

In this system, the armed forces constituted a routine political actor, which eventually began to operate as a "military party" and representative of state autonomy—rather than merely a referee or agent of last resort. Between 1930 and 1971, the average president served only two years and ten months of the mandated six-year term.[23] Between 1930 and 1983, Argentina had 24 Presidents (16 of whom were military officers) and experienced 26 successful military coups.[24] After an exhaustive study of the history of military intervention in Argentina, Alain Rouquié concluded that Argentine governments fell into three categories: "those that derived their support from the military (like the Peronist regime until 1951–52), those that governed [by] neutralizing the military (like the [multiparty and electorally restricted] Justo Concordancia) and the rest, whose destiny it is to be overthrown by the military."[25]

The military's role in politics was originally confined to defending its own institutional interests and those of the system against threats to the conservative status quo. The armed forces began to condition policy during the labor mobilizations of the early twentieth century: in 1919's Semana Trágica, the government of President Hipólito Yrigoyen violently suppressed a general strike following military threats to withdraw support from the government.[26] The first military coup, in 1930, displaced a subsequent Yrigoyen administration and presided over a conservative restoration to safeguard the interests of the agricultural oligarchy.

But the "liberating revolution" that overthrew the populist Juan Perón in 1955 marked a new phase of military rule. The armed forces no longer confined themselves to seeking veto power among civilian political forces, but sought to restructure society through "tutelary intervention."[27] The military government of General Pedro Aramburu (1955–58) systematically attacked Peronist institutions, economics, and activists. The regime of General Juan Onganía (1966–70) further increased the scope and scale of military intervention, pledging to remain in power indefinitely. "Following the Brazilians, Onganía sought to create a modernizing autocracy that would change society from above, with or without popular backing."[28]

All of the politically organized forces of civil society accepted and at times encouraged military intervention. The (actual or anticipated) losers of electoral contests frequently turned to the military and participated in the resulting regimes: conservatives during the 1930's, nationalist proto-Peronists in 1943, some Radicales in 1955, and a broad spectrum of civilians by 1966. The military, in turn, participated in a variety of ways in civilian regimes, ranging from technical and economic management of large state sectors to periodic muscle-flexing to impose military policy preferences.[29] In 1966, 77 percent of Argentines approved of the coup that brought General Onganía to power, and the armed forces—which had decided to intervene some time before—waited for critical levels of both internal cohesion and popular support before overthrowing yet another unrepresentative civilian government.[30]

The Legitimacy Crisis of Democracy

As a response to political and economic breakdown, a systemwide legitimacy crisis developed, which came to assume an independent role in perpetuating instability and inspiring antisystem violence. Both inflation and military intervention shortened time horizons and eroded the norms of short-term risk and sacrifice necessary for long-term social cooperation (Guillermo O'Donnell's "impossible game"). In general, institutions bore little relation to practice in a highly formalized and mobilized system. And the most powerful institutions—the military, the Executive, the Church, and the unions—were precisely the least pluralistic and least accountable to society at large.[31]

Even periods of civilian rule were undermined by restrictions on democratic rights and the proscription of majoritarian political forces. Between 1930 and 1983, Argentina experienced ten states of emergency, comprising approximately thirty years of the fifty-year period.[32] Federal intervention in the provinces frequently supplanted elected provincial authorities. And even the popular, freely elected Juan Perón had purged the judiciary, restricted the press, and abolished university autonomy.[33] When elections took place, they were rarely free and inclusive. The conservative restoration was maintained throughout the 1930's with rigged elections.[34] The Peronist party was proscribed from participating in elections from 1955 until 1973. Thus, the Radical party president Arturo Illia came to power in 1963 with only 25 percent of the vote (in a system with compulsory suffrage).[35]

Responses to these conditions were reflected and exacerbated by ideology, as neither of the dominant intellectual currents—liberalism and nationalism—provided support for institutions, and both rationalized the resort to political violence. Sectors of the elite wanted free markets but not free elections; "economic and political liberalism do not necessarily imply each other: since the Depression, most Argentine supporters of economic liberalism have backed political authoritarianism."[36] More generally, dominant groups took on a Church-influenced, reactionary worldview characterized by exaggerated fears of popular mobilization and little confidence in institutional channels for emerging sectors. One analyst labeled this preemptively reactionary ideology "anticommunism without Communists."[37]

Popular nationalism (usually expressed through Peronism) shared some aspects of this distrust of institutions, compounded by decades of exclusion from the political system. In 1971, Perón assured guerrilla supporters that he approved of violence and did not believe in elections. Earlier, in the waning days of his first administration, the historic leader of Argentina's majority had declared: "The watchword for all Peronists, whether as individuals or within an organization, is to reply to a violent action with one more violent. And when one of ours falls, five of theirs will fall."[38]

Political Violence and the Repressive State Apparatus

The original and predominant source of political violence in Argentina was the state, and every political force that held state power engaged in some form of human rights violations. The historical pattern of human rights abuse in Argentina includes (roughly in order of appearance) judicial torture (inherited from the Spanish legal code), inhumane imprisonment, police brutality, para-police civilian "death squads" covertly supported or tolerated by the state, and state terror. Repression was intensified by, but by no means limited to, periods of military rule. Significant antecedents of the state terror practiced during the Proceso military dictatorship date from the 1930's (establishment of the autonomous Special Section of the police), the first Peronist period (undocumented arrests and scientific use of torture), and the Onganía regime (military participation in both overt repression and a covert parallel apparatus). According to the Liga Argentina por los Derechos del Hombre (Argentine League for the Rights of Man; La Liga), the nation's oldest human rights organization, "Only during very brief periods, during the presidencies of Yrigoyen, Alvear, and Illia, can one affirm that human rights were fully in force."[39]

Inhumane prison conditions and episodes of police brutality were continuing features of the Argentine penal system, but they became more widespread and politically targeted following the early twentieth-century wave of labor mobilization and strike activity.[40] Torture of political prisoners intensified during the 1930's, following the first military coup. General José Uriburu founded the "Special Section" of the police; a 1931 report claimed that 1,900 police worked with the Special Section, and that prominent individuals, including legislators, dissident generals, and an ex-president, had been tortured.[41]

Torture of dissidents continued throughout the Peronist era, although the identity of the victims changed to students, Communists, and dissident labor activists. A doctor called to the Special Section by police was told that the central list of detainees accessible to the judiciary did not include those in the Special Section, and that "the papers you see here are *denuncias* [registered complaints]—the judges send them back to us."[42] In 1950, in response to public pressure, a congressional bicameral Commission on Torture was formed to investigate—but ironically, the commission ended up shutting down protest organizations, notably La Liga.[43]

The number of detainees rose after the 1955 "liberating revolution" coup that overthrew Perón.[44] Lawyers and judges interviewed generally cited personal knowledge of increasing incidents of police torture dating from the late 1950's. Human rights violations again increased in scope and severity following the 1966 coup that brought Onganía to power.[45] And isolated cases began to appear of labor organizers and lawyers who were not officially detained but remained missing; in 1971, an unofficially detained teacher in Rosario was told, "You have disappeared."[46]

During the early 1970's, significant levels of antisystem violence appeared for the first time in Argentina. The level of violent strikes and protest increased dramatically, but more important, several leftist guerrilla groups emerged, staging kidnappings, bank robberies, assassinations of Army and police personnel, and eventually urban bombings.[47] The largest group, the Peronist Montoneros, kidnapped and killed the former military president General Pedro Aramburu in 1970, assassinated "collaborationist" union leaders and military officers during the years that followed, engaged in urban bombings that claimed scores of victims, and even mounted (dramatic but unsuccessful) attacks on military installations. The smaller, Trotskyist and later Guevarist ERP (Ejercito Revolucionario del Pueblo) waged a rural insurgency in outlying, semitropical Tucuman province, and also launched several unsuccessful assaults against Army garrisons.[48]

Right-wing counterterror quickly followed; by early 1971, there was an average of one "disappearance" every eighteen days.[49] The right crystallized into the death squad Alianza Anti-Comunista Argentina—popularly known as the Triple A—which killed thousands of leftists during this period.[50] By 1974, the Triple A was concentrating on the political (rather than guerrilla) left—especially lawyers and intellectuals, and there was evidence of covert official sponsorship.[51] Victims were abducted by individuals with police credentials, the police did not respond to the attacks, and there were links to personnel and resources derived from the Ministry of Social Welfare.[52]

Official military involvement in counterinsurgency, political repression, and government increased in tandem. In a famous incident at Trelew in 1972, a group of escaped guerrilla prisoners were shot after surrendering.[53] The Army was officially called into Tucumán province in February 1975; by November, military control of the counterinsurgency program had been extended to the entire country.[54] Around the same time, a National Security Council was created under Army control, and an active-duty officer was appointed minister of the interior.[55] By 1975, the military had already established clandestine detention centers in Tucumán, where torture and murder of political dissidents as well as suspected guerrillas were common.[56] A federal police chief who had urged centralized, open, "legitimate" repression was replaced; apparently, at one point President Isabel Perón herself was voted down by the Army when she proposed a system of (open) summary military trials and executions for guerrillas.[57]

Human Rights Resistance

Prior to the Proceso, this history of repression had generated some human rights activity, but no broadly based human rights movement. La Liga, which provided legal and material aid to political prisoners, had existed since the beginnings of military rule during the 1930's.[58] While La Liga provided critical services to victims of state violence, and periodically denounced patterns of abuse of human rights, it gained little domestic recognition or support (largely because of its close association with the Argentine Communist party). By the late 1950's, another attorneys' group had formed, the Centro de Abogados Pro-Imperio del Derecho.[59] During the 1960's and early 1970's, various ad hoc committees formed by relatives of Peronist political prisoners emerged, only to disband following the release of specific groups of prisoners.[60] A lawyers' Forum for Human Rights formed during the early 1970's was crushed by the death-squad assassination of many of its members.[61]

Why is it, then, that a broadly based, permanent social movement for human rights emerged and gained widespread recognition during a period of repression worse than any previously experienced? One factor is the nature of the repression itself. Another critical factor is the response and failure of other social institutions. Finally, the Argentine human rights movement of the late 1970's emerged in and made use of a distinct international context. The "international regime" of official international bodies and private organizations such as Amnesty International allowed relatively powerless domestic actors to circumvent their own governments and appeal directly to the international system. Each of these elements is examined below.

Prelude to the Proceso: A "Dirty War"?

The early 1970's contained all of the elements that had led to previous periods of military rule: economic crisis, institutional instability, and lack of systemic legitimacy. But several new elements were present that help account for the unprecedented nature of the Proceso, or Process of National Reorganization (1976–83). Both popular protest and antisystem violence had reached new levels—and the guerrillas directly targeted military officers and their families. The perception of threat by both dominant groups and the military was heightened by the internal breakdown of Peronism, the force that had thus far channeled the aspirations of excluded majorities. Finally, the international context of the early 1970's was receptive to new, more pervasive forms of authoritarianism.

Following the collapse of a series of military regimes, Juan Perón returned to power in 1973, almost twenty years after his ouster. But the populist leader could no longer manage the internal contradictions of his multifaceted movement, which had grown during a generation of exile.[62] Perón's landing at Ezeiza airport foreshadowed the fate of the nation, as armed bands from both sides of Peronism turned the welcome rally into a massacre.[63] Perón's death in July 1974 left a howling political vacuum; his widow, the politically inexperienced and personally unstable Isabel Perón, became president. Under Isabel, all semblance of political and economic stability was lost. In eighteen months, she filled Argentina's eight ministries with thirty-eight appointees.[64] Skyrocketing inflation followed by draconian austerity measures produced the first general strike under a Peronist government. Inflation, partly fueled by the oil crisis's effect on import prices, reached 738 percent in 1975; by early 1976, inflation was the equivalent of 3,000 percent a year.[65]

But the military went beyond the historic scenario to justify a new level of intervention, and the state terror that followed, with the argument that Argentina during the early 1970's was involved in a "Dirty War" against the guerrillas, in which unorthodox tactics and the deaths of civilian bystanders were inevitable.[66] There is ample evidence to refute this claim. First of all, the guerrillas never posed a serious threat to the territorial or institutional integrity of the state; they never controlled or administered any region of the country or mounted a force of sufficient size to do so.[67] Furthermore, whatever threat the guerrilla movements did present to the security of members of the military and police, their families, and ordinary citizens (probably in that order) had substantially diminished before the 1976 coup, following the 1975 defeat of the ERP in Tucumán and Montonero reverses.[68] The concrete practices and methodology of the Proceso also fail to support the claim of a "Dirty War" and were actually biased against nonviolent political activists.[69] It is improbable that the armed forces were able to detain thousands of violent guerrillas while suffering minimal casualties, or that "anti-guerrilla" operations produced deaths and disappearances but virtually no injuries among enemy forces.[70]

Although objective conditions did not constitute a "Dirty War," the new form of authoritarianism of the Proceso was linked to unprecedented perceptions of threat by the military and key political actors. The military's decision to yield to Peronism during the early 1970's had been catalyzed by a series of popular uprisings that seemed to show a new and evolving worker-student alliance.[71] And in 1971, almost half of the public felt that guerrilla activity was "justified." "Peronism was at the same time the worst threat to the dominant classes and their only hope to control the threat."[72] But not only was Peronism in general disarray, elements of Peronism came to threaten military interests directly. During his 1973 brief interregnum, Perón's delegate Hector Cámpora decreed an amnesty for imprisoned guerrillas—which increased the potential for violence, violated one of the military's conditions for ceding power, and generally convinced the right that it had nothing to gain from the rule of law.[73] The Montonero guerrillas turned to political action through the Peronist Youth, as Juventud Peronista rallies suddenly grew from 5,000 to 100,000.[74] By mid 1975, the military and key sectors of the bourgeoisie had diagnosed Argentina's problem as populism unleashed from the state, and the solution as a strong state pursuing economic liberalism and war.[75]

A final element contributing to a new level of repression was the influence of international conditions and alliances during the early 1970's. Latin America as a region was rapidly succumbing to the comprehensive authoritarianism of "market militarism" (neighboring Brazil in 1964, and Chile in 1973).[76] The U.S.-sponsored National Security Doctrine depicted Argentine domestic political conflict as a surrogate for a larger East-West struggle.[77] Argentine leaders and U.S. policymakers wished to avoid the international outcry that had followed the open repression of political activists following the 1973 coup in Chile, so that the covert technique of disappearance was favored.[78] And there is some evidence that the junta was encouraged by Henry Kissinger's failure to mount objections to repression following the 1976 Argentine coup.[79] Argentine rightists also received support from a shadowy international network of neo-fascists centered in the Italian P-2 secret society.[80]

The Proceso

Although generally and accurately classified as a bureaucratic-authoritarian regime, the Argentine Process of National Reorganization (1976–83) combined features of several regime types: reactionary defensiveness, sweeping totalitarian aspirations, and a high level of personal corruption.[81] But the dictatorship's bureaucratic-authoritarian character was reflected in its demobilizational program and justification as a temporary (if indefinite) expedient necessary for the ultimate restoration of democracy.[82] "The new dictatorship was the most radical of all military experiments in Argentine history. It was determined to become more impersonal, autonomous, permanent, repressive, and deeply 'structural' than anything before."[83]

This time, the military government sought a comprehensive transformation of every aspect of Argentine society so as

to restore the essential values that serve as the foundation for the leadership of the State, emphasizing the morality, competence, and efficiency indispensable for reconstructing the content and image of the nation, the eradication of subversion, and the promotion of national economic development based on a balance and responsible participation of various sectors, with the goal of assuring the subsequent installation of a republican, representative, and federal democracy, adequate to the situation and demands for progress of the Argentine people.[84]

To this end, the founding statutes of the Proceso—which superseded the Constitution—dissolved the Argentine Congress and provincial governments, removed the Supreme Court, forbade all party and union activity, and suspended emigration rights. Measures shortly thereafter reinstituted the death penalty and subjected civilians to trial by military courts and "detention at the disposal of the Executive" (without a trial).[85] To an unprecedented extent, military officers assumed control of every branch of government and civil society; and power was divided evenly among the services.[86] And this time, the military regime was prepared to remain in power as long as necessary to guarantee its objectives.

The first substantive goal, "the eradication of subversion," was framed by a right-wing nationalist political philosophy informed by the national security doctrine. But Argentine theorists went further, arguing that Argentina was the site of a "Third World War" against communism.[87] The cohesion and legitimacy of military rule were closely tied to this "war," in the absence of (and subsequently defeat in) external conflict.[88] The guerrillas existed, but if they hadn't, the Proceso would have had to invent them.[89]

The war against the guerrillas thus became a total war against subversion for the soul of the nation, in which ideological and social hegemony were just as important as military victory. In response to foreign journalists' questions about the disappearance of a handicapped woman clearly incapable of armed activity, President Jorge Videla responded: "A terrorist isn't just someone with a gun or bomb, but also someone who spreads ideas that are contrary to Western and Christian civilization."[90] The military's defense of its vision of "Western Christian civilization" included a crypto-fascist glorification of patriarchal family, religion, and traditional women's roles—including motherhood.[91]

The second goal, "the promotion of national economic development," entailed the adjustment of the Argentine model of accumulation to the world market. Economic adjustment involved a reversal of the Peronist sectoral transfer: taking income out of the urban sector and returning it to Argentina's internationally competitive agricultural exporters. It therefore entailed a reduction in the numbers and political power of the industrial working class. The Proceso economic package included the elimination of export taxes on agriculture, a reduction in import tariffs, wage restraints, liberalization of foreign exchange and financial markets, and rationalization of public sector activities.[92] The liberalization of financial markets resulted in an increased role for finance capital and speculation—and, ultimately, capital flight and debt.[93] Foreign exchange and import policies produced a decline in (formerly protected) national industry.[94] And the preceding factors plus wage restraints led to a significant decline in working-class incomes.[95]

These measures (especially exchange rate policies) initially boosted middle-class purchasing power, so that the period is sometimes referred to as one of *plata dulce* ("sweet money"). This burst of affluence helped garner support for the military and decreased concern about repression. But the "sweet" times did not last (see below). And although economic adjustment clearly benefited some sectors, it did not serve its avowed purpose of restoring Argentine national prosperity: 25 percent of Argentina's economic decline from 1930 to 1989 occurred during the Proceso (1976–83).[96]

The pursuit of total war against subversion along with orthodox economic adjustment led to state terror.[97] The best description of the relationship between the military's perceptions and the security and economic rationales for repression is that the national security doctrine legitimized coercion and the creation of a state security apparatus, while economic ideology served as a perceptual filter in the selection of the victims.[98] The military openly acknowledged that the success of its economic policies required insulation from "political pressures"; Secretary of State Guillermo Walter Klein stated that the political economy of the Proceso was "incompatible with any kind of democratic system and only applicable if backed by the de facto government."[99] The disempowerment of Latin America's strongest working class would require high levels of coercion.[100] "The subjection of any politically mobilized class entails an uncommon level of brutality because it involves not only the elimination of the class's current generation of political activists but also the destruction of those institutions (political parties, labor unions, university faculties, peasant coops) that could serve as centers of dissent," Lars Schoultz notes.[101] This provided the link to the war against subversion; as one general stated: "[Now] we must control the educational, industrial and neighborhood environment, which is where what is left of terrorist delinquency has taken refuge."[102] In Argentina, the doctrine adopted by the Proceso "included as a goal implantation of generalized terror in the population to ensure that the guerrilla couldn't move like a 'fish in the water.' It was these concepts that were the basis for the policy of disappearances."[103]

State Terror

Numerous national and international observers have documented the existence of widespread, decentralized, officially sponsored human rights violations of horrific character and proportions under the Argentine military dictatorship.[104] Although repression was most intense during 1976–79 and had peaked by 1980–81, dozens of new disappearances were reported as late as 1983, and both illicit detainees and political prisoners were held through the 1983 transition elections.[105] The pattern of repression falls under the rubric of state terror; the deliberate use of coercion by the state to create fear among a target group of citizens through the demonstration effect of attacks on a group of victims with whom the target groups identify.[106] Victims included pregnant teenagers, paralyzed intellectuals, French nuns, and some of the military's own diplomats—and the target group was all of Argentine society. The characteristic technique of state terror in Argentina was "disappearance," carried out by task forces composed predominantly of military personnel (but occasionally including civilians).[107] "Disappearance" involved the kidnapping of unarmed citizens (usually in the middle of the night, from their family homes) by a gang of armed men, followed by forced removal of the victims to clandestine detention centers, extensive torture, and mistreatment, and (almost always) murder. Task forces secured a "green light" within their zone of operations, so that local police were aware of and refused to respond to the assault. Although the kidnappers usually sought a specific person, other family members or visitors often "disappeared" in lieu of or in addition to the intended victim.[108]

The 1984 official report of the Comisión Nacional sobre la Desaparición de Personas (CONADEP) confirms almost 9,000 cases of disappeared persons who have never reappeared, but acknowledges that the true total is probably higher because of cases in which families were unable or unwilling to report the disappearance and cases in which entire families or groups of witnesses disappeared. Several human rights activists in working-class areas indicated personal knowledge of two to three times the number of cases reported to CONADEP in their areas, and a few cases in rural areas were still being reported in 1988. Even an amplified total will not include persons who were openly executed (usually in an alleged "armed confrontation" with the military) or persons whose death following their disappearance has been confirmed.[109] The record of cremations at Buenos Aires' largest cemetery, during a period unmarked by significant epidemics or natural disasters, is suggestive: from 13,120 in 1974 before the coup the number increased to 30,000 annually in 1978 and 1979, declining somewhat to 21,381 in 1980.[110]

The vast majority of the disappeared were taken to clandestine concentration camps, held and tortured for weeks or months, and then killed. CONADEP documented the existence of a national network of approximately 340 secret detention centers. The report summarizes:

The characteristics of these centers, and the daily life led there, reveal that they had been specifically conceived for the subjection of victims to a meticulous and deliberate stripping of all human attributes, rather than for their simple physical elimination. To be admitted to one of these centers meant to cease to exist. In order to achieve this end, attempts were made to break down the captives' identity; their spatio-temporal points of reference were disrupted, and their minds and bodies tortured beyond imagination.[111]

Torture, especially the administration of electric shocks with cattle prods for periods as long as several days at a time, is a constant feature of victims' accounts. Extreme beatings, near-drownings, hangings, burnings, rape, and mock executions were other forms of torture commonly practiced on prisoners.[112] The use of torture was scientific and systematic; for example, many victims received medical examinations during the course of a torture session to determine if they could withstand further mistreatment. But torture was only loosely related to a search for information—and was not intended as a method of execution. Victims were removed from the detention centers ("transferred") before being killed. While mass graves have been uncovered showing that many were shot, a substantial number were thrown from military helicopters into the Atlantic or the Rio de la Plata, and it is likely that many were cremated.

In estimating the scope and incidence of state terror in Argentina, it is important to consider the tens of thousands of persons directly affected by varying combinations of torture, murder, rape, kidnapping, and inhumane and illegitimate imprisonment, as well as the systematic violation of civil, political, and property rights prevalent in the society at large. In addition to the disappeared, the majority of the 8,000-plus Proceso-era political prisoners were also detained illicitly and often held and tortured for several days before being registered. Many "officialized" prisoners who had been arrested during the 1974–75 period also suffered torture and extremely inhumane conditions of imprisonment during the Proceso. Occasionally, registered prisoners ordered released subsequently disappeared.[113] A final category of (undocumented) victims of state terror includes persons kidnapped and tortured but released within a matter of days or weeks, as occurred with many trade union delegates.

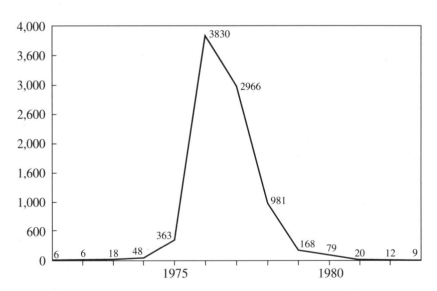

Fig. 1. The Pattern of Detentions and Disappearances, 1971–1983. (Source: CELS Centro de Documentación)

The repression was carried out under orders from the highest military authorities, implemented by an extensive military hierarchy, and coordinated among the various services.[114] The scope, scale, and systematic character of the repression constituted a conscious policy of state terror, not one attributable to the "excesses" of zealots or sadists, as was later argued by the military.[115] Although full records have never been recovered, survivors of some facilities report that centralized, microfilmed records were kept, and documents such as signed orders for arrest and the seizure of property have been located.[116]

Each military task force had a permanent membership, but other officers were rotated through to strengthen the "blood pact" of repression. An officer who disagreed with the methods (although not the goals) of the repression was pressured to participate, with the comment, "This one is too clean."[117] Although large proportions of the armed forces had knowledge of or provided logistical support for clandestine detention centers, those officers who engaged directly in torture constituted a relatively isolated group.[118] Guards were often drawn from police or prison forces, and conscripts were rarely involved.[119]

While the general strategy of repression was centrally planned and coordinated, each service, each military zone, each concentration camp, and even each task force had considerable latitude in deciding whom to detain, whether and how much to torture them, whether to officialize, release, or execute them, and how to dispose of their children and property.[120] This added a further element of randomness to the repression and militated against the success of lobbying or pressuring central governmental authorities. As one who was a political prisoner at the time (and subsequently, a Peronist legislator) put it: "In those days, the country was feudalized; there were guys decorated by the First Corps, kidnapped in the Second, killed by the Third, and vindicated by the Fifth."[121] And repressors received substantial personal rewards for their participation, including looting of the property of disappeared persons, and systematic appropriation and illicit adoption of children born to pregnant women in clandestine concentration camps.[122]

The targeting of victims for repression simultaneously reflected the regime's bureaucratic-authoritarian mission, the methodology of state terror, elements of a totalitarian apparatus, and personal caprice.[123] By its nature, state terror is often tied only loosely, if at all, to official repressive policies (in this case, the repression of guerrilla activity):

The ultimate targets of terrorist strategies are people who can recognize themselves as potential victims because they are members of a social group selected by the terrorist actors. . . . Thus, in many cases, targets of both state and non-

state terrorism become targets simply because they are members of some as-
cribed or achieved category, rather than for anything they have done personally. Hence, while terrorism is not arbitrary or indiscriminate, it may certainly
be impersonal.[124]

The disappeared included many persons extremely unlikely to engage
in guerrilla activity (and presenting a minimal threat to state security if
they did). Of the victims whose cases were registered with CONADEP,
1.65 percent (about 148) were children under the age of 15 and 1.41
percent (around 126) persons over the age of 60. About 269 were
pregnant women, and at least a dozen were disabled persons, several
of whom were completely paralyzed.[125]

In keeping with the need to disempower the working class, the regime disproportionately persecuted union activists.[126] In pursuit of the
total war against subversion, the dictatorship victimized anyone with
the capacity to question its ideological hegemony—especially journalists, academics, lawyers, and psychiatrists.[127] The persecution of these
occupational categories and neofascist military ideology combined to
produce disproportionate and exacerbated victimization of Argentina's
Jewish community.[128] Special conditions such as international recognition, foreign citizenship, and membership in the clergy did not protect
targeted victims from disappearance, torture, or—in most cases—murder.[129] The decentralized and unaccountable repressive apparatus soon
assumed a "life of its own": victims were persecuted merely for social
connections with other victims, or for affiliation with organizations er-
roneously labeled guerrilla front groups.[130] And members of task forces
sometimes even selected victims from the general population to satisfy
personal grudges, sadism, or acquisitiveness.[131]

Conclusion

The nature of the repression thus contributed to the rise of the
human rights movement. The sheer scope and scale of repression had
no precedent in Argentine history. For the first time, members of the
Argentine middle class with relatively high political expectations and
resources were victimized in large numbers. The deliberate randomness of state terror also caused a small but crucial group of previously
ignorant or acquiescent actors to question its legitimacy. Finally, the
technique of "disappearance," although it temporarily paralyzed resistance, eventually stimulated protest precisely because it blocked the
resolution of intolerable family uncertainty and loss.[132]

Most Argentines—like most witnesses to this century's other holocausts—trusted their government, refused to see what was happening, avoided conflict, and in any case blamed the victims.[133] But a few did not; they risked death to engage in irrational, seemingly futile resistance. In the flames of repression, the Argentine human rights movement forged a new way of doing politics.

Chapter 3

The Emergence of the
Human Rights Movement

"What we did wasn't courage; we had no choice."
Las Madres member

I n Argentina, ordinary citizens took to the streets and defied a powerful and murderous dictatorship. Political voice was evoked by intolerable uncertainty; hope and anger conquered fear.[1] They turned
to protest because their families and communities had been shattered,
their neighbors were silent, and their own government denied their
existence. Their public dramatization of personal anguish and quixotic
principled challenge to the ruthless exercise of state power barely registered in their own society, but it was sustained and amplified in the
international arena. As a result, the human rights agenda was taken up
both internationally and by a reawakened civil society in Argentina,
and the dictatorship ultimately collapsed. Symbolic protest combined
with structural crisis to bring down the dictators and shape an unprecedented transition to democracy.

The Reactions of Civil Society

The majority of Argentines avoided exploring or expanding their
inevitable peripheral awareness of the repression and accepted the military's justification for its activities. When confronted with evidence of
disappearances, the typical response was "Por algo habran hecho" or
"En algo anduvo" ("They must have done something"). But tens of
thousands of citizens were directly affected by the repression, and tens
of thousands more—their families, friends, neighbors, and colleagues—were indirectly affected and still capable of resistance. Their

options were limited, and the traditional structures of Argentine society—the legal system, the unions, the Church—all failed to offer a satisfactory response to this unprecedented situation. The form and distribution of disappearances interfered with the functioning of the family. Forty-five percent of the documented disappeared were under the age of 25 (the vast majority of whom would have been living at home) and 62 percent of the documented disappeared were detained in their own homes in front of witnesses—usually family members.[2] "Behind each disappearance is a family, often destroyed or dismembered, and always a family that is assaulted in its right to privacy, to the security of its members, and to respect for the profoundly affectionate relations that are the reason for its existence," notes the CONADEP report *Nunca más*, which goes on to cite cases of family members of suspects being tortured, held as hostages, or even themselves made to disappear.[3] The family became the only space available for the expression and interpretation of social conflict; it is thus no accident that three of the most influential of the ten human rights groups correspond to family roles (Las Madres, Las Abuelas, and Familiares de los Desaparecidos).

Citizens affected by violence of ambiguous provenance often turned to the legal system. Upon taking power, the dictatorship had dismissed all judges, replaced the Supreme Court and appeals courts, and subjected lower-ranking members of the judiciary to reconfirmation and a loyalty oath to the statutes of the Proceso.[4] Later, the dictatorship suddenly imposed the requirement that petitions of habeas corpus be signed by an attorney.[5]

The courts generally denied writs of habeas corpus and appeals for persons detained by the Executive to exercise their constitutional "right of option" to exile.[6] There were widespread allegations of judicial complicity in failure to investigate detainees' allegations of mistreatment, uncritical certification for burial of unidentified bodies, and registration of illicit adoptions.[7] On the other side of the bench, there were additional obstacles. In a series of legal actions, proceedings were suspended "in 8 cases owing to disappearance of attorney; in 20 cases owing to death [of client]; in 24 cases owing to exile; [and] in 21 cases owing to imprisonment," according to a Familiares report. Proceedings "in 27 cases [were] affected by terrorist intimidation of the attorney . . . in only 11 cases, did the action take its normal course, and these took place in the period following 1980."[8]

The only glimmers of judicial responsiveness to human rights violations came in a handful of habeus corpus appeals that reached the Supreme Court; the most successful was the ruling ordering the publisher Jacobo Timerman freed by the military.[9] A more typical situation was that of a lower-court judge, later an active defender of human rights under democracy, who was troubled by hundreds of complaints of kidnappings by armed gangs claiming a connection to the security forces. When this judge (more active than most) approached the secretary of justice, he was warned not to interfere with military affairs. His only recourse—he felt—was to "disqualify himself to rule on the case," thus forcing the cases up to a higher court.[10]

Trade unions had long been one of Argentina's strongest social institutions, and traditionally combined the roles of labor representation and political opposition.[11] Since the repression affected workers and unionists disproportionately, it was natural that some sought support from their unions. But the most combative unionists themselves disappeared, and the bulk of the remaining union leadership largely collaborated with the dictatorship.[12] "Despite internal differences, rank-and-file pressure, and the opposition stance that the 25 [dissident confederation] were assuming, the relationship between the dictatorship and the union leadership was good, across all sectors."[13]

Strikes, sabotage, and rank-and-file resistance to repression continued throughout the Proceso, without penetrating the union hierarchy until the transition era.[14] A leader of a minority union movement that argued for the release of political prisoners and acknowledgement of the disappeared pleaded with his fellow union leaders, "We can no longer continue compromising below; it could produce uncontrollable reactions and we shall be unjustly blamed. One must remember that the workers suppose that we are complacent. The risk is that less patient leaders will appear."[15]

Finally, many approached the Church for spiritual comfort and with some hope of mediation. But despite the fact that members of the clergy were themselves disappearing, and the support provided by some dissident churchmen and women, the Church as an institution was at best complacent and at worst complicitous.[16] In addition to its long-standing doctrinal support for military rule and the "Dirty War," the Argentine Church continued to operate a military vicariate and initially refused to receive the relatives of the disappeared. Of more than eighty bishops, only four engaged in any human rights advocacy.[17] More ominously, members of the clergy were seen at torture centers, in at least one case performing a Mass for shackled and hooded detainees—and urging them to confess.[18]

Eventually, the Church did designate a member of the military chaplaincy to receive relatives of the disappeared at a site controlled by the military—and despite the conditions, thousands came, without results.[19] In addition, the Episcopal Council eventually sent a series of carefully worded private letters to the junta, expressing concern over the unresolved issue of disappearance, "which seems to show that the government does not have an exclusive hold on the use of force," but never engaged in any public criticism of the regime.[20] As a foreign observer summarized it, "The impact to date on human rights activities by Argentine churches has been the least effective of all other church groups in the subcontinent."[21]

The failure of the Argentine Church is particularly important in explaining the emergence of the human rights movement. At least two of the human rights groups (SERPAJ and Movimiento Ecuménico) and several key activists (Emilio Mignone, the Fernandez Meijide family, and a number of Madres and Abuelas) began movement activity after unsuccessfully approaching Church officials.[22] The human rights movement then assumed the Church's traditional role in elaborating symbols, rituals, and metaphors to explain and resolve death and injustice.

A Brief Guide to the Human Rights Movement

The Argentine human rights movement consists of ten organizations whose main purpose was or is the defense of the rights of the person.[23] These groups have formed various alliances or informal *lineas* in relation to government policy. During the Proceso, those who limited their demands to information contrasted with those who demanded government accountability; during the constitutional period, the dividing factor has been willingness to participate in or support government policies that most groups agree are incomplete. Members of the human rights groups also distinguish among groups and activists: between *afectados* (those directly affected by the repression) and non-*afectados*. However, the groups can be functionally divided into civil libertarians, family-based organizations, and religious movements.[24]

Civil Libertarians

Two civil libertarian groups, the Liga Argentina por los Derechos del Hombre and Asamblea Permanente por los Derechos Humanos (APDH), were founded before the 1976 coup, and a third, the Centro de Estudios Legales y Sociales, includes many members whose activism began in the Asamblea or as individuals before 1976. If not previously involved in political parties or government, most members of these organizations were active in law, education, or other professions that provide some basic political skills. All of these groups used collection and reporting of evidence of human rights violations and legal activity as their main strategies.[25]

The civil libertarians based their activity on an appeal to universal principles and respect for legal norms. Their emphasis on legal activities played a consciousness-raising role and helped to build (domestic and international) organizational networks.[26] These groups have a relatively structured relationship to political parties. Although La Liga has no formal ties to the Communist party, it is widely seen as a party organ, while the APDH includes open representatives of the Radical, Socialist, Intransigent, and Christian Democratic parties on its Directive Council. The leadership of both the APDH and CELS suffered repression by the military, but in both cases were ultimately released because of international pressure.

The Liga was founded in 1937 and, as noted, had been active prior to the Proceso; it was a co-founder of the International Federation for the Rights of Man, which holds a permanent seat at the United Nations, and had long stressed international solidarity. Although the founders of the Liga included Radicals and socialists, the organization's reputation as a representative of Communist party positions helped to inspire the 1975 founding of the multiparty Asamblea Permanente as an alternative human rights forum. During the Proceso, the Liga's position of "critical dialogue" with the dictatorship and concentration on traditional political prisoners (rather than the disappeared) and the legal system led *afectados* meeting in Liga offices to found Familiares de Desaparecidos y Detenidos por Razones Políticas. Despite its perceived insufficiencies, the Liga took a leading role in the few successful legal actions of the era.[27]

The Asamblea, or APDH, was founded in 1975 in response to the growing death-squad violence and repressive legislation of the second Perón administration. Its elaborate multisectoral structure attempts to incorporate official representatives of every party and social group in Argentine society, drawn from throughout the country. In contrast to the Liga, the Asamblea does not maintain any formal international affiliations.

The APDH was the largest and most active civil libertarian organization during the Proceso. During the dictatorship, this group systematically recorded information on almost 6,000 disappearances, providing the documentary basis for international appeals and domestic investigations during the Alfonsín period. Although it did not provide individuals with legal defense, the APDH also participated in legal action and public education; its leaders credit the organization with blocking the application of the Ley de Presunción de Fallecimiento ("presumption of death" law; see further below) and with leading opposition to the military's proposed self-amnesty.[28]

The Centro de Estudios Legales y Sociales was formed by a group of lawyers—notably the dissident lay Catholic Emilio Mignone—who broke away from the Asamblea in 1979, generally seeking a more aggressive and less "evenhanded" approach to state terror. CELS has combined the Liga's function of legal defense with the Asamblea's role in documentation, with some differences in emphasis. Legally, CELS sought to establish state involvement in the repression as well as challenging specific government actions and legislation. In terms of documentation, CELS was less active than the APDH in processing cases but took a greater role in analyzing data and establishing patterns. CELS has also established the most complete human rights archive in Argentina, including books, periodicals, an extensive clippings file, and its own publications. CELS has no formal relationship with any political party or sector, but maintains extensive international affiliations, including ties with the International Committee of Jurists (Geneva) and International League for Human Rights (New York).[29]

Family-Based Groups

The family-based groups are the Madres de Plaza de Mayo, Abuelas de Plaza de Mayo, and Familiares de Detenidos y Desaparecidos por Razones Políticas. These groups were all founded in the midst of and as a direct result of state terror. Very few of their members were politically or professionally active before joining the human rights movement. Their main strategy was highly symbolic political protest. This has included the famous weekly vigils, petitions, and visual representations concerning the disappeared, and a leading role in organizing several dozen mass demonstrations since 1982. They base their activity on a personal sense of loss, the rights of families to protect their members, and the obligations of the state to those families.

The best-known human rights group is the Madres de Plaza de Mayo.[30] Las Madres were the first and most active family-based human rights movement in Argentina, and their emergence marked a historically and internationally new form of social organization. The Mothers originally met in the halls of government offices while seeking information as to the whereabouts of their disappeared (adult and adolescent) children. By April 1977, fourteen of these politically inexperienced middle-aged women had decided to engage in public protest in the central political space of the nation: the Plaza de Mayo in Buenos Aires. Las Madres established a form of ritual weekly vigil in the capital's central square, marked by their use of highly evocative symbols such as poster-sized photographs of their missing children and the wearing of white scarves (derived from diapers) to represent motherhood. As their num-bers grew from dozens to hundreds by 1978, the Mothers added peti-tions, pilgrimages, and paid newspaper announcements (*solicitadas*) to their protest repertoire: one petition gained 24,000 signatures in the midst of severe repression. Government repression was severe throughout 1979, but by 1980 Las Madres had retaken the Plaza with a more determined stance of passive resistance, and by 1981 they were leading mass demonstrations of thousands, and then tens of thousands.

Las Madres engaged in political theater and challenged the regime's legitimacy in its own terms to attain domestic acceptance and interna-tional appeal. Their first published advertisement ("We do not ask for anything more than the truth") recalled President Jorge Videla's state-ment on a visit to the United States that "Nobody who tells the truth will suffer reprisals."[31] The Madres' first newsletter was even more explicit in framing their demands in terms of the regime's own claims and the activists' social legitimacy:

We don't even ask for their freedom. We are just trying to get [someone] to tell us where they are, of what they are accused, and that they be judged in accor-dance with the law and the legitimate right of defense, if they are considered to have committed any crime. That they not be tortured. . . . Could there be any plea more elemental, more correct, more human, more Christian?[32]

The Mothers consciously contested the imagery being promoted by the "Western, Christian" Proceso; they made pilgrimages to sites of popu-lar Marian devotion and evoked the suffering of mothers seeking chil-dren crucified by a state that claimed to be Christian but did not even allow the family to bury its dead.[33] Las Madres' challenge was particu-larly directed at the military, which had historically styled itself a Ma-rian institution. The legitimacy of Las Madres was such that it even mitigated street-level repression. Mothers would turn on the police sent to break up their protests, saying, "Aren't you ashamed to attack de-fenseless mothers? Don't you have children?"—often causing the police to hang back.[34] Through this new form of protest, the Mothers moved from a desperate search for their individual children to an identity-based social movement protesting on behalf of "every mother's son."[35]

The Abuelas de Plaza de Mayo (grandmothers of the disappeared) arose in tandem with Las Madres, since participants initially identified themselves primarily as women whose adult children had disappeared. But within a few years, the Abuelas began to realize that the disappearance of entire families (their children and grandchildren) and the kidnapping of pregnant women were neither exceptional nor temporary. By 1978, the Grandmothers began to focus on the fate of their missing grandchildren as a separate issue. At that time, the Abuelas focused on legal activities and general appeals to conscience to solicit information from the general public on the location of their grandchildren, while continuing to participate in the Madres' protests. A 1978 paid announcement stated: "We appeal to the conscience and the heart—of those who have or know of our disappeared grandchildren. . . . God enlighten those who receive the smiles and affection of our grandchildren to respond to this anguished call to conscience."[36] Legal actions were generally unavailing during the Proceso, but the Abuelas' particular legitimacy, international links, and some information established during this period laid the groundwork for the restitutions and institutional reforms of the Alfonsín era.[37]

The final family-based group, Familiares de Los Detenidos-Desaparecidos y Presos por Razones Políticas, differed from the above groups in several ways. First, the Familiares ("relatives") included male relatives and did not engage in ritual protest centered on female identity. The Familiares also included many relatives of officially recognized political prisoners, pursuing their release and improvement of human rights and inhumane conditions in the regular prison system. Finally, as the organization's name indicates, this group treated the repression as a political strategy and its victims as political actors, rather than appealing to "apolitical" principles such as the rule of law or the sanctity of the family.[38] The group gathered and published information, provided assistance to prisoners and their families, and participated in multisectoral mass demonstrations, but generally played less of a public and symbolic role than the Madres and Abuelas.[39]

Religious Movements

SERPAJ, the Movimiento Ecuménico por los Derechos Humanos, and the Movimiento Judío por los Derechos Humanos make up the religious human rights movements. Both SERPAJ and the Movimiento Ecuménico arose because (lay or clerical) religious activists were unable to provide pastoral services within traditional religious structures to those affected by repression. The Movimiento Ecuménico and Movimiento Judío also incorporated dissident religious figures who consciously sought to use their status and religious identification to repudiate and delegitimize repression, notwithstanding the acquiescence of the dominant religious community. Each of these movements bases its work on a philosophical commitment to a broad vision of social justice—in the cases of both SERPAJ and the Movimiento Ecuménico, there are explicit references to liberation theology.

SERPAJ (Servicio Paz y Justicia) was founded in 1971 as a pan–Latin American movement for social justice inspired by liberation theology; since 1974, it has been headed by the Argentine Adolfo Perez-Esquivel. The human rights crisis in Argentina and its effect on SERPAJ's base-level constituency soon came to dominate the organization's regional

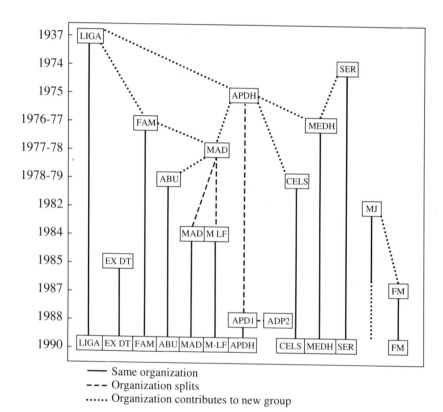

Fig. 2. The Organizational Development of the Argentine Human Rights Movement. (Abbreviations: LIGA, La Liga; EX-DT, Ex-Detenidos; FAM, Familiares; ABU, Abuelas; MAD, Madres; M-LF, Madres–Linea Fundadora; APDH, Asamblea [1 + 2]; CELS, CELS; MEDH, MEDH; SER, SERPAJ; MJ, Movimiento Judío; FM, Fundacíon para la Memoria)

agenda, and other issues were postponed. SERPAJ activities during the dictatorship concentrated on providing organization, assistance, and education to the marginalized grass-roots sectors most affected by the repression. For example, a 1977 publication provides a list of national and international human rights organizations and model forms for filing a habeas corpus petition and complaint with the OAS Human Rights Commission.[40] SERPAJ also helped to form the Asamblea and the Movimiento Ecuménico.[41]

The Movimiento Ecuménico por los Derechos Humanos (MEDH) was formed in 1976 by dissident members of the Catholic clergy unhappy with the Church's lack of responsiveness to its parishioners, along with several leaders of Argentina's long-standing mainline Protestant community. Unlike the lay activists in SERPAJ, clerics belonged to the MEDH as official representatives of their congregations, and the group was closely linked to the World Council of Churches, so that its mere existence made it an important symbolic counterweight to the role of the Argentine Church. In addition to serving as a source of alternative theological interpretation and religious legitimacy for the human rights movement, the MEDH provided extensive material, spiritual, legal, and psychological assistance to families affected by the repression, especially in the provinces.[42]

The panorama of the religious human rights organizations is completed by the Movimiento Judío por los Derechos Humanos. Since Argentina's large Jewish community was disproportionately affected by repression, and Jews were disproportionately active in the human rights movement, this sector of the movement inevitably sought a vehicle for recognition of its identity. For various reasons, the Ecumenical Movement could only bridge the inter-Christian gap and failed to provide a space for Jews as a community. Jewish activists therefore began working together in 1977, formalizing their movement in 1982. Under the leadership of the journalist Herman Schiller, the Movimiento Judío lent a distinctively Jewish presence and interpretation to multisectoral events.[43]

International Responses

Both Argentine state terror and the emergence of the human rights movement generated significant international response. International organizations, foreign governments, the media, and citizens of other nations helped the Argentine human rights movement to survive and shifted the agenda of the dictatorship. The nature of the symbolic protest and information projected by the movement allowed it to en-

gage an international audience. The informal (and at times unconscious) division of labor within the human rights movement successfully
combined political theater, which mobilized domestic awareness and
lobbying in Europe and the United States, and documentation, which
served as the concrete basis for international policy decisions like the
U.S. aid cutoff and 1979 inspection visit of the OAS Human Rights
Commission (see below). International actors provided the movement
with protection, legitimacy, information, and resources.

The family-based sector of the movement communicated with the
international system both symbolically and directly. The image of grieving
mothers' silent weekly vigil was a challenge to the legitimacy of the
Argentine regime that was heard round the world. Members of Las
Madres visited the United States, Canada, and Europe in 1978 at the
height of the dictatorship. In 1979, Las Madres sent delegates to the
Catholic Church's Puebla Conference, the Organization of American
States, and the United Nations, and representatives of the group testified before the U.S. Congress. Las Madres were nominated for the
Nobel Peace Prize in 1980. When members of Las Madres toured Europe during the year of the transition to democracy (1983), they were
received as dignitaries by the prime minister of Spain, President Fran-
çois Mitterand of France, and the pope.

Meanwhile, "insider" civil libertarians were gathering information
documenting the nature and scope of human rights violations. The
most international of these groups, CELS, established with impetus
from the Washington-based Center for Law and Social Policy and a
grant from the U.S. Agency for International Development, is affiliated
with the International Commission of Jurists (Geneva) and the International League for Human Rights, and has subsequently received
funding from the Ford Foundation. The founder of CELS, Emilio Mignone, had worked for the Organization of American States in Washington during the 1960's, and thus had extensive international connections. CELS was founded in distinction to the preexisting APDH precisely to increase the international ties of concerned lawyers and affiliated activists.[44] As a result, CELS (and APDH) lists of the disappeared
served as the basis for OAS and U.N. activities in Argentina, and material prepared by CELS was incorporated substantially in the 1989 OAS
Report on the Situation of Human Rights in Argentina.

The impact of the Argentine human rights movement's contact with
international actors was magnified by the existence of an "international
human rights regime" that was greater than the sum of its constituent
states, international organizations, and NGOs (nongovernmental orga-

nizations).[45] The international human rights regime created an information network and a principle of "moral interdependence" that helped propagate the human rights movement's concerns across national boundaries.[46] This new pattern of international cooperation on human rights developed critical strength during the era of the Argentine Proceso (1976–83): the Carter administration displayed a new commitment to human rights by the regional hegemon, multilateral human rights forums grew stronger, and—most important—nongovernmental transnational organizations played an increasing role.[47]

Every type of actor in the international human rights regime participated in diplomatic pressure on Argentina. Under Jimmy Carter, no Argentine junta leader was ever invited to the United States on an official state visit, whereas U.S. Deputy Secretary of State Warren Christopher sought out the CELS leader Emilio Mignone and Las Madres on visits to Argentina. U.S. Assistant Secretary of State for Human Rights Patricia Derian constantly criticized the Argentine juntas' human rights violations and made several trips to Argentina, openly advocating human rights groups demands. When U.S. Secretary of State Cyrus Vance visited Argentina in 1977, he handed Argentine leaders a list of 7,500 cases of disappearance to investigate; the list had been prepared by the NGO Argentina Information and Service Center.[48]

The United States imposed economic linkage on Argentina, governing both bilateral aid and multilateral lending.[49] The most dramatic case was a 1977 U.S. aid cut, followed by a withdrawal of all military aid and multilateral sanctions in 1978. The United States voted against 23 of 25 Argentine multilateral development bank loan requests between 1977 and 1980, and by late 1978 the Overseas Private Investment Corporation (which insures against political risk for private investors) would no longer consider applications for Argentina.[50] Much of the general legislation linking U.S. votes in multilateral aid and lending institutions to human rights monitoring was passed at this time, informed by the Argentine case.[51] Even when the 1978 U.S. arms ban was lifted by the Reagan administration, Congress insisted on country-specific conditions in the International Security and Development Act, naming Argentina and requiring human rights certification for the resumption of aid—including an accounting for the disappeared (a key human rights movement demand).

The United States also linked bilateral relations to participation in multilateral human rights forums and successfully pressed Argentina to admit representatives of the International Committee of the Red Cross to its prisons. Argentina's admission of the OAS Human Rights

Commission was linked to a U.S. decision to unfreeze Export-Import Bank funds that the U.S. company Allis-Chalmers needed to invest in Argentina.

International and regional organizations added their response to human rights violations in Argentina. The United Nations tracked individual cases, challenged patterns of repression, and established new mechanisms. The United Nations ultimately pursued 7,000 cases in Argentina.[52] U.N. involvement in Argentina began over the dictatorship's persecution of refugees under the protection of the U.N. High Commission on Refugees; the commission evacuated some of these potential victims, and the United Nations passed a resolution condemning Argentina's violation of international norms in 1976. By 1978, evidence presented by NGOs led to a specific recognition and condemnation of the practice of disappearances. Eventually (in 1980), the United Nations established a Working Group on Forced Disappearance, largely in response to the situation in Argentina; the Working Group was backed by the U.S. representative (the former head of a human rights NGO) and structured to allow greater participation by affected individuals and human rights groups than preexisting mechanisms based on governmental representation. The United Nations was particularly responsive to Las Abuelas' campaign to trace their missing grandchildren, representing this issue to the Argentine government on several occasions. As Argentina's ambassador noted, Argentina's status as a pariah was such that France vetoed Argentina's candidate for U.N. secretary-general on the basis of Argentina's human rights violations.[53]

Both the general credibility and specific claims of the human rights movement were bolstered by the 1979 inspection visit of the OAS Human Rights Commission, a multilateral, technically neutral body, which confirmed and expanded the reports of thousands of disappearances. Furthermore, the OAS report's closing recommendations echoed human rights movement demands: investigation, trial, and punishment for all deaths attributable to government agents, restoration of the right of habeas corpus and the option of exile, lifting of the state of siege, and government action to "facilitate the contribution" of human rights organizations.[54] The Organization of American States received evidence of disappearances from the human rights groups APDH, Familiares, La Liga, MEDH, and CELS.[55]

There is an extensive debate on the wider consequences of this pattern of pressure on human rights in Argentina.[56] While some cite the restraining effect of U.S. diplomatic and economic linkage, others question its effectiveness, consistency, and unintended consequences.[57] International pressure clearly inspired nationalist resistance in the short run, but international delegitimation produced long-run shifts in discourse and the establishment of new institutions (treated below) that may have weakened the dictatorship.

And international pressure had clear and positive results for the development of the human rights movement: the international system shielded activists, legitimized protest, and transferred resources to the Argentine movement. President Carter tossed the APDH's telegram reporting the recent disappearance of the Asamblea leader Alfredo Bravo across his desk to General Jorge Videla, president of the first junta, who was then paying a state visit to the United States. Bravo's detention was officialized, and he survived the dictatorship.[58] Similarly, the entire leadership of CELS was released from prison following generalized international protest.[59] When the CELS leader Emilio Mignone was arrested, the police assured witnesses that he would not disappear—because he was too well known. The Washington Center for Legal and Social Studies (and many individuals) contacted the State Department, while the Ford Foundation lobbied the U.S. Embassy in Argentina. The U.S. Embassy then warned Videla and the Argentine Foreign Ministry that the CELS arrests could hurt Argentina in the U.N. Human Rights Commission.[60] Madre Renée Epelbaum was picked up by a death squad during the World Cup Soccer Championships, but released because of the presence of foreign witnesses.[61] By 1981, SERPAJ had established political contacts in Europe as "repression insurance," which proved successful shortly thereafter in securing the release of a group of rank-and-file activists.[62]

The international system also granted legitimacy to the human rights movement. The award of the 1980 Nobel Peace Prize to the (previously obscure) SERPAJ leader Adolfo Perez-Esquivel gave the Argentine people pause. International media coverage of and papal meetings with Las Madres had a similar effect. International peers used their own domestic legitimacy to create transnational alliances to pressure more accessible regimes: women's groups protested on behalf of the Mothers in France and Holland, while the International Commission of Jurists and World Council of Churches used their own legitimacy and expertise to defend their Argentine counterparts.

Finally, international actors provided the Argentine human rights movement with concrete information and resources. The sympathetic secretary of the U.S. Embassy, Tex Harris, provided Las Madres with the schedule of visiting North American dignitaries.[63] The Mothers initial overseas contacts were suggested by foreign journalists, and[64] a Dutch group purchased the building that served as their meeting place and organizational home. The Abuelas received technical advice in their search for their grandchildren from scientific institutions in the United States, France, and Sweden.[65] Even the calculation of the number of victims was shaped by lists prepared by Amnesty International, the (New York) Lawyers' Committee on Human Rights, and other international groups.[66] It was a foreign visitor who introduced one of Las Madres most dramatic slogans: *Con vida los llevaron, con vida los queremos* ("You took them away alive, we want them back alive").[67]

International pressure contributed significantly to the emergence of the Argentine human rights movement. The international system sustained and amplified the human rights challenge long enough for civil society to reemerge. The military's response to this challenge fused with economic mismanagement and the Malvinas crisis to delegitimate the dictatorship.

Military Responses to Human Rights Activity

Direct government responses to human rights activity during the Proceso involved a contradictory combination of practices and institutions: the repression of activists and simultaneous establishment of administrative and legal measures to "resolve the problem of the disappeared." An important indirect response to both movement and international pressure—a shifting pattern of discourse—helped to delegitimate the dictatorship and facilitate the transition.

Repression of the human rights movement touched every organization, affecting both the leadership and grass-roots membership. Many members of the original leadership of Las Madres (nine people) "disappeared," while the Movimiento Ecuménico lost two nuns, several priests, and a Protestant minister.[68] The co-founder of the Asamblea, Alfredo Bravo, was kidnapped, tortured, and imprisoned for several years, as was Adolfo Perez-Esquivel of SERPAJ, while the leadership of CELS were arrested but then released.[69] Several Liga lawyers disappeared, and a secretary of the Familiares was kidnapped, tortured, and forced to give false statements to the press denying her disappearance and alleging connections to guerrilla forces.[70] Rank-and-file members of Las Madres were arrested repeatedly following demonstrations, and various *afectados* were detained to prevent their contact with human rights organizations.[71] The offices of the Asamblea, CELS, La Liga, and Movimiento Ecuménico were raided, chiefly before the 1979 visit of the OAS inspection commission.[72] This repression removed activists from the movement, but did not crush the movement itself.

Meanwhile, the regime tacitly acknowledged the claims of the human rights movement by establishing mechanisms designed to coopt growing concern about human rights violations. Ironically, each government initiative only generated more activism. The military government opened a national office to register claims of disappearance, housed in the Interior Ministry.[73] Later on, the military authorities promulgated a law that would have permitted disappeared persons to be declared dead without their families' consent and proposed a system of pensions for the families.[74] The human rights movements brought legal challenges to the "presumption of death" law that resulted in its nonimplementation, while completely rejecting the pensions.[75] Eventually, the government even removed small numbers of police and military officers for "excesses" or "abuse of power."[76]

Finally, the military responded symbolically to symbolic challenge. The shifting pattern of discourse involved both public and internal statements and encompassed both the tenor of routine communications and specially staged public relations events.[77] In keeping with the regime's transient authoritarian mandate, the military acknowledged human rights as a political ideal—laying the basis for subsequent challenge of its legitimacy by the human rights movement. Shortly after the coup, President Videla said, "For us, respect for human rights comes not only from law and international declarations, but results from our profound Christian conviction on the fundamental dignity of man."[78] From 1976 until around 1978, the dictatorship's response to human rights protest began with a refusal to admit the problem, combined with attempts to discredit activists. After several years of human rights protest (around 1978–81), the official position changed to acknowledgement of the phenomenon of disappearance combined with a refusal to explain it (or vague reference to "excesses") and a nationalist portrayal of international criticism as an "anti-Argentine campaign." In a 1979 Army Day speech, the Army commander in chief, Roberto Viola, explained, "We've accomplished our mission—that is the only and sufficient explanation. The country and the Armed Forces know the price . . . the dead, the injured, the detained, 'los ausentes para siempre' [the forever absent]."[79] Finally, as internal military consensus wavered, and through the Malvinas War, a clear strategy emerged of emphasizing the existence of a "dirty war" that required unconventional techniques. On a 1981 visit to the United States, Viola responded to international criticism, "I think that you are suggesting that we investigate the security forces—absolutely out of the question. This is a war and we are the winners. You can be certain that in the last war if the armies of the Reich had won, the war crimes trials would have hap-

pened in Virginia, not in Nuremberg."[80] Growing military awareness
of possible accountability for the repression led to rumors of the release
of information to families, and attempts to "privatize" the issue of human rights violations as a matter strictly between the military and the
families.[81]

The military also promoted public relations efforts designed to counter
the effects of human rights criticism. The junta hired a U.S. public
relations firm to improve its image abroad.[82] While Admiral Emilio
Massera was commander in chief of the Armed Forces, he founded a
disinformation center in Paris that published blind ads, with no sponsor
listed; forged material attributed to human rights groups; and attempted to infiltrate exile organizations. Back at home, the admiral's
torture center at the Naval Mechanics School forced detainees to work
writing and translating propaganda material for the domestic and international press.[83] Like many repressive regimes before and since, the
dictatorship used sports as a source of cathartic mobilization and nationalist stimulation. The government organized a soccer celebration to
coincide with and distract from the OAS Human Rights Commission's
1979 inspection visit to Argentina.[84] The official use of the 1978 Soccer
World Cup to promote nationalism marked the high point of this strategy, rivaling the 1936 Berlin Olympics in domestic impact.[85]

Internally, too, the military began to suffer increasing loss of cohesion over a series of issues, among them human rights and the criticism
it generated. A 1980 speech to the troops prominently mentioned human rights, but carefully reinterpreted the issue as "aftereffects of the
aggression realized by terrorist organizations to dissolve Argentine society."[86] A later internal junta project for the institutionalization of military rule spoke of a legitimacy crisis, noted the existence of human
rights criticism (especially international and Church pressure), and
recommended eliminating any cause for criticism.[87] This military loss
of mission became a critical factor in the transition to democracy.[88]

The Transition to Democracy

The collapse of Argentina's military dictatorship and the 1983–84
transition to democracy resulted from a combination of economic decline, external military defeat, and a domestic legitimacy crisis. Although the fall of the dictatorship cannot be directly attributed to the
human rights movement, it is important to emphasize the role human
rights protest played in delegitimating the regime before the Malvinas
defeat and conditioning the character of the transition that followed.

In turn, the transition that resulted opened a space for further development of the human rights movement challenge.

General Videla had handed over power to General Viola in March 1981, just as the consequences of economic mismanagement were catching up with a regime that had been unconstrained by the demands of civilian sectors. The juntas' economic programs led to a vast and precarious increase in the role of finance and borrowing, along with an overvalued exchange rate. This combination produced a trade deficit, capital flight, and near-collapse of the deregulated banking system in 1980.[89] As a result, the foreign debt tripled between December 1979 and March 1981, the government took on $5 billion worth of private-sector debt, and inflation hit 131 percent and the peso depreciated 600 percent during 1981.[90] During the last quarter of 1981, GNP was down 11.4 percent, industrial production had fallen 23 percent, and real wages had dropped around 20 percent.[91] By the end of the year, Viola—the leader slated to stabilize and institutionalize the Proceso initiated by Videla—had been ousted by General Leopoldo Galtieri, a hard-liner.

The economic crisis fused with long-standing dissatisfactions, many tied to the repression, to inspire increasing resistance from key civil sectors. By March 1981, the corporate organizations representing both rural agricultural exporters (the Sociedad Rural) and urban manufacturers (the Unión Industrial Argentina) had issued statements highly critical of Proceso economic policies. A private elite group released a report criticizing the regime's lack of legitimacy, citing both institutional problems and international isolation resulting from human rights criticism.[92] Labor was also reviving; in November 1981, a Mass for St. Cayetano—the patron saint of labor—drew 50,000 with the slogan "Peace, Bread and Work." Even the Church was changing: "In March 1981, after five years of silence, tolerance and complacency, the Conference of Argentine Bishops issued a document (Church and National Community) criticizing the excesses of repression and pointing out the dangers of usury."[93] But perhaps most important, all of Argentina's major political parties joined forces and issued a call and program for return to civilian rule. This multiparty front for democracy, the Multipartidaria, issued a proposal that explicitly attacked the dictatorship for the denial of human rights and demanded information on the disappeared, processing of untried prisoners, an end to the state of siege, and implementation of the constitutional rule of law (*el estado de derecho*).[94]

Seen against this background, the catalytic factor in the transition—the invasion of the Malvinas—had roots in and implications for the social crisis.[95] The loss of the war did not cause, but accelerated the transition: "A victory in the war would have bought some time for the regime; the defeat simply hastened a degenerative process already underway."[96] Although plans to invade the Malvinas had been established long before, several massive multi-issue demonstrations in March of 1982 (including both the human rights and labor movements) speeded the invasion.[97] The decision to invade the highly symbolic but strategically insignificant islands was colored by the military's internal loss of mission and external legitimacy crisis: "From being the army of the 'Dirty War,' they would turn into patriots. . . . The war against subversion would be sanctified as the necessary prelude to the war for the Malvinas."[98]

Once the dictatorship had been goaded into this disastrous episode, related factors came into play. Simply the fact that the timing of the invasion was pushed forward because of social pressure probably contributed to the lack of planning and coordination that resulted in defeat. In general, the loss of the Malvinas War can be traced to many characteristics of the Argentine Armed Forces that were shaped by their experience as a repressive power: feudalized command structures, massive corruption, lack of experience or inclination to engage in direct combat.[99] Planes that had been used against the guerrillas in Tucumán proved inappropriate for war with an external power. Alfredo Astiz—the naval officer infamous for his infiltration and kidnapping of Las Madres—ignominiously surrendered his command. The only military success in the islands was one the military had practiced extensively on the mainland: the taking of the seat of government.[100]

The loss of the Malvinas had swift and decisive results in Buenos Aires. The mobilized nationalist throngs that had rallied round the flag remembered their discontent and were transformed into angry mobs calling for the overthrow of the junta.[101] The dictatorship itself fell into disarray over recriminations concerning the defeat; the Navy and Air Force bolted from the junta, forcing the Army to designate a new president without support from the other services—and with a clear mandate to oversee a transition to civilian rule. And when lingering incidents of repression occurred, human rights groups protested openly, received social support, and often succeeded in forcing the release of disappeared citizens or the officialization of their imprisonment.[102] Overall, the result was "the delegitimation of the military, both as a professional organization and as a political actor. This was, paradoxically, a result of using force in both the domestic and international arenas."[103]

The junta headed by General Reynaldo Bignone that took power in mid 1982 was in many respects a caretaker administration, but the military took clear steps to resolve the increasingly volatile issue of human rights and the emerging question of accountability. In November 1982, the new regime tried to broker a national accord to govern the transition, including accountability for the disappeared and the Malvinas debacle—but the political parties refused, instead mobilizing the masses against the pact in December.[104] Around the same time, the first mass grave of unidentified bodies was discovered in La Plata, the SERPAJ leader Perez-Esquivel led a mass demonstration against the accord, and the CGT trade union confederation called its first general strike since the 1976 coup.[105]

Elections were scheduled for October 1983; in April, the military tried again, issuing its *Documento final de la junta militar sobre la guerra contra la subversión y el terrorismo* ("Final Document of the Military Junta on the War Against Subversion and Terrorism"), which dealt extensively with the disappeared, asserting that many of them were guerrillas who had gone into exile, that some had been buried as unidentified bodies in an unconventional war, and that any remaining unresolved cases should be considered dead "for legal purposes." The military affirmed that all operations had been conducted under orders, called for national reconciliation, and reserved itself to the judgment of history.[106] In May, the human rights movement headed a march of 30,000 rejecting the *Documento final*.[107]

Finally, in September, with time running out before the October elections, the junta issued a retrospective amnesty for all acts committed during the war against subversion—theoretically applicable to both sides of the "Dirty War."[108] The law was criticized by representatives of political forces across the civilian political spectrum.[109] The "auto-amnesty" was later struck down as one of the first acts of the newly elected legislature, but even before the transition, various judges had declared it unconstitutional.[110]

The transition elections of October 1983 marked not only a change of regime, but a fundamental change in the character of political life. Although the human rights groups did not make any presidential endorsements, they attended all political rallies and colored the agenda of the campaign. The unprecedented and overwhelming victory of the Radical party in open elections was influenced by Alfonsín's use of human rights as a campaign issue, and a widespread perception that Peronism represented a return to a violent past.[111] The Peronist candidate for president, Italo Luder, had signed the order requiring the Armed Forces to "annihilate" subversion, and refused to repudiate the self-amnesty they had declared.[112] Herminio Iglesias, the Peronist candidate for governor of Buenos Aires, was associated with reputedly violent sectors of the labor movement. He is believed to have alienated large numbers of undecided voters by burning a coffin symbolizing the Radical party during the closing campaign rally.[113]

Meanwhile, Alfonsín's speeches regularly incorporated references to peace, legality, and human rights.[114] He pledged to repeal the self-amnesty and to put the military on trial. Alfonsín also linked the repression to a corporatist analysis of Argentine society by denouncing a "union-military pact" to broker the transition.[115] Describing the change in political identity symbolized by Alfonsín's victory, the Argentine sociologist Emilio de Ipola concluded, "For the Radicales, there are citizens but no corporations; for the Peronists, there are corporations but no citizens. The 1983 elections were the 'revenge of the citizens.'"[116]

Conclusion

This "triumph of the citizens" ushered in the beginning of a new era for the Argentine polity, defined by distinct parameters and a transformed agenda. We can assess this change in terms of the basic conditions of Argentine political development outlined at the beginning of the preceding chapter. One parameter had not changed: the Argentine model of accumulation was still unstable, still contested by rapidly remobilizing social forces, and further strained by the loss of capital, intensification of foreign exchange constraints, and exhaustion of the development models introduced by the Proceso. But the other three conditions were different. The military was no longer accepted as a legitimate political actor. The gap between the norms and institutions of representative democracy had been bridged for the first time in half a century. And for the first time in Argentine history, a social force had emerged to resist the political methodology of repression and to insist on state accountability for its consequences. The Argentine human rights movement had forged a new way of doing politics, based on symbolic politics, legitimacy challenge, and international links. This new movement would shape the foundations of the system emerging from the ashes.

Chapter 4

Establishing Truth:
¿Dónde están?

A government that respects human rights is almost always
the legacy of persistent national political struggles against
human rights violations. Most governments that respect human rights have been created not from the top down, but
from the bottom up.
                     Jack Donnelly, "International Human Rights"

The scope and success achieved by state-sponsored human rights
reform in Argentina are historically and internationally unprecedented. Nowhere else in the world have former military rulers been
tried for human rights violations by an elected civilian government.[1]
Argentina's public and systematic investigation of its recent past was
more thorough than that of any other emerging democracy. Although
problems persist and reform was eventually limited well short of its full
potential, the human rights record of the Alfonsín administration stands
as the best in Argentine history, among the best in Latin America, and
compares favorably to that of other democratizing nations.[2] These unprecedented and significant reforms would have been weaker, or later,
or would perhaps not have happened at all without the Argentine human rights movement.

Legitimacy Challenge and
Human Rights Reform

Following the model outlined in Chapter 1, the human rights movement's impact on the establishment of a democratic regime derived
from the use of norms to affect institutions and, through those institutions, to affect practices. As discussed in Chapter 1, institutions are
amenable to social change to the extent that they involve independent
criteria of legitimacy and predictability. The human rights movement
transformed state institutions by introducing systematic challenges to

the legitimacy of the new Alfonsín regime and to the legitimacy of specific institutions. These challenges usually took the form of introducing new concerns to the political agenda. Once the human rights movement had opened an institutional channel for its demands, some activists influenced the operation of institutions from within by providing information and personnel, while others continued mobilizing as outsiders, to pressure for and resist the new institutions' policies.

The human rights movement achieved recognition by the new and newly democratic regime, which was particularly susceptible to human rights movement demands: the Alfonsín administration was accountable to a civil society and an international community that already acknowledged the legitimacy of human rights claims. Regime-level movement demands reflected the nature of the human rights agenda and its link to democratic accountability. As discussed in Chapter 1, human rights claims coincide with the bases of democratic legitimacy in invoking ethical boundaries and accountability for the exercise of state power. This was expressed succinctly in one human rights group's statement, in reference to human rights prosecutions, that "the State has the duty of protecting society."[3] President Alfonsín acknowledged this claim in his opening speech to the legislature, calling on the nation "not only in the name of the legitimacy of origin of a democratic government, but also of the ethical sense that sustains that legitimacy" and saying that "[today] the government resumes its tradition as the defender of the rule of law and civil liberties."[4]

At the regime level, the human rights movement demanded state accountability for controlling coercion, investigating and explaining the fate of citizens who had been under state jurisdiction, providing equal justice (including compensation for past victims of unequal justice), and institutionalizing mechanisms for long-term accountability in each of these areas. The movement framed these demands as challenges to the legitimacy of the existing Argentine democracy, proclaiming: "This is the democracy we want: truth, freedom, justice and [the right to] life."[5] The demand for the truth took the form of a question: "¿Dónde están?" ("Where are [the disappeared]?"). This demand asked for information about the disappeared but also implied accountability.[6] Democratic, equal justice meant freedom for the surviving victims and an end to immunity from prosecution for the repressors. The human rights movement slogans related to justice were: *No a la impunidad* ("No to impunity!"), *Juicio y castigo a los culpables* ("Trial and punishment for the guilty"), and *A los asesinos, la carcel ya; a los compañeros, la libertad* ("For the murderers, prison; for our comrades [the political prisoners], freedom"). Finally, the movement echoed a larger social response to the

revelation of the full scope and depth of state terror in the slogan
¡Nunca más! ("Never again").

Alfonsín came to power on the basis of a platform that specifically
recognized and validated these bases of democratic legitimacy. In his
summary closing campaign speech, he recognized human rights as the
moral basis for political community, calling for a "democracy that re-
sponds to the dignity of man . . . in terms of both civil rights and human
needs" and promising to work "to secure democracy, which serves the
dignity of man" and to establish "a democracy with real power . . . to
defend the rights of all." (In his later message to the legislature, cited
above, the connection is even more explicit: "We have a goal: life, justice
and freedom. . . . We have a method: democracy.") Alfonsín linked
security and state accountability, saying: "Our program [nuestra pro-
puesta] is [to provide] peace, democracy, the rule of law and the restitution of authority . . . we will exercise the authority of democracy, which
is based on respecting the rights of all."[7] A powerful Radical campaign
slogan, Somos la vida, somos la paz ("We are life, we are peace"), alluded
to the legitimacy of both the human rights movement and the New
Testament.

In his closing speech, Alfonsín went on to acknowledge each of the
regime-level legitimacy claims made by the human rights groups, within
the terms of his own call for democracy. Human rights required security through ethical boundaries to state coercion. Alfonsín said: "We
must end rulers who overstep their authority [mandones]; we must end
violence; we must end the abuse of power [prepotencia]," and added that
"[our commitment to] peace means that we will never engage in atrocious and illegal repression." The human rights groups asked for truth,
and Alfonsín noted: "There is a teaching [predica] of democracy, a discourse, a language that is the teaching and the discourse of the truth."
The human rights groups demanded equal justice, and Alfonsín affirmed: "This is our program, the clear program of the 'estado de derecho,' the rule of law . . . so that all men will bow [inclinarse] before the
law and no man will ever be obliged to bow before another man in
Argentina." The human rights movements were recognized as the legitimate representatives of these rights; the Radical party leader who introduced Alfonsín at the historic rally specifically identified human
rights groups in the crowd as a key constituency.[8]

The identity and history of the Alfonsín administration thus both
validated the movement's regime-level legitimacy challenges and shaped
an Executive institutional agenda that was favorable to movement challenges. The Argentine human rights movement found a receptive Executive, since the Alfonsín administration had a preexisting, principled

commitment to human rights and institutional recovery that had been shaped but not created by the human rights movement. The new administration—and the Radical party from which it drew—included large numbers of lawyers, intellectuals, and former exiles who were already sensitized to the importance of legal guarantees against the abuse of power.[9] Although few had a personal history of persecution, several presidential advisors and the president himself had defended political prisoners prior to and during the early years of the Proceso.[10] Alfonsín himself was an early member of the civil libertarian APDH and consistently supported its goals throughout the Proceso, but he had retreated to formal and indirect participation well before the transition. Nevertheless, Radical figures close to the president (such as the Foreign Ministry official and later congressional deputy Horacio Ravenna) continued to be active in the human rights movement and served as an informal channel of influence.[11]

Legacies and Strategies

Although the Alfonsín administration's own agenda and the requisites of the transition thus coincided to some extent with human rights movement claims, movement and government actors differed fundamentally in their analysis of the sources of state terror and consequent strategies for democratization. The unfolding of events did not change either group's strategy so much as reveal the differences in their underlying logics, with significant consequences for the movement's ability to effect reforms. As both the movement and the administration sought to implement similar transition-era agendas, distinct ideologies emerged, and movement influence was limited.

The Executive's shared basis of legitimacy with the human rights movement was rooted in the common values and ideals of democracy; but normative claims usually come in ideological packages that include interpretations of history, strategies for reform, and prescriptions for the future. The human rights movement depicted state terror as a massive and disempowering exercise of state repression rooted in fundamental social contradictions, while the Radical analysis stressed the globalized political culture of violence that had generated both guerrilla activity and the repression that followed. For the human rights movement, the state, which had been the source of repression, was the logical target for change and the ultimate guarantor of security. For the Radical administration, bringing about lasting change was as much a matter of introducing a democratic political culture to a society that had generated repressive institutions as of constructing institutional guarantees. Since the human rights movement believed that repression had been rooted in illegitimate power relations among social forces, the movement emphasized direct restructuring of power relations (such as punitive measures against the military). On the other hand, the administration view that repression arose from a lack of legitimate institutions dictated a strategy of institutionalization around and through existing social actors. Finally, the origins of the movement promoted an analysis that linked resolving the legacies of the past to progress in the present, while the Alfonsín administration believed that Argentina must transcend the past to create the future.[12]

A presidential advisor, responding to a question about guarantees of human rights for the future, reflected the administration position, contending that: "The guarantees are things like the Inter-American Convention, constitutional reform, and, most important, the preservation of democracy. Human rights violations can't be committed without an institutional context. But democracy also depends on a definitive change in the people's level of consciousness and tolerance."[13]

An activist summarized the human rights movement's position thus: "We need to confront the past in order to build the future. Without trials and the establishment of responsibility, it [the repression] could happen again. Institutional changes are good, but they aren't enough; for example, the Costa Rica Pact [Inter-American Human Rights Convention] is great—but who will enforce it? This is why we need changes of personnel in the police, the army, the judiciary, the secretary of interior."[14]

These divergent ideological packages generated distinct strategies for reform. During his campaign, Alfonsín announced a nine-point plan for human rights reform that included a ban on secret detentions, the reintroduction of habeas corpus, the freeing of detainees held without trial, and legal prosecutions of *those who had given or exceeded orders* during the repression.[15] As early as 1980, members of the Asamblea recall Alfonsín making this critical distinction among three levels of responsibility for the crimes committed: those who gave orders, those who simply followed orders, and those who—although perhaps following orders—committed atrocities.[16] Although the general outlines of Alfonsín's human rights policy were established early on, since the Radical electoral victory was rather unexpected, most of the forms and mechanisms of human rights policy were not worked out until the "lame duck" period of October–December 1983.

Upon assuming office in December 1983, the Alfonsín administration sent a "trials package" to Congress that included the annulment of the military's self-amnesty, followed by a reform of the military code of justice and a decree mandating the trial of the members of the first three juntas.[17] By Executive decree, the president created CONADEP, the national investigatory commission on the disappeared. He introduced civil libertarian legislation to eliminate the death penalty, strengthen habeas corpus, punish torture by public officials as murder, and criminalize "attempts against the constitutional order." And Alfonsín promoted the ratification of the Inter-American Human Rights Convention (the San José Pact), the UN Covenants on Civil, Political, Economic, Social and Cultural Rights, and the Convention Against Torture.[18]

The human rights movement had long demanded an investigation of the whereabouts of the disappeared; during the transition, this demand focused on the creation of a bicameral parliamentary commission.[19] During 1983, many of the human rights organizations (Familiares, Abuelas, APDH, CELS, MEDH, and SERPAJ) formed a technical commission to pool data on the repression and prepared to forward this information to the new government—specifically, to the anticipated bicameral commission.[20] The movement stressed punishment for *all* of those responsible for the repression, condemned the military's attempt at a self-amnesty, and demanded wide, civilian trials of all of those implicated in the repression. It demanded the immediate release of all political prisoners inherited from the dictatorship (pending review of their cases), as well as the location and restitution of all missing children. And the human rights movement asked for a systematic retirement of Proceso-era members of the judiciary and police, as well as a law declaring forced disappearance a crime against humanity.[21]

Investigatory Efforts

The National Commission on the Disappearance of Persons (CONADEP)

During the transition, all of the human rights organizations called for the establishment of a bicameral legislative commission to investigate human rights abuses committed by the military dictatorship. The only previous investigations of human rights violations had been carried out by legislative commissions;[22] such a commission would have been amenable to popular and human rights movement pressure through elected legislators, and would have had the power to subpoena accused repressors as witnesses.[23] Several Radical legislators supported proposals for a bicameral commission during their electoral campaigns, and during a December 1983 Madres' march on Congress, the House majority leader, Cesar Jaroslawsky, indicated that the new government would establish a bicameral commission.[24] Legislative proposals to establish a bicameral commission were introduced by (Renovador) Peronist, Christian Democratic, and Partido Intransigente legislators.[25]

Bicameral legislative commissions *were* established in several provinces, including Entre Rios, Jujuy, and Tucumán.[26] In December 1983, the province of Buenos Aires established a permanent provincial bicameral commission with investigative powers, headed since 1987 by Horacio Ravenna (the president's informal liaison to the APDH). This provincial-level bicameral body was active in pressuring the provincial Executive for police and penal reform, promoting symbolic and educational projects, and building a nonpartisan consensus on human rights.[27]

But at the national level, instead of the bicameral commission, the Executive introduced a project to establish a special blue-ribbon panel, appointed directly by the president. A presidential advisor explained that the president was well aware of the movement's demands for a bicameral commission. But when the president and his advisors met with the minister of the interior (then Antonio Troccoli) during December of 1983, they decided that a bicameral commission would be inefficient and politically uncontrollable—in the sense of being open to claims outside of the major party bipartisan consensus.[28] Troccoli himself claimed CONADEP was to "channel and institutionalize those demands" but to keep the issue out of the judiciary.[29] So the administration chose the "commission of notables" plus military trials formula. This was modified slightly when legislators began lobbying presidential advisors regarding the functions of such a panel; Alfonsín then suggested adding a role for legislators on the commission.[30]

The president directly appointed ten well-known public figures to serve on CONADEP, of whom five were prominent in the human rights movement: Carlos Gattinoni (MEDH), Gregorio Klimovsky (APDH), Marshall Meyer (APDH, Movimiento Judío), Ricardo Colombres (APDH), and Jaime de Nevares (APDH). In addition, the human rights movement eventually provided most of the staff for the commission. The Depositions Department was headed by Graciela Fernandez Meijide (APDH) and the Procedures Department by Raul Aragon (CELS). These activists had access to the information assembled by the 1983 human rights movement Technical Commission, logistical experience in documenting disappearances, and the necessary emotional fortitude. The government members of CONADEP quickly decided to lobby the human rights organizations to secure their cooperation.[31] The Asamblea leader Graciela Fernandez-Meijide described how she and a segment of the movement decided to drop the demand for a bicameral commission and instead to push the newly created institution further than the government intended.[32] Alfonsín had mandated the designation of three legislative representatives from each chamber, but only the Radical-dominated House appointed legislators to serve. Two of the three, Hugo Piucil and Santiago Lopez, were also members of the Asamblea.

But the bulk of the human rights movement, led by the *afectados*, objected to the substitution of CONADEP, a nonrepresentative body whose mandate was limited to the passive receipt of documentation, for the originally envisioned bicameral commission. The Madres de Plaza de Mayo and the Nobel laureate Adolfo Perez-Esquivel refused to participate.[33] Hebe de Bonafini, president of Las Madres, claimed that they rejected CONADEP because it lacked real power. She asserted that the movement had no objection to the CONADEP appointees, but that only a bicameral commission would have been accountable to the people; so that the report "didn't end up in a box."[34] The establishment of CONADEP marked the beginning of the post-transition divisions between those human rights movements willing to work within the system and those that chose to continue their role as outsiders, which often coincided with a division between civil libertarian groups like the APDH and *afectados* such as the Madres.

CONADEP worked for nine months, and documented almost 9,000 cases of unresolved disappearances. It identified 340 clandestine detention centers and evaluated patterns of disappearance among adolescents, conscripts, members of the clergy, and missing children born to detainees.[35] The commission traveled to fifteen provinces and half a dozen foreign countries, collecting more than 1,400 depositions. In the provinces, CONADEP was particularly dependent on the work of local human rights activists; in one case, it discovered the mass abduction of 200 people in one night in a small town in Jujuy because the local chapter of Las Madres called the commission and requested a site visit.[36] Assisted by survivors (many of whom later organized as the Association of Ex-Detainees), CONADEP identified and visited the sites of former secret detention centers, morgues, hospitals, and prisons and examined military, police, and prison records—filing around 1,300 requests for further information.[37]

The majority of CONADEP's requests to the military were never answered, and those answers received often claimed an improbable ignorance concerning basic military activities (for example, certain commanders claimed not to know the current military assignments of subordinates implicated in the repression).[38] In a famous incident in June 1984, General Pedro Mansilla refused CONADEP access to army bases under his command in Cordoba that had been identified as clandestine detention centers. The head of the commission, the writer Ernesto Sabato, appealed directly to Alfonsín, who was forced to remove the general from his command.[39] Members of CONADEP received constant death threats; the Cordoba office of CONADEP was bombed in August 1984, and in April of 1985 there were bombings of the homes and offices of delegates in three cities.[40]

Based on the information it had collected, the commission issued a two-volume report (*Nunca más*), produced a television show, and brought hundreds of cases against repressors implicated in multiple testimonies. CONADEP brought a total of 1,087 cases directly to the federal appeals courts.[41] The *Nunca más* report has sold over 250,000 copies in Argentina alone; the author has seen the report in settings ranging from a remote farmhouse in Entre Rios to supporting a heraldic crest on the bookshelf of a member of the Buenos Aires elite. Almost 2,000 copies of the report were distributed to government officials, national and international human rights organizations, and embassies.[42] When the members of the commission turned in the final report on September 20th, they were accompanied by a human rights demonstration of 70,000 supporters.[43] Similar support marches took place throughout the country; in Rosario, Argentina's third-largest city, the gathering was called the "March for Truth and Justice."[44]

The July 4th "¡Nunca más!" television broadcast was seen by over a million people, and the film was subsequently shown by private groups throughout the country. The show, a simple and haunting presentation of a handful of representative testimonies—including a Madre, an Abuela, and the Asamblea's Enrique Fernandez Meijide—was marred by displays of internal and external opposition to the work of the commission. With the approval of the president, the minister of the interior, Antonio Troccoli, insisted on adding introductory remarks "designed to temper the impact of the program by reminding the viewers of the onslaught of revolutionary violence that had caused the repression."[45] Troccoli provided the first public demonstration of the government's "evenhanded" reading of the Proceso when he asserted that the "¡Nunca más!" program failed to show "the other side—the excesses of subversion."[46] Then, during the broadcast, a bomb was thrown at the government television station and an undetermined number of troops around Buenos Aires engaged in unplanned maneuvers.[47]

Many aspects of the results of the work of CONADEP were controversial. First, the human rights movement feared that CONADEP's necessary underrepresentation of the true numbers of the disappeared would be seen as the final figure and thus used to downplay the scope of the repression.[48] Indeed, official and international sources now routinely speak of 9–10,000 disappeared. Second, the commission staff had assembled a list of approximately 1,500 persons implicated in the repression from the testimonies received. Although the list was turned in to the president, the members of the panel decided not to release this information to the public, on the grounds that it was not confirmed and exceeded their mandate. But part of the information was later leaked to and published by the newsweekly *El Periodista*. When the published list included the name of the papal nuncio, the president intervened to deny the legitimacy of the entire repressor list.[49] Finally, the CONADEP report concluded that there was no evidence that any disappeared persons who had not reappeared were still alive. This contradicted persistent rumors of unlocated survivors within the human rights movement. These rumors were based on episodes such as a series of apparently authentic phone calls received by a family *between December 1983 and March 1984* from a woman kidnapped in July 1977. (Alfonsín, it will be remembered, assumed office in December 1983.)[50]

Exhumations of Unidentified (NN) Bodies

Another series of investigatory efforts definitively established the fate of many of the disappeared: the exhumation of unidentified ("NN") bodies. Vast numbers of undocumented corpses were interred between 1976 and 1983.[51] By late 1983, several judges had ordered exhumations of NN bodies, but existing official Argentine forensic scientists were unprepared for this type of work; they conducted excavations with bulldozers, which traumatized family members and destroyed evidence. These dramatic and grisly revelations were highlighted in the popular press, and provided many people's first concrete evidence of the nature of the repression.[52]

But human rights organizations, especially the Abuelas—who sought to establish legal proof of childbirth from the exhumations—turned to the international system for help. In May 1984, they approached the American Association for the Advancement of Science and asked for expert assistance. The forensic anthropologist Clyde Snow and the Berkeley geneticist Mary Claire King traveled to Argentina. King developed a blood test for the establishment of genetic grandpaternity. Snow trained Argentine students in forensic exhumation techniques and formed a team of newly trained students, who continued the exhumations in his absence.

Members of the Forensic Anthropology Team were called as expert witnesses in a series of significant trials.[53] Within the framework of the Argentine legal system, the exhumations acquired particular importance in substantiating charges of homicide—since the statute of limitations on kidnapping was already running out by the mid 1980's. By 1988, the Forensic Anthropology Team had begun the systematic exhumation of a common grave containing dozens of bodies in the province of Buenos Aires, to provide broader documentation of the patterns of the repression.[54]

The NN exhumations caused controversy within both the government and the human rights movement. Most members of the human rights movement, including the religious groups, civil libertarians, and many *afectados*, supported exhumations to provide legal evidence, closure for families, and irrefutable historical documentation.[55] But Las Madres and the Ex-Detainees, scarred by the insensitive methods used earlier and fearing premature and inadequate closure, objected to the exhumations. Las Madres' leader Bonafini explained: "We reject exhumations, because we want to know who the murderers are—we already know who the murdered are."[56]

While Buenos Aires provincial authorities supported exhumations (under both Radical and Peronist administrations), the national subsecretary of human rights became embroiled in a heated territorial dispute with the Forensic Anthropology team. Buenos Aires province's under secretary of justice (a Radical) organized seminars for judges all over the country on modern forensic techniques.[57] Buenos Aires province's minister of government (a Peronist) sent the Forensic Anthropology team his personal police guard and new video cameras when their excavation was inexplicably sabotaged.[58] But the national subsecretary of human rights denied the Forensic Anthropology Team access to official records and created a rival official Technical Commission, which was recognized by the Supreme Court.[59] Although rivalries did not seriously impede the progress of exhumations by either group (and events have minimized the legal potential of any future exhumations), the conflict provides graphic and literal evidence of the Alfonsín administration's determination to leave the disappeared buried.

Through registering normative claims and providing expertise to both Executive and judicial institutions, the human rights movement got the truth. The revelation of the truth was limited by the Executive in an attempt to maintain an "evenhanded approach" and to make the revelation a catharsis—not a catalyst. But truth implied accountability, and the human rights movement demanded justice.

Chapter 5

Establishing Justice:
¡No a la impunidad!

> We Argentines have tried to gain peace based in forgetting
> and failed. . . . We have tried to search for peace through
> violence and extermination and failed. . . . With this trial
> and condemnation [of the military juntas], the responsibility
> rests with us to found a peace based, not in forgetting, but
> in remembering, not in violence, but in justice.
>
> *El diario del juicio* (Journal of the Trial)

The trial of the country's former military rulers for human rights
violations was the high watermark of state reform in Argentina
and the outstanding distinguishing feature of the Argentine case. These
and related human rights trials illustrate the role of agenda-setting and
legitimacy challenge in unleashing institutions that take on a "life of
their own." This dynamic evolution of human rights reform in Argentina fits the framework discussed in Chapter 1, in which democratization is both a condition for and outcome of symbolic protest. In keeping
with this approach, the transition to democracy must be viewed as a
disaggregated process of small, linked steps that result in indetermi-
nate, multiplicative social change.[1]

First, the human rights movement transformed the public agenda
through the expression of reform demands framed in terms that invoked the bases of democratic legitimacy: in this case, equal justice.
This challenge was particularly effective during the transition period
when pre-Proceso institutions were being rehabilitated and dormant
institutional structures (like the legal system) were being put back to
use. At the institutional level, the human rights movement had more
success with the judiciary than with any other branch of government,
because the judiciary possessed a unique combination of legitimacy,
autonomy, and institutional incentives.

The basis of the judiciary's institutional legitimacy—equality before
the law—coincided with a central demand of the human rights movement. At the same time, the judiciary could respond to the movement
unfettered, since it has the most relative autonomy from the power
relations of social forces (and thus from military pressure). The judicia-

ry's unique institutional mandate is the collection and assessment of information. Information thus gives the judiciary an independent source of power, and we have seen that a strategy of persuasion on the part of a social movement involves the projection of both cognitive and affective information (roughly, in the Argentine case, by civil libertarians and family-based branches of the movement respectively).[2] And since judges also served as investigators in Argentina's legal system, the brunt of demands by the human rights movement for investigation were channeled through the judiciary. Like the Executive, the judiciary had a shared basis of legitimacy with the human rights movement; but the narrower focus, lack of competing agendas, and professional norms of the judiciary made it more amenable to movement influence.

The Trials of Military Officers:
Juicio y castigo a los culpables

Trial of the military officers responsible for the repression of the Proceso was a long-standing demand of the human rights movement. Alfonsín had long discussed limited trials, which were planned as a self-purification of the leadership of the armed forces initiated by the assertion of civilian presidential authority (rather than through popular pressure on the courts). Carlos Nino, one of the president's advisors, explained that from the beginning, the new government had planned on a limited number of exemplary trials—"somewhere between 20 or 30 and 100 or 150."[3] The Alfonsín administration's goals were the reestablishment of the rule of law and military self-discipline, so that it was important to use existing and relatively nonpolitical institutions and legal figures, rather than a Nuremberg-style special tribunal or controversial charges such as genocide or sedition. The administration stressed that it was not trying the military as an institution, but rather members of the institution who had violated the law.[4]

Thus, the package of mechanisms chosen to initiate the trials was the congressional derogation of the military's attempted retroactive self-amnesty, a set of presidential decrees mandating the trials of the first three military juntas, and a reform of the military code of justice introducing appeal to civilian courts.[5] Human rights activists criticized the mechanisms chosen even within the terms of the Radical political project:

[Alfonsín's] strategy is plagued by a basic contradiction between the political task at hand—the reestablishment of the rule of law and of civilian control over the military—and the means chosen to carry out that task, namely removal of the human rights prosecutions from the civilian court system and the establishment of a set of special rules by which military personnel need answer in the first instance only to the military itself.[6]

The legislature introduced critical modifications of the president's proposal for reform of the military code that were vastly to increase its impact. Following Alfonsín's original concept of three levels of responsibility for the repression, the president's project mandated an automatic presumption of obedience to apparently legitimate orders in favor of the accused. In House committees, this presumption was changed to an optional defense, available only to lower-ranking officers "without decision-making capacity." The House also specified automatic jurisdiction for the civilian appellate court in the case of "negligence or unjustifiable delay" by military courts. Further and more significant changes were made in the Senate, where the Radicales lacked a majority and were thus forced to bargain with small provincial parties. This is how the tiny Movimiento Popular Neuquino (whose leader had two sons who had disappeared) qualified even the modified "due obedience" (obediencia debida) defense to exclude anyone who had engaged in "atrocious and aberrant acts," which provided the basis for the wider trials to follow.[7]

The highest military court—the Supreme Military Council—was given six months to issue a sentence but was subsequently awarded several extensions. However, the council refused to call prosecution witnesses or investigated the witnesses, gave defense witnesses desultory interrogations, and delayed throughout 1984. Human rights activists, led by CELS, petitioned the federal court of appeals for Buenos Aires to take over the case.[8] The *Nunca más* report appeared on September 20th, and the military council's final extension was due to expire in October. It was in this context, in late September, that the military council issued a report stating that it could not judge the alleged crimes committed because the orders issued in the "war against subversion" were "unobjectionable." This controversial statement prompted the specified appeals court, the Buenos Aires federal appeals court, to assume jurisdiction over the trials of the juntas—under pressure from the human rights movement, public reaction to CONADEP, and its own reawakening sense of institutional prerogatives.[9]

The trials of the juntas lasted from April through December 1985: the court heard a total of 78 days of testimony from 833 witnesses, and excerpts from the day's testimony were broadcast on the television news every night for nine months.[10] The trial itself was open to the general public and press, and the trial was conducted in an oral, public format unprecedented in Argentine jurisprudence.[11] The six judges came from a credible variety of political backgrounds, and the witnesses included not only the expected victims, activists, and accused, but also three pre-Proceso presidents (one military and two civilian), prominent Church and labor figures, and an array of international experts and policymakers.[12]

The impact of the testimony was sharpened in several instances by the graphic accounts of survivors, including a woman who had given birth in chains in a concentration camp; an adolescent who was the sole survivor of the incident known as "La Noche de los Lapices" ("The Night of the Pencils"), in which half a dozen adolescents were kidnapped in La Plata because they had petitioned for subsidized bus fares for high-school students;[13] and the mother of a disappeared son who was herself kidnapped because of her efforts to locate him (and subsequently forced while still detained to give a widely disseminated interview discrediting the human rights movement and denying her own disappearance). A military officer removed for "failure to share the philosophy of the armed forces" described his visit to a concentration camp. Civilian complicity was highlighted in testimony by a group of labor leaders who "could not remember" whether members of their unions had disappeared,[14] and by Church officials questioned about their alleged presence at concentration camps. The ferocious irony of the repression was revealed in two cases of disappeared Proceso-era diplomats, one apparently murdered because she discovered links between the former junta member Admiral Massera and the Montonero guerrilla group.[15]

As with CONADEP, the trials aroused controversy and opposition. Investigating military courts and police pursued procedures designed to exert a "chilling effect" on prosecution witnesses. A courthouse in Rosario was assaulted and records destroyed.[16] A coup plot was discovered just before the trial, and 250,000 people responded to President Alfonsín's call for a popular demonstration in support of the trials.[17] On March 20th, a bomb was discovered at the home of the president of the federal appeals court that was to hear the case, and another set of bombings in October preceded both the sentencing and the midterm elections. During the trials, the defense attempted to discredit and intimidate witnesses; defense counsel several times referred to prosecution witnesses as "the detained." Unidentified individuals threatened witnesses with various forms of violence, published threatening letters and petitions—and in some cases even brought trumped-up legal charges against witnesses through sympathetic judges in other jurisdictions.[18]

The assistant prosecutor during the trials, Luis Moreno Ocampo, maintained that "without the human rights organizations, there wouldn't have been a trial." Owing to the magnitude of the case and the limited time and resources available, the prosecutor's office conducted an investigation based on the evidence collected by CONADEP, which in turn was based on the work of the human rights groups. In many cases, the CONADEP records were "in a form that was not legally helpful," so that the prosecutor often went back to human rights organizations for additional information and/or referred directly to the 1983 Technical Commission report. The prosecutor worked with the human rights organizations to identify "leading cases": cases that had an abundance of proof, cases that showed national and interservice patterns of repression, and cases that spanned the entire 1976–83 period (this was especially critical for the last junta, where there were fewer cases). The human rights groups coordinated the prosecutor's search for further corroboration and acted as a liaison with victims and families.

Human rights groups, especially the Ex-Detainees, helped the prosecutor's office to locate witnesses. Prominent *afectados* such as Emilio Mignone (CELS), Estela Carlotto (Abuelas), Teresa d'Israel (Familiares), Lucas Orfano (La Liga), Bishop Gattinoni (MEDH), and Graciela Fernandez Meijide (APDH) served as witnesses; the prosecutor cited the Fernandez Meijide and D'Israel cases in his summary. Human rights activists presented their own cases, helped to establish patterns of repression, and denied the defense the argument of ignorance by documenting their own efforts during the Proceso (for example, Lucas Orfano had presented 22 writs of habeas corpus).[19]

In addition to this argument of officers' ignorance of "excesses" that occurred under their command, the defense argued that the alleged violations had been committed in the context of an unconventional "Dirty War." Operationally, this war had been pursued in a decentralized fashion, without central coordination of specific repressive strategies by the juntas. Furthermore, the defense contended that the repression had been pursued under a mandate from the preceding civilian government, which had issued a decree ordering the "annihilation" of subversion.[20]

The prosecution argued that the members of the juntas, as order givers in a hierarchical institution, were the indirect authors of all of the human rights violations committed during their rule.[21] The degree of interservice and even international cooperation in detentions, as well as the uniformity of repressive procedures, was said to demonstrate the existence of a joint criminal plan at the junta level.[22] Finally, the prosecution sought to disprove the existence of a state of war—and to argue that in any case, the acts committed also violated the laws of war. In the words of the prosecutor, "either there was no war, as I believe, and we have before us common criminals; or there was—and we have before us war criminals."[23]

More broadly, the prosecution argued for the values of the human rights movement (although the prosecutor did not consciously align himself with any political force). The movement led a massive demonstration timed to coincide with the reading of the accusation in September.[24] In his summation, the prosecutor described himself as representing the voices of 9,000 disappeared, for whom this trial served as the only possible reparation. Beyond the condemnation of the accused, he asked for the condemnation of violence as a political instrument. And most of all, the prosecution argued for a principle taken for granted in most legal proceedings—the legitimacy of the rule of law. Citing the testimony of the newspaper publisher Robert Cox, the prosecutor reminded the court that all of the disappeared were innocent—because none had been tried. The court was reminded of the emotional plea of one mother whose son had disappeared, "My son deserved a trial like this one!" The accusation closed with the words "*¡Nunca más!*"[25]

The sentence condemning five of the nine defendants—General-Presidents Jorge Videla and Roberto Viola, Admirals Emilio Massera and Armando Lambruschini, and Air Force Brigadier Orlando Agosti—legally established the existence of massive, illegal, abhorrent repression corresponding to central direction. The sentence specifically rejected the defense argument that the offenses had taken place during a "Dirty War" and concluded that no war had existed after 1976. However, the argument of coordinated planning by junta (as opposed to planning by service) was rejected, as was the prosecution of the (last) Galtieri junta for concealment of evidence. Thus, sentences varied by defendant and by service with the attribution of responsibility; four of the nine defendants were acquitted, only two defendants were given life sentences, and one received only four years (for eight counts of torture and three of robbery). Many activists believed that the sentences were too lenient, and Las Madres led a courtroom protest.[26]

The trials also established the political and institutional independence of the renascent judiciary. A key provision of the sentence, "Punto 30," added that the trials had uncovered evidence implicating many more repressors, and that the courts were now legally required to go beyond the original trials decree in investigating these crimes. Judge Jorge Torlasco, who coauthored the provision, explained: "We were faced with over 9,000 legally proven crimes, and five defendants convicted. Just from the evidence presented directly at the trials, about 100 other agents could be identified and their legal responsibility established."[27] There is some evidence that the Alfonsín administration had planned to issue an amnesty right after the trials of the juntas, but was deterred by social opposition and judicial independence.[28]

Meanwhile, the administration *was* pursuing other "exemplary trials." In 1984, Alfonsín issued another decree ordering the trial of General Ramón Camps, the notorious military commander of the Buenos Aires police; in December 1986, Camps was found guilty of 600 counts of homicide and sentenced to 25 years in prison by a civilian court.[29] General Luciano Menéndez, who had supervised the repression throughout the Cordoba region, was finally arrested after a 1984 incident in which he attacked human rights demonstrators at a talk show with a knife.[30] International searches were ordered for the former zone commander General Carlos Suarez-Mason and the death squad organizer and former Minister of Social Welfare José López Rega (both eventually extradited from the United States).

But exemplary trials could not meet social demand; the scope of the trials had already escaped the control of the Executive and the judicial process had assumed a life of its own. Victims and their families (often through human rights organizations) were flooding the courts with claims: by mid 1984, an estimated 2,000 complaints had been filed (more than 400 by CELS alone); by mid 1986 there were at least 3,000 cases just in the military courts.[31] The appropriate jurisdiction for these claims was unclear, and similar cases were being treated inconsistently. Cases were being brought by victims' relatives, human rights organizations, nonmovement attorneys, and foreign governments.[32] By early 1985, around 650 military officers were named defendants—at least one-third still on active duty and increasingly drawn from the middle ranks—leading to growing military tension.[33]

In response to these pressures, in early 1986 the minister of defense instructed the military prosecutor to issue a set of administrative instructions to the military courts. The administration presented the Instructions as a device to unify, speed up, and ensure uniform treatment of the various cases pending: they included the grouping of trials by Proceso-era military zones and new interpretations of the sentencing of the juntas and the concept of "due obedience." But the members of the civilian appeals courts claimed that the instructions were constructed so as to result in massive acquittals or immunity from prosecution on technical grounds.[34] One of the members of the federal appeals court that had tried the juntas, Jorge Torlasco, resigned in protest (and two more of the six members threatened to resign). The human rights movement led massive demonstrations, which were attended by leading Radical party legislators.[35] In a June 11th press conference,

Alfonsín "corrected" the instructions point by point. The incident once again stimulated the judiciary, and several of the ten designated provincial appeals courts took over important human rights cases pending in the military courts of their regions (including the Camps and Menéndez cases mentioned above).[36]

Throughout 1986, prosecutions continued wending their way slowly and unpredictably through the courts, and the president's advisors prepared several plans to limit future trials and defuse military tension. On the one hand, the appeals court of Bahia Blanca was threatening to charge the Ministry of Defense with contempt of court for failure to provide information on charged personnel; on the other, a bomb was discovered on Alfonsín's route during his visit to a military base in Cordoba. The government sought to restore predictability and reassure the military, without imposing an open amnesty. The introduction of the Punto Final proposal to limit the trials procedurally was timed to follow the sentencing of General Camps in December of 1986.[37]

The Punto Final legislation specified that no future charges could be brought against any defendant that were not processed within sixty days (the first thirty days would fall in January, the traditional vacation period). It was believed that this would procedurally limit future trials to a handful of serving officers. The human rights movement spearheaded opposition to the measure; during the second week of December, over 50,000 demonstrators marched on Congress, again accompanied by sympathetic legislators from almost every party.[38] A second member of the appeals court that had tried the juntas, Judge Guillermo Ledesma, resigned in protest.[39] The CONADEP commission and the CGT trade union confederation came out against the Punto Final proposal.[40] Even members of the administration (Carlos Nino and Eduardo Rabossi) and the youth branch of the Radical party sent letters and petitions of protest.[41] CELS lobbied, while Madres in white scarves occupied the gallery of the Senate and threw leaflets. For 48 hours while the legislature was debating the bill, Ex-Detainees staged a concentration camp at the entrance to Congress, standing hooded and in chains.[42]

The Radical party's annual convention was scheduled to take place two days before the final vote, and the president met with Radical dissidents and demanded party discipline.[43] In addition, the Radical senator leading the debate "clarified" the law to explicitly allow continued prosecution for child-stealing, citing committee sessions and conversations of "long hours with different sectors of national life, with the Abuelas of Plaza de Mayo."[44] In the House, the Peronist opposition split along traditional-Renovador lines, and a significant number of Renovador Peronists absented themselves in protest.[45] Thus, the bill passed the Senate through an unusual coalition of Radical loyalists, conservative Peronists, and provincial parties. Punto Final passed the House with an absolute minority, since almost 40 percent of the members of the lower chamber were absent during the final vote.[46]

But once again, the human rights movement flooded the courts; and once again the traditionally passive judiciary reacted against Executive attempts to limit the trials by processing record numbers of defendants.[47] After the Punto Final deadline had expired, almost 400 cases had been processed.[48] Prosecutor Moreno Ocampo attributed this to the sheer force of the evidence presented by the human rights movement and in the trials of the juntas. He cited several cases in which jurists who had been appointed by the military were overwhelmed and pushed past their denial of the repression by this "force of the facts" and its challenge to the legitimacy of the legal system.[49]

Nevertheless, passage of the Punto Final law was seen as a major defeat by the human rights movement, since it prevented the prosecution of the vast majority of the 1,300–1,500 repressors already identified from testimonies. For example, during 1986, CELS had published *Terrorismo de estado: 692 responsables*, identifying 692 implicated individuals, documenting their precise role in the repressive apparatus, and linking this role to personal responsibility through testimony from victims. This set of cases was reduced by one-third after Punto Final became law.[50] A typical situation was that in the province of Entre Rios, where approximately forty defendants had been identified; after Punto Final, only six or seven of these could still be prosecuted.[51] Several prominent figures within the human rights movement, such as Renée Epelbaum—head of the Madres–Linea Fundadora and the mother of three missing children—were definitively blocked from access to the legal system.[52]

Ironically, the Punto Final law did not even sufficiently reduce military tension, since accused military officers were still being called to court (both in connection with the hundreds of remaining cases and in order to adjudicate the terms of Punto Final in specific instances), and the mere process of being judged inspired political objections by the military. A few months after the Punto Final deadline, in April 1987, one of the remaining indicted middle-ranking officers, Major Ernesto Barreiro, refused to answer a civilian summons and took refuge with a regiment in Cordóba. His refusal to go to trial sparked a widespread military rebellion, whose leader, Aldo Rico, occupied the Campo de Mayo military complex on the outskirts of Buenos Aires. While the majority of the armed forces remained technically loyal, they refused to suppress the rebellion or to fire on fellow officers. The Semana Santa crisis was resolved after Alfonsín negotiated directly with the leaders of the rebellion at Campo de Mayo. The "due obedience" legislation was introduced within weeks, on May 13, 1987.[53]

The so-called Obediencia Debida law returned to the original concept of a presumption that the accused were "just following orders," except for a few very high-ranking officers who clearly held decision-making posts as heads of zones. The new law narrowed the concept of "atrocious and aberrant acts" (which could not be presumed to be legitimate orders) to exclude torture and murder, but maintained the possibility of prosecution for rape and child-stealing.[54] A Radical legislator leading the debate defended due obedience in terms of the human rights agenda by stating that the Radical administration had already achieved *no impunidad* through the earlier trials, but parted company with the human rights movement over *juicio y castigo a los culpables* (trial and punishment for the guilty).[55]

Despite wide social opposition, the Obediencia Debida law passed the legislature relatively quickly in the atmosphere following the Semana Santa military uprising.[56] "I am totally convinced that we have no alternative," the Progressive Radical Federico Storani explained. Chastened by their experience with Punto Final, the Renovador Peronists actively opposed the measure this time rather than walking out. But the Renovador Peronist Antonio Cafiero (subsequently a presidential candidate) complained: "We are not deliberating freely . . . once more the society of fear and 'conditional liberty' has been installed among us. . . . There are new lists of citizens [to be repressed] circulating. . . . We know that there is an invisible army pressuring [us] . . . to compel us to legislate against [our] conscience."[57]

The highest-ranking remaining official from the human rights movement, Education Under Secretary Alfredo Bravo—who had been tortured and imprisoned by the military and had worked with Alfonsín in the APDH—resigned in protest. The human rights organizations appealed to the Supreme Court, which held that the measure was constitutional and did not violate the principle of equality before the law in June 1987. Human rights organizations, notably CELS and SERPAJ, appealed both the due obedience legislation and specific cases subsequently dismissed under its terms to the Interamerican Commission on Human Rights of the Organization of American States and the World Court.[58]

A human rights movement publication estimates that 450 pending cases were reduced to 50 by the immediate application of the due obedience law.[59] Returning to the previous example in the province of

Entre Rios, after forty prosecutions were reduced to seven by Punto Final, all seven were dropped under the principle of due obedience. Although the legislation could not be applied retroactively, it could be and was applied to cases still under appeal, so that dozens of *convicted* murderers and torturers were released on appeal under the Obediencia Debida law.[60] By October 1988, 17 officers remained under trial, with half a dozen others yet to have their status determined. None of these cases were brought to trial during the remainder of Alfonsín's term.

Shortly after Alfonsín's successor, Carlos Menem, assumed office in July 1989, the new president pardoned all military officers with human rights prosecutions pending. Menem also pardoned dozens of military officers involved in military rebellions and a handful of former leftist guerrillas. In December 1990, despite widespread public and international opposition, these pardons were extended to the former rulers already convicted of human rights violations.[61]

Missing Children: Justice for the Next Generation

The Abuelas de Plaza de Mayo led an effort to locate, identify, and restore children missing as a result of the disappearance of their parents. Of the several hundred documented cases of missing children, the Abuelas located almost fifty prior to and during the Alfonsín administration. Public support played an important role in locating missing children; over 5,000 reports were provided by the general public.[62]

In those cases where the children had been illegally adopted by repressors, the biological families and human rights organizations sought restoration of the missing children to their biological families (usually grandparents). Judges consistently awarded custody to the biological families in almost twenty cases of this sort. These decisions were based on the rights of the children to their natural families and the rights of the families to reclaim their members, since criteria of parental environment or child welfare were never introduced (and in most cases, the children had not been mistreated by the adoptive parents).[63]

Judge Ramos Padilla, who acted in five of the nineteen restorations, confirmed that the Abuelas played a key role. The Abuelas brought all five cases, conducted the investigation that provided the circumstantial evidence, and developed the physical basis of proof (genetic blood-typing to establish grandpaternity). The Abuelas' team of child psychologists worked closely with court-appointed experts. But most of all, he said, the Abuelas "raised his consciousness" about the children's rights to their origins and identity. As a result of his work with the Abuelas through five cases, he learned that "you can't base a family on lies, secrets and a view of children as objects."[64]

However, more recent cases show an eroding judicial consensus on restorations, as the children age and the general climate of opinion on human rights issues deteriorates. During 1987, a case in which the adoptive parents were not clearly involved in the repression produced a crisis in the Supreme Court before resulting in the restitution of the child to her natural family. In the 1988 Juliana case, nonrepressor adoptive parents who had aided in the search for the child's natural family were pitted against the extensive biological family. Custody was switched several times, and the ultimate decision favoring the adoptive parents introduced traditional criteria of contested adoptions.[65] Nevertheless, restitutions continued, and by 1992 a total of four dozen children had been restored to their biological families.[66]

The Abuelas criticized the Alfonsín administration for taking a passive role in the search for missing children; in November 1988 the president finally met with the Abuelas and subsequently ordered the creation of a special prosecutor for cases involving missing children.[67] The Executive had earlier responded to the Abuelas' and international pressure for a national genetic data bank to facilitate the identification of biological grandpaternity by promoting a legislative project to establish the data bank. Finally, in a related move, the legislature mandated the provision of a special pension for the dependents of disappeared persons. The pension for relatives of the disappeared was introduced by Senator Alfredo Napoli (a member of the APDH), and later passed in a conference version worked out with Deputy Piucil (also an APDH member and formerly of CONADEP) in an informal APDH Legislative Committee.[68]

Justice Delayed: The Political Prisoners

Since the military had released large numbers of political prisoners during 1982 and 1983, only several hundred (of the peak total of 8–10,000) remained in prison at Alfonsín's assumption of power.[69] The majority of these had been either illegally arrested, tortured, denied due process, judged by military tribunals, held under state of siege provisions, or charged under Proceso-era codes, and all had experienced inhumane conditions of imprisonment. The human rights movements, and the prisoners themselves, demanded their release pending a systematic review of their cases. The prisoners engaged in two hunger strikes, one for 49 days, with support from the human rights movement—including marches of up to 25,000.[70] However, the administration preferred the indirect mechanism of a special parole formula for Proceso-era prisoners, which acknowledged the inhumane prison conditions without reviewing the cases.[71] The resulting commutation of sentences of political prisoners represented a compromise between various legislative proposals by Deputy Augusto Conte, representing the human rights movement, and the Executive.

The sentence commutations freed all but fourteen of the political prisoners. These prisoners became a cause célèbre for the human rights movement, which saw the continued incarceration of victims of human rights abuses under a democratic government as a particular affront to both due process and substantive justice. Each case had to work its way up to the Supreme Court, which eventually ordered the cases reopened by the original judges.[72] Meanwhile, eight of the fourteen prisoners served out their sentences. As of 1988, six remained in prison; approximately the same number as the total of imprisoned military officers at that time.[73]

Other Attempts at Legal Redress

In addition to the direct prosecution of former repressors, equal justice and state accountability involved various kinds of redress for the surviving victims of the Proceso: the few survivors of temporary disappearances, political prisoners, and missing children. Several victims who survived a temporary disappearance brought civil suits, usually against enterprises that had denied them wages or reinstatement. These suits often claimed that the victim had been denounced or even turned over to the repressors by the former employer.[74] The scope for civil prosecutions has been limited, since many of the employers involved are state enterprises, and civil suits against the state must be brought within two years of the alleged crime (in these cases, within two years of the transition). Although a pilot judgment for complicity was obtained against Ford Argentina, it was subsequently invalidated on technical grounds.[75]

Scattered orders for indemnification were obtained against both state and private enterprises, but no victims received compensation as a result of civil suits under the Alfonsín administration.[76] Under the Menem administration, legislation was passed in December 1991 granting compensation to official political prisoners held "at the disposition of the Executive" during the Proceso. An estimated 4,000 victims will receive the equivalent of U.S.$27 per day of detention in government bonds; the measure does not provide compensation to survivors of disappearances.[77]

The Establishment of a Democratic Regime

The human rights movement demanded past, present, and future truth, justice, and accountability from the democratic regime. The regime responded with reforms that provided "truth and partial justice" with respect to the past; in the following chapters, we shall examine the extent to which accountability was institutionalized for the future. The significance of the investigation and adjudication of human rights movement claims must be evaluated both in terms of the final results achieved and in terms of the historical value of these phenomena (not only as they occurred, but also in establishing precedents).

A former Alfonsín advisor explained the consequences of the trials as: specific factual findings, institutional disapproval, confidence in the universality of democratic principles, and military adaptation. He stressed that the Argentine trials served both deterrent and expressive functions.[78] At the level of norms, the trials and investigations broke the Proceso's monopoly on the truth and rewrote history, by presenting the horrors of the past framed by the legitimacy of democratic justice.[79] The reforms inaugurated a new level of institutional legitimacy by submitting the military to equal justice and seeking procedural justice for the losers of an ideological struggle for the first time in Argentine history.[80] And at the level of national and international precedent, the example of the trials serves as a deterrent to those who would violate human rights in the future. By rewriting history, legitimating institutions, and establishing the boundaries of state accountability, the trials and investigations served to define democratic citizenship.[81]

The pardons mitigate but do not eliminate the value of the trials. History cannot be erased; just as a jury will remember testimony even if it is "stricken from the record."[82] In this sense, a human rights movement figure who was a witness at the trials explained before the sentencing: "The trial is already an example of moral value. A society, a fragile democracy, judging three ex-presidents and the heads of its armies, for having subjected the citizenry. . . . The trial is already, morally, a thing achieved."[83]

The introduction of new norms and the operation of new institutions to secure accountability for the past was a necessary, but not sufficient, step in guaranteeing human rights for the future. Institutionalizing human rights reform in the new democratic regime would require both the extension of state control of the coercive forces and the establishment of mechanisms within the state to monitor and enforce the restraint of state coercion within legitimate boundaries. Institutionalization and its limits would determine the movement's ability to meet its final objective: *¡Nunca más!*

Chapter 6

Reforming the State:
¡Basta de patotas!

> The Argentine people have not taken the Bastille.
> Raúl Alfonsín

The Argentine people rallied to democracy with the repudiation of state terror; during the 1983 electoral campaign, this was expressed in the slogan *¡Basta de patotas!*—"Enough thuggery!" In order to consolidate the reforms introduced by the human rights movement, democratic accountability must be extended to the state's core coercive power. The institutionalization of human rights accountability in Argentina thus presented two different kinds of problems. First, the democratic regime lacked full control of the forces of coercion—the people had not taken the Bastille.[1] In Argentina, this meant both that a coercive agency of the state (the military) was not subject to democratic accountability and that the state was unable to provide security from extra-institutional and antisystem violence. Second, within the areas fully under government control, the influence of the human rights movement was limited (as was that of civil society in general). These limitations were owing both to programmatic differences between the human rights movement and the Alfonsín administration and to the inherent incapacity of the new social movement to penetrate state structures effectively.

The Argentine transition to democracy was highly conditioned by continued military veto power, institutional legacies, and lack of resources. Argentina was a form of tutelary democracy; contestation stopped at the barracks door. Civilian authority was not autonomous in dealing with any issue that affected the military's self-defined "vital interests."[2] A history of authoritarian rule had weakened the most representative institutions of political society. "At the heart of the transition, constitutional power founded in democratic legitimacy coexists with corporatist forces that were strengthened by institutional weaknesses or absences."[3] Meanwhile, chronic economic crisis limited the resources available for establishing new institutions or procedures and raised the level of social conflict, threatening the absolute as well as relative interests of all political actors.

Within this context, the impact of the human rights movement was limited by the fact that its program diverged from that of the administration and by the new social movement's inability to translate its program into a source of influence on the democratic regime. The Alfonsín administration's strategy for consolidating the incomplete transition to democracy was global, procedural, and incremental. Alfonsín's policies were directed at a general "culture of illegality" and asserted that it "would be absurd to expect to overcome military intervention through military self-criticism or through action by society on the military. Military intervention can only be overcome from a global reflection by Argentine society on itself."[4]

While the administration certainly recognized the problem of continuing corporatism, reform strategies treated the military as a group of problematic individuals to be subordinated to a new set of rules rather than an estate to be dissolved.[5] As "citizens in uniform," the military would be subject to the "logic of the law."[6] One analyst concluded that the problem with Alfonsín's strategy with respect to the military was that he assumed "that officers would behave as individual rational maximizers," but instead they chose "esprit de corps, which in fact is a conception of the armed forces as an entity independent of the government and placed above the law."[7]

In keeping with an incremental approach, Alfonsín's policy was reactive. The Alfonsín administration believed that time would improve rather than diminish the prospects for democracy, so that various kinds of holding actions were justified in response to threats to democracy.[8] President Alfonsín saw the completion of his term as the overriding goal of his administration. The government's midterm summary of its policy accomplishments was titled *Tres años ganados*—"Three Years Won." In a representative statement, Alfonsín said: "I have always thought that the decisive proof of the success of the path initiated in 1983 was to arrive at the elections of 1989."[9]

For the human rights movement, in contrast, truth and accountability for the past were not enough, as long as the forces responsible for the repression continued into the present and shadowed the future. At post-transition demonstrations, the movement clamored for civilian control of the military: "¡Alfonsín, vos sos el Presidente; hacé que los milicos nos devuelvan nuestra gente!" ("Alfonsín, you are the president; make the military return our loved ones!") In keeping with the human rights agenda—and in contrast to the administration's policy of self-administration of reform by the military—the movement called for equal judicial treatment for all citizens. Rejecting Alfonsín's global analysis, the movement traced human rights violations and military rule to the identity of specific actors, making military promotions as important as military procedures.[10] As a symbolic movement with absolute, ethically based demands, the movement found itself in perpetual conflict with the incremental, reactive policies of the administration.

Furthermore, the human rights movement's most potent weapon was relatively ineffective in the area of civil-military relations. In the final analysis, the movement was unable to challenge the legitimacy of a key actor in the transition, the Argentine military, which had in fact extended its own, antidemocratic basis of legitimacy to the entire state apparatus. Argentine coercive institutions reverted to the "logic of necessity" in the presence of any perceived threat to security. Nevertheless, the normative element in the military uprisings illustrates a struggle between these distinct bases of legitimacy.

The differing influence of the components of the human rights movement illustrates the nature of these limitations. The most expressive groups (especially the *afectados*) were the most constrained by them, but the more traditional civil libertarian organizations continued to play some role.

The monopoly of legitimate force is the very essence of the state, but in Argentina, the exercise of decentralized state terror had eroded both the control and the legitimacy of coercion. Any successor regime would face the task of dismantling or deactivating the repressive apparatus, composed of the military, some elements of the police, members of the intelligence services, and "free-lance" civilians. A democratic regime would be required by its mandate to induce these forces to submit to the rule of law, and to survive it would need to transform their interests from undermining democracy to defending it.

The Military

A ver, a ver, quien dirige la batuta—
El pueblo unido o los milicos hijos de puta.

We'll see, we'll see, who calls the tune—
the people united or those military sons of bitches.
Human rights movement refrain

The Argentine military is much more than an inadequately supervised coercive agency; rather, the military's historic role has been that of an autonomous corporate body operating as a parallel source (and intermittent holder) of state power. The Argentine military closely approximates Juan Rial's dependent capitalist ideal type: autonomous from the state, alienated from civil society, predisposed to intervene to safeguard "the nation," antiliberal, and authoritarian; moreover, it ranks high on Alfred Stepan's ranking of military institutional prerogatives.[11] Historically, internal political intervention was part of the military's mission. The Executive exerted little control or coordination, while the military operated a massive state enterprise (Fabricaciones Militares) and autonomous parallel legal and educational systems. The Armed Forces, which refer to themselves as "the military family," even established special neighborhoods for military families. The Argentine military has been a classic case of a "total institution" for its members, and a veto-holding corporation in its relationship to the rest of Argentine society.[12]

The normative concomitant of the military's role as a parallel source of state power is the view of the Armed Forces as a source of national identity that precedes the state: the "moral reserve of the nation."[13] A general later indicted for massive human rights violations wrote in the official corporate military journal:

Our Armed Forces . . . are integrators of the national being and of the historic and supreme goals of the nation and are thus profoundly immersed in the people and its problems. If we add these two conclusions, [the military's] habitual protagonistic role and its profound sense of the nation, an explanation arises for its many interventions.[14]

The form of military rule—the *estado de excepción*, which contrasts with the *estado de derecho*—substitutes a logic of necessity for the justification of political community in legitimacy.[15] The power of this idea of national security as national identity is illustrated by the controversy caused when Alfonsín referred to the Armed Forces as "children of the Constitution"—rather than founding fathers of the nation.[16]

The combined experience of unsuccessful military rule and defeat in the Malvinas conflict left the military delegitimized and deeply divided. The Air Force chief of staff, speaking just after the Semana Santa military rebellion, traced Argentina's military crisis to the military's "loss of legitimacy."[17] Thus, since the transition, the military has struggled to establish vindication of the past as a source of institutional cohesion, and the logic of necessity as the parameter for democratic legitimacy.[18] The Semana Santa military rebellion was called "Operation Dignity." In every rebellion, a key demand has been the recovery of military honor in the media. Even Alfonsín-appointed Chief of Staff José Dante Caridi asserted that the military sought understanding and "affection" from society.[19]

Argentina's transition to democracy did not spring from, correspond to, or produce a democratic military. The military withdrew from politics because the exercise of political power was detrimental to military cohesion. Within the military, overlapping factions defined the core interests of the institution in terms of traditional perquisites of power, the national security doctrine, (Peronist or fundamentalist) nationalism, technocratic modernization, or Martinian constitutionalism.[20] Only the last (and smallest) group can be said to have any intrinsic commitment to democracy; during the uprisings, factions labeled themselves the "national army" and "the constitutional army."[21] By diminishing military unity, these contradictory conceptions had facilitated the transition—but they subsequently formed alliances to veto human rights trials and block the consolidation of military reform.

The Armed Forces were never democratized; rather, the military as an institution made a conditional commitment to subordinate itself to civilian rule, based on its vision of corporate interests and subject to revocation when those interests were threatened.

From the government standpoint, the steps necessary to professionalize the armed forces were, in essence, those which would lessen their ability to intervene in politics as well as their interest in doing so. From the standpoint of the military, the steps necessary to reprofessionalize itself (which it also considered a primary goal) were those which would rebuild its professional expertise and capability. . . . Since the military failed to achieve what it perceived as one of the potential benefits of constitutional democracy (i.e. its reprofessionalization as an institution, in the absence of external political obligations), its distrust of democracy, at least in its present form, was renewed and led to the organization of a powerful politicized bloc within the army.[22]

As Stepan's indicators would predict, the main areas of contestation were accountability for human rights violations, budget, mission, structure, and civilian control.[23]

Military Reform

Military reform figured prominently on the agenda of both the Alfonsín administration and the human rights movement. The movement, administration, and academic analysts agreed that the military needed to become "citizens in uniform"; and that this would require a combination of restructuring, reorientation of strategic doctrine, and reeducation.[24] However, the human rights movement argued for selective promotions and trials to remove antidemocratic actors, whereas the government had an additional interest in professionalization and technological modernization. But professionalization is not necessarily democratizing: it increases the potential scope of intervention, strengthens some military factions at the expense of others, and was often self-managed in the Argentine case.[25] Military reform and resistance significantly restricted the strategies available to the human rights movement; in consequence, the movement generally played a limited and reactive role in the military reform process, which was dominated by the Executive.

Alfonsín moved swiftly to assert civilian control and reduce military resources. The president retired at least half of the high command—and often did not replace them. The military budget was cut by 30–40 percent, and the number of conscripts drastically reduced (from 120,000 to 45,000). The new administration reorganized the Joint Chiefs of Staff to inject more civilian supervision, reorganized the Ministry of Defense, and appointed a civilian as the head of the "military-industrial complex" (Fabricaciones Militares).[26]

However, these significant reforms were not matched by internal restructuring. The military had inherited structural patterns from its role as a repressive political force, such as the predominance of land (rather than air or naval) forces, the deployment of forces around the capital rather than in border regions, and occupational and residential isolation; and these were not addressed systematically or successfully. There is still a disproportionate emphasis on infantry, communications, and light weapons that are useful for repression rather than international conflict. The bulk of the military budget has been devoted to personnel—so that budget cuts immediately lead to moonlighting by military officers. While the number of youths subject to conscription has been reduced, the treatment of conscripts has not been made subject to adequate civilian supervision.[27] This incomplete reform package has led to intense military dissatisfaction; the sociologist Ernesto Lopez uses the metaphor of a "starving elephant": resources have been diminished, but the nature of the beast (and thus its appetite) remains unchanged.[28]

Meanwhile, the Alfonsín administration introduced a new defense law in an attempt to promote new norms and a new basis for institutional legitimacy. The new law, passed in 1988 after several years of parliamentary debate and modification, attempted to rewrite the mission of the Armed Forces so as to repudiate the so-called national security doctrine. Specifically, it forbade the military to use internal intervention as a "hypothesis of conflict" or training scenario.[29] Some human rights groups engaged in lobbying in connection with the defense law.[30] The Armed Forces were invited to comment on the legislation; all objected to being excluded from internal aggression, and the services differed on their visions of the role of military intelligence in internal conflict.[31] The limitation of domestic military involvement would have implied practical changes in military training and procurement. In addition, the defense law mandated the passage of new internal security and intelligence laws, all aimed at increasing congressional supervision of coercive forces.[32] However, the unexpected resurgence of guerrilla violence in the January 1989 attack on the La Tablada military barracks—which reintroduced the military's argument that it faced a security threat—resulted in the creation of a National Security Council with significant military participation and essentially derailed the new defense law.[33]

The other normative military reforms attempted by the Alfonsín administration concerned the key area of military education. The human rights movement recognized military education as a priority reform area, but again the movement was able to exert little influence. The scope of the problem is illustrated by a text produced by the official corporate military body Circulo Militar (and apparently still in use at Argentine military schools during the Alfonsín period) that traces domestic political conflict in Latin America to the superpowers—specifically, to the Soviet struggle for ideological hegemony, asserts that in a revolutionary war there is little distinction between political and military conflict and that intellectuals serve as the channel for ideological penetration, criticizes liberalism as an unsatisfactory and anomalous feature of U.S. national identity, and proclaims the supremacy of Catholic nationalism as a political philosophy.[34]

In response to this situation, the Defense Ministry created a commission to reform military education with participation from each service.

The ministry coordinator explained that in the case of the high-school-level military academies, the commission was able to remove or transfer a few of the most antidemocratic teachers and to reduce the number of courses with ideological content to two (History and Civic Education). But ministry control was limited: each service writes its own curriculum, and each service designates a junior officer as "advisor" to each class of cadets, who lives with the students and influences them far more than their formal instructors. As the commission realized that the problem was as much the isolation as the content of military education, the Defense Ministry increased attempts to integrate military and civilian education. Several services preempted these efforts by signing exchange pacts with selected civilian universities—but these pacts generally incorporated military students as a bloc, thus defeating the purpose of the reform.[35]

The major area of conflict between the Alfonsín administration and the human rights movement, and the major area of movement participation, was the promotion of military personnel accused of human rights violations. In Argentina, military promotions below the rank of colonel are determined by each service autonomously. Promotions to colonel and above are proposed by a Joint Chiefs of Staff commission to the president, who then submits them to the Senate for confirmation—and officers who are not promoted are automatically retired. Control of the Senate by right-wing Peronists during the Alfonsín period ensured that the president was the only real filter for military promotions.

The human rights movement lobbied steadily against the promotion of officers indicted or implicated in the repression.[36] In 1984, the human rights organizations presented a list of 896 officers implicated in the repression to Congress.[37] The movement had a few early successes: Adolfo Perez-Esquivel managed to block the promotion of General Mario Davico, and the Centro de Estudios Legales y Sociales reported the Senate's rejection of three of a group of six officers denounced by the human rights movement during 1984.[38]

But the Executive generally remained impervious to human rights movement protests, focusing on military loyalty rather than human rights record or democratic conviction as a criterion for promotion. When the first batch of military promotions were submitted in March 1984, the human rights organizations prepared a report showing that at least 20 of the 219 were implicated in human rights violations. After all of the promotions passed, following Executive pressure on the Senate, one Radical advisor resigned—since he had been tortured by one of the officers promoted.[39] Even José Dante Caridi, the loyal officer Alfonsín appointed chief of staff after the Semana Santa uprising, had been promoted over the objections of the human rights movement.[40]

Another case that generated massive controversy was that of Navy Lieutenant Alfredo Astiz, whose military accomplishments included the surrender of his command during the Malvinas conflict. Astiz was clearly linked to the disappearances of the Swedish teenager Dagmar Hagelin, the original leadership of Las Madres, and two French nuns, but had been acquitted by a military court on a technicality. Alfonsín did request that the Navy not recommend Astiz for promotion—but the president was ignored, and he did not subsequently veto the proposed promotion. The promotion of Astiz caused international as well as domestic protest, including condemnation of Argentina in the UN Human Rights Commision.[41]

Virtually the only sign of voluntary change within the military has been the foundation of CEMIDA, an association of democratic military officers. Founded by several hundred retired officers in late 1984 and in response to the 1985 trials of the juntas, CEMIDA sought to democratize both the military itself and civil-military relations. To this end, it published proposals for military reform, made policy statements in support of democracy and civilian trials for military officers, called for "tribunals of honor" to judge implicated but legally immune officers such as Lieutenant Astiz, and sponsored educational activities. CEMIDA framed the problem of military intervention in terms of nationalism, U.S. influence, and the national security doctrine. A retired officer who had trained in both the United States and in a U.S.-sponsored program in Argentina said: "In the United States, alongside the American officers, the training was never oriented towards internal security. But here it was different." The organization has had some coincidence of goals but no formal interchange with both the human rights movement and progressive elements of the Peronist party.[42]

While CEMIDA represented a public break with the monolithic stance of the armed forces vis-à-vis civilian society, the organization was rejected by an overwhelming majority of the members' military comrades. In November 1984, CEMIDA's offices suffered a powerful bombing, which appears to have been linked to clandestine forces within the military. Since military courts retain jurisdiction over retired officers, several members of CEMIDA were prosecuted by their services for alleged violations of the Honor Code in connection with statements critical of the current military leadership. In 1987, the Circulo Militar resolved to name all of the junta members convicted of human rights violations as honorary members. The president of CEMIDA resigned in protest; other members of CEMIDA who argued against the move were suspended from the Circulo Militar "military family."[43]

This panorama of ineffective and incomplete reform attempts, along with the steady pressure of human rights prosecutions, turned the "starving elephant" into a wounded and angry beast. The Alfonsín administration had not succeeded in transforming the role of the Armed Forces, but at the same time the military's traditional interests were being threatened by the democratic regime. This common threat provided the necessary institutional cohesion for the military to reassume an active role in conditioning the consolidation of democracy.

Military Uprisings

As a result of the human rights trials and military reform attempts, the six years of the Alfonsín administration saw a steady stream of military incidents, capped by three full-scale military uprisings: Semana Santa, Monte Caseros, and Villa Martelli.[44] The military uprisings served to narrow the political space available for human rights reform and the consolidation of democracy. The three military rebellions each reflected distinct military factions' perceptions of threats to military interests (crosscut by rank and service loyalties)—interests surprisingly linked to military legitimacy.[45] The Semana Santa uprising, for example, represented an alliance between national security doctrine–inspired middle-ranking officers still subject to trial for human rights violations and nationalist "professionals" who objected to military reform. The nationalist professional element predominated at Monte Caseros, without attracting much active support from other elements. And the Villa Martelli uprising presented a dangerous combination of the (sometimes right-wing Peronist) nationalists with professional grievances and nationalist "ultras" representing a fundamentalist ideology with a power-seeking political program.[46]

The first military uprising during the democratic period, the Semana Santa military rebellion, was a direct response to the continued prosecution of junior officers for human rights violations following the Punto Final legislation.[47] Alfonsín's strategy of a limited military housecleaning foundered on the rock of the military's unity through the blood pact of repression. One of the rebel leaders asserted: "There may be people who say their hands are clean, but if we did something wrong, we are all accomplices; because all, absolutely all, of us knew what we were doing or what others were doing."[48] In institutional terms, a junior officer dismissed during the Proceso explained that the trials were inherently threatening: because in a hierarchical organization, the individualistic and egalitarian standards of civilian justice endanger institutional cohesion.[49] During early 1987, following the Punto Final indictments of hundreds of officers, various (class-year) cohorts of Army officers swore to defend their comrades against trial and contacted like-minded groups through their class presidents. These junior officers were predominantly drawn from the infantry—especially the paratroopers, and most were commanded by classmates of Aldo Rico (the lieutenant colonel who was to assume leadership of the uprising).[50]

The rebellion was sparked when Major Ernesto Barreiro, who had been the "principal interrogator" at the La Perla clandestine detention center, was cited by the Cordoba Federal Appeals Court on April 15, 1987. Barreiro took refuge with his regiment, which refused to deliver him to justice. Meanwhile, Lieutenant Colonel Rico—who believed that the military was institutionally imperiled by budget cuts and "betrayed" by discredited leadership—marched down from his base in Missiones Province and took over the Buenos Aires Infantry School complex. Infantry regiments in Cordoba, Tucumán, Neuquen, and Santa Cruz all declared themselves in rebellion.[51] The rebels identified themselves as the true warriors who had defended Argentina in two wars (the Malvinas and the "Dirty War"); they dressed symbolically in combat gear and covered their faces with camouflage paint.[52]

Initially, the rebels' demands were unclear. Subsequently, they stressed that they were not attempting a coup d'état and only intended to carry out a severe form of protest (which they likened to a general strike).[53] But the uprising was widely (and correctly) perceived as a threat to the basic democratic character of the regime—and it elicited an unprecedented defense of democracy from all sectors of Argentine society. Alfonsín called on the people to come to the Plaza to defend their government, and hundreds of thousands responded. Representatives of every major political party, union, and business organization signed a pledge of democratic commitment (*acto de compromiso democratico*), and publicly declared their support for the government.[54] Both national and provincial legislatures went into permanent session. Thousands of unarmed citizens surrounded the Campo de Mayo rebel headquarters, peacefully blockading the base with their bodies.[55]

Throughout the Easter weekend, huge numbers of citizens from all walks of life kept a vigil for democracy. When Alfonsín addressed them, the Plaza once more became the site of political theater. On Holy Thursday, the president, invoking the founding Popular Assembly (Cabildo) of the nation, affirmed the values of equality before the law and declared, "Democracy in Argentina will not be negotiated."[56] The subordination of the military became linked to the president's assertion of personal authority: on Sunday, he announced that he was going to Campo de Mayo—alone—to receive the rebels' surrender.[57] And when he returned to the Plaza as the head of a reconciled national family, Alfonsín signaled the end of the crisis by wishing the assembled crowds a Happy Easter, urging them to "go home and kiss your children," and assuring them that "the house is in order."[58]

But the barracks were not in order. During the course of the rebellion, the democratic regime discovered the dimensions of military corporate solidarity: even those troops not involved in the rebellion would not fire on their fellow officers.[59] The chain of command had been broken, and junior officers refused to obey their (loyal) commanders.[60] At least one general raised enough loyal forces to initiate an attack, but the outcome was unclear—as was the attitude of the other services.[61] The civilian government faced a passive collapse of authority.[62]

Before the presidential visit that resolved the conflict, Alfonsín's military commander, Ríos Ereñu, had appealed to Aldo Rico on the basis of the military's corporate interest in democracy, defined in terms of legitimacy:

Don't you see that we've passed from being a 'repressive army' to an institution respected by society? . . . The only possible path is respect for the *estado de derecho* and dialogue. . . . [We've won] the instructions to the prosecutor, the Punto Final, a [pending proposal legislating] due obedience, and you know that the majority of those cited won't be convicted or the charges will be dropped under statutes of limitations. . . . [Rico responded negatively, and Ríos continued:] Do you think this is the way to get an amnesty? People consider this an insult, the people are in the streets. Look at the newspapers, Rico.

Holding out a newspaper photograph of the multitudinous, diverse popular demonstration in the Plaza, Rico pointed out a banner of the Montoneros [a virtually defunct former guerrilla group]. He shouted back: "That is not the people, that is the enemy!"[63]

The content of the president's meeting with Rico is not known, but the rebels sought an end to human rights trials, a change of military leadership, cessation of an alleged media campaign against the prestige of the military, and no prosecution for the rebellion itself. Afterward, Rico claimed that these conditions were met in essence, while the government asserted that the meeting served only to clarify already planned policy changes and exercise presidential authority.[64] Within weeks of the rebellion, Alfonsín introduced the due obedience legislation drastically limiting further human rights trials, especially among the junior officers involved in the rebellion. Alfonsín's military chief, Ríos Ereñu, did resign, but was replaced by a general unsympathetic to rebel concerns (José Dante Caridi).[65] The rebels were prosecuted, but they were charged in a military court rather than under the new defense of democracy law. And when the president returned to the Plaza, he revived military prestige when he referred to the mutineers as "heroes of the Malvinas."

After Semana Santa, Caridi initiated a series of military transfers and purges against the followers of Rico. Fifteen generals were retired and nine unit heads were relieved. By October of 1987, almost 40 percent of infantry regiments had been affected by the transfers.[66] In late September of 1987, there was yet another military incident—officially explained as a poorly planned training exercise but claimed by Rico followers as a response to their punishment for Semana Santa.[67] By January 1988, Rico was convinced that the pact ending the Semana Santa rebellion had been broken, and he determined to rally his followers before their institutional position could be eroded further. Rico left the base where he had been detained (without being stopped) and holed up on the country estate of a Proceso-era minister. Several weeks later, military judges ordered Rico rearrested. But when the authorities arrived, Rico had gone—and taken refuge at the army base in Monte Caseros.

In the Monte Caseros uprising of January 1988, a series of infantry regiments throughout the country again declared themselves in rebellion. But this time, support for Rico was much more limited, since the due obedience law had removed the threat of human rights trials.[68] However, a small group of ultrarightist Air Force and civilian intelligence personnel did take advantage of the uprising to briefly take over an air base and the domestic national airport, Jorge Newberry.[69] Again, civilian support for the democratic regime was swift and unanimous.[70] But this time, Alfonsín did not mobilize the masses (perhaps fearing backlash from the disillusionment following the due obedience law).

The other critical difference between Semana Santa and Monte Caseros was the willingness of loyal troops to put down the uprising; the corporate cohesion of the military had been undercut by the concessions made following the previous rebellion. On Sunday, January 17th, Caridi advanced on Rico, leading troops drawn predominantly from the cavalry and artillery. Surprised and disheartened by a direct military attack, Rico surrendered after a brief skirmish. Hundreds of officers were detained, and dozens were tried or disciplined during the first half of 1988.[71] In response to the airport takeover incident, the Air Force command was reshuffled.[72] In addition, military salaries were raised significantly.[73]

But a group of officers associated with Rico had eluded capture and gone underground; their names surfaced in connection with bombings, robberies, and extortions.[74] In September, a Riquista officer retired by Caridi created an institutional crisis by appealing the sanction to a civilian court. The matter was resolved by Alfonsín, acting as commander in chief, who returned the case to military courts.[75] Throughout October, the scheduling of the few remaining human rights trials and pending promotions caused tension in the ranks.[76] In November, massive caches of arms of unclear provenance were discovered.[77]

The next rebellion (Villa Martelli) was catalyzed by a controversial colonel who had been passed over for promotion rather than by the Riquistas. The name of Colonel Mohamed Alí Seineldín, an ultraright fundamentalist stationed in Panama, did not appear on the promotion lists—but Seineldín himself turned up in Argentina in early December 1988. The rebellion began with the unusual desertion of an elite Coast Guard unit (with a large supply of weapons) on December 1st.[78] Several Army regiments joined in, including one led by the son of the former dictator Jorge Videla, and a group headed by Seineldín took over the Campo de Mayo base, site of the Semana Santa uprising, on December 2d. An unsuccessful attempt was made to free both Videla, who was serving a prison sentence for human rights violations, and Aldo Rico, the leader of the two previous rebellions. Since President Alfonsín was out of the country when the Villa Martelli uprising broke out, Vice President Martinez supervised a meeting between Chief of Staff Caridi and Seineldín, after which Martinez announced that the mutiny had been resolved.[79]

But when Alfonsín returned on Saturday, December 3d, the situation worsened. What had seemed to be the resolution of the crisis turned out to be only a truce. The day was filled with tense meetings between rebel and loyalist leaders of the military command. By nightfall, a group of rebels had left the Campo de Mayo base in tanks and taken over the Villa Martelli army base, situated in a residential neighborhood in suburban Buenos Aires where civilian casualties were likely in the event of conflict. Alfonsín ordered the uprising put down by force.

Meanwhile, the beleaguered government once more called on the people to fill the Plaza and defend democracy. The human rights movement, lately ignored by the government, was pressed into service to provide legitimacy for the call: "Dictatorship or democracy! Prevent the return of the terror!" Although civilian support for the government was strong and multisectoral, many fewer mobilized to defend it than at Semana Santa. But as at Semana Santa, hundreds of local residents and political activists surrounded the rebel base, again unarmed—but increasingly determined to repudiate the rebellion.

The rebellion peaked on yet another long Sunday. Throughout the morning, police and loyal troops attempted to clear the area surrounding the base of civilians; demonstrators were determined to remain and observe the attack, in order to prevent any negotiation from taking place. Tension was high, and some of the frustrated demonstrators attacked the rebel troops with rocks. Loyal troops fired on the rebels during the afternoon, but around dusk, hostilities suddenly ceased and the rebels surrendered. Three civilians had been killed and thirty-five injured. That evening, Alfonsín spoke to the nation: he announced that the rebellion was over thanks to "an act of God" ("Dios puso su mano") and assured the public that there had been no negotiation. Many scholars, journalists, and the *carapintadas* themselves believed otherwise.[80]

Seineldín's demands, the subject of the alleged pact that ended the uprising, included replacement of the chief of staff, an end to human rights trials, better salaries, and minimal prosecution for the rebellion. Once more, the rebels were charged in a military rather than civilian court, and received primarily disciplinary sanctions. Within two weeks, the military received a 20 percent pay raise.[81] By the end of the month, Army Chief of Staff Caridi had resigned. And no significant human rights prosecutions were pursued during the remainder of Alfonsín's term.[82]

Although the military did not actively engage in human rights violations during the Alfonsín administration, the major coercive agency of the state was able to resist the institutionalization of democratic accountability: the repressive apparatus was deactivated but not dismantled. But the human rights agenda is not exhausted by the demand that the state refrain from violating human rights; it also assigns the state a role as a guarantor of security. Beyond the illegitimate violence carried out by legitimate state agents, human rights in Argentina were threatened by citizens who had access to the means of coercion but remained beyond the control of the state.

Ongoing Violence:
La mano de obra desocupada

Although the formal structure of military task forces was dissolved by the military before the transition, the individuals who had operated official death squads ("task forces") continued to engage in lesser forms of unofficial violence: bombings, beatings, and even kidnappings of political activists.[83] Early in the Alfonsín administration, the minister of the interior, Antonio Troccoli, was confronted by human rights activists who cited continuing incidents of violence that seemed linked to former members of the task forces of the repression. Troccoli responded that after all, there were now a large group of "displaced workers" who had participated in the repression—*"la mano de obra desocupada."*[84] These domestic mercenaries combined with long-standing sponsors of political violence such as military intelligence agents, Argentine Nazis, and right-wing Peronist thugs.[85] The human rights movement documented and publicized these incidents, periodically called for reform of the intelligence services, and published lists of individuals implicated in the repression.

The scope of the continuing violence was substantial: one chronology lists over 500 incidents during the first two years of the Alfonsín government.[86] In 1984, there were about a dozen politically targeted bombings, most involving human rights reform.[87] In 1985, a state of siege was declared following a right-wing bombing campaign that threatened schools, bus stations, and other public places, and the son of General Camps was arrested on conspiracy charges.[88] A 1987 wave of dozens of attacks culminated in the bombing of sixteen sites connected with the ruling Radical party.[89] A wave of bombings in March and April 1988 that focused on movie theaters was followed by the arrests of the neo-Nazi group Alerta Nacional.[90] A December 1988 study, which includes political violence in strikes and other milieus not necessarily linked to the dictatorship, documents 876 incidents with 42 fatalities—the third-highest level of political violence in South America.[91]

The intelligence services were the main state agency implicated in these incidents. Argentina is rife with intelligence services: each branch of the military and police has its own intelligence service (including the Coast Guard, Border Guard, and National Penitentiary Service), along with the civilian state intelligence service (SIDE).[92] A Defense Ministry official explained that at the transition, these services were so oriented toward internal repression that they were virtually incapable of providing reliable foreign intelligence.[93] The Alfonsín administration placed the national intelligence coordination center under civilian control and retired dozens of SIDE's military operatives, but was unable to reform the military intelligence services.[94] In fact, a reforming head of the civilian intelligence service admitted that he "lacked the capacity to determine" whether the military services continued to engage in internal intelligence.[95] When the same civilian official invited each military service to designate a representative for the new system of intelligence coordination, the Army sent Lieutenant Colonel Enrique Venturino—subsequently known as the chief aide to Aldo Rico.[96] The intelligence services—agencies of the state—were also implicated in the *carapintada* uprisings that sought to overthrow it.[97]

Former intelligence agents have been linked to extortion and traffic in arms and drugs, and the former head of the civilian intelligence agency claimed that members of military intelligence were responsible for bombings, beatings, and intimidation of political activists.[98] An official familiar with reports of the incidents confirmed human rights movement claims that the attacks showed access to knowledge only available to police or intelligence services.[99] When a Nazi group was detained for bombings, two of the seven were found to be former members of the intelligence services.[100] Another group of Nazis was linked to an Air Force officer implicated in the airport takeover during the Monte Caseros military uprising.[101] Human rights groups identified a provocateur at the "Bloody Friday" CGT general strike as a former concentration camp operative.[102]

The majority of the above incidents were bombings, but the best-known illustration of continuing violence by "free-lance" former repressors is the Sivak scandal. Osvaldo Sivak, a wealthy and prominent businessman, was kidnapped for both political and extortionary purposes in 1979 by Buenos Aires federal police officers linked to the repression.[103] Sivak was rescued by another faction of the police, but his kidnappers were never punished, and made their way into various intelligence agencies.

Then, in 1985, Sivak disappeared again. His wife, suspecting police complicity again, approached the Executive for help in 1986. She was directed to a special section of the Ministry of Defense that was investigating kidnappings—which promptly attempted to extort money from the Sivak family. Marta Sivak, herself an attorney, reported the problem to the Ministry of the Interior, which engaged in a cover-up. It was only after Marta Sivak, through personal influence, persuaded a legislator to launch a congressional investigation that the kidnappers were discovered and the ministries discredited.[104]

Once again, the kidnappers included members of the Buenos Aires federal police; in fact, one of them was a "rescuer" from the first kidnapping. Sivak's body was discovered shortly thereafter. The ensuing scandal led to the resignation of the new defense minister[105] and strengthened the hand of a recently appointed reforming federal police chief, Juan Pirker. But Marta Sivak, who has founded a citizen's action group to promote democracy as a result of her experiences, sees evidence of the "work of the unemployed" in a series of other Alfonsín-era extortionary kidnappings.[106]

The right to life and basic security in Argentina continued to be threatened by former state agents, quasi-state agents, persons with illicit access to state resources, and sponsors of political violence subject to only sporadic detection and control. The human rights movement called attention to this problem—and was one of its chief victims. But as with the military, the nature of the coercive agency admitted little role for outsiders or even branches of government other than the Executive.

The basis of state power in Argentina was not restructured, and human rights reform was thus incompletely consolidated. Democratic accountability could not be extended to coercive institutions as long as antidemocratic actors retained veto power. Time eroded, rather than reinforced, the consolidation of democracy because the level of substantive social conflict overwhelmed the legitimacy of democratic procedures. The very incrementalism and pluralism of democratic actors and procedures weakened their influence vis-à-vis authoritarian actors and legacies.

The Argentine people had not taken the Bastille—or the barracks. The human rights movement played a critical role in highlighting and questioning the implicit limits of civilian control of the military and associated forces, helping to push back each resurgence of violence. But coercion could only be contained, not controlled. The democratic state was neither fully accountable for the control of coercion nor fully accountable to the society in whose name it governed. Given these structural limits, the human rights movement could only try to institutionalize its agenda in the state. The trials and investigations had addressed the past, while the present evolved toward stalemate. In challenging the state apparatus to consolidate democracy, the human rights movement looked to the future.

Chapter 7

Institutionalizing Safeguards:
¡Nunca más!

You must first enable the government to control the governed; and in the next place oblige it to control itself.
James Madison, *The Federalist Papers*, No. 51

Human rights reform in Argentina was linked to the establishment and legitimacy of a new democratic regime, but regime transition had preceded rather than followed the transformation of state structures. Alfred Stepan distinguishes three spheres of political activity: civil society (social movements), political society (parties, legislature, and contestation), and the state (the ongoing administrative, legal, and coercive system).[1] While the reforms of the establishment phase of a democratic regime had centered on the relationship between civil society and political society, the consolidation of human rights reform would also require a restructuring of the relationship between political society and the state.

In Argentina, a democratic regime was established atop a partially authoritarian state riddled with inherited and continuing repressive features. This system was then faced with immediate challenges to military interests, the maintenance of public order, and the reemergence of antisystem violence. Within this context, the human rights movement pressed for the democratization of the state. Invoking democratic legitimacy, the movement threw its weight against government tradition, bureaucracy, and convenience (albeit with a declining level of symbolic protest) and opened a space for the establishment of human rights safeguards.

The human rights movement program for the institutionalization of human rights included police reform, increased congressional representation, new legislation, renewal of the judiciary, a permanent bicameral commission on human rights (originally proposed as an investigatory commission), and the promotion of international conventions on forced disappearance and missing children. The Alfonsín administration focused on more general measures to consolidate democracy: international treaties, constitutional reform, civil libertarian legislation, and reform of police and judicial *procedures* (rather than personnel). Durable human rights reform has taken place at each of these levels, but the movement had the most direct influence in police reform and the legislative arena.

Given this difference in programs and strategies, the human rights movement's limited success in the institutionalization of change can be attributed in large part to the inherent limitations of a symbolic, expressive new social movement. The new social movement was more effective in settings of transition or crisis than during the daily operation of long-standing institutions. This limitation is linked to the early establishment of movement influence through civil society and the international system, which did not transfer readily to the state itself. The call to institutionalize accountability to a social movement constituency based in civil society was most powerful in the most representative—and weakest—institutions of the state. Despite these significant barriers, the movement established a basis for the recognition of new rights and a continuing challenge to traditional repressive practices.

Police Reform and Penal Reform

> "If they told me that [the former Buenos Aires police chief General Ramón] Camps had tortured some low-life [*un negrito*] that no one knew, [I'd say] go right ahead [*vaya y pase*]. But how would it occur to him to torture a [well-known] journalist like Jacobo Timerman!"
>
> Father Christian von Wernich,
> former police chaplain, in *Madres de Plaza de Mayo*, December 1984.

The police had been less directly and exclusively involved in the repression than the military, and the police force more closely fits the model of an inadequately supervised but essentially legitimate coercive agency. Although the police had been heavily militarized, the human rights movement could play a reforming role—since the institutional basis of legitimacy of the police was tied more to justice than external threat, and accountability (to the judiciary) was an established tradition. Also, the Alfonsín government did remove military chiefs of police when it assumed power. Those aspects of police practices that threatened human rights sprang from a combination of legacies of the Proceso and traditional abusive practices. Thus, the extension of human rights claims to the police went beyond deactivating repression to question the traditional treatment of suspects—especially the poor. This shift in human rights focus toward "endemic violations" has been paralleled in many other democratizing nations in Latin America, especially Brazil. In this sense, the human rights movement challenge began to move from the control of coercion to the institutionalization of human rights safeguards.

The Centro de Estudios Legales y Sociales, along with the Asamblea Permanente por los Derechos Humanos and several concerned judges, launched a campaign against police abuse in 1986. A CELS study documented almost one thousand deaths from police violence; in many cases, police contentions of an armed confrontation were contradicted by the accounts of witnesses or forensic evidence. The study also correlated patterns of unexplained shootings to specific jurisdictions, supervising officers, and waves of political pressure (including the pressure of the CELS campaign).[2]

The jurisdiction of the Buenos Aires federal police includes the federal district of Buenos Aires, federal territories such as Tierra del Fuego, and any place where a federal crime has been committed. The federal force has been troubled primarily by corruption, extortion such as the Sivak kidnapping, and the excessive use of force in situations of public unrest (rather than abusive behavior toward suspects in custody).[3] However, some of the outlying (poorer) areas of the capital were implicated in the CELS study, and several suspicious deaths of political or union activists have been attributed to the federal police.[4]

When Chief Juan Pirker assumed the leadership of the Buenos Aires federal police, he instituted a quiet crackdown on police violence; for example, Pirker transferred the chief of what the CELS study showed to be one of the worst areas—who had been the head of a concentration camp.[5] At the federal level, the Ministry of the Interior did not modify the internal police regulations on the use of deadly force or standards for promotion but did introduce reforms designed to extend judicial supervision of police procedures and reduce discretionary police power.[6] The ministry organized a series of meetings over two years between judges and high-ranking police officials. Finally, the education of the federal police was reformed to emphasize the role of "rights and guarantees" in three of their 28 courses (which are now taught by professors rather than retired police officers), incorporate continuing education seminars by law professors on "the problem of illegal pressures," and introduce a course in public relations.[7]

In the marginal and working-class areas of greater Buenos Aires and the province of Buenos Aires, there have been extensive reports of police shootings of unarmed suspects and abuse of suspects in custody by the force formerly commanded by General Ramón Camps, the Buenos Aires provincial police. An investigating judge pointed out that by 1986, there were two or three suspects killed *per day* and referred to a "de facto death penalty" for common crime.[8] The greater Buenos Aires neighborhoods of Budge, Dock Sud, Gran Bourg, and San Francisco de Solano are each associated with an unsatisfactorily explained police killing of unarmed (often activist) youths, followed by the intimidation of witnesses and neighbors who protested.[9]

In the province of Buenos Aires, so many police were arrested (primarily for corruption) that a special wing of Caceros prison was reserved for them. The Radical provincial administration (1983–87), working with the provincial bicameral human rights commission, passed sweeping reforms requiring judicial review of "probable cause" for detention, registration of detainees within six hours of arrest, and allowing for habeas corpus to be filed for preventative purposes as well as for action or omission. They also incorporated some changes in police education and introduced proposals for changes in the prison code. Marco DiCaprio, the provincial undersecretary of justice who sponsored these reforms, had defended imprisoned lawyers during the Proceso, worked closely with the APDH, Abuelas, and SASID, and counts an Asamblea activist among his chief legislative aides.[10]

But when a Peronist provincial administration came to power in 1987, widespread police abuse (and corruption) continued. During the first four months of the new administration, 105 police officers were retired; by the time the Peronist provincial minister of the interior resigned in late 1988, only 2 members of the original police command were still serving.[11] The provincial bicameral human rights commission instituted inquiries over the unexplained deaths in Budge, Dock Sud, and San Francisco de Solano. In these cases, neighborhood defense committees modeled on the national human rights movement formed spontaneously and persisted under difficult conditions.[12]

In the provinces (each under the control of its own provincial police force), several cases surfaced of suspicious deaths while in police custody. Continuing abuses are probably worst in the northern provinces, where they are unlikely to be publicized or punished. In other parts of the country, reports of abuse continue—but they are often punished once publicized (usually by human rights groups).[13] In one case, all sixteen police who had been on duty in a Rosario police station when the suspect's death occurred were temporarily arrested.[14] In Cordoba, several officers denounced their superiors for keeping a detainee chained up without food or water for three days.[15] At one point, the entire police command of La Rioja (Menem's province) was replaced because of allegations of human rights violations, and similar incidents and penalties occurred in Entre Rios.[16] Chilean refugees have been abused in the border provinces, but the level of abuse of Argentine citizens appears to be low in this region, and Mendoza is the only province to offer police a course on human rights.[17]

Under the Menem administration, Americas Watch (with CELS), Amnesty International, and the U.S. State Department continue to report widespread police abuse. Although complaints of police brutality have generally been ignored by the government, resistance by civil libertarians and neighborhood groups continues.[18] In mid 1992, the province of Buenos Aires did fire hundreds of police officers for human rights violations.[19]

The prison system was also the target of human rights reforms.[20] Prisoners' rights and human rights organizations objected to the presence of Proceso-era officials, including the former head of a concentration camp who ran a prison in the provinces.[21] It is worth noting that as of 1984, 1,200 federal prisoners (about 60 percent of the total) were serving preventative detention, and had not been convicted of any crime. There was also a series of prison mutinies during the Alfonsín administration, many involving claims of abuse.[22]

Early reform attempts included the appointment of a civilian head of the Penitentiary Service, who engaged in inspection visits and transferred members of the prison intelligence service, but the new official resigned in 1985.[23] In 1986, in response to continuing complaints, the national subsecretary of human rights formed a prison inspection commission consisting of representatives of the APDH, MEDH, CELS, and La Liga, which issued a critical report published by the Asamblea.[24] Working with human rights organizations, the Buenos Aires provincial minister of the interior, a Peronist, ordered a series of transfers in the Penitentiary Service, following incidents in which detainees were abused.[25] In the province of Santiago del Estero, a provincial congressional human rights commission investigated inmates' complaints of abuse by violent inmates on the orders of prison officials and secured the transfer of the victims.[26] A prison dispute in Mendoza was also mediated by the provincial congressional human rights commission.[27]

In criticizing the operation of traditionally legitimate institutions such as the police and prisons, the human rights movement helped institutionalize democratic accountability for legitimate coercion. But in many cases, the pace and extent of reform was dependent on the presence of sympathetic officials, whose influence did not outlast their tenure in office: the new intelligence service and prison service heads resigned to fill other posts, the new federal police chief died, the Buenos Aires provincial administration changed hands in midterm elections, and the Peronist reformer was subsequently forced out of office. In order to secure long-term state accountability for human rights, the movement would have to restructure the basic institutions of governance.

Legal Reforms

An early triumph of the human rights movement was the election on a human rights platform of the congressional deputy Augusto Conte, a member of the Partido Democrato Cristiana (DC), the father of a *desaparecido*, and one of the founders of CELS. Conte was elected with the votes of human rights activists who joined the Christian Democrats on his behalf, some of whom later served as his staff.[28] He campaigned on a platform that included international and domestic conventions on forced disappearance, establishment of a bicameral commission, civilian trials and a systematic plan of retirements for the military, commutation of sentences for political prisoners, and a legislative motion to force the Executive to seize and publish military archives concerning the disappeared.[29] Although it is difficult to trace specific legislative victories to Conte himself, he played a powerful role in setting the congressional agenda, leading floor debates, and representing movement interests in committees.[30]

Subsequently, representatives of the DC and Partido Intransigente and both Peronist and Radical reformers continued to be sympathetic to human rights movement concerns, but the human rights movement was unable to develop consistent alliances with the major parties—Conte's term marked the peak of its direct congressional representation.[31] More general attempts at human rights movement lobbying of the legislature were generally neutralized by military lobbying.[32] Thus, legislative human rights reform was dominated by the Executive.

The legislative protection of the rights of the person in Argentina involved both repealing repressive legislation and regulating repressive practices introduced during the Proceso and addressing continuing systemic problems. Immediately following the transition, the Executive introduced legislation informed by the abuses of the repression to eliminate the death penalty (included in the so-called defense of democracy law), extend habeas corpus to prisoners condemned by military tribunals and during states of siege, and punish torture by public officials as murder.[33] Although the latter measure was initiated by the Executive and written by Alfonsín's advisors, it was announced following a march by Las Madres on the newly elected Radicals, in which Las Madres turned in 3,000 case histories and demanded a bicameral commission to investigate human rights abuses.[34] A later measure, rooted in the Proceso experience but institutionalizing the rights of future generations, was the establishment of the National Genetic Bank for identifying the biological relatives of missing children. The National Genetic Bank was an Executive project, passed in 1987, which involved substantial input from the Abuelas de Plaza de Mayo.[35] The human rights movement legislative project to criminalize forced disappearance was introduced by Conte but not passed by Congress.[36]

But erasing the legacies of the Proceso was not enough, since the Argentine legal system contained historically accepted but arbitrary and inequitable features.[37] Attempts at restructuring to guarantee civil rights included a law limiting preventative detention to two years, a maximum period of three days for holding detainees incommunicado, the granting of equal authority to women in representing the family to the state, and legislation forbidding racial, ethnic, or religious discrimination.[38]

Civil libertarians, among them human rights activists, continue to argue that preventative detention and incommunicado status are in and of themselves questionable practices that should be eliminated rather than regulated.[39] It is estimated that 60–65 percent of the Argentine prison population is serving preventative detention. One jurist explained that in many cases, the months or years of preventative detention serve as a de facto sentence, with the trial as a revision of time served rather than a determination of culpability.[40] In addition, the human rights movement has continued to campaign in areas not covered by these reforms, such as discretionary police power to hold suspects for up to 24 hours (or over the weekend) in order to "verify their records" and police chiefs' ability to impose sentences of up to 30 days for "offenses against public order" (in 1984, there were almost 30,000 cases of this type).[41]

Judicial Reform and Judicial Autonomy

Many of the police, penal, and legal reforms discussed above were intended to increase accountability through judicial supervision. But this introduced the issue of the nature of the judiciary. In Argentina, judges at all levels are chosen by the Executive and confirmed by the

Senate. The military dictatorship had replaced most of the judiciary and forced all new appointees to swear allegiance to the military's political program, the statutes of the Proceso, which explicitly superseded the Constitution. Accordingly, during the transition, the human rights movement demanded the retirement of Proceso-era judges, who were seen as complicitous with the repression.[42] But about 90 percent of the judiciary were retained—the general policy was to confirm judges unless there was special evidence against them.[43]

However, many members of the judiciary were unexpectedly supportive of human rights concerns, at least insofar as they involved the reestablishment of the *estado de derecho*. Although those few judges who had defended the rule of law during the dictatorship continued to do so under democracy, there seems to be little correlation between Proceso-era passivity and the tone of current rulings: for example, half of the judges who condemned the juntas and both prosecutors had held judicial posts during the Proceso. Judges of disparate convictions, such as Eugenio Zaffaroni and Juan Ramos Padilla, engaged in unprecedented judicial activism in pursuit of human rights.[44]

Judicial support for human rights derived from an autonomous institutional environment that facilitated the expression of personal and professional convictions, not from the history of individuals. Jorge Torlasco, a judge who presided in the junta trials, said, for example, that his original choice of profession was determined by a "sympathy for the protection of persons," and that during the Proceso, when he felt that he could not carry out a judge's duty to investigate he had simply removed himself from the case.[45] Judge Ramos Padilla, who was active in both missing children and NN exhumation cases, pointed out that most of the activist judges who have supported human rights come from the same generation as the disappeared. Both the "force of the facts" they encountered and the nature of the transition to democracy infused many of his colleagues with a sense of historical responsibility.[46] Judge Julio Virgolini, the organizer of a judicial reform movement called the Green List for a Democratic Judiciary, described the context of reform: the personal and professional risks in defending human rights decreased dramatically.[47]

In the province of Buenos Aires, the former minister of government Luis Brunatti created a Judicial Appointments Advisory Council to encourage just such professionalism and accountability in future appointments, in a manner sensitive to human rights movement concerns about judges' professional history.[48] At the national level, reforms were proposed to make the judiciary both more accountable and more efficient: all trials would be oral and public, and the jury system would be introduced for some kinds of cases. A special class of magistrate would be introduced to deal with petty crime, in order to reduce judicial caseloads and further supervise the police. And in each case, a special judge would be assigned to safeguard the rights of suspects.[49]

But some members of the judiciary used their new autonomy to perpetuate the values they had exercised during the Proceso, as the human rights movement had predicted, through selective prosecution of victims and human rights activists. The most prominent case of this type was that of Graciela Daleo, who was kidnapped, tortured, and imprisoned in the Naval Mechanics School (ESMA) clandestine detention center for almost two years. She survived to testify at the trials of the juntas and became an active member of the Ex-Detainees Association. She was then subjected to preventative imprisonment for several months, under an obsolete statute, for an alleged connection to a guerrilla kidnapping, on the basis of anonymous accusations and evidence obtained illicitly.[50] Another example of judicial harassment is the charge of "disrespect" (*desacato*) filed by a Proceso-era judge against Ernesto Sabato (the former head of CONADEP), Augusto Conte, and the Nobel laureate Adolfo Perez-Esquivel for their criticisms of the judge's failure to investigate habeas corpus cases under the military regime.[51] During 1984, the human rights activist who was to become Entre Rios's subsecretary of human rights, then an employee of the judiciary, was prosecuted for "unauthorized political activity" under a 1933 statute.[52] A final example is one judge's attempt to make the father of the disappeared Swedish teenager Dagmar Hagelin pay the court costs involved in his ultimately futile attempt to prosecute Navy Lieutenant Alfredo Astiz.[53]

The human rights movement's failure to secure the key demand of judicial renewal did not prevent judicial reform or the emergence of a judiciary committed to civil rights as a concomitant of the rule of law. However, the institutional autonomy necessary to safeguard that commitment cut both ways—and sometimes worked against the human rights movement. But the establishment of *new* state institutions in a form that did not correspond to movement demands *did* dilute the realization of human rights reform.

Executive Institutions

A Subsecretariat of Human Rights was created as a successor to the CONADEP investigation, alternative to the human rights movement's desired permanent bicameral commission, and permanent state institution to supervise human rights policy.[54] Many of the agency's initial staff were drawn from CONADEP (and thus included many of the human rights activists who had decided to cooperate with CONADEP). The subsecretary of human rights, with a staff of around 30 people, was established under the Ministry of the Interior by Executive decree.[55] The main functions of the subsecretary are to manage the CONADEP files, receive denunciations of current human rights violations, and promote educational activities related to human rights. Since the passage of the legislation mandating a pension for the relatives of disappeared persons, the subsecretary has also been responsible for certifying the claimed disappearance to the Ministry of Health and Social Action (which dispenses the pensions).[56] The subsecretary does not carry out any preventative inspection or supervision of police or penal facilities.

The Subsecretariat of Human Rights is divided into two sections, Prevention and Promotion. The Department of Prevention takes citizen complaints, communicates with the judiciary, and manages the CONADEP files. By 1988 it had received around 700 complaints of continuing violations, which were assessed for admissibility and forwarded to the judiciary. Since most denunciations were not forwarded and since complainants can approach the judiciary directly, the only advantage in registering a human rights claim with the subsecretary is that an Executive branch institution may enhance the claim's priority with other institutions.[57]

The CONADEP files are closed to the public and only available to designated representatives of human rights movements when they request a specific file (files are organized by victim). The CONADEP records are not accessible en masse and are closed to journalists, researchers, and international organizations.[58] Furthermore, members of some of the human rights movements report difficulty in accessing the records. The subsecretariat has certified around 2,000 disappearances for the purpose of granting pensions, including about 70 new cases not included in the CONADEP files.[59]

The Department of Promotion prepares educational and media projects, answers inquiries from the general public, and analyzes existing legislation to suggest human rights reform. The subsecretary organized a series of teacher-training workshops on human rights. The legislative review project has proceeded more slowly; in 1988 (four years after the founding of the subsecretariat) the author was informed that the organization hoped to have a preliminary evaluation prepared by the following year.[60]

The subsecretary is not well-known to the general public, and is not well regarded by many in the human rights movement.[61] The subsecretariat has suffered a lack of staff and resources, which has hindered its work. Between 1984 and 1986, the new agency was provisional and thus forced to borrow office space and furniture from the Municipality of Buenos Aires. Staff turnover has been unusually high, partly because of low salaries and a government hiring freeze; there are eight vacancies in a staff of around thirty. During 1988, the director of the Prevention section had been on sick leave for six months.[62]

It is interesting to contrast the work of the only existing provincial-level subsecretary of human rights, in the (Renovador) Peronist-ruled province of Entre Rios. Entre Rios's subsecretary was a well-known human rights activist, and several members of her small staff were activists and/or *afectados*. In response to a flood of denunciations, she began a program of regular prison inspections. She worked with the provincial minister of the interior to retire or remove police officers accused of human rights violations, and generally to incorporate respect for human rights into police promotion criteria. The subsecretary also organized a series of public neighborhood meetings to discuss community security and police abuse, headed by a panel composed of herself, the provincial minister of justice, the local police chief, a Church representative, and leaders of neighborhood organizations. Entre Rios's subsecretary has sponsored various workshops and seminars—many of which stress social rights, in keeping with the Peronist vision.[63]

At the systemic level, various proposals for constitutional reform have attempted to establish new forms and principles for existing institutions in a manner that would safeguard both democracy and human rights. Alfonsín and his Council for the Consolidation of Democracy promoted an overall change in institutional relationships through the mechanism of constitutional reform to stabilize the democratic system. The most prominent feature of this proposal was the replacement of the presidential system with a mixed parliamentary model in order to strengthen the legislature and allow for reelection of the president. In response, SERPAJ—in association with the CGT Human Rights Secretariat—outlined a proposal for constitutional reform to increase guarantees of both civil and social rights, and to promote broader popular participation in the political process.[64] Members of La Liga, in turn, prepared analyses of problems of constitutional law relevant to human rights, such as the constitutional provision for a state of emergency (the source of the *estado de excepción*) and the necessity for postratification congressional enactment of international treaties.[65] To date, none of these proposals has advanced beyond the stage of public debate.

Finally, the administration itself promoted and publicized a commitment to international human rights standards, with a high degree of congruence with human rights movement goals. This served both to bolster Alfonsín's domestic legitimacy and to counterpoise the international human rights regime to domestic (military) pressures.[66] Argentina has now ratified every significant international treaty on human rights, including the San José (Costa Rica) Interamerican Treaty on Human Rights and the Convention Against Torture.[67] Argentine representatives to the UN Human Rights Commission introduced the human rights movement-sponsored initiative to have forced disappearance declared a crime against humanity.[68]

A Subsecretariat of Human Rights has also been created under the Foreign Ministry, with a staff of about a dozen personnel—about half of whom are diplomats. This office helps to evaluate Argentine participation in human rights–related treaties, reports to international monitoring bodies, and coordinates diplomatic activity related to human rights (such as extradition requests for missing children residing in Paraguay). Originally, the Foreign Ministry subsecretariat coordinated its activity on behalf of missing children with the Abuelas, but a breakdown of this arrangement during 1988 caused controversy and criticism of the agency by UN officials.[69] A representative of the subsecretariat also advises the Refugee Evaluation Committee of the Immigration Department.

As of December 1988, the military was antidemocratic but tenuously subordinated to civilian rule, the police were intermittently abusive but amenable to reform, and continuing incidents of violence marred the quality of life but did not threaten the basic democratic nature of the system. New treaties and institutions were more symbolic than substantive, but the human rights movement had gained representation and civil libertarian measures in the legislature, many judges were sympathetic to human rights concerns, and the *estado de derecho* was intact. Elections were scheduled for May 1989. But before the end of the transition, marked by the transfer of power from one democratic regime to another, the state of human rights would be put to the test.

La Tablada: Human Rights under Fire

On January 23, 1989, the guerrilla violence that had preceded and served as a rationale for the dictatorship reappeared unexpectedly. Several dozen ultraleft nationalist members of the Movimiento Todos por la Patria (All for the Fatherland movement), apparently believing that a military coup was imminent, attacked the La Tablada military base, with the ultimate goal of sparking a massive popular uprising. The attack was completely unforeseen, and it took the military almost two days to defeat the guerrillas. Over 40 people were killed (including both attackers and military), more than 100 were injured, and 20 attackers were taken prisoner.[70]

The motivations and history of the guerrillas remain somewhat unclear. When they entered the base, they shouted slogans and scattered leaflets supporting the right-wing nationalist military rebels Rico and Seineldín, perhaps as a diversionary tactic. Some of the leaders of the attack had been linked during the 1970's with the ERP (the weaker and more Marxist of the guerrilla groups, which was militarily defeated in 1975 and had played no political role since). The Movimiento Todos por la Patria had been an intemperate but democratic force from its founding in 1985 until a split in 1987–88. It now appears that one faction went underground after this split. And, most significant for the human rights movement, the founder of the Movimiento Todos por la Patria and attack leader, Jorge Baños, was an attorney for CELS.

The La Tablada guerrilla attack affected human rights and the human rights movement in Argentina in four ways. First, the resurgence of political violence shifted the social discourse away from the consolidation of democracy to the military's "logic of necessity." James Nielson, the Proceso-era editor of the *Buenos Aires Herald*, described the reintroduction of the threat as a "return to normal" background conditions for the struggle for human rights, following an extraordinary interval of peace. The guerrillas were referred to as "subversives" in the media, and the work of the CONADEP investigatory commission was attacked and linked to "subversion."[71] Alfonsín declared that the attack could have led to civil war.[72] When the president visited the site of the attack, he was asked if his presence was motivated by concern for the safety of prisoners and replied, "No . . . a judge was already there. So that our concern was not that but rather connected to the need to be with the people [of the Armed Forces] and to congratulate those who carried out this important action and saved the country, I believe, from really important evils."[73]

Second, there are credible allegations of human rights violations by the military during the course of the attack. The military did not call on the police or National Guard, responded with maximum deadly force, and ignored attempts to surrender. Several of the attackers were captured with minor injuries but subsequently disappeared and were presumably executed by the military, and several corpses were impossible to identify. While detained by the military, prisoners were beaten and tortured.[74] These violations are not only disturbing in and of themselves, but reflect an immediate return to the methodology used during the dictatorship: prisoners were stripped, bound, and hooded; Argentine suspects were irregularly detained by Argentine police in Brazil; unidentified security agents made unannounced nocturnal raids in poor neighborhoods (in search of fugitives).[75] Argentina's attorney general disqualified these allegations as "late" and "a campaign to discredit the investigation, a defense tactic," but promised to investigate—although delinking the investigation of abuses from the determination of responsibility for the attack.[76]

The La Tablada attack led to the founding of new institutions that undercut the consolidation of human rights reform, but nonmilitary institutions retained the legal framework of the *estado de derecho*. A National Security Council was created, composed of military officers, to advise the president and direct antiguerrilla policy—in direct contradiction of the new defense law, which forbade military participation in internal political conflict. New antisubversive legislation was introduced, which restricts civil liberties.[77] On the other hand, the suspects were tried with full due process (once under civilian jurisdiction) and most of the police investigations carried out were legally correct and judicially supervised. But the earlier failure to overhaul state institutions clouded the legitimacy of democratic procedures: during the trials of the guerrillas, a defense attorney impugned the testimony of one of the commanding officers at La Tablada, since the attorney had been tortured during the Proceso in a military unit under the officer's command and the officer had met one of the accused under similar circumstances.[78]

Finally, the association of Jorge Baños with the human rights movement served to discredit the movement and created a crisis of neutrality. All of the human rights groups except Las Madres (main branch) were quick to condemn the attack and to disassociate themselves from all forms of violence.[79] CELS, which was both the most neutrally civil libertarian organization and that most directly associated with the attack, announced that it would not defend the guerrillas, but would monitor the trials for due process.[80] La Liga, with a long history of defending political activists regardless of their advocacy or use of violence, assumed the legal defense of the attackers and filed a writ of habeas corpus for the missing prisoners.[81] The APDH met with the attorney general to express concern about the human rights violations alleged.[82] But as a *Buenos Aires Herald* analysis suggested:

For them [opponents of the human rights movement], La Tablada proved what they had said [all] along: that the human rights movement was but a cover-up for obscure subversive conspiracies and all their members were bloodthirsty terrorists in disguise. . . . It will now be much more difficult for those of us who believe no person under any circumstances can be justifiably tortured or murdered to make our point.[83]

Journalists, activists, and scholars reported a pronounced change in public acceptance of the legitimacy of human rights organizations and the human rights agenda following the attack; Las Madres received death threats.[84] Adolfo Perez-Esquivel announced a fast to protest the manipulation of the La Tablada attack to persecute human rights and grass-roots activists and militarize internal security.[85] The APDH met with Alfonsín to denounce right-wing attacks, reflecting the president's willingness to endorse a multiparty, moderate defense of civil liberties—but no concrete policy changes.[86] The only public official willing to defend the human rights movement was the outgoing Argentine representative to the UN Human Rights commission.[87]

Argentine democracy and its human rights institutions survived the attack at La Tablada: the resurgence of guerrilla activity did not provoke widespread repression, the guerrillas were put on trial, and the human rights groups played a legitimate role in monitoring the state's use of force. But under fire, the system reverted to military management of internal conflict, abuse of detainees—and even disappearance. The true test of the institutionalization of human rights is a situation like La Tablada, when unpopular extremists violently attack a pillar of state power. Human rights in Argentina did not fully pass that test.

Conclusion

The human rights movement played a much more limited and reactive role in institutionalizing than in initiating human rights reform. The sources of coercion were beyond the reach of movement legitimacy challenge or state control. The Alfonsín administration preempted movement demands for institutional safeguards, reducing the movement's appeal to civil society and outsiders. Within the state structures of the *estado de derecho*, the most influential institutions (the Executive and judiciary) were the least representative and least amenable to movement influence. And the movement's defense of those whose rights were most threatened associated the human rights agenda with unpopular and politicized issues.

The partial institutionalization of human rights reform highlights the compound nature of the human rights movement's program: a call for the rule of law and democratic procedures, the transformation of state and society to guarantee the rights of the person, the concrete defense of those whose rights are threatened, and a reinterpretation of the meaning of citizenship. The human rights movement helped bring to power a democratic regime that could introduce the rule of law but could not definitively transform the state. Since significant structural issues were not addressed successfully, it is unclear how the tentative transformations achieved will respond to changes of administration, acute economic crisis, and the threat of renewed guerrilla conflict. Thus, we turn to what may be the most enduring legacy of Argentina's human rights movement: outside the state, in the creation of citizens.

Chapter 8

Democratizing Civil Society

And although the decline[s] of periods of insurgency are
sometimes accompanied by the reversal of elite reformism,
they often leave a residue of policy and cultural change, of
new social actors within the political community, and of new
forms of collective action that have been forced into the
routine repertoire of participation.

Sidney Tarrow, *Struggle, Politics and Reform*

Resistance to authoritarian rule, human rights reform, and democratization in Argentina all came from and resonated most deeply
in civil society. The location of the motor of social change in civil society,
as well as the content of that change, had important implications for the
redefinition of citizenship. Human rights reform in civil society provided one of the bases for the establishment of democracy in Argentina
and has continued to serve as a key referent for the uncertain process
of consolidation. And just as the attempt to transform the state intertwined human rights with civil-military relations, the attempt to transform society embedded questions of human rights in the larger issues
of democratization.

Civil society consists of all of those institutions, patterns, and expressions of social life outside of the state apparatus.[1] While political parties
are the most widely recognized politically consequential forces in civil
society, in a corporatist society such as Argentina, vertically organized
functional bodies also play an important political role. But civil society
also consists of more diffuse channels of interaction and communication, such as media and education, which may generate social change
and new institutions. In Argentina, the human rights movement helped
to change civil society at three different levels. First, the movement
contributed to the creation of democratic citizenship a reassertion of
the autonomy of civil society and the possibility of a public sphere.
Second, the human rights movement transformed collective norms and
values. Finally, preexisting social institutions changed as they absorbed
human rights activists and the human rights agenda (see Chapter 9).

It is difficult to assess the significance of these changes. In terms of the model of the development of the impact of a social movement outlined above (see Table 1), the Argentine human rights movement has clearly achieved social recognition and some reform. The passage of both political and generational cycles will be required to determine to what degree the movement has generated stable, widespread collective learning. However, signs of the emergence of a permanent subculture of resistance to authoritarianism can be discerned in extra-institutional settings (whose future influence is difficult to predict).

Beyond the unclear weight of the changes that have taken place, there have been important limitations on the human rights movement's ability to reshape civil society, based in both larger social patterns and specific behavior and perceptions of the human rights movement. First, the new consensus on democracy sits lightly atop underlying patterns of internalized authoritarianism and a traditional, instrumental sectoral logic.[2] Second, society as a whole quickly turned its attention to problems considered more pressing and salient, predominantly economic crisis.[3] Finally, the lack of government responsiveness to popular human rights demands, especially the suspension of trials of military officers despite massive civilian mobilization in defense of democracy at Semana Santa, produced a cumulative alienation among those sectors most inclined to support both democracy and the human rights movement.[4]

Strategic choices and the inherent limitations of the human rights movement itself also checked the movement's impact on civil society. Once the movement won the initial phase of human rights struggle for "the right to have rights," the determination of the *content* of human rights introduced a politicized and ideological dimension that restricted the movement's appeal. In broad, general terms, the APDH, CELS, MEDH, and Las Abuelas concentrated on documenting and addressing specific past and current human rights violations. But Las Madres, La Liga, SERPAJ, the Ex-Detainees, and the Familiares adopted a more radical ideological perspective on human rights violations, which dictated their broader policy stances and forms of political action. A leader of La Liga explained the latter position: "There can be no theory of abstract human rights outside of social structure. There are some social and economic structures that favor and others that frustrate human rights."[5] Several groups' association with a leftist analysis provided minimal benefits to the movement, discredited the entire human rights movement in the minds of many Argentines, and associated the human rights movement with the crisis of the Argentine left—including memories of leftist violence.[6]

Ironically, the movement also suffered as the apolitical and absolutist character of symbolic politics made bargaining and the formation of alliances much more difficult. The movement's attempt to maintain its moral authority through highly symbolic demands led to a public image of intransigence, and political styles that were uniquely effective under dictatorship became a movement handicap under democracy. Las Madres' insistence on *aparición con vida* ("Bring them back alive") and rejection of government-sponsored reforms (such as economic compensation for surviving relatives) fostered divisions within the movement and a social image of inflexibility. Within the movement, the Madres' position against NN exhumations alienated families seeking legal proof and spiritual comfort, while the rejection of "posthumous commemorations" frustrated sectors intent on memorializing the disappeared. A member of the breakaway faction of Las Madres (Linea Fundadora) accused its leader of a "discourse of the barricades—which was effective and appropriate in its time, but has become less so."[7] A prominent and sympathetic journalist described the evolution of Las Madres, the leading edge of the movement in the public mind, as being "from Las Locas [the Madwomen] to Las Heroicas [the heroines] and back again."[8]

But despite internal differences and waning influence, activists agreed on one final goal: establishing the memory of their loss and their struggle in Argentine collective history. Three activists from the Familiares, all in their sixties and seventies, said that while other groups continue to demand "trial and punishment for the military," they have retained the original question, "Where are the disappeared?" They believe that their task is to establish this question as "part of the national patrimony, so that it won't die with us."[9] A leader of the Asamblea, when challenged to address the future of the movement, responded similarly: "What is the role of education in the face of an armed military and an indifferent people? To maintain memory—because you can act despite fear if you have *conciencia* [moral consciousness]."[10]

The Recovery of Public Space

For some, the recomposition of civil society is in and of itself a form of democratization, "the invisible transition."[11] One of the deepest legacies of authoritarian rule was the blurring of public and private—the demobilizing privatization of the public sphere and totalitarian invasion of the private.[12] Marcelo Cavarozzi characterizes the Argentine model since 1966 as one of strong governments attempting to "cure" society of dissident projects and force civil society back through the state, while Guillermo O'Donnell points out that state terror in Argentina attacked society as such.[13] It is in this context that a recent study emphasizes the Argentine human rights movement's role in the transition to democracy as the recovery of civil society from the logic of the state.[14]

The human rights movement helped to recreate a public sphere in Argentina, where a purely interest-based, short-term pursuit of advantage had emerged as the dominant orientation to civic life; a political culture almost lacking in the concept of a long-term, collective public interest.[15] A high level of factionalism and the "institutionalization of violence as the standard mechanism for conflict resolution" were related legacies of authoritarianism.[16] Thus, the human rights movement played an important role in establishing the possibility of democratic politics: the movement was one of the few political forces in Argentine history dedicated to nonviolence, intent on recovering the ethical limits of the political, and composed of individuals undertaking great personal risk in pursuit of a principled vision of the common good.[17]

But beyond the significance of the mere *occurrence* of norm-based change through a new social movement, the *content* of human rights movement norms reshaped democratic political discourse and identities in Argentina. Political discourse "does not just put words to what already exists, but produces new relations of meaning, constituents of political culture and of the political goals of the population."[18] In general, the key components of the emergent democratic political culture in Argentina were the revaluation of institutions and the recovery of history in political discourse.[19] The revaluation of institutions assumed special importance in Argentina since participation rights had preceded effective institutional guarantees of contestation.[20] The human rights movement associated the delegitimation of military rule with the revaluation of institutions and "guarantees"—such as an independent judiciary and free press.[21]

The establishment of a democratic national identity following authoritarianism must be based on a reinterpretation of the past to avoid its repetition.[22] Authoritarian repression often seeks to rewrite and conceal the history of its victims; as it transforms citizens into subjects, state terror seeks to eliminate even the memory that there were victims.[23] The Argentine human rights movement helped to recover the past by reclaiming the identity of the disappeared as citizens. On the eve of the 1983 transition elections, the movement printed a stunning eight-page newspaper supplement resembling pages from voter rolls, listing thousands of disappeared persons, their dates of disappearance, and their national identity document numbers, with the caption WHERE

WILL THE DISAPPEARED VOTE?[24] Beyond that, the movement began to overcome polarization by its refusal to distinguish among classes of victims; either between victims who had engaged in violent or nonviolent activism, victims who were activists or "mistakes," or "innocent" missing children and their (possibly activist) parents.[25]

Following the transition to democracy, a key challenge for a new democratic social movement is to shift from an oppositional orientation toward the state to a role in the democratization of social space.[26] In the discussion that follows, we shall trace this democratization—and the human rights movement's representation of the disappeared as "invisible citizens"—through the media, public opinion, new social forms, and education.

"The Official Story": Changing Norms in the Media

In the years following the establishment of democracy in Argentina, the Argentine media witnessed a cathartic explosion of revelations of human rights violations, reinterpretations of the past, and the emergence of a diverse and critical spectrum of new sources of information. These changes were most visible in the print media and film. Shifts in discourse in the media were especially significant in Argentina because of its high level of literacy and traditionally high levels of access to and interest in broadcast media, and because the Proceso had attempted to hegemonize all channels of expression to an unprecedented degree.[27] The human rights agenda was reflected in and shaped this rewriting of "the official story."

During the dictatorship, most of the media echoed the "official story" of a Dirty War against subversion and refused to publish information on human rights abuses or the human rights movement.[28] The major sources of information on human rights issues were the (limited circulation) English-language *Buenos Aires Herald*, Jacobo Timerman's *La Opinión* (until his 1977 arrest), and starting in 1978, the satirical monthly *Humor*. *Humor*, the most accessible of these sources, published interviews with dissident figures such as Monseñor (later Bishop) Miguel Hesayne, the CELS activist (and later deputy) Augusto Conte, SERPAJ's Nobel laureate Adolfo Perez-Esquivel, the noted author (and future head of CONADEP) Ernesto Sabato, and the Madres de Plaza de Mayo.[29] Each of these sources continued its coverage following the transition: for example, the *Herald* continued to run its column "The Law," which included comments such as: "The armed forces should carry out acts of genuine contrition all over the country and the nation should build a monument to the Mothers of Plaza de Mayo."[30]

They were joined by a new daily, *Pagina Doce*, and a new weekly, *El Periodista*. *Pagina Doce*, with estimated sales of 60,000, devotes at least one page to human rights issues every day, runs several weekly columns on the topic, and has been generally supportive of human rights movement positions. *El Periodista*, which specializes in investigative journalism, has provided the public with controversial documents such as CONADEP's list of implicated military officers and continuing, in-depth coverage of legal and civil-military issues, as well as sympathetic interviews with human rights activists. Although the mainstream mass-circulation dailies (*Clarín*, *La Nación*, and *La Prensa*) have engaged in much more episodic and less favorable coverage of human rights issues, major legal developments, reforms, and demonstrations have received some mention, and movement spokespersons are generally cited in these contexts. Another interesting development is the diffusion of human rights coverage to specialty publications: for example, the (Renovador) Peronist monthly *Unidos* has published interviews with political prisoners, critical analyses of Punto Final, and specific coverage of the human rights movement.[31]

Argentina's large and popular film industry showed even more dramatic changes. As early as 1982, several popular films exposed and reinterpreted the generalized violence, corruption, and losses of the past (*La invitación*, *Plata dulce*, and *Volver*). By 1984, *Los chicos de la guerra*, which "attempts to reconstruct the history of a generation . . . [who] live[d] in a country where, with few exceptions, civic freedom, human rights, [and] the possibility of dissent and free speech have been suppressed," was seen by over 75,000. The next year, the internationally acclaimed *Official Story*—recounting the raising of the consciousness of a history teacher who has unwittingly adopted the missing child of a *desaparecida*—was seen by over 800,000 Argentines in 1985 alone. In 1986, *La noche de los lapices*, the quasi-documentary story of a group of disappeared adolescents, and *El exilio de Gardel*, a surrealistic, *Cabaret*-like treatment through tango of repression and exile, each drew over half a million viewers. This treatment of human rights themes continued throughout the Alfonsín period: in 1987, *Los dueños del silencio*, an Argentine-Swedish co-production, depicted the case of the disappeared adolescent Dagmar Hagelin, and 1988 saw the release of at least eight human-rights-related films.[32]

Overall, films treating the themes of Proceso-era repression and criticizing authoritarianism in Argentina constituted about one-quarter of all films released between 1984 and 1986 (and almost a third of serious films).[33] In these films, human rights activists and topical issues appear frequently: the Abuelas receive sympathetic treatment in *The Official Story*, the mother of a missing adolescent is shown protesting in the Plaza de Mayo in *La noche de los lapices*, and human rights marches in Paris are counterpoised to repression in Argentina in *El exilio de Gardel*. In 1988 *La deuda interna* linked Argentina's "internal debt" to its provinces, the disappeared, and the victims of the Malvinas conflict through the story of a boy from an impoverished provincial village whose unionist father is disappeared—and who himself grows up to fight and die in the Malvinas. The same year, *La amiga* depicted the emergence of a Madre from a highly movement-oriented perspective. Documentaries have played an important role as well; *Juan cómo si nada hubiera sucedido* shows the journalistic investigation of a disappearance, including interviews with witnesses and implicated military officers, while *A los compañeros la libertad* (a human rights movement slogan) documents the cases of the political prisoners.

State television has been a critical but contested media forum for changing norms. The 1984 broadcast of CONADEP's "¡Nunca más!" report testimonial drew 25 percent of viewers, and the 1988 television broadcast of *La noche de los lapices* attracted 84 percent of the viewing audience (around four million people, the highest rating received by any television broadcast for several years).[34] Official news broadcasts regularly treated human rights issues in the context of historical occasions or court cases, but rarely offered direct coverage of human rights activism or movement activities. All of Argentina's television channels ran public service announcements produced by Amnesty International throughout December 1988, which featured public figures presenting articles of the Universal Declaration of Human Rights. And Jacobo Timerman, Argentina's best-known victim of the repression and the former editor of *La Opinión*, hosted his own interview-format television program on the government channel.[35]

But the government station declined to broadcast a worldwide concert tour to promote human rights sponsored by Amnesty International, and references to the Madres were edited out by the private station that carried the program.[36] And in the wake of the December 1988 Villa Martelli military uprising, the scheduled broadcast of a series of controversial films with human rights themes (including *Los chicos de la guerra*, *Cuarteles de invierno*, *Los dias de junio*, and the Radicales' own *La republica perdida II*) was cancelled by state programmers. One positive sign of changing values in Argentine civil society was the subsequent protest by both human rights activists and all of the relevant media intermediary organizations.[37]

Collective Learning

Beyond the emergence of a new space for democratic discourse and a new discourse on human rights, can we discern a wider process of collective learning in Argentina derived from the human rights experience? Public opinion has shown a clear consensus on movement-inspired values such as delegitimation of the military and accountability. New organizations defend a universal right to life, nonviolence, and the attempt to promote a shared collective history. And community reactions to those involved in repression display a continuing awareness of this history.

Although public opinion data have shown general support for human rights movement positions, human rights as such have little salience and human rights organizations little general recognition.[38] The strongest and most consistent responses lie in the low prestige of the military and high support for comprehensive trials. The military generally ranks last in indicators of institutional confidence: in 1985, 51 percent of the Argentine public believed that the military contributed nothing to or hurt the country; in 1986, 69 percent expressed low confidence in the military as an institution; in 1988, 64 percent believed the military were doing nothing to solve the problems of the country.[39] Similar skepticism about the coercive forces was evinced by the response to a 1987 question: "If a police statement says that two criminals were felled resisting the authorities, and the neighborhood association says they were killed without justification, who would you believe?" Almost half of respondents said they would believe the neighborhood association, and only 19 percent that they would believe the police version of events, while 20 percent said they would believe neither.[40]

Support for trials of the military eroded slightly over time, but still registered in the 70–80 percent range through the late 1980's. And in 1988, 73 percent still strongly supported the principle that "all the military who violated human rights are responsible, whatever their rank."[41] Opinion has been sharply polarized on the trials limitations at Punto Final and Semana Santa (around 40 percent both supporting and opposing them), with 46 percent describing the due obedience law as either "an advance by the military on society" or "a justification of human rights violations."[42]

General support for democracy was also firm, despite negative assessments of democratic performance.[43] In 1988, one poll registered 79 percent approval of the statement, "Democracy is the best political system for a country such as ours"—although only 56 percent agreed that "democracy is allowing us to solve our problems."[44] Another inquiry the same year showed that 70 percent of respondents rated the economic situation as the same or worse than under the military, but nevertheless 84 percent affirmed that "a government [chosen] through votes is preferable to any other form of government."[45] Edgardo Catterberg notes a disturbing disparity between support for participatory and libertarian aspects of democracy, but such disparities have not impeded democratic consolidation in cases such as that of Italy, for example, as long as systemic support for democracy is strong.[46]

Neighborhood and community human rights commissions flourished following the Proceso, and SERPAJ played a role in catalyzing some of this grass-roots activity.[47] While most base-level organizations are now dormant, they created a network and experience of community organization that was important for a society emerging from a "culture of fear" and that may be reactivated in the future. In communities affected by police abuses, commissions of victims' relatives formed, following the pattern of *afectados* from the Proceso. More generalized social resistance to police abuse has also emerged. Most of these groups do not have formal relationships with the national human rights organizations.

An example of a persisting neighborhood organization is the Quilmes Human Rights Commission, which sponsors talks, debates, and video screenings in a working-class neighborhood of greater Buenos Aires. Talks have included the identification by Las Madres of a "Gallery of Repressors" from photographs and, later, participation in an ethical tribunal of repudiation (see below). In 1982, the founding members of the Quilmes Commission had formed part of a support group for the Madres, and members continued to attend the Madres' weekly vigils. Local churches, unions, and student centers hosted the debates. Members also made regular visits to political prisoners. Since 1987, the group has also sponsored an informal youth club that discusses current events.[48]

Other organizations show the influence of principles and discourse introduced by the human rights movement. The Servicio de Asistencia Integral al Detenido (SASID) is a prisoners' rights organization dedicated to "the enforcement of human rights in relation to persons detained for common crimes."[49] The movement was founded by prisoners during the Proceso, and was influenced by prison abuses of that time, including the detention of political activists for common crimes (which the co-founder experienced).[50] SASID incorporates the human rights movement's claims of respect for legal principles and limits to state repressive power. The group distributes flyers listing the rights of suspects and detainees, as well as sources of legal aid (including the APDH).[51]

An internal document issued from prison highlights "the adoption of peaceful methods of struggle by individuals accustomed to expressing themselves through violence."[52] One of the key organizers is also a member of the Peronist party's Human Rights Secretariat. Although SASID also has no formal relationships with human rights organizations, the group makes referrals to the APDH, CELS, and MEDH.[53]

The Fundación para la Memoria is a group of relatives of victims who are attempting to found a permanent memorial to the disappeared. They envision a museum and documentation center "like the Anne Frank House or Yad Vashem [the Holocaust memorial in Israel]." Many of them are mothers of disappeared children, some former members of the Madres and/or Movimiento Judío. The group has received some support from members of CELS and the APDH, but plans to avoid institutional relationships with human rights organizations in order to minimize political conflict and to emphasize memory rather than political action.[54]

During the Menem years, several new groups emerged to deepen democratic citizenship. Groups like Citizen Power, Citizens in Action, and Conciencia all promote citizen participation, civil rights, and government accountability. Citizen Power was founded by the trials prosecutor Luis Moreno Ocampo and focuses on access to the judicial system.[55]

Following shifts in public opinion and the establishment of new organizations, perhaps the clearest example of the *application* of new norms is seen in the phenomenon of social repudiation of repressors. In at least five specific cases, community leaders organized to condemn and shun former repressors who had never been prosecuted or had been acquitted under the due obedience law, through symbolic "ethical tribunals" and declarations of them as persona non grata. Héctor Febres, indicted for 23 cases of torture but released under the due obedience law, was assigned to the Coast Guard Prefecture of Concordia, Entre Ríos—where he was recognized by witnesses. Local human rights groups, political parties, unions, and student groups organized protests against his presence, and persuaded the city council to declare Febres persona non grata.[56] In a less successful case, a former alleged torturer was discovered heading a prison in a remote southern district on the Chilean border. A mistreated prisoner alerted the town human rights secretary, who unsuccessfully pressured the municipal authorities to take action. Party youth groups, the local CGT, and the Methodist Church took up the case; by the end of 1988, they had collected 500 signatures urging repudiation in a town of several thousand.[57]

Two doctors accused of participating in torture have also been condemned by their communities. In Quilmes, activists sponsored an ethical tribunal to hear evidence against Dr. Jorge Bergez, who had been convicted but released under the due obedience law, culminating in censure by his medical association. A similar case in the south was that of Doctor Fermín de los Santos, who had testified before CONADEP regarding his activities before recanting.[58] As discussed in Chapter 9, the priest Christian von Wernich experienced community condemnation for his Proceso-era activities, culminating in a municipal resolution requiring him to leave his parish of Bragado within 48 hours.[59]

There are other, more diffuse signs of a collective attempt to come to terms with the human rights experience. The following exchange with a group of working-class adolescent boys in Quilmes who had just watched the film *La noche de los lapices* (the story of the disappearance of a group of adolescents) shows historical identification, awareness of options for resistance—and cynicism as to the ultimate outcome.

> *Boys:* They're just like us. It could happen to us.
> *Question:* What would you do if something like this happened to one of your friends?
> *Boys:* Organize, protest.
> *Question:* How?
> *Boys:* You know, mobilize in the street. I guess you could publish a *solicitada* [newspaper announcement, often used by the human rights movements], but no—that takes too much money for people like us.
> *Question:* What about legal action?
> *Boys:* No, it's very bureaucratic, it takes forever; and in the end, there's no justice here.[60]

Education

How will this collective learning be passed on to the next generation? Educational reform assumes special significance in a society in transition, since education is the social institution exclusively dedicated to the preservation of collective memory and the transmission of norms. In Argentina, generations of military rule had produced an authoritarian educational system, disproportionately staffed by the wives of military officers, in which the treatment of history generally stopped before 1930 (the year of the first military coup). During the Proceso, some politically active—or merely iconoclastic—students were denounced to the repressive agencies by their own teachers and school authorities.[61] The educational situation was not automatically addressed by the establishment of a democratic regime: in 1985, parents complained that a high-school civics text asserted that "order must be imposed by superior force" and characterized the 1976 military coup as a natural response to a power vacuum.[62]

Human rights organizations and a variety of other social forces recognized the importance of educational reform, and many wrote reform proposals. But state authorities were sensitive to counterpressure from conservative forces such as the Church.[63] And centralized policy implementation was difficult in education, since primary schools are under metropolitan or provincial jurisdiction, secondary schools are governed by the national Education Ministry, tertiary schools are both public and private, and the Church and military both administer large parallel educational systems. The Ministry of Education did in fact adopt a comprehensive educational reform program designed by the APDH that incorporated human rights at all levels and in all subject areas, but it was never implemented.[64]

However, various initiatives at each level did contribute to important changes in education. At the primary level, the municipality of Buenos Aires engaged in a curriculum review in 1984–86, culminating in a more flexible program.[65] With this new discretion, some elementary schools put into use a new series of substantively and pedagogically progressive civics primers; titles include *Los derechos de todos* (The Rights of All), *¿Que es esto de la democracia?* (What Is Democracy?), and *¿Porque es una república Argentina?* (Why Is Argentina a Republic?).[66]

But the most sweeping reform at the primary level has been a set of programs on free expression and critical thinking. In 1984, an innovative journalist began working with elementary school students to produce their own magazine, and by 1988, the Ministry of Education and over 300 schools were involved. The magazine, *Tenemos la palabra* ("We Have the Floor"), has published issues on the rights of children and topical issues. The initiative was expanded in 1986 to a "Newspapers in the Schools" program, in which 6th and 7th graders read and analyze each of the major dailies in school once a week. Finally, in 1987, municipal radio began an affiliated children's show, produced by rotating groups of elementary school students and broadcast each week to all schools in the district. A 1988 show, "Elections," included a discussion of children's right to make choices that affect their lives, a person-on-the-street poll, and reflections on the meaning of democracy.[67]

At the secondary level, reform has taken place in both curriculum and student life. A new civic education text written by Emilio Mignone, founder of CELS, has been adopted by many schools (30–40,000 copies have been sold). The second-year text devotes three units out of seven to "The Democratic Way of Life" (liberty, equality, human dignity), "The Constitution" (the rights of citizens), and "Breakdowns of the Institutional Order" (a complete history of military governments in Argentina, concluding with the defense of democracy law). The third year, which is devoted exclusively to civil society, includes a unit on Human Rights, which lists human rights organizations and national and international mechanisms for redress of human rights abuses.[68] Human rights has also been incorporated in secondary school teacher training.[69]

Almost every high school student center has some sort of human rights structure or activity, although levels of involvement vary widely. On the anniversary of the "Night of the Pencils" (the disappearance of six high-school students who had been advocating the introduction of reduced student bus fares), municipal authorities declared the day a memorial on which Buenos Aires high schools would study human rights each year. And thousands of secondary students marched alongside human rights activists in memory of other students who had died before some of the marchers were even born.[70]

Similar measures have been introduced at the tertiary level. Human rights courses have been introduced in a variety of public and private institutions throughout the country; most are taught by former or current human rights activists. One of the more comprehensive programs, at the greater Buenos Aires University of Lomas de Zamora, has been taught by the Liga lawyer Eduardo Barcesat; Bishop Novak, co-founder of MEDH; the APDH activist Enrique Fernandez Meijide, father of a *desaparecido*; and Deputy Horacio Ravenna.[71] Over a thousand students participate in this program each year. Almost all major law schools have instituted courses on human rights and/or constitutional guarantees, and all law students are required to take a course on the subject of the *estado de derecho*.[72]

Student response to these courses has been favorable, and like their secondary counterparts, university student centers routinely include a human rights committee or secretary.[73] The student center of the University of Buenos Aires College of Sciences sponsored a mural to commemorate disappeared colleagues.[74] At the same university, the School of Sociology elected an unusual representative—the imprisoned ex-detainee and trials witness Graciela Daleo. Ms. Daleo, who had survived over a year in a clandestine detention center only to be preventatively detained under democracy by a Proceso-era judge, had been nominated as a protest candidate by almost every student slate.[75]

Conclusion

As new social movement theory predicts, the Argentine human rights movement played an important role in democratizing civil society. The human rights movement helped to reestablish public space and the possibility of democratic politics. Widespread activity in a variety of venues shows a flowering of dialogue on human rights issues. Many references have been framed in terms of the human rights agenda or the human rights movement—and the discussion has also entered a more generalized social frame of reference.

One of the key accomplishments of Argentina's human rights movement has been the promotion of a memory, consciousness, and discourse of human rights throughout civil society. But new norms must be translated into practices and institutions. Thus, we now examine how this new discourse has been treated by the existing institutions of civil society and to what degree it has been institutionalized.

Chapter 9

Transforming Social Institutions

> Civil society in Argentina, perhaps to a greater extent than
> elsewhere in Latin America, possesses its own superior logic,
> a logic which has repeatedly demonstrated a remarkable
> capacity to resist and defeat attempts to impose authoritarian
> rule and to reorder society. . . . Whether this capacity to
> resist authoritarian rule can be articulated into a viable
> alternative project of redemocratization is another matter.
>
> William Smith, "Reflections on the Political
> Economy of Authoritarian Rule and Capitalist
> Reorganization in Contemporary Argentina"

The institutionalization of collective learning is a critical but slippery
dimension of social change. As the discussion in Chapter 1 suggests, new social movements' greatest potential may lie in catalyzing
changes in the political consciousness of civil society. But changes in
norms are most effective when they create or reshape institutions with
an independent source of power. Thus, an assessment of social movement impact must consider the movement's effect on other social institutions. A new social movement can transform other social institutions
in three ways: by shifting their agenda, entering their ranks, or forming stable alliances.[1]

The Argentine human rights movement's legitimacy challenge resonated beyond the state. The new social movement modality allowed the
Argentine movement to shift the agenda of some of the hegemonic
institutions of civil society. The establishment of human rights institutions, programs, or adjuncts in a wide range of social settings shows the
degree to which human rights came to be considered a necessary referent for civic identity.

But the reemergence of social institutions under democracy in Argentina also coincided with a steady decline in human rights movement
membership. Still, this is a more general and less detrimental development than it may appear. New social movements generally draw in a
larger population of sympathizers around the core membership; this
penumbra ebbs and flows with social conditions.[2] Transitions to democracy also tend to generate a surge and decline in social movement activ-

ity.[3] The drop in human rights movement membership registers activist circulation as well as demobilization.

Some centrifugal impulse was inevitable within the Argentine movement, as the common struggle against repression had brought together a diverse collection of individuals with distinct, crosscutting interests. More specifically, many had turned to the human rights movement as a "space of resistance" at a time when parties, unions, and other social organizations were closed to them. Many of these activists returned to their former venues marked by their experiences in the human rights movement. Even as elements of the movement dispersed, its energy was not lost; rather, it diffused out into the reawakening institutions of civil society.

However, the overall influence of the human rights movement on social discourse was not matched by a corresponding influence on social institutions and alliances. Diffuse (and potentially ephemeral) changes in collective consciousness have outpaced institutionalization, and the establishment of new institutional bodies has exceeded incorporation in existing institutions or alliance formation. The general level of activity, and the specific role of human rights activists, was lower in parties and corporations than in the media and education. Furthermore, the institutional impact of the movement was greatest in the weakest institutions (parties rather than corporations). And certain sectors—notably the military and economic elites—never accepted the legitimacy of the human rights agenda.[4] The institutionalization of movement influence in civil society is the final arena in which to assess the human rights experience in Argentina.

Political Parties

There is a general consensus that political parties in Argentina have been historically weak institutions.[5] Many believe that the strengthening of political parties, especially vis-à-vis interest groups, is an inherent element of democratization—and that the relationship between social movements and political parties is a key determinant of movement influence.[6] But the relationship of the social movements that catalyzed the transition with reemerging political parties is a complex and contingent one.

The most credible and influential sectors of the human rights movement (the family-based groups) had always been the least politicized. But under democracy, the lack of both ideologically and socially compatible alliance partners for the movement among majority parties and corporations meant that a sector of the human rights movement turned to the minuscule and doctrinaire electoral left for support. The most extreme example of this phenomenon is the case of the Madres de Plaza de Mayo, whose domestic supporters and newsletter staff now include a high proportion of members of small leftist parties. Las Madres, originally one of the most apolitical groups, adopted an analysis of human rights that posits a direct relationship between capitalism, imperialism, and repression, and a stance of implacable opposition to the Radical government.[7] This political orientation was also partially responsible for the split between Las Madres and Las Madres–Linea Fundadora in 1986.[8]

At the other end of the movement ideological spectrum, the APDH came under increasing criticism and suffered a 1988 schism because of its image of uncritical support for the Alfonsín administration. Asamblea dissidents complained that the organization hesitated to criticize government policy, especially current human rights violations, in order to retain its Radical membership. There were repeated moves to oust President Alfonsín from the APDH Council of Presidents, especially following the Punto Final and Obediencia Debida legislation, but these proposals were always defeated on the argument of a trade-off between influence and ideology.[9]

Vicente Palermo maps a set of possible relationships between parties and social movements based on the mode of social movement representation in the parties (indirect representation versus direct participation) and the degree of social movement autonomy. With the two cases cited above marking the poles of movement-party relations, most of the Argentine human rights movement seems to fall into Palermo's scenario of indirect representation combined with confrontational autonomy.[10] As a result, most parties have only informal ties to the human rights movement, largely based on activist circulation and agenda absorption. Nevertheless, both major and most minor political parties have at some point established human rights commissions within their parties.

The Unión Cívica Radical (UCR): Radicales

The establishment of a human rights commission within the Radical party can be said to some extent to represent an extension of a historical commitment by the party. However, Radical claims to an unsullied heritage of civil libertarianism are open to question, since the Radical party at various opportunities did support the electoral proscription of the Peronist majority party and the Radical president Arturo Frondizi

(1958–62) presided over the Army-sponsored CONINTES security plan, which significantly curtailed civil rights.[11] Ricardo Balbín, head of the party during most of the Proceso and Alfonsín's predecessor in that position, was not particularly sympathetic to the human rights movement, and on one occasion blithely asserted that the disappeared "must be dead by now."[12] However, during the dictatorship, the Radical party newspaper in exile, La República, consistently and comprehensively covered human rights issues as early as 1981, including favorable accounts of the activities of human rights organizations.[13]

The UCR's Human Rights Commission was founded in 1986 as a structure of the Radical Youth branch of the party. This drew on a coherent group of activists already committed to the human rights agenda, but it has limited partywide influence: Radical Youth holds only one seat on the party's National Committee, which is occupied by a liaison rather than by the Radical Youth president. The concept of the human rights commission and many of its activists originated in the (Buenos Aires) provincial capital of La Plata.[14] Many of the Human Rights Commission activists had belonged to the APDH, especially the La Plata branch, and the commission established a special relationship with the Asamblea.[15]

At its height, the UCR Human Rights Commission had ten members—and at times as few as four. The group's major activity was to stimulate discussion within the party by issuing position papers on human rights-related issues. The commission's positions often differed markedly from government policy, and these differences periodically became public. Its objections to the 1986 instructions to the military prosecutor contributed to the "correction" of the instructions.[16] It successfully initiated the creation of a special government Commission on Missing Children, under the auspices of the Human Rights Subsecretariat. With less success, the group advocated the human rights movement's proposals for case revision for political prisoners, declaration of forced disappearance as a crime against humanity, and opposition to the promotion of military officers accused of human rights violations. The UCR commission also opposed the Punto Final limitations on the prosecution of military officers, specifically citing the possible appearance of new "NN" unidentified graves. But by the time the Obediencia Debida legislation was introduced in 1987, the UCR commission reluctantly supported the measure as the best solution to a bad situation, and turned its attention to consolidating the popular defense of democracy that had emerged during Semana Santa.[17]

A secondary activity of the UCR Human Rights Commission was public education. The group sponsored neighborhood discussion groups and screenings of CONADEP's "¡Nunca más!" television program throughout the country, often in conjunction with the local APDH. Along with the civil libertarian wing of the human rights movement, the commission began to analyze prison conditions, the rights of minors, and even the foreign debt in terms of human rights. And in the wake of repeated military uprisings, the Radical group joined human rights activists to call for the creation of citizens' "committees for the defense of democracy."[18]

Although the UCR Human Rights Commission reflects human rights movement influence and a healthy degree of party autonomy from government, it was clearly a minor force within the Radical party as a whole. Party quiescence was partially attributable to the displacement of Radicales with human rights concerns toward sources of government (as opposed to party) positions. But with a few notable exceptions, the mainstream Radical position was unswerving support for government policy and increasing alienation from the human rights movement as such.[19]

However, the Radical party continued to identify itself as the party that defended human rights, even when human rights were electorally irrelevant or controversial.[20] This was in part an accurate reflection of the party's historical commitment to constitutionalism and civil liberties, and in part a device to shift attention from criticisms of its economic policy, but it also represented a rewriting of Radical identity under Alfonsín.[21] One of the stated purposes of the UCR Human Rights Commission was to defend the claim staked out in this area; to "prevent the theme of human rights being used exclusively by any sector or political party."[22] The party produced and broadcast a two-hour documentary, *La república perdida* ("The Lost Republic"), reinterpreting Argentine history as a fifty-year cyclical struggle between democracy and authoritarianism, commencing during the lost, halcyon era of pre-Perón Radical rule. The extent of this change can be seen in the changing standpoint of Antonio Troccoli, a former interior minister and a member of the party's old guard, who during the Proceso had assured a representative of U.S. President Jimmy Carter's State Department that Argentina suffered no human rights violations, except the continuing problem of subversion.[23] After the triumph of Alfonsinismo in the UCR, Troccoli felt called upon to affirm that "there have never been any human rights problems under any Radical administration. . . . To be Radical is to favor human rights."[24]

The Partido Justicialista (PJ): Peronists

The Peronist party faced an even more mixed human rights heritage. Perón himself had founded a "special section" of the police that routinely engaged in torture, his widow Isabel presided over a government closely linked to the Triple A death squads, and the 1983 Peronist candidate for the presidency, Italo Luder, had signed the 1975 decree authorizing the military to "annihilate" subversives.[25] On the other hand, since most of the disappeared were workers and some Peronist organizations were targeted by the military, it is likely that many of the victims of the repression were Peronists.[26] And the Peronist party did approach the Interamerican Commission on Human Rights of the Organization of American States during its 1979 inspection tour of Argentina. Still, a widespread association of Peronism with violence and lack of respect for individual liberties contributed decisively to the Peronist defeat in the 1983 transition elections.

It is thus especially significant that the Peronist party also founded a Human Rights Secretariat, which has been better institutionalized and more oriented toward service activities than its Radical counterpart. The development of human rights structures within the Peronist party is intertwined with the rise of the Renovador Peronist reform movement.[27] As with the Radicales, former Peronists who had been working with human rights organizations brought the issue back to the party, sponsoring a Peronist Human Rights Meeting at the first post-transition party congress in 1983. Proponents of the Renovador reform movement had supported human rights movement proposals such as the establishment of a bicameral investigatory commission, and the Peronist Human Rights Secretariat was founded when the Renovadores gained power in the Buenos Aires party organization in 1985.[28]

The Peronist secretariat is larger and more active than the Radical structure. About twenty-five members participate on a regular basis, with three or four staff members engaged in daily human rights activities. A large proportion of activists are *afectados*, and several were or remain active in human rights organizations (common projects have been undertaken with both CELS and MEDH). Both national-level and metropolitan secretariats hold direct, permanent seats on their respective party Directive Councils. And the Peronist party's constitution now specifies that each local ward office (*unidad basica*) must have its own human rights secretary.[29]

Compared to the Radical commission, the Peronist body appears to have played less of a role in internal policy debates, but it has engaged in service activities never taken up by the UCR institution. The PJ secretariat processes complaints by party members of current human rights violations, generally involving questionable detentions in marginal areas of the capital, and has provided round-the-clock coverage for legal assistance and referrals. Like the Radical body, the Peronist secretariat has had an active educational program. In addition to base-level talks and seminars, which often focus on social rights, representatives of the party secretariat have attended political events sponsored by human rights organizations.[30]

The Peronist discourse on human rights has differed significantly from a classical civil libertarian position (the Radical position). Peronism links individual freedoms to its preexisting commitment to social rights; "Peronism conceives of human rights [as possessing] an eminently social nature and origin" and deriving from the (abrogated) 1949 Constitution. In keeping with the Peronist vision of the state as community, rights are depicted more as citizen entitlements than as guarantees against state power. The central tenet of Peronist human rights activism is Evita's statement, "Where there is a need, there is a right." But under a Radical government, Peronist human rights activism *was* an oppositional vehicle. Party statements and documents criticized almost every aspect of Radical government human rights policy and the Radical interpretation of history, attributing human rights successes exclusively to the pressures of social movements.[31]

The final aspect of democratic political discourse—revaluation of institutions—has historically been weak in Peronist political culture, since exclusion from institutional competition led to a decline in respect for the rules of the (rigged) game.[32] In this regard, the treatment of the human rights issue by Renovador Peronists has had a clear democratizing influence. In the 1983 presidential primaries, the proto-Renovador presidential candidate Antonio Cafiero endorsed human rights trials for the military with the slogan, "Neither forgetting nor vengeance, justice."[33]

At the general party level, the Peronist record on human rights issues has broken down along traditional-Renovador lines. While Renovador figures such as Deputies Roberto Digon, Manuel de La Sota, and Manzano have been clear and consistent supporters of human rights movement positions, traditional Peronists—especially in the Senate—have advocated military interests, and a group of ultranationalist Peronist Youth physically attacked members of Las Madres in 1983.[34] This highlights a wider problem of policy unpredictability because of the breadth and populist ideological flexibility of Peronism.[35] Until 1988, the party included both the violent neo-Nazi group Alerta Nacional and former left-nationalist Montonero guerrillas. In a typical edition *Jotapé*, the militant journal of the Peronist Youth, featured both an interview with the head of the CGT Human Rights Committee and the claim that critics of Peronism were "ideological terrorists."[36]

The 1989 presidential victory of the lapsed Renovador Carlos Menem has further tested the durability of the Peronist commitment to human rights. In his electoral campaign, Menem stressed his own experience as a political prisoner to counter rumors of a planned amnesty for the military (which he implemented once in office). Menem also denounced the Radical candidate, Eduardo Angeloz, for his early support of the military dictator General Videla.[37] On the other hand, Menem asserted early on, "We are working for liberation and we are not going to talk of democracy or dictatorship. . . . What good is democracy, if workers have no jobs?"[38]

When questioned about the effects of a Menem victory on the Peronist human rights program, the PJ human rights secretary claimed that the political coloration of a Peronist government would make no difference, since human rights were institutionalized within the party at all levels.[39] But another member of the secretariat admitted in a private conversation: "As a human rights activist, I know that we will probably have less protection of individual liberties under Menem than under the current government. But as a Peronist, I know that a Peronist government will make basic structural changes that get at the sources of human rights violations—and that's where I put my hope."[40]

Minor Parties

The Partido Intransigente (PI), a democratic socialist party that originally formed in a schism with the UCR, is the largest minor party on the left, and the minor party that has been the most active in human rights at the party level. The PI's concern with human rights predates the Proceso: human rights feature in its 1975 platform, and the 1983 document incorporates most of the human rights movement's demands. In 1984, the PI was the first party to found a human rights commission, whose founding members were drawn largely from CELS and the APDH. The Intransigente Human Rights Commission had about 40 members, and constituted one of the largest bodies within the party. In this case, activist circulation was two-way; the presidents of the Cordoba and Mar del Plata CONADEP investigatory commissions were from the Partido Intransigente, and activists from the PI Human Rights Commission also joined and even founded human rights movement organizations.[41]

The PI commission met every week through 1987. This commission, like its major party counterparts, sponsored educational activities and attended human rights marches, but the group also developed human rights proposals for the party's legislators and worked with neighborhood human rights groups. The PI helped to establish some of these neighborhood groups during 1984–85, while the party's conventions served as a meeting ground for human rights activists from all over the country. Intransigente legislators presented a series of exemplary legislative projects on human rights. Party activists also claim that the PI served as a mediator within the Asamblea, between Radicales and leftists attacking government policy.[42]

The major limitations on the influence of the Intransigente commission were intrinsic to the nature of the party itself. At its peak, the legislative bloc was composed of five congressional deputies, and little of the legislation they proposed—on any subject—was passed. The PI also experienced an internal crisis beginning around 1987, as the coalition of center leftists, former members of the revolutionary left, and crypto-Peronists began to unravel—and the party's human rights activities with it.[43]

On the other side of the political spectrum is the right-wing Unión Democratico del Centro (UCD), Argentina's largest minor party, which received around 15 percent of the vote during the late 1980's.[44] The leader of the UCD, Alvaro Alsogaray, is a former military officer who served under several military regimes, and the party has long been considered the respectable outlet for military and elite interests. Therefore, it is telling that the UCD founded its own Human Rights Commission in 1988.[45] A UCD activist, one of the party's few *afectados*, said that an informal working group on human rights had operated since around 1982, linked to the party's Youth Movement (like its Radical counterpart). Around five people were involved, and most activity consisted of a series of consultations with legal officials.[46]

The UCD has had an antagonistic relationship with the human rights movement; but the founding of the Human Rights Commission and statements on related issues do reflect a contradictory and defensive response to the human rights agenda. Alsogaray has repeatedly called for a vindication of the military's role in the "war against subversion," but his daughter and heir apparent, Deputy Maria Julia Alsogaray, has gone on record in favor of limited human rights trials.[47] A UCD municipal councilor attempted to block a memorial to a bishop allegedly assassinated by the military and condemned the murdered Church leader as "an agent of international Marxism"; a fellow party member, however, defended capitalism in terms of a liberal "human right to property."[48] Amidst a barrage of unfounded charges against the human rights movement, the UCD Human Rights Commission member interviewed gave a coherent liberal definition of human rights and repeatedly expressed his support for both democracy and social democratization.[49]

Political parties, articulating the changing norms of civil society, incorporated human rights activists and elements of the discourse of the human rights movement. But the organization of civil society in Argentina has traditionally taken place more through corporate bodies—labor, the Church, and the military—that maintain a direct and privileged relationship with the state and influence over their members. Some of these institutions, too, responded to the human rights movement's challenge.[50]

Corporations

The Unions

Like the political parties, each of the corporations was called upon to process the history reclaimed, the demands made, and the reforms catalyzed by the human rights movement. The task was particularly urgent for the labor movement, since large numbers of union activists had figured among the disappeared, while labor leadership had taken an ambiguous position.[51] A number of interviewees from the human rights movement, political parties, journalism, and labor itself emphasized the significance of human rights activity within the labor movement, and several offered the hypothesis of a shifting of human rights activism—from the human rights movement to political parties to the unions—during the Alfonsín period.

An important feature of human rights activity by labor is that it began at the grass roots, among union members affected by the repression and/or associated with the human rights movement. In 1982–83, the telephone workers' union, FOETRA, became the first union to found a human rights commission; the commission's leader had been active in both Las Madres and the Asamblea. Shortly thereafter, municipal employees, graphics workers, journalists, actors, public health workers, and government employees' unions established their own commissions. By 1984–85, there were 25–30 union human rights commissions, which had formed a joint coordinating body. As this body became more active, the central labor confederation, the Confederación General del Trabajo (CGT), decided to incorporate this preexisting human rights activism. The CGT Human Rights Secretariat was founded in 1987.[52] Not only had most union-level leaders passed through the human rights movement, but a key CGT secretariat figure concurrently held a post in the government Human Rights Secretariat, and an important union-level activist remained a staff member of SERPAJ.[53]

The CGT body supplemented, but did not substitute for, the human rights activities of its member unions.[54] Both union and CGT human rights commissions had full-time staff, daily office hours, and weekly meetings. The CGT secretariat was composed of representatives from each member union, and an average of fifteen delegates attended its meetings. The commission has pursued complaints of human rights violations against union members, attended human rights movement events, sponsored educational activities, issued policy statements, and contacted government officials on human rights issues.[55]

At a meeting of the CGT Human Rights Secretariat Directive Council that I attended, the unions present represented about 300,000 members.[56] Topics discussed included the plight of the political prisoners, support for a week-long Latin American Federation of Families of the Disappeared (FEDEFAM) conference in Buenos Aires, a complaint from a Chilean union member threatened with deportation because of his political activities, and a constitutional reform proposal being co-sponsored by the CGT and SERPAJ.[57] The CGT human rights secretary had already met with the government secretary of justice and the (Renovador) Peronist Deputy Manzano on behalf of the political prisoners, and several representatives had visited the prisoners themselves. At the meeting, various bills being considered in Congress to review the cases of political prisoners were discussed, and a disagreement was aired between union delegates circulating a petition to the secretary of justice and the CGT leadership, which favored a more gradual negotiating strategy. The state workers' union (ATE) agreed to provide facilities for the opening of the FEDEFAM conference. And the delegates decided to protest the deportation of the Chilean worker, even though he was a member of a leftist party who had engaged in controversial activities within the union. "We don't agree with him, but his life would be in danger—so we must be in solidarity," one delegate concluded.[58]

Although the Human Rights Secretariat clearly represented a minority voice within the CGT, the larger body has thus far lent institutional support to the secretary's activities. Under Alfonsín, this was facilitated by the coincidence of interests between the labor movement as a whole and human rights activists in criticizing government policy. But the climate of opinion has also changed. "These days no unionist will speak against human rights or our committees," one delegate explained.[59] The labor movement has worked most closely with SERPAJ, because of their common interest in grass-roots social issues and the fact that some activists have common backgrounds. In contrast, labor and Las Madres have had a stormy relationship, in part because of personal differences and the outspoken styles of leadership figures on both sides. However, the CGT has been supportive of the Abuelas' claims in cases involving missing children. Labor in general has had little interest in the civil libertarian groups: union activists, who are mostly Peronists, have expressed particular misgivings about the Liga and its close association with the Argentine Communist party.

Despite tremendous variations within the union movement, it is a large and influential social sector, many of whose members have learned important lessons through the human rights experience. The head of the CGT Human Rights Secretariat acknowledged this learning process:

Thus I believe that, after all that has happened to us Argentines, human rights must be the foundation [*materia primaria*] of our civic life, because there is nothing greater than the right to life, to liberty, to security of the person, to work, to health, etc. Many times we sinned by omission and with our silence allowed things to happen in our country that hurt us and that we repent.[60]

In response to military attempts to vindicate the past, the secretary asked, "What is it the people should vindicate? The kidnapping of children of disappeared men and women; the torture and rape of pregnant women; the murder, executions and mutilations of thousands and thousands of workers and grass-roots militants [*luchadores populares*]."[61]

During the military uprisings, the labor movement decisively supported democracy to an unprecedented degree.[62] When Peronist-identified elements of the military came "knocking on the union hall door" during the Villa Martelli uprising, the CGT refused to meet with them, stating: "Our position is staked on the defense of democracy and the constitutional way, and the CGT is no place for anyone who isn't a worker."[63] As a union human rights activist put it, "We have learned that any civilian government—the worst civilian government—is better than military rule."[64]

The Church

The Argentine Catholic Church has not been available to the human rights movement as an institutional source of support. Despite the principled activism of a coherent minority of bishops and scattered parish priests, the mainstream of the Church has yet to engage the issue of human rights or its own accountability during military rule. The failure of the country's major norm-creating institution to ally with a symbolic social movement professing ideals endorsed by the universal Church— and the marked contrast in this respect with other Latin American experiences—must be understood in the context of the Argentine Church's historical role.

The Argentine Church has historically espoused a neoconservative Catholic nationalist doctrine.[65] Its restrictive vision of democracy is clear from *Democracia, responsibilidad y esperanza*, a 1984 publication of the Argentine Episcopal Conference, which states: "Pluralism presupposes respect for others in an atmosphere of responsible liberty. This has its limits. . . . It is unquestionable that the leading role of persons, of families, of intermediate associations and of institutions should be oriented and instructed by the authorities, whose specific goal is to lead the people to the achievement of the common good."[66] The ideology and political role of the Argentine Church have been linked with a favored corporate status, enhanced under military rule. Argentina is officially a Catholic country: the Church has received state subsidies, a privileged role in state policy on education, and informal veto power in many areas of social policy. The relationship has been reciprocal, as the state played a role in appointing bishops, established a large and influential military chaplaincy, and called on the Church for doctrinal legitimation of counterinsurgency.[67]

During the Proceso, prominent members of the clergy collaborated with the military.[68] For example, General Ramón Camps, the former head of the Buenos Aires Police, later convicted of hundreds of counts of homicide, prefaces his account of the Timerman case with a letter thanking the archbishop of La Plata for his help and support.[69] In response to widespread criticism and disillusionment with the Church's passivity during the Proceso, the Episcopal Council published a record of the Church's statements on human rights during the dictatorship (largely private letters to the military).[70] One Church official sympathetic to human rights concerns explained that the general discourse among the bishops has changed under democracy to one of obligatory concern with human rights (in part owing to the influence both of the pope and of the Chilean and Paraguayan Churches), but that the biggest single improvement in the Church position has resulted from the deaths of several antidemocratic figures (Bishops Antonio Plaza, Adolfo Tortolo, and Victorio Bonamín).[71]

The general Church approach to accountability for the past has been a doctrine of "reconciliation," which the human rights movement saw as a code for amnesty for the military. The doctrine of "reconciliation" explicitly criticized the discourse of the human rights movement: "We feel that it is very important to underline in the current circumstances that true reconciliation does not lie only in truth and justice, but also in love and forgiveness."[72] And members of the military subsequently adopted the Church discourse to gain legitimacy for their demands; in one account, the Semana Santa rebel leader Aldo Rico was advised by Military Vicar José Medina to couch his demand for an amnesty in terms of "reconciliation."[73]

The timing and context of Church statements on "reconciliation" and continuing contact with rebellious and convicted military officers contributed to a general reading of Church support for military demands. For example, the first statement the Church issued after the Villa Martelli military uprising (five days later) warned that "national unity is impossible without a prior reconciliation among Argentines," but that it would not be the Church's role "to indicate the appropriate legal instruments to achieve it."[74] Church officials entered the rebel camp at Semana Santa, and the bishop of La Plata visited the convicted junta members in prison.[75] And after the first rebellion, Vicar Medina declared that, "the war against subversion . . . from a moral perspective, was a just war, because the existence of the nation depended on it."[76]

However, the Church has not been able to attain reconciliation within its own ranks, as illustrated by two cases of unresolved accountability for the role played in the past by its own clergy. In 1976, La Rioja's Bishop Enrique Angelelli—one of the few Argentine clergymen sympathetic to "Tercermundista" liberation theology—was killed in a highly suspicious car accident. Angelelli was returning from the funeral of two priests of his diocese who had been murdered by military task forces and is alleged to have collected evidence linking the military to the murders. Debate over the fate of Angelelli and the course of judicial investigations into his death racked the Argentine Church and highlighted the targeting of clergy by the dictatorship, the reclaiming by the Church of clerics with social concerns, and the Church's unavoidable involvement in legal and institutional processes.[77] The Angelelli case also created an indirect link with human rights organizations—especially the MEDH—which had called for an investigation while the Church itself was still accepting the official version of the cleric's death.

In a different sense, the case of Father Christian von Wernich also pitted popular and human rights pressure against the ecclesiastical hierarchy. Wernich had been the police chaplain for the province of Buenos Aires and personal confessor to General Ramón Camps, and he himself had been implicated in human rights violations by testimony from survivors of clandestine detention centers, including allegations at the trials of the juntas that the priest had lured detainees to their deaths under the guise of a negotiated exile. In late 1988, Wernich was assigned to a small parish that included the families of some of his alleged victims. Massive popular protests and repudiation by all social sectors in the parish followed, including appeals to the papal nuncio. The Church hierarchy treated the case strictly within channels, refusing to acknowledge any special dimension to the situation; as of December 1988, Wernich had not been removed or transferred—although his Masses were being boycotted by the local community.[78]

Within this panorama of reluctant democratization and general institutional ambivalence on human rights issues, whatever human rights activism exists in the Church has been closely linked to the human rights movement. Several dissident bishops have worked directly with the human rights movement, including Bishops Jaime de Nevares of Neuquen (APDH), Jorge Novak (MEDH), and Miguel Hesayne (APDH). Bishop Novak of Quilmes (greater Buenos Aires) presides over a working-class diocese of approximately 1,200,000 people. A founding member and co-president of MEDH, Novak alone registered 2,800 cases of disappearances during the Proceso (almost a quarter of CONADEP's total), and held a monthly Mass for affected families, which was often attended by Las Madres. Novak held an unprecedented memorial service for two French nuns and the original leadership of Las Madres in the church where they had been kidnapped by the military. Bishop Novak regularly attends human rights marches, teaches courses on human rights in both lay and ecclesiastical settings, and has monitored and condemned police abuse within his diocese.[79]

Bishop de Nevares sat on the CONADEP investigatory commission and has consistently worked to raise public consciousness. For example, in a widely disseminated homily following the introduction of the Punto Final legislation, de Nevares condemned both the social consequences and moral foundations of Punto Final, proclaimed justice and equality before the law as important religious values, and called for popular resistance to rollbacks of human rights reforms.[80] In his home province of Neuquen, de Nevares allied with the sympathetic Governor Zapag (of the provincial Movimiento Popular Neuqueño) to form a provincial environment noted for receptivity to human rights claims.[81]

At the parish level, a small number of concerned priests have also engaged the issue of human rights, often in highly symbolic ways. One of the most dramatic experiences occurred during Holy Week 1988 in Tilcara, a picturesque village in northern Argentina whose colorful celebrations attract thousands of tourists. The Canadian parish priest, who had been visited for several years by local human rights movement activists and had been engaged in base-level work in his community, began the Holy Week celebration by washing the feet of several Madres, asking for their forgiveness of "the Church's cowardice." On Holy Friday, his sermon linked the persecution and death of Jesus to the fate of the disappeared. Finally, during the traditional procession bearing images of Christ, the priest tied a white scarf on the image of the Virgin Mary and explained that the suffering mother was represented by the Madres present.[82]

The priest was immediately attacked by local elites (especially the ultraconservative organization Tradición, Familia y Propiedad) and the absentee owners of summer homes, who convened a "People's Tribunal" against him in the town square. Base-level parishioners and human rights organizations came to the priest's defense: Las Madres (Línea Fundadora), the Abuelas, SERPAJ, and La Liga all sent representatives to Tilcara. In response to the local controversy, the bishop pressured the priest's formal superiors in Canada, and eventually he was suspended until his (already pending) transfer. But no one removed the white scarf from the Virgin of Tilcara.[83]

Conclusion

Human rights reforms touched almost every social institution and arena in Argentina, and have arisen and persisted independent of the state of public policy. Like the agenda of most social movements, human rights consciousness spread from a small core group of those affected and concerned to reach most members of Argentine society, and then receded back to a slightly expanded core. But the experience left a residue of new conceptual frameworks, historical reference points, and repertoires for collective action. However, this legacy is still ignored or contested within the dominant institutions of civil society and has not yet been institutionalized in a consistent and enduring way. The human rights discourse remains the property of a marginalized subculture and a diffuse collective consciousness.

Civil society has changed in unexpected and critical ways of unclear magnitude. And even massive changes in civil society do not have a clear or predictable impact on political outcomes; the relationship between state and society is among the many issues unresolved by Argentina's incomplete consolidation of democracy. But if democracy fails or if repression returns, the legacy of the human rights movement will ensure that this time society will respond with more than silence. Scattered citizens and latent groups will ask questions—questions taught to them by the human rights movement. The Argentine armed forces have long recognized their hegemonic role in shaping collective identity by referring to themselves as "the moral reserve of the nation"; now, in a different sense, it is the human rights movements that serve as the "moral reserve of the nation."

As we have seen, the development of the human rights discourse in Argentina implicated, overlapped, and framed the wider question of democratization. The human rights movement played a critical role in the establishment of a democratic regime, institutions, and citizenship. But this has not been enough to consolidate democracy in Argentina. The question of the impact of the human rights movement on democratization and the prospects for democracy and human rights in Argentina are addressed in the closing section of this inquiry.

Chapter 10

The Human Rights Movement
and Democratization

> But I remain convinced that it is only by recognizing in the
> institution of human rights signs of the emergence of a new
> type of legitimacy and of a public space, only by recognizing
> that individuals are both the products and instigators of that
> space, and only by recognizing that it cannot be swallowed
> up by the state without a violent mutation giving birth to a
> new form of society, that we can possibly hope to evaluate
> the development of democracy and the likely fate of freedom.
>
> Claude Lefort, *Democracy and Political Theory*

We are now in a position to evaluate the accomplishments of Argentina's human rights movement, and to analyze the implications of the movement's activity in the context of a transition to democracy. The role of the movement can be assessed in terms of its historical significance during the critical period of the Alfonsín administration, as a source of legacies for democratization, and as a model for democratization elsewhere. Finally, the international learning sparked by the human rights movement will be explored.

The Impact of the Movement

As we saw in Chapter 3, the human rights movement's accomplishments were rooted in its role as a resistance to authoritarian rule. First and foremost, the human rights movement survived one of the most repressive regimes of its era and provided a critical counterpoint to a "culture of fear." The movement's use of symbolic politics and political theater secured social recognition of the claim and collective identity of human rights activists, while protest personalized and "reappeared" the disappeared. The combination of this symbolic protest and the collection and dissemination of information about the scope and severity of human rights violations undermined the authoritarian regime's international legitimacy. While the movement did not cause the transition to democracy, human rights protest helped to precipitate and intensify the effects of the Malvinas defeat, which catalyzed the transition. Furthermore, once the military had conceded civilian control, the human rights movement conditioned the character of the resulting transition through an influence on the tenor of the electoral campaign and ultimate Alfonsín victory, as well as specific challenges to military attempts to limit accountability for human rights violations.

When a democratic regime emerged in Argentina, the human rights movement launched a triple challenge to the legitimacy of the government and its institutions, a challenge for truth, justice, and the institutionalization of human rights, based on the movement's own expertise and mobilization. Chapter 4 documents how the demand for truth ("Where are our children?") was met by the establishment of a national investigatory commission on the disappeared and the exhumation of unidentified bodies. Chapter 5 shows how the call for equal justice brought unprecedented trials of the former military commanders and other officers accused of human rights violations, restitution of missing children to their biological families, and extraditions of several key figures. Through these reforms, the human rights movement exercised an unexpected degree of influence on reemerging institutions: the outstanding example is the stimulation of judicial autonomy through human rights trials.

Chapters 6 and 7 turn to the institutionalization of human rights reform in the state. This involved both establishing binding state control over coercive agencies and incorporating human rights movement influence in Argentina's legal and bureaucratic apparatus. As we have seen in Chapter 6, there were significant limitations to the civilian government's ability to exercise full authority over the military and "free-lance" repressors; and these limitations in turn narrowed the parameters of human rights movement activity. Chapter 7 shows how the human rights movement did play a role in presenting and implementing the furthest-reaching, most problematic challenge—the institutionalization of state accountability for the protection of human rights. The Alfonsín administration responded with police reform, civil libertarian legislation, international human rights treaties, and the establishment of a human rights secretariat. Going further, the human rights movement extended its critique to demand accountability for traditional, "apolitical" state repressive practices, such as police and prison abuses.

The Argentine human rights movement, as discussed in Chapters 8 and 9, also played a unique role in civil society. The movement transformed political discourse, traced in the media, public opinion, and educational reform. Attempts to institutionalize movement influence in civil society have been less successful but are visible in the establishment of party, neighborhood, and union human rights commissions. There are some indications that the human rights movement has consolidated its role in maintaining collective memory and fostering collective learning.

Once democratic institutions had been established and attempts were being made to consolidate democracy in Argentina, the human rights movement assumed a much less visible and more reactive role. The movement did serve as a latent pressure group for human rights safeguards in a new and ambiguous crisis of political violence, the 1989 resurgence of guerrilla activity at La Tablada. Human rights activists were still able to mobilize when faced with a clear challenge. On several occasions, the movement convoked over 40,000 people in opposition to Menem's pardon of military officers accused or convicted of human rights violations. The movement's position was echoed by civil society; public opinion polls showed around 70 percent of the population opposed to the measure.[1] Nevertheless, the movement failed to secure significant state responses in these areas, as the parameters of consolidation were framed increasingly by military veto power and economic crisis.

The impact of Argentina's human rights movement is summarized in Table 3, which can loosely be compared with Table 1. Internally, the movement achieved survival, mobilization, collective identity, and the circulation of activists to other spheres of civil society. In civil society, the movement gained recognition, delegitimized the military, reformed some social institutions, and transformed collective memory. The human rights movement spurred state reform through legitimacy challenge, the provision of information and expertise, and a role as a pressure group. Reforms were both symbolic and structural, but never embodied participation rights or a movement role as interlocutor to the state. At the governmental level, the movement helped set the agenda for transition, continually challenged the legitimacy of the regime, and eventually served as a source of legitimacy for democracy. Finally, the Argentine human rights movement mobilized the international human rights regime, contributed to its elaboration, and continues to provide an international model for other movements.

Table 3 also displays one of the findings of this study of a social movement during a transition to democracy: the shifting location of social change produced by the movement throughout the process of transition. During authoritarian rule, most of the effects of movement activity came from above and below: through the international system, civil society, and within the movement itself. With the transition, movement influence on civil society intensified, and the movement assumed an agenda-setting role in regime change, while international attention

TABLE 3
The Impact of Argentina's Human Rights Movement

	STAGES OF DEMOCRATIZATION		
Authoritarian (1976–82)	Transition (1982–83)	Establishment (1984–86)	Consolidation? (1986–89)
International Attention Documentation Intl. "human rights regime"			Model
Regime Delegitimation	Agenda setting	Legit. challenge	Legit. source
State Discourse shift	Accountability	Reform	Safeguards Endemic abuses
Society Recognition	Mobilization	Discourse shift Reform	Memory Learning
Movement Collective ID Mobilization Survival	Participation	Diffusion	Empowerment?

waned. Policy reforms and other conventional measures of impact peaked during the phase corresponding to the establishment of democratic institutions. But as new institutions were forced to address continued structural problems, the consolidation of democracy was stalemated, movement influence on the state declined, and change lingered most strongly as social and international memory.

Although none of these accomplishments can recover the thousands of victims whose fate originally inspired the movement, some of them may contribute to the rehabilitation of the ultimate victim—Argentine society as a whole. The underlying basis of torture is the obliteration of truth, human will, and accountability.[2] The recovery of these attributes as dimensions of social life is the most fitting form of reparation and prevention. The Argentine human rights movement has linked the resolution of the human rights issue to the larger question of democratic accountability for the legacies of authoritarian rule by labeling human rights "the internal debt" (*la deuda interna*).[3] In contrast to Argentina's external debt, in which the state assumed the consequences of private loss, the state's response to the internal debt of human rights has been an ethical privatization of the consequences of public policy.[4] But for human rights—as for the other debt—the consolidation of democracy has been constrained by every attempt to pay the interest and by an absolute inability to repay the principal.

The Movement's Contribution to Democratization

What are the implications of these achievements and limitations of Argentina's human rights movement for democratization in Argentina? At one point, Argentina's first democratic president—frustrated with the "destabilizing" demands of the movement—labeled Las Madres "anti-democratic."[5] Yet the same democratic leader called on the human rights movement as a source of democratic legitimacy during every military crisis faced by the new regime. And one activist summarized the movement's analysis: "To deepen the struggle for human rights *means* to deepen democracy."[6]

This controversy highlights two linked tensions inherent in the process of democratization: democratic stability versus deepening, and governability versus institutionalization. Democratization is a dual process of maintaining governability while establishing democratic institutions.[7] As human rights activists pressed for the establishment of democratic institutions (like equal justice), their demands inevitably strained governability. Similarly, movement attempts to enhance democratic accountability inspired destabilization attempts by antidemocratic actors such as the military. The human rights movement, then, embodied one of the axes of democratization. While we may debate the trade-off achieved between these dimensions at any point in the democratization process, the presence of a force demanding democratic deepening is not anti-democratic but essential. As Scott Mainwaring reminds us, "Although the stability of democracy does not depend on being responsive to popular movements, the quality of democracy does."[8]

To further analyze the movement's contribution to democratization, movement achievements can be mapped against a set of processes that develop the fundamental dimensions of democracy: contestation, participation, accountability, and civilian control over the military.[9] These dimensions of democratization can be measured against social movement participation, accountability to civil society, and regime contestation.

New Social Movements and Democratization

Many theorists of new social movements in the Third World contend that the nontraditional identity and strategies of new social movements may make them bearers of a democratic political culture. These authors generally link the democratizing effect of new social movements to participation, both because the movements encourage participation by marginal actors and because their informal, nonhierarchical structures provide an example and experience of grass-roots democracy.[10] However, the Argentine experience provides mixed support for this hypothesized broadening and deepening of participation.

First, participants in the Argentine human rights movement were politically but not socially marginal: most activists were literate, Europeanized members of the *porteño* middle class. Since socially marginal groups were disproportionately affected by repression, it can be argued that the human rights movement represented the *interests* of marginal actors, but the movement was not composed of citizens who had previously been generally or automatically denied access to the dominant institutions of society. Furthermore, during the course of the transition, Peronism quickly reassumed its historic role as both the representative and participatory channel for popular sectors.

The human rights movement did encourage participation by one previously marginalized group—women. The Argentine human rights movement was disproportionately composed of women, most of whom had previously been politically inactive housewives. Many interpretations of the movement have focused on the symbolic use of female identity.[11] But while protest may have empowered some women, the Argentine human rights movement was by no means a feminist movement. Las Madres and the other family-based movements were "feminine rather than feminist"; that is, they were movements that valued and employed traditional sources of maternal identity but never questioned the sexual division of labor.[12] The participation of women is one way in which we can say that the human rights movement expanded democracy, but it did not systematically challenge the principles by which women were excluded from the political sphere.

New social movements are said to bring new actors into the political system. At the same time, the experience of democratic participation in new social movements is believed to democratize the political system. But how democratic was the experience of participation in the Argentine human rights movement? The degree of internal democracy in the Argentine movement may have been overestimated by early observers because of the embryonic stage of movement development observed and the limits of the authoritarian environment. The new social movement ideal of fluid, nonhierarchical participation has not been achieved (or even aspired to) by most of Argentina's human rights organizations. La Liga is probably the most centralist organization, perhaps owing to its association with the Communist party. Personalism in Las Madres was one of the main factors in the split with the Linea Fundadora, while the Movimiento Judío and SERPAJ are also strongly oriented by the personalities of their founders (although the much larger SERPAJ does appear to be fairly decentralized). Las Abuelas, CELS, and MEDH are among the least personalistic and most internally democratic organizations, but within a traditional nonprofit group structure that includes formal offices, hierarchies, and divisions of labor. Familiares probably comes closest to the new social movement ideal of informal organization and weak hierarchy ("We have never voted," one organizer boasted), but it is one of the smaller and least externally influential groups.[13] The experience of movement participation is only democratic by comparison to other forms of social organization in Argentina—corporatism and political parties.

Furthermore, the relationship between institutional and noninstitutional democracy has not been fully explored. Will the experience of participation in democratic social movements translate into system-level democracy?[14] In the case of the human rights movement, activist circulation to state institutions, parties, and unions provides a limited opportunity to test the claimed relationship. In some venues (such as the CGT) these former human rights activists do seem to serve as advocates for democratization, but in others (such as the UCR) their effect has been minimal.

The system-level impact of the incorporation of the mass of human rights activists is even less clear. While social movement theorists tend to equate participation with empowerment, unsuccessful participation may equally well generate alienation and disillusionment. Several movement leaders, for example, have suffered debilitating episodes of clinical depression. A few have even committed suicide in despair over their personal and political losses: Alfredo Galetti in December 1983; Augusto Conte in February 1992.

But activism can be therapeutic; one activist referred to the human rights movement role in reconstructing her identity, saying, "My family now are the Madres de Plaza de Mayo."[15] And activism can provide democratic citizens with hope, dignity, and patience in the absence of concrete political gains. As the widow of a *desaparecido*, living in a small town in one of the least developed regions of Argentina, put it: "Not too much has changed, and we certainly haven't gotten justice; but we keep working away slowly—like little drops of water. . . . That is the history that no one can take away from us."[16]

"Democracy as a Form of Society"

Beyond the participation effects of new social movement activity, human rights movements may have more general effects on accountability and contestation. In this sense, democratic theory goes beyond the treatment of democracy as a regime type to characterize democracy as a relationship between the state and civil society. Lefort invokes the "Tocquevillean concept of democracy as a form of society."[17] A democratic form of society will involve the possibility of autonomy in civil society (and thus, contestation vis-à-vis the state), a minimal version of the liberal ideal grounded in the "right to have rights," and a sense of inclusive shared identity as citizens.[18]

From this perspective, the mere existence and persistence of the human rights movement have contributed to the creation of an autonomous civil society (contrasting with the tradition of corporatism in Argentina). And the human rights movement did help to establish the possibility of nonviolent and non-power-seeking responses to the state in Argentina. The movement channeled loss into democratic channels; it is noteworthy that despite tremendous frustration with those channels, there have been no incidents of personal vengeance against repressors on behalf of the victims.[19]

The human rights movement also played a key role in introducing the concept of civil rights to Argentine society. The sociologist Oscar Landi noted that previous waves of mobilization successfully installed social rights and voting rights as referents for Argentine collective identity and asked if human rights have achieved this status.[20] A partial reply is provided at the micro level by the pollster Edgardo Catterberg, who distinguished support for participatory and liberal (civil libertarian) aspects of democracy in Argentina. Catterberg found that support for democracy focused on the participatory dimensions, with much lower levels of liberalism—although it is encouraging that liberal attitudes were higher among younger citizens.[21]

Finally, the human rights movement has contributed to the consolidation of democracy through its attempt to promote an inclusive sense of citizenship. Democracy is more than just a set of new rules of the game; it is a relationship among citizens with a shared identity.[22] A democratic social identity is inclusive and historical; the political community is composed of all citizens, past and present.[23] As a union leader who lost his son explained, "Without memory, there is no democracy."[24]

This sense of inclusive citizenship is the social foundation for democratic accountability. In the past, in Argentina "the nation was embodied as a political position [*linea*], through which a determinate group gained identity and self-consciousness from the 'anti-national' character attributed to the other. In this way, every form of national political organization ended in being an apartheid."[25] The Argentine human rights movement's insistence on recovering the history of a "lost generation" and reclaiming the identity of the disappeared as citizens helped to reconstruct an inclusive and accountable sense of national identity.

Human Rights, Regime Type, and Agenda Challenge

In the case of a human rights movement, the nature of movement demands may democratize the system by challenging the basic conception of regime type. For the Argentine human rights movement, movement demands called into question a model of democracy that installed procedural democracy (contestation and participation) but delayed the resolution of questions of civil-military relations and accountability. Thus, the very aspects of protest that Alfonsín found destabilizing contributed profoundly to democratization: by promoting a substantive vision of democracy, an alternate reading of the transition, and a challenge to Radical claims to hegemonize democracy.

A democratic regime may mean varying combinations of: (1) a regime characterized by continuous and predictable civilian rule, (2) a government chosen by fair and open elections, (3) the reliable operation of a set of "democratic" principles and institutions (such as an independent judiciary), (4) popular sovereignty and participation, and (5) an embodiment of "democratic" values (such as equal justice for all, or respect for human rights).[26] The nature of the human rights issue ties democratic legitimacy to performance, not just procedures: human rights "hold against all types of states, democratic as much as any other: if one's government treats one as less than fully human, it matters little, if at all, how that government came to power."[27] The human rights movement demanded that the realization of human rights be considered one of the defining characteristics of a democratic state.[28]

The movement held the new regime accountable for the realization of democratic values, advocated a regime model that differed sharply from those offered by other political actors, and highlighted the conflicts and trade-offs between different aspects of democratic ideals. For the military, transition to democracy meant open elections leading to civilian rule, retaining a corporate military veto over superficially democratic institutions. Most Peronists defined democracy chiefly in terms of popular participation. The development of the Alfonsín administration's human rights policy seems to show that the vision of democracy based on an elected civilian government originally encompassed procedural democracy but was transformed into a defense of civilian rule that at times required the sacrifice of democratic values like equal justice.[29] But human rights movement criticism sent up flares to mark the retreating frontiers of democracy and exerted some countervailing pressure on behalf of substantive democracy.[30] An activist explained: "We must remind this government of its responsibilities; because it was won with the blood of our children."[31]

In this sense, the human rights movement promoted an alternative to the Alfonsín administration's reading of the transition. Alfonsín's human rights policies were based on a prioritization of procedural democracy as a necessary condition for the consolidation of full contestation and accountability. But the human rights movement contended that regime change and procedural democracy would not be self-sustaining if contestation were not fully developed; "democracy is not enough."[32] In contrast to earlier criticisms by the left of "mere bourgeois democracy," the human rights critique of a stage theory of democratization did acknowledge the significance and necessary role of regime change and procedural democracy.[33] But it incorporated a sense of an intrinsic link between decision-making mechanisms and the identity and capabilities of participants.[34]

More specifically, the human rights movement contributed to democratization by questioning the Radical claim to a monopoly on democracy. The association founded in the 1983 transition elections between Radicalism, Alfonsín himself, and a democratic regime developed into a political and electoral strategy asserting a unique historical mandate for the UCR.[35] Other political forces contested this attempt to personalize and partisanize democracy. "With us, democracy will be more," was a 1987 Peronist campaign slogan, for example.[36] But the human rights movement was uniquely qualified to challenge Alfonsín's status as the sole interpreter of the democratic ideal, since the movement represented precisely those values on which this identity had been founded. In this way, the human rights movement challenge helped to pave the way for the true mark of democratic consolidation: the peaceful alternation of opposition political forces.

Following the 1988 Villa Martelli military uprising, government posters proclaimed: "Democracy is among us. It is here to stay." In a variety of ways, the human rights movement helped to establish "democracy among us." The corollary claim—the durability of democratization—must be examined more closely.

Durability of the Human Rights Legacy

Given the partial and shifting nature of the accomplishments of the human rights movement, how can we assess the long-term legacy of activism—both in terms of human rights and of the larger questions of democratization it implies? An evaluation of the durability of change requires further examination of both the movement and its democratic context.

The Argentine human rights movement has demobilized significantly: membership and activities are sparse. Does this mean that the movement has exhausted its political force—or are cycles of protest like waves breaking on a beach, which deposit layers of social change as they recede and "help redefine the parameters of political struggle?"[37] The movement has shown chronological adaptability in surviving over a decade through a change of regime and two changes of administration, but has faced problems with both functional adaptability (redefining goals) and generational succession.[38] The movement's social (rather than policy) goals—raising the base level of respect for human rights and expectations concerning state conduct—continue to be met at higher levels than at any time in Argentine history. Menem's pardons of the military sparked not only human rights protest, but legislative challenges, resignations of party and government officials, and a precipitous drop in the president's popularity.[39] Another illustration of the new level of expectations was a series of spontaneous local protests against police misconduct in 1990.[40]

But absent continuing movement pressure and participation rights, we must also examine their institutional legacy. Are mechanisms available for the guarantee of rights and redress?[41] We have seen that the civil libertarian legislation and checks on civilian branches of government introduced by Alfonsín represented substantial guarantees, but that Executive branch implementation has been weak and easily overridden by military veto power. This trend has continued under the successor Menem government; accountability has been diluted as convicted military officers have been pardoned and the Executive has attempted to purge the judiciary.[42] The erosion of guarantees has not yet allowed widespread repression or impeded freedoms of expression and protest, but it leaves the future of human rights in Argentina highly dependent on the future of civil-military relations and the *estado de derecho*.

The human rights legacy, then, will be tied to an assessment of the stability of democracy. But such an assessment must begin with a recognition of the accomplishment and precedent of even a single season of democracy in Argentina. Prior to the Alfonsín administration, Argentina had not experienced a complete six-year presidential term of fully inclusionary democracy in two generations. Following Alfonsín's 1983 election, Argentine voters participated freely and peacefully in a 1984 plebiscite on the Beagle Islands and in 1985 and 1987 midterm elections that resulted in significant gains for opposition political forces. Finally, in 1989—for the first time in over half a century, a freely elected civilian president handed over power to another freely elected civilian representing the opposition. This unprecedented democratic experience survived three military uprisings and inflation that reached almost 5,000 percent in 1989.[43] Even the resurgence of guerrilla activity in early 1989 did not bring appeals for military rule.

Unfortunately, all of this by no means precludes a return to military rule; in the recent past, far more established democratic regimes in Chile and Uruguay succumbed readily to authoritarianism. And sectors of the military have advocated quasi-authoritarian solutions to the economic crisis.[44] However, the combined legacies of human rights activism and a season of democracy would make a coup more difficult and costly.[45]

The Argentine military has never before sustained a military regime on purely corporatist grounds. Military rule has always been justified in terms of "national interest," but the human rights challenge to military legitimacy has made such claims much more problematic. Again, the human rights movement's reminder of the price of alternatives to democracy may strengthen democratic legitimacy in the face of social and economic problems.[46] The availability of a reliable democratic alternative to official policies has probably served as a safety valve, and should continue to provide an outlet for the frustration generated by the economic crisis and social consequences of adjustment.[47]

In addition, the military has never acted without at least tacit international support. In part as a result of human rights activism, the international climate is now highly critical of authoritarian rule and supportive of democratization. Specifically, U.S. policy is subject to built-in human rights provisions and an attentive foreign policy constituency.

Finally, in the event of a military coup, the human rights movement's latent organizational strength, experience, credibility, and international networks have raised the potential costs of repression for any regime contemplating a return to state terror. The experience of human rights trials and social repudiation catalyzed by the human rights movement, as well as the institutional fractures repression created within the military, serve a deterrent function. Thus, the lasting influence of

Argentina's human rights movement cannot and will not prevent the military from returning to power (or significantly conditioning policy)—but it will mean more awareness, more resistance, and probably less repression in the long term.

Generalizing from the Argentine Experience

The Politics of Human Rights and Transitions to Democracy

What lessons, cautions, and considerations may the Argentine experience offer for other countries in transition to democracy? First, the Argentine case urges careful attention to timing as a nonrenewable resource. The Alfonsín administration generally believed that the passage of time would work in favor of the consolidation of democracy.[48] But the human rights movement and others pressed for early, sweeping reform.[49] The pattern of early relative success of human rights reform in Argentina and subsequent revival of military resistance seems to support the argument for rapid reform. "Under these circumstances, one could argue that the government's excessively moderate stance on human rights gave the military the respite they needed to regroup."[50] This analysis may be fruitfully combined with a search for critical policy junctures and institutional branch points.

In the Argentine case, there are several outstanding examples of lost opportunities. One is the form of the 1984 reform of the military code, which initiated trials in military courts, slowing down the trials, increasing uncertainty, and buying time for the military, while dissipating popular support. Another was the 1987 passage of the Obediencia Debida legislation, despite massive social and international opposition during the Semana Santa military uprising. The general lessons that can be abstracted from these particular junctures include the dangers of delay in judicial processes following regime change and the need for the rapid institutionalization of the ephemeral resource of popular mobilization in transforming civil-military relations.

On a related point, the Argentine experience speaks to the debate on the value and effects of democratic pacts.[51] The Argentine transition was notable initially for its lack of pacts and range of democratic indeterminacy. But each military challenge brought implicit or explicit limits to contestation and accountability. In Philippe Schmitter and Guillermo O'Donnell's terms, the "military moment" lingered on to condition every phase of the transition. The Argentine model, first considered a case of transition by collapse from above and reform from below, ended up as a kind of slow, twisting pact—a "transition tango." Precisely because of the path-dependent nature of democratization, this default model offered neither the guarantees of a true pact nor the latitude of a representative struggle among social forces. Furthermore, the Argentine scenario evolved undemocratic "rules of the game" that implicitly endorsed (by rewarding) periodic appeals to force.

Argentina's delayed model of consolidation also reveals some important characteristics of institutions. Key advances in human rights reform came about through the unexpected power and autonomy of institutional structures as they developed over time, such as the legislature (nullifying the military's self-amnesty and expanding the reform of the military code), the CONADEP commission, and the judiciary. In each instance, social movement pressure directed at a specific institutional context strengthened the impact of reform. Thus, the Argentine case also directs attention to the ways in which noninstitutional factors—especially civil society and the international system—interact with institutional components of the political system.

But excessive reliance on inappropriate or limited institutions can also handicap a transition. The Alfonsín administration's exclusive use of the judiciary to assert accountability and civilian control over the forces of coercion proved short-sighted.[52] The administration's reluctance to assert Executive political control over undemocratic actors in the military, police, and intelligence services did not inculcate respect for judicial procedures. Failure to address coercion through the Executive perpetuated access to the resources of state power, which facilitated continuing human rights violations and attacks on the democratic regime itself.

The Argentine experience is more than just a study of human rights reform and transition to democracy; it is an exploration of the role of social movements in producing human rights reform. What can the Argentine case tell us about the relationship between protest and reform?

Human Rights Protest and Reform

We have seen that Argentina's human rights movement played a critical and consequential role in producing human rights reform. In Argentina, protest was a necessary and sometimes a sufficient cause of reform. Does this reflect a general relationship? Is a human rights movement *necessary* to achieve human rights reform? And if so, is social movement activity *sufficient* to achieve human rights reform?

In order to generalize from the Argentine case, we must reiterate general definitions of a social movement and human rights reform. Following the discussion in Chapter 1, a social movement is a set of organizations pursuing universalistic goals through collective action. A human rights movement will be one whose principal purpose is or was the defense of the rights of the person. A human rights movement can be characterized as strong or weak depending on some combination of the numbers of people involved, persistence of protest, use of multiple channels of dissidence, broad social base, symbolic power, degree of human rights focus, and general social legitimacy.

Human rights reform will involve measures such as trials, investigations, memorials, institutional reorganization (police, military, etc.), educational reform—and of course, the level of continuing repression. Reform will be stronger if it involves multiple arenas, institutionalized mechanisms, and covers past, present, and future abuses.

Since human rights reform has taken place with and without the presence of a human rights movement, a controlled comparison will yield at least four outcomes, bounded by the strength of reform and the level of movement pressure. The first outcome, repression without response, may be useful as a control case but shows little change in either variable. Most of these cases, such as Khmer Rouge Cambodia, involve the total destruction of civil society. But some pacted transitions to democracy, like that in Spain, also illustrate a lack of both movement pressure and human rights reform. The second outcome, reform without movement mobilization, usually involves external imposition of reform. This was the case of the Nuremberg trials and denazification process in Nazi Germany, war crimes trials in Japan, Vietnam's invasion of Cambodia and subsequent memorials and investigations, and similar measures following Tanzania's invasion of Amin's Uganda. Absent foreign intervention, it is difficult to find a case of human rights reform without the presence of a human rights movement. A human rights movement seems to be a necessary condition for reform.[53]

But not all human rights movements produce reform. The third outcome, a successful movement, may be seen in Argentina, parts of Eastern Europe, and perhaps South Africa. But the fourth result, a movement that does not produce reform, is found in China, Peru, and Uruguay. Movement outcomes remain highly uncertain in Guatemala and South Korea. How then, may we distinguish the sufficient conditions for human rights reform, which enable some movements to succeed while others fail to secure reform?

This is a question that clearly goes beyond the scope of this inquiry and merits further investigation. However, the Argentine case can serve to draw our attention to some variables that facilitated reform in that country. Thus, factors to examine will include the interaction of human rights protest with international influence, democratizing institutions (especially the judiciary), and the social legitimacy of protesters. One of these factors—international influence—suggests an important qualification of the comparative framework outlined above, which is at the same time the final accomplishment of the Argentine human rights movement.

International Learning

Finally, we must examine the international context and contribution of the Argentine human rights movement. Comparative cases of human rights protest and reform are not independent; from a social science perspective, they are "contaminated" by international learning and diffusion. But this methodological weakness is a practical political strength, because the Argentine human rights movement gave the world a new protest repertoire. To generalize from the Argentine case, we must finally examine this global legacy.

First, the historical comparative cases influenced Argentina. The very nature of the repression was shaped by earlier experiences of state terror in Brazil, Chile, and Greece. International response was also related to the Chilean experience, which had laid the foundation for U.S. human rights policies. During the transition, the Alfonsín administration drew mixed lessons from the Nuremberg trials. On the one hand, the Argentine trials were carefully framed within the existing legal system to avoid the format of a special tribunal. On the other hand, the Argentine prosecution emulated the legal strategy of military leaders' indirect responsibility for human rights violations. And at least one human rights group (SERPAJ) consciously emulated a Gandhian resistance strategy of "active nonviolence" (although without focusing on civil disobedience).

But what of the international influence of the Argentine experience itself? International learning has occurred at the multilateral, regional, bilateral, and country levels. Among the "lessons" are mechanisms, strategies, and repertoires for reform.

As a result of the Argentine experience, international organizations have become more active in human rights and more sensitive to the phenomenon of "disappearance." The United Nations established a working group on forced disappearance and generally increased its level of human rights activity. The Argentine human rights movement has consciously sought to expand the role and accessibility of the United Nations in cases involving human rights.[54] The OAS inspection mission to Argentina also strengthened the OAS Interamerican Human Rights Commission. The Argentine human rights movement introduced a proposal to the OAS that would declare disappearance a universally extraditable crime against humanity, not amenable to amnesty. The OAS ruled Argentina's trials limitations in violation of international law, in response to an appeal by the Argentine human rights movement.[55]

More generally, Argentine human rights protest combined with other national movements to shape a new international climate of issue awareness and legitimacy—especially in the United States. The extradition of the Argentine General Carlos Suarez Mason from the United States for human rights abuses contributed to the growing body of international human rights law.[56] Human rights activism in and about Argentina helped to trigger positive changes in U.S. policy, especially human rights linkage for aid reviews (including economic and military assistance, criteria for U.S. participation in multilateral organizations, and reporting requirements).

Argentine human rights organizations have also lent direct assistance to activists in other countries. Nongovernmental organizations based in the United States and Europe such as Amnesty International and Americas Watch learned strategies and built networks through the Argentine movement. The Argentine Forensic Anthropology team has provided technical expertise in the treatment of unidentified corpses in Peru, Guatemala, and the Philippines. Argentine human rights groups have joined with their counterparts across Latin America to form FEDEFAM, the regional federation of relatives of the disappeared. This federation has sponsored regional conferences through which local human rights groups exchange monitoring, lobbying, and coping strategies.[57]

However, the very success of the Argentine model has also inspired defensive measures by states seeking impunity for human rights violations. In neighboring Uruguay, the example of Argentina's trials helped to secure a popular referendum to overturn the transition pact granting amnesty to the military, despite tremendous government resistance. But the negative lesson of Argentina's military uprisings contributed heavily to the measure's ultimate defeat. The outgoing Chilean regime issued explicit warnings against Argentine-style trials of military officers.[58] And the first major legislative initiative of El Salvador's Cristiani government sought to penalize lobbying of international organizations to denounce human rights violations.[59] And yet, we can see everywhere signs of the "human rights revolution." In East Germany, protesters stormed secret police headquarters to secure the release of files. Across eastern Europe, former dissidents have pressed for investigations, trials, and reparations. Police forces have been reorganized in South Africa. "Truth commissions" have issued reports in Chile and El Salvador.

It is a revolution led by unlikely standard bearers. Around the world, there are women in headscarves, marching slowly, carrying life-sized photographs of their disappeared. They are still marching in Argentina, and family-based human rights movements are marching now in Chile, Peru, Colombia, El Salvador, South Africa, Lebanon, and Soviet Georgia.[60] Across different cultures and conflicts, they are marching to the same beat: truth, justice, the right to life.

In Argentina, an Abuela still searching for her kidnapped grandchild described "the conditions necessary to achieve *nunca más*." Her vision included social justice and military reform, but stressed "a moral restructuring. This comes from truth and justice. Only truth and justice can rebuild and consolidate democracy."[61]

In South Korea, a group of relatives of political prisoners were arrested for their protest at the trials of police officers convicted of human rights violations. The father of one victim explained, "It's not the verdict or the sentences I'm interested in. This trial did not disclose the truth."[62]

And on another continent, in Uganda, human rights hearings on the atrocities committed under Idi Amin concluded: "These hearings are to help us understand the past so we don't make the same mistakes. But at some point, we have to come to terms with accountability, don't we? At some point we must ask ourselves, aren't we obstructing justice if we hide the truth? I hope we are learning."[63]

The politics of human rights will continue as long as states do unspeakable violence to their citizens to maintain power. The purpose of this study has been to show that citizens have an unexpected road to resistance: symbolic politics. At some times and in some places, truth and values can create their own kind of power. There are limits to its reach and robustness, but it is a kind of power that can send ripples of social change reverberating through a political system. Further study of the sources, uses, effects, and conditions of symbolic power can illuminate a dark side of the study of politics. More important, it may help the disenfranchised to find their voice.

Glossary

Glossary of Spanish Terms, Names, and Acronyms

The following glossary is provided to aid the reader in three senses. First, since Argentine politics contains particular or anomalous features that must be developed within the study in a historical or conceptual context, the glossary serves as an introductory overview of key terms and concepts. For example, in Argentina, the terms "Radical" and "Liberal" have meanings diametrically opposed to their standard usage in English. Second, since material within each section refers to material developed in previous sections (especially in Chapter 2), the glossary will assist readers of isolated portions of the text. Finally, since the repetition of full explanations of key terms would lengthen the manuscript considerably, the glossary serves as a source of reference for readers unfamiliar with Argentine politics.

Alfonsín—Raul Alfonsín, president of Argentina (1983–89). Alfonsín, a member of the Radical party (see listing), was the first constitutional president elected following the 1976–83 military dictatorship.

Abuelas—Abuelas de Plaza de Mayo (Grandmothers of the Plaza de Mayo): a human rights organization founded during the military dictatorship, composed of women whose grandchildren and/or pregnant daughters were kidnapped by the military during the dictatorship. The organization seeks to trace children who may have been illicitly adopted and restore them to their surviving biological families.

afectados—Family members of persons imprisoned, tortured, or kidnapped during the dictatorship. Within the human rights movement, this term is used to distinguish people or groups that became active because of a personal experience with repression.

Asamblea—Asamblea Permanente por los Derechos Humanos (Permanent Assembly for Human Rights): a multiparty, multisector civil libertarian organization founded in 1975. The APDH coordinated the documentation of disappearances during the dictatorship and continues to advocate a wide range of human rights.

CELS—Centro de Estudios Legales y Sociales (Center for Legal and Social Studies): a human rights organization that both documents patterns of abuse and provides legal assistance to those affected. The CELS also challenges legislation and judicial rulings it deems unconstitutional or antithetical to civil liberties.

CGT—Confederación General del Trabajo (General Labor Federation): the central coordinating body for Argentina's labor unions. The CGT is closely allied with, although not officially a part of, the Peronist party (see listing).

CONADEP—Comisión Nacional sobre la Desaparición de Personas (National Commission on the Disappearance of Persons): a blue-ribbon presidential panel created in 1983 to investigate the fate of the thousands of Argentines who had "disappeared" during the military dictatorship. Its report, *Nunca más*, documented a nationwide system of repression.

DC—Partido Democrata Cristiana (Christian Democratic party): a small social democratic party. Of the two minor parties most sympathetic to human rights movement claims, only the DC has elected a representative on a human rights platform.

desaparecido—a person who "disappeared" during the military dictatorship. It has been established that the majority of these persons were kidnapped by special military task forces, taken to clandestine detention centers, tortured, and later murdered.

denuncia—a complaint that an abuse of legal or human rights has occurred, along with supporting documentation. In contrast to its English cognate, "denunciation," the Spanish term has formal legal significance.

Due obedience—see *Obediencia debida*.

ERP—Ejercito Revolucionario Popular (People's Revolutionary Army): one of the two major guerrilla groups during the 1973–76 period leading up to the military dictatorship. The ERP, the weaker of the two groups, was predominantly rural and had an ideology influenced by Che Guevara.

estado de derecho—either "constitutional government" or "rule of law" (historically, usually equivalent). During the transition to democracy, the concept of *estado de derecho* became the focus of claims for due process and institutionalization of the democratic state.

Ex-detainees—Asociación de Ex-Detenidos-Desaparecidos (Association of Former Detainees): a human rights organization composed of some of the few surviving "disappeared." Founded in 1985 after the trials of the juntas, the Ex-Detenidos' main goal is to bear witness to the atrocities they experienced.

Falklands—see Malvinas.

Familiares—Familiares de Los Detenidos-Desaparecidos y Presos por Razones Políticas (Relatives of Those Disappeared and Detained for Political Reasons): Another family-based human rights organization. Familiares differs from other such groups in that it was the only organization for relatives of the thousands of political prisoners held during the dictatorship. Political prisoners, in contrast to *desaparecidos*, were officially acknowledged by the government, although often subject to torture and other abuses—and official political prisoners generally survived the dictatorship.

Intransigente—see PI or Partido Intransigente. Not equivalent to the English word "intransigent."

juntas—Military rulers, specifically the four sets of commanders who ruled Argentina between 1976 and 1983. Each junta consisted of a representative from the Army, Navy and Air Force; the Army leader was the president.

Justicialismo, Justicialista—see Peronism. The ideology and official name of the Peronist party.

La Liga—Liga Argentina por los Derechos del Hombre (Argentine League for the Rights of Man): a civil libertarian organization dating from the 1930's. It is closely associated with, although not officially affiliated with, the Argentine Communist party.

La Tablada—Apparent resurgence of long-dormant guerrilla activity in a January 1989 attack on the La Tablada army base.

Liberal—See UCD. Not equivalent to the English word "liberal." In the Argentine political spectrum, *liberal* connotes a supporter of free-market economics and (usually) "open" foreign policy.

Linea Fundadora—Madres de Plaza de Mayo–Linea Fundadora (Mothers of the Plaza de Mayo–Founding Line): an offshoot of the Madres (see below), formed in 1984 as the main group radicalized. The Linea Fundadora sought to preserve a position of openness toward the government and certain other groups, which the main body saw as irremediably compromised.

Madres—Madres de Plaza de Mayo (Mothers of the Plaza de Mayo): the best-known human rights organization, formed in 1977 by mothers whose (adult and adolescent) children had been "disappeared" by the military. The Madres are known for a ritual form of protest in which they march around the Plaza de Mayo in Buenos Aires, wearing white scarves and carrying poster-sized photographs of the disappeared. Since a 1984 split, the hard-line faction of the Madres has retained the use of the original name.

Malvinas—The 1982 Falklands-Malvinas War with Britain was pursued by Argentina's military dictatorship to recover a set of islands in the South Atlantic historically claimed by Argentina but controlled by Britain and populated by English speakers. The loss of the Malvinas War served to discredit Argentina's military rulers and to catalyze the transition to democracy.

MEDH—Movimiento Ecuménico por los Derechos Humanos (Ecumenical

Movement for Human Rights): a religious human rights organization with the membership of (dissident) Catholic and Protestant official religious figures and congregations. The distinctive role of the MEDH has been the provision of pastoral services and charity to persons and families directly affected by the repression.

Monte Caseros—Military rebellion in January 1988, the second of Alfonsín's administration. A lieutenant colonel who refused to be brought to trial took refuge in the Monte Caseros Army base but surrendered after a brief skirmish with loyal troops.

Montoneros—the largest guerrilla group during the 1973–76 period preceding the military dictatorship. The Montoneros, who were Peronist ultranationalists of socialist orientation, pursued a strategy of urban terrorism that killed hundreds.

Movimiento Judío—Movimiento Judío por los Derechos Humanos (Jewish Movement for Human Rights): a religious human rights movement drawn from the ranks of Argentina's large Jewish community. The Jewish Movement was distinct from the Ecumenical Movement since "ecumenical" generally means inter-Christian in the Argentine context.

NGO—nongovernmental organization.

NN—*Ningun nombre* (no name): label given to unidentified bodies buried during the dictatorship. The discovery of mass graves of *NN* bodies provided concrete evidence of military human rights abuses.

NSM—new social movement.

Obediencia Debida— ("due obedience"): a law passed in June 1987 that limits legal accountability for human rights violations committed under the military dictatorship to commanding officers and explicitly excludes those who were "just following orders."

PC—Partido Comunista (Communist party): the Argentine Communist party, which is a minor and relatively conservative force within the left. The PC, whose influence peaked during the 1930's, has pursued an internationalist, pro-Soviet line.

Peronism—A populist, nationalist movement and political party founded by General Juan Perón (who governed Argentina from 1945 to 1955 and again from 1973 to 1974). Peronism has come to represent a non-socialist philosophy of workers' rights and state ownership within a Catholic, nationalist framework that honors the role of (national) capital. Peronism has usually commanded a majority during the postwar period but has often been excluded from power. The movement's ideology is not easily classified on a left-right political spectrum; unifying characteristics of movement supporters include a commitment to popular interests, mass mobilization, and a nationalist development strategy and foreign policy.

PI—Partido Intransigente (Intransigent party): a small democratic socialist leftist party, originally formed as an offshoot of the centrist Radical party (see below). One of the two minor parties most sympathetic to and representative of the claims of the human rights movement.

PJ—Partido Justicialista: see Peronism. Official name of the Peronist party.

Plaza de Mayo—the main public square of the capital city of Buenos Aires. The Plaza de Mayo is surrounded by the seats of power: the Casa Rosada Presidential Palace, the Cabildo Founders' Hall, the main cathedral, and the major bank headquarters. It has been a traditional site of public protest, including the 1945 uprising that brought Peron to power.

Proceso—Proceso de Reorganización Nacional (Process of National Reorganization): the political program of the 1976–83 military dictatorship. The Proceso was an unprecedented and sweeping plan for the political, economic, and cultural transformation of Argentine society in accordance with a demobilized, capitalist, dependent, "Western Christian" ideology. The term Proceso has come to be used by a variety of observers to capture the pervasive nature of repression and social control experienced by Argentines during the dictatorship.

Punto Final—legislation passed in December 1986 that limited the scope of future trials of military officers for human rights violations. The Punto Final law specified that trials could only be pursued in cases where indictments had been issued within sixty days of the passage of the legislation.

Radical—Unión Cívica Radical (UCR) (Radical Civic Union): Argentina's second major political party, which ruled during the transition to democracy (1983–89). The Radical party, which is not at all "radical" in the sense of the English term, is a centrist party that draws support primarily from Argentina's large middle class. The UCR is identified with a commitment to the rule of law, "good government," and mixed economic and foreign policies.

Renovador—Peronismo Renovador (Renovation Peronism): A progressive tendency that arose among a new generation within the Peronist party as a response to the traumas of the dictatorship and Peronism's unexpected defeat in the 1983 transition elections. Renovation Peronism emphasizes the social democratic elements of Peronism, downplays the Catholic-derived social conservatism, seeks greater internal democracy within the movement, and explicitly recognizes and supports human rights claims.

Semana Santa—the Holy Week 1987 military rebellion by junior officers opposed to both human rights trials and military reform. Semana Santa, the first military uprising during the democratic period, inspired unprecedented massive support for the civilian government, but was followed by the adoption of the "due obedience" legislation limiting future trials.

SERPAJ—Servicio Paz y Justicia (Peace and Justice Service): a pan-Latin American social movement loosely based on liberation theology, whose Argentine branch became active in promoting human rights during the dictatorship. Its Argentine founder, Adolfo Perez-Esquivel, received the 1980 Nobel Peace Prize for the work of SERPAJ, especially its role as a human rights organization in Argentina.

UCD—Unión del Centro Democratico (Union of the Democratic Center): a right-wing, Liberal (in the Argentine sense [see above]) political party. Argentina's largest and fastest-growing minor party; often a supporter of military positions on human rights issues.

UCR—see Radical; the Radical political party.

Villa Martelli—The third and final military uprising during the Alfonsín period, in December 1988. The Villa Martelli rebellion, led by a right-wing ultranationalist colonel, was the first uprising in which civilians were killed.

Reference Matter

Notes

Full authors' names, titles, and publication data for works cited in short form are given in the Selected Bibliography, pp. 255–82.

Introduction

1. The CONADEP government investigatory commission has documented 8,960 cases of persons who "disappeared" who are still missing; see Comisión Nacional sobre la Desaparición de Personas, *Nunca más: The Report of the Argentine National Commission on the Disappeared* (New York: Farrar, Straus & Giroux, 1986), 447. CONADEP itself believed that the official count of the disappeared significantly underrepresents the true figure, and the human rights movement has generally claimed a figure closer to 30,000. For a review of the debate on the numbers of disappeared, see Brysk in Cingranelli, ed.

Chapter 1

1. In terms of social science methodology, the construction of such a general model is a hermeneutically informed rather than strictly positivistic exercise. While this study seeks to identify causal relationships among actors and processes (positivism), it acknowledges the limits of models derived from the natural sciences in modeling voluntaristic and communicative human behavior—including politics. These limits can be addressed by interpretive techniques that seek to recover the meanings of political practices to their participants, and to uncover the internal coherence of ideas, intentions, and forms of expression by political actors (hermeneutics). See Gibbons, "Introduction: Politics of Interpretation," in id., ed., *Interpreting Politics*.

2. On universalistic goals, see Gamson, *Strategy of Social Protest*, 62. For a

related discussion of "purposive" incentives, see Wilson, *Political Organizations*, 9, 33–35, 46. Also see Rochon.

3. K. Webb et al., in "Etiology and Outcomes of Protest," adopt a model based on the "political tendance"—a set of groups that share a challenge and some overlap of leadership, constituency socialization, and organizational learning. Within a tendance, multiple strategies are normal. Also see Wilson, *Political Organizations*, 296, on the division of labor within a social movement. Marwell and Oliver, 12, situate social movements within a wider collective campaign involving political parties, international organizations, and other actors.

4. During the period under study, all of the Argentine groups would agree on this definition as a minimal set of common goals. There is a vast literature on defining human rights. This definition draws on Articles 3 and 5 of the Universal Declaration of Human Rights. For leading treatments, see Dworkin, *Taking Rights Seriously*; Donnelly, *Universal Human Rights* and *Concept of Human Rights*; Claude, *Comparative Human Rights*; Gewirth, *Human Rights: Essays on Justification*; Nickel, *Making Sense of Human Rights*; and Forsythe, *Internationalization of Human Rights*.

5. The family-based groups are the *Abuelas*—Abuelas de Plaza de Mayo (Grandmothers of the Plaza de Mayo); *Familiares*—Familiares de Los Detenidos-Desaparecidos y Presos por Razones Políticas (Relatives of Those Disappeared and Detained for Political Reasons); and *Las Madres*—Madres de Plaza de Mayo(Mothers of the Plaza de Mayo [two factions since 1984]). The civil libertarians, a category including many relatives of victims who undertook a different mode of activism, are the *Asamblea*—Asamblea Permanente por los Derechos Humanos (APDH) ([Permanent Assembly for Human Rights); *CELS*—Centro de Estudios Legales y Sociales (Center for Legal and Social Studies); and *La Liga*—Liga Argentina por los Derechos del Hombre (Argentine League for the Rights of Man). Religious movements include the *MEDH*—Movimiento Ecuménico por los Derechos Humanos (Ecumenical Movement for Human Rights; *Movimiento Judío*—Movimiento Judio por los Derechos Humanos (Jewish Movement for Human Rights); and *SERPAJ*—Servicio Paz y Justicia (Peace and Justice Service). For obvious reasons, the group founded by *Ex-Detainees*—Asociacíon de Ex-Detenidos-Desaparecidos (Association of Former Detainees) is sui generis. A capsule description of each group is provided in the Glossary that follows the main text. Fuller accounts of organizational development, including functional strategic divisions and the history of organizational contact, may be found in Chapter 3.

6. This early literature is extensively reviewed in the first two chapters of Oberschall, and also in McAdam, *Political Process and Black Insurgency*, ch. 1. A systematic model of grievance and mobilization is in Davies, while Gurr presents the classic "frustration-aggression" hypothesis. A succinct critique and response may be found in Waterman. Waterman's resource-mobilization-like "political" explanation of collective action explicitly excludes explanations based on mass socioeconomic frustration, organizational dynamics and career ladders, psychocultural factors, modernization, and "strain" (582–86).

7. I include rational choice, resource mobilization, political economy, and

political process approaches under the rubric of economistic models. While recognizing the important differences among these perspectives, the common classification highlights their shared assumptions of individual, rational actors, material and structural bases of power, and the predominance of political process over political content.

8. See Hirschmann, *Exit, Voice and Loyalty*, and Olson, *Logic of Collective Action*.

9. The basic theory is presented in Tilly, *From Mobilization to Revolution*; the social context, network resources, and dynamic and interactive character of collective action are developed in Tilly's "Models and Realities of Collective Action." A classic application is Popkin, *Rational Peasant*.

10. See Gamson for a systematic application of this kind of model to movement success. Also see Tarrow, *Struggling to Reform*, 17, 19–28; id., *Struggle, Politics, and Reform*; and Marwell and Oliver.

11. Disruption is emphasized by Piven and Cloward, DeNardo, and Tarrow. But Tarrow, moving out of a resource mobilization perspective to incorporate symbolic politics, describes disruption as a combination of drama, symbolism and uncertainty—not just numbers mobilized or threat of violence. See *Struggle, Politics, and Reform*, 6–7.

12. See Chapters 2 and 3. On repression of the family see Comisión Nacional Sobre la Desaparición de Personas, *Nunca más*, 11, 284, 321–22. On the silence of the Church, see Mignone, *Iglesia y dictadura*.

13. Bousquet, *Las locas*, 47, 80.

14. See Lipsky, 1155–57, on the role of reference publics and Oberschall, 304, on reference publics' ready response to symbolic concessions.

15. See Moore, *Injustice*; Janeway, *Powers of the Weak*; Scott, *Domination and the Arts of Resistance*; Hartsock, *Money, Sex and Power*.

16. Wilson incorporates "solidary incentives," in *Political Organizations*. Tarrow simply codes symbols as a kind of resource. Popkin tells us that the rational peasant is critically influenced by "credibility, moral codes and visions of the future" (262). Charles Tilly's work does recognize a residual role for symbolic modes of collective action, through repertoires: "a model in which the accumulated experience—direct and vicarious—of contenders interacts with the strategies of authorities to make a limited number of forms of action more feasible, attractive and frequent than many others which could, in principle, serve the same interests" ("European Violence and Collective Action since 1700," 176).

17. See Pizzorno, "Political Exchange and Collective Identity"; Cohen, "Strategy or Identity"; Evers, "Identity," p.56.

18. See Melucci, "Symbolic Challenge," and Offe, "New Social Movements."

19. See Dalton and Kuechler, eds., 298; D. Slater, "Social Movements and a Recasting of the Political," 2–3; Rosenthal and Schwartz, "Spontaneity and Democracy in Social Movements"; Laclau, "New Social Movements and the Plurality of the Social," in Slater, ed. Since the members of new social movements are often women, some theorists have linked the assertion of difference to a feminist logic—that is, a women's stance toward politics—which may or

may not involve "women's issues." For an application of this perspective to the Argentine human rights movement, see Elshtain, "Antigone's Daughters," 59: "Maternal thinking, like Antigone's protest, is a rejection of amoral statecraft and an affirmation of the dignity of the human person."

20. For a systematic review, see Escobar and Alvarez, "Introduction: Theory and Protest in Latin America Today." Representative treatments include Elizabeth Jelin, ed., *Los nuevos movimientos sociales*; Mainwaring and Viola, "New Social Movements"; and Slater, ed., *New Social Movements in Latin America*. Eckstein suggests that Latin America's "bureaucratic centralist" heritage may influence protest to avoid direct challenges to the state and focus on "nonpolitical" issues, in *Power and Popular Protest*, 53.

21. For Latin America, a fruitful approach is a recognition of the emergence of postmodernity in societies which are not yet postmaterial. See Eyerman, "Modernity and Social Movements," 37–54, for a characterization of postmodernity in terms of growth of the state, mass media, and knowledge industry; Rafael de la Cruz arrives at a similar framework for NSMs in Latin America as the result of a triple rupture of state, economic, and cultural models, in "Nuevos movimientos sociales en Venezuela." Hegedus highlights the "planetarization" of such movements and their broad social impact.

22. Existing studies of the movement tend to fall into the new social movement framework, particularly those which focus on the Mothers of the Disappeared. See Schirmer, "Those Who Die for Life"; Navarro, "Personal Is Political."

23. One indication of the early emergence of this dilemma is a provision in Las Madres founding charter, written in 1979, when political parties were banned under the dictatorship, that forbid the founders from joining political parties (see Feijóo and Gogna, 87).

24. See Downs, "Up and Down with Ecology." Jacobo Timerman suggested an "information cycle" interpretation of the declining strength of human rights activity under Alfonsín (interview, July 28, 1988). These cycles may be related to a more general pattern of social protest cycles, see Tarrow 1989. The competing interest basis for mobilization in Argentina was economic.

25. Eventually, family-based movements, civil libertarians, and religious activists were drawn back to their original concerns, which had been temporarily unified by resistance to state terror. Even within the family-based branch of the movement, the Mothers' and Grandmothers' organizations mark the ideological extremes of the movement. Some of the difference is strategic, since Grandmothers of missing children can still benefit from working with the government. But this division also reflects diverging interpretations of the common symbolic identity of motherhood: although many members of both groups are the same chronological age, they identify with different generational roles.

26. Alvarez and Escobar emphasize the need for further research on this question, commenting: "The symbolic politics of social movements, in short, merits much closer social scientific scrutiny than it has heretofore received" ("Theoretical and Political Horizons of Change," 328).

27. See Ralph Turner, 147–49.

28. Note the similarity to Brian Smith's treatment of change in the Chilean Church as comprising changes in "norms, structures and behavior," in *Church and Politics in Chile*, 7. In his view, new value orientations lead to institutional reform, which produces behavior change; he also stresses the pivotal role of institutionalization.

29. Mainwaring and Viola, 17. It is important for this case to emphasize that political discourse includes what is NOT said, and that the "style of doing politics" includes the decision to withdraw from political activity. Note that since discourse is a social interaction and doing politics is active rather than attitudinal, the individual-level surveys used by previous studies of "political culture" will not adequately capture this dimension of social change.

30. Giddens contends that actors' "practical consciousness" gives them the power to change social systems (114). Also see Tilman Evers, 51. Practices can lag behind reform through routinized domination, but practices can also precede reform through humanizing exceptions to authoritarian institutions or values.

31. While this was certainly the case in Argentina, it raises the larger question of whether this is necessarily the case—as argued in some feminist interpretations of women's human rights protest. The extension of mothering into the public sphere is an important element in many forms of women's political activity and presents a healthy challenge to rational actor approaches' tendency to assume that individuals must consciously decide to identify with any collective interest. However, the argument that mothers naturally or universally have an overriding interest in their children's survival must be tempered with an appreciation of the strategic uses of maternal legitimacy, and explain why mothers routinely send their children off to war. On these points, see Elshtain, *Women and War*; Navarro; Chaney, *Supermadre*.

32. An example of the legitimacy and assumption of nonthreatening character that the military granted to mothers in their maternal role is the pattern of mothers being admitted to military bases and police stations to search for their children, while lawyers and other relatives were excluded. See Feijóo and Gogna, 91. This legitimacy could be characterized as charisma, since the classic treatment in Weber deals with the role of priests and stresses the connection with a central experience such as a rite of passage (motherhood would seem to qualify), in Eisenstadt, ed., xxv, xl, xli.

33. Corradi, "Mode of Destruction," 63.

34. See Corradi, Fagen, and Garretón, eds., *Fear at the Edge*. On fear and violence as "power deflation," Arendt, "Communicative Power," 64–65; for an application to the Argentine case, see Corradi, "Culture of Fear in Civil Society," 113.

35. The study by Guillermo O'Donnell and Cecilia Galli is discussed in Corradi, "Culture of Fear in Civil Society," 119.

36. Ibid., 124. The "development of cultures of solidarity" bears important similarities to the process of counterhegemony discussed below as a source of change.

37. For literature on this point from a variety of perspectives, see Rosen-

berg, *Reason, Ideology, and Politics*; Edelman, *Symbolic Uses of Politics*; George, "Operational Code"; Victor Turner, *Dramas, Fields, and Metaphors*; Drescher, Sabean, and Sharlin, eds., *Political Symbolism in Modern Europe*; Feldman, "Stories as Cultural Creativity."

38. Taussig, "Culture of Terror—Space of Death," 494.

39. In a related framework, Snow and Benford describe changing consciousness as a form of reframing, with the achievement of "frame resonance" linked to communicative coherence, credibility, and narrative fidelity.

40. An overall summary of the dramaturgical perspective is found in Hare and Blumberg. Search involves a relatively powerless protagonist overcoming obstacles to remedy a personal loss (ibid., 18–19); the antecedents of search for a lost child are probably traceable to Demeter. Anne Pescatello ties the tradition of the *mater dolorosa* in Latin America to the Christianization of goddess myths in which a grieving mother-goddess appears with a son who dies (*Female and Male in Latin America*, 92). The cross-cutting dramatic theme of a struggle over burial rights pitting the family against the state first appears prominently in the Western tradition in Antigone; this parallel has been explored by several Argentine intellectuals, notably Oscar Terán.

41. Jelin, *Women and Social Change in Latin America*, 5.

42. Another indication of the cultural resonance of the Plaza de Mayo as a setting for protest was the "offer" by the dictatorship's police to allow the Madres to continue their protest—if they would move to some other plaza; see Feijóo and Gogna, 92.

43. This implication of a symbolic logic of collective action stands in sharp contrast to economistic approaches that model the goals of protest as virtually interchangeable "political goods" or "preferences"—to be "purchased" once sufficient resources are accumulated. For an extreme example, see DeNardo. Some sophisticated rational actor approaches do recognize that the content of the goals of collective action conditions the strategies, opportunities, and constraints of social movements. See Wilson, 330.

44. See Rossi, 168–70, and Gewirth, 3, 5, 8. On Argentina, see the interview with Adolfo Perez-Esquivel, founder of SERPAJ, in López Saavedra, *Testigos*, 110.

45. For a general discussion of principled human rights activism, see Fruhling, "La defensa de los Derechos Humanos en el Cono Sur."

46. For the classic formulation of the state as the holder of the legitimate monopoly on violence, see Weber, *Theory of Social and Economic Organization*. In his discussion of genocide, Irving Horowitz treats the "special relationship between the state and its monopoly on life-taking propensities . . . [the] presumption of taking life as a unique capacity, morally and legally, of the authority system within a society" (*Taking Lives*, xiii). The Interamerican Commission on Human Rights of the Organization of American States invoked this principle in its 1980 report on Argentina, in response to government criticism that the commission was "one-sided" in its focus on state terror: international organizations have a mandate to protect the citizen from the state, and it is the state's

responsibility to protect the citizen from unofficial terrorism (*Report on the Situation of Human Rights in Argentina*, 25–26).

47. Under authoritarian or totalitarian rule, the protection of human rights may require the state to limit its coercive activities, but under a weak authoritarian or even democratic regime, human rights may require an *extension* of state power over the coercive activities of private or semi-private agents. The lack of legitimate political project inherent in the authoritarian regime type is first discussed in Linz, "Totalitarian and Authoritarian Regimes." For applications of human rights to the legitimacy of authoritarian projects in Latin America, see Gomez, "Derechos humanos, politica y autoritarismo en el Cono Sur," 145, and Lechner, *Los derechos humanos como categoria politica*, 98–99.

48. For a full treatment of the impact of the transnational human rights alliance in Argentina, see Brysk, "From Above and Below," *Comparative Political Studies*, Fall 1993.

49. Human rights violations are characterized as "crimes against humanity." Many international agreements invoke respect for human rights as an implied condition of sovereignty; see Montealegre, 189, 206–7. The defining characteristics of human rights (preceding any specific claims) are that they are rights, are universal, stand independent of national recognition or implementation, imply duties, and establish minimum standards (Nickel, 3). The international system is often seen as a "court of last resort" for human rights (Donnelly, *Concept of Human Rights*, 21).

50. An international regime is generally defined as a nonbinding collection of arrangements and institutions that shape state behavior. "International regimes are defined as principles, norms, rules and decision-making procedures around which actor expectations converge in a given issue-area" (Krasner, 1). Donnelly applies this model to the international organizations and mechanisms concerned with human rights in "International Human Rights: A Regime Analysis." Also see David Forsythe, *Human Rights and World Politics*, 211.

51. Lipsky introduced the use of reference publics as a source of leverage for protest groups, 1144–50.

52. Cobb and Elder, 85.

53. On agenda limitation as a form of power, see Bachrach and Baratz, "Decisions and Non-Decisions," 632. Also see the discussion of Bachrach and Baratz's "mobilization of bias" in Giddens, 89.

54. Success in agenda-building has been linked to: the use of nontraditional tactics and broad, evocative symbols, the support of outsiders and an issue that is inherently ambiguous, long-range, nontechnical, unprecedented, and carries wide social significance. See Cobb and Elder, 40–50, 94–96, 112.

55. See Landi, "La transición politica argentina y la cuestión de los derechos humanos," 40, on the logic of the system in regard to the public-private distinction and responsibility for human rights violations.

56. Interview, Northern Argentina, Nov. 2, 1988.

57. Reprinted in Bennett and Simpson, *The Disappeared and the Mothers of the Plaza*, 41.

58. Arendt, *Human Condition*, 50–58.

59. The Argentine military regime refused to acknowledge state responsibility for and participation in kidnappings, even publishing accounts that handcuffed persons had died in guerrilla shoot-outs. See Gillespie, *Soldiers of Peron*, 235. Details of the practice and denial of repression are provided in Chapter 2.

60. Interview, July 28, 1988. Jacobo Timerman is an Argentine newspaper publisher, prominent in the Jewish community, who was kidnapped, tortured, officially imprisoned, and eventually released by the military dictatorship. His account of these experiences, *Prisoner Without a Name, Cell Without a Number*, raised international awareness of human rights abuses in Argentina.

61. See Eisenstadt, ed., *Max Weber: On Charisma and Institution Building*, esp. 87, on the role of formal justice. An Argentine illustration is the prosecution response to the former military rulers' claim that their trials were invalid since the alleged victims were subversives: "The law punishes homicide and does not distinguish by the ideology of its authors or its victims" (Strassera and Moreno Ocampo, *Será justicia*, 85–86).

62. In fact, the Madres' first paid advertisement specifically cited a statement General Videla had made during a visit to the United States promising to tell the truth. See Bennett and Simpson, 160. The ad appeared in *La Prensa*, Oct. 5, 1977.

63. Even the failed attempt to capture the Malvinas that precipitated the collapse of military rule has been seen as a last-ditch attempt to legitimate the Dirty War through victory in a "clean" war against a foreign enemy. See Rozitchner, *Malvinas: De la guerra sucia a la guerra limpia*, esp. 97–98.

64. Interview, Buenos Aires, Aug. 12, 1987.

65. On the role of democratic accountability in defining citizenship and legitimating democracy, see O'Donnell and Schmitter, *Transitions from Authoritarian Rule—Conclusion*, 7.

66. Interviews with a representative of Las Abuelas, Aug. 8, 1987; Mar. 25, 1988.

67. Tarrow comments that there is "little consensus on what constitutes social movement success, with some researchers regarding simple survival as an indicator of success in a hostile world, while others insist upon systemic social change as their standard" and defines success as "policy innovation addressing the protestors' stated needs" (*Struggling to Reform*, 4–7). In the most comprehensive treatment in the resource mobilization tradition, Gamson codes outcomes as "advantages" and "acceptance," which are operationalized as "the fate of challengers and the advantage gained for beneficiaries" (*Strategy of Social Protest*, 28).

68. Piven and Cloward measure the emergence of a protest movement as a combination of a transformation of consciousness and behavior (*Poor People's Movements*, 3–4). A leading political process theorist has introduced the concept of a group process of "cognitive liberation" as a critical mediating variable in the emergence of protest, which incorporates delegitimation, perception of the need for change, and efficacy (McAdam, 2, 36–59). Similarly, Moore iden-

tifies critical elements of resistance as the reversal of self-enforcement of oppression and redirection outward, the development of new standards to explain suffering and demonstrate an alternative, personalizing the responsibility of authority and "contract voiding" (*Injustice*, 113).

69. General discussions of the panoply of changes involved in assessing impact are found in both Klandermans, ed., *Organizing for Change*, and Huberts.

70. For a related overview of internal movement development, see Offe, "Institutional Self-Transformation," in Dalton and Kuechler.

71. Oberschall, 243.

72. "Reforms producing institutionalized participation are both more durable and more productive of further reforms, than substantive rights" (Tarrow, *Struggle, Politics, and Reform*, 94; see also *Struggling to Reform*, 15–17, 45).

73. Boschi, *On Social Movements and Democratization*, 7, 12.

74. Munck, 28, stresses that Latin new social movements generally emerge in a context of regime change, and that for Latin NSMs, regime type is both a dependent and independent variable. From a modified resource mobilization perspective, Tarrow's depiction of political opportunity structures will also pick up many aspects of democratic transitions: openness of polity, stability of political alignments, elite tolerance, and even protest cycles. Tarrow moves beyond the resource mobilization tradition and approaches this analysis when he states that groups can help to create their own opportunities. See *Struggle, Politics, and Reform*, 34–36.

75. Earlier literature on democratization, such as Schmitter, O'Donnell, and Whitehead's study, mentions social movements but does not explore their role. The recent emphasis on pacts and negotiations has an inherent elite bias, seen in works as diverse as DiPalma, Przeworski, and Higley and Gunther. The best attempt to model the role of social movements from the democratization literature is Garretón, *Dictaduras y democratización*, 72, which suggests that different kinds of actors will predominate during the transition and consolidation phases of democracy. "Destabilizers" are necessary to introduce mobilization and contestation to catalyze the transition itself, but democratic consolidation requires "concertation": coordination of diverse constituencies under new rules of the game and a common social project.

76. Munck, 32.

77. Interview, Aug. 17, 1988.

78. Besides outright repression, a government can attack the group, discredit group leaders, appeal to members past the leaders, coopt leaders, provide symbolic reassurance, take token action, create a new organization to symbolize concern with the issue, coopt movement symbols, grant anticipatory concessions to preempt mobilization or disruption, feign constraint, or just postpone action (see Cobb and Elder, 125–29; a similar set of responses appeared earlier in Lipsky, 1150–57). The latter tactic relies on the "law of passive advantage"; since movements always have fewer resources and a lower level of organization than governments, delay—especially ambiguous delay—can only erode movement cohesion (see Lofland and Fink, 99).

79. Wilson, 15, makes the general point that organizations are both empowered and limited by their formative experiences.

80. Mainwaring and Viola, 20.

81. "These organizational pressures frequently mean that a protest tactic originally adopted to enable a group to get into a bargaining relationship with another party can be carried out in ways that make bargaining difficult, if not impossible" (Wilson, 293).

82. Leaders also experienced persecution, economic insecurity, lack of formal status, disruption of family life, and uncritical movement admiration—all of which exacerbated the development of inflexible, insensitive tendencies among some movement leaders. See Oberschall, 148, on the situational factors that aggravate inflexible leadership. In Argentina, a prime example is the bitter split between two factions of Las Madres. Many observers in and out of the movement attribute the split to the personal qualities and leadership style of the president of Las Madres, Hebe de Bonafini.

83. Alfonsín, "Building Democracy," 121.

84. Flisfich, 110.

85. In his historical study of the development of human rights, Claude identifies a "secure and procedurally regularized legal system" as the one universal precondition for the development of human rights (*Comparative Human Rights*, 10).

86. Garretón characterizes this recomposition, revaluation, and (subsequent) remobilization of civil society as the "invisible transition" to democracy (see *Reconstruir la política*, 35, 40–43). Civil society will be treated further in Chapters 8 and 9.

87. See Bermeo, "Democracy and the Lessons of Dictatorship," 273–91.

Chapter 2

1. See Glossary for acronyms, brief descriptions, and translations of the names of Argentine human rights organizations, political parties, and other key political institutions. Table 2 lists Argentina's regimes in chronological order.

2. This analysis bears some similarity to Guillermo O'Donnell's characterization of the "constants" of the Argentine social and historical legacy: the dependence of the Argentine economy on international trade and capital movements, the strong disaffection of vast sectors based on highly significant cleavages and unequal distribution of political resources, a high degree of incongruence between political behavior and formal institutions and ideologies, the application of democratic "rules of the game" only when they produce the "correct" government (i.e., one acceptable to dominant social forces), and strong resistance by established political actors to the participation of new actors, even when such participation involves relatively low risks. See O'Donnell, *Modernization and Bureaucratic-Authoritarianism*, 118–32.

3. A classic treatment of these themes is Halperin Donghi, *Argentina en el callejón*.

4. This parallels the oft-cited paradox of German sponsorship of the Holocaust and raises fundamental questions concerning the relationship between modernity and repression.

5. See Solberg, "Land Tenure and Land Settlement."

6. Like the United States, Argentina eliminated rather than enslaving and assimilating its Indian population—contrasting sharply with the typical Latin American (especially Andean) experience. At the height of European immigration (around 1880–1920), immigrants made up almost one-third of the population of Argentina. The percentage of immigrants to native population was approximately twice that found in the United States. See Crassweller, *Perón and the Enigmas of Argentina*, 46.

7. For an analysis of the differences between immigration to Argentina and to other "lands of recent settlement," see Waisman, "Argentina: Autarkic Industrialization," 61. The political influence of the rural immigrant population is discussed in Solberg, *The Prairies and the Pampas*, 29–31.

8. By 1914, almost 30 percent of Argentines were middle-class (Solberg, *The Prairies and the Pampas*, 20). On the nature and role of Argentina's middle class, see Rock, "Radical Populism and the Conservative Elite, 1912–1930," esp. 69. The Argentine middle class did serve as the original impetus for democratic reform, but in a careful alliance with the economic elite.

9. See Waisman, *Reversal of Development in Argentina*, esp. xii, 66–77.

10. While in Canada, the Argentine intellectual Jorge Sábato was asked to explain the divergent paths of the two nations; he responded, "Can any of you name the commander of the Canadian Army? Because I can name—from memory and in order—the names of the last 25 Commanders of the Argentine Army. That is the difference between our countries" (Giussani, *Los días de Alfonsín*, 21).

11. See Rock, "Survival and Restoration of Peronism," 207. Rouquié presents a contrasting argument, claiming that coups were preceded by rapid growth, but he eventually links military intervention to other indicators of financial crisis (*Poder militar*, 389–97).

12. See Waisman in Peralta-Ramos and Waisman, 101.

13. Rock, *Argentina in the Twentieth Century*, 6.

14. See Diamand, "Overcoming Argentina's Stop-and-Go Economic Cycles"; William Smith, *Authoritarianism and the Crisis of the Argentine Political Economy*, esp. ch. 2.

15. Thus, political crises have predictably followed the decline in the early twentieth century of the hegemony of Britain (Argentina's former major customer), barriers to the export of Argentine beef (especially in 1928 and 1974), and droughts in 1951–52. However, classical trade dependency has decreased since World War II and has been replaced by a major increase in financial dependency since the 1970's (Waisman, *Reversal of Development*, 66).

16. Interview, Aug. 5, 1987. Historians note that the Argentine agricultural oligarchy had fallen behind in research, transport, and marketing even before

industrialization produced the unbalanced model (Solberg, *The Prairies and the Pampas*, 4). Also see Cortés Conde on institutional and technological backwardness in Argentine industry preceding the Peronist wave of import substitution.

17. Waisman, *Reversal of Development*, 123. The first administration of Juan Perón (1946–55) is generally credited with the definitive introduction of import-substituting industrialization, as well as the corporatist organization of the working class, which granted unions a privileged relationship with the state.

18. On the alternation between policy strategies, see DiTella and Dornbusch, eds., *Political Economy of Argentina, 1946–83*, esp. the introduction, and Diamand, "Argentina's Stop-and-Go Economic Cycles."

19. See Diaz Alejandro, *Essays on the Economic History of the Argentine Republic*.

20. On this point and its relationship to inelasticities, see ibid., and Diamand, "Overcoming Argentina's Stop-and-Go Economic Cycles."

21. Since Peronist policies of the 1940's had redistributed income to both urban workers and industrialists, the dominant Peronist/anti-Peronist cleavage was more accurately a conflict between opposing polyclass coalitions than a class conflict through the 1960's. See Little, "Popular Origins of Peronism," and Rock, "Survival and Restoration of Peronism" in Rock, ed.

22. See O'Donnell, *Modernization and Bureaucratic-Authoritarianism*, 138–48, and Rock, "Survival and Restoration of Peronism," 195.

23. See Rouquié, esp. "Hegemonía militar, estado y dominacíon social," in Rouquié, ed., *Argentina hoy*, esp. 18–26, 45.

24. See William Smith, *Authoritarianism and the Crisis of the Argentine Political Economy*, 267.

25. Rouquié, *Poder militar*, 340. For governments of Argentina, 1930–90, see Table 2.

26. Crassweller, *Perón and the Enigmas of Argentina*, 62.

27. See Cavarozzi, "Argentina's Political Cycles," 31–32.

28. Rock, *Argentina, 1516–1987*, 346–47.

29. See Rouquié, *Poder militar*, esp. 341, 368, 316–25.

30. See O'Donnell, *Modernization and Bureaucratic-Authoritarianism*, 115, 163. The pattern of delaying a planned coup in order to garner civilian support was repeated in 1976.

31. See ibid., 118–47; Waisman, "Argentina: Autarkic Industrialization," 70; Rouquié, *Poder militar*, 380, 420.

32. The dates of states of siege are recorded in Villalba Walsh, 123.

33. Crassweller, *Perón and the Enigmas of Argentina*, 191–203.

34. See Rock, *Argentina, 1516–1987*, 214–17. "Ballot rigging became a pandemic practice in the 1930's" (217).

35. Ibid., 344.

36. Waisman, *Reversal of Development*, xii.

37. This is the main thesis of Waisman, *Reversal of Development* (see 175–78 for a discussion on the role of the Church as an ideological filter). Also see Rosales, "La reconciliación," 45–50. The phrase "anticommunism without Communists" appears in Rouquié, *Poder militar*, 356.

38. Crassweller, *Perón and the Enigmas of Argentina*, 349, 281.
39. See Villalba Walsh, 21.
40. The "Brigada de Orden Social" arm of the Buenos Aires police was founded following the first general strike, in 1902. This was coupled with the appearance of ultra-nationalist armed gangs and strike-breaking death squads, such as the Liga Patriotica and the *gendarmeria volante* of La Forestal (1920–21). See Rodriguez Molas, *Historia de la tortura*, 85–88. During the famous Semana Trágica of January 1919, a general strike in Buenos Aires led to anti-labor, anti-immigrant, and anti-Semitic riots by the Army, police, Liga Patriotica, and members of the elite, resulting in hundreds of deaths. See Rock, "Lucha civil en la Argentina"; also see Mirelman, 61–63. A few years later, in 1920–22, a group of striking rural workers in Patagonia were brutally repressed by the military; somewhere between 1,000 and 1,500 were killed. See Bayer, *La Patagonia rebelde*. Sources include an interview with a representative of La Liga, Apr. 6, 1988.
41. Rodriguez Molas, *Historia de la tortura*, 87–92. Between 1931–34, it is estimated that around 500 prisoners (5 percent of the prison population) were tortured. It was also at this time that the *picana electrica*—the electric cattle prod found on Argentine ranches—was introduced as an instrument of torture (100–103).
42. Ibid., 117, 160. Testimony from 1948 cites precursors of Proceso-era techniques such as the hooding of victims and the playing of radios to cover screams.
43. Villalba Walsh, 41.
44. Rodriguez Molas, *Historia de la tortura*, 127, 130, 132. Under questioning by the Senate, President Arturo Frondizi's minister of the interior admitted that the routine use of torture by police continued under the successor civilian government.
45. Villalba Walsh, 68. After troops assaulted the university, Onganía claimed that there were no political prisoners in Argentina—and was presented by the CGT labor federation with an 8-page list.
46. Rodriguez Molas, *Historia de la tortura*, 212. A La Liga attorney cited the similar cases of Juan Ingalinella (1955), the labor organizer Felipe Vallese (1962), and the lawyer Nestor Martins (1970), who disappeared with his client (interview, Apr. 6, 1988). The police officer accused in the Vallese case subsequently became the head of a concentration camp during the Proceso (*Pagina Doce*, Aug. 23, 1988).
47. For figures on the level of strikes, demonstrations and acts of political violence, see O'Donnell, *El estado burocrático-autoritario, 1966–1973*, 437–48.
48. For a general account of the Montoneros, see Richard Gillespie, *Soldiers of Perón*. Martin Edwin Andersen argues that the Montoneros were penetrated by Argentine military intelligence, which distorted their original political strategy and program, in *Dossier secreto*, esp. the chapter on López Rega. The Tucumán insurgency and repression is also profiled in Andersen; see the chapter titled "Tucumán: A Rumor of War."
49. Rock, *Argentina, 1516–1987*, 355.

50. For figures on Triple A victims, see González Janzen, *La Triple A*, 19; Rock, *Argentina, 1516–1987*, 363–64; Bennett and Simpson, 65; Amnesty International, *Argentina: The Military Juntas*, 3.

51. See Richard Gillespie, *Soldiers of Perón*, 155; González Janzen, 16, and Verbitsky, *La posguerra sucia*, 28. Gillespie claims that the Triple A had killed at least 200 by September 1974 and notes that often police guards would leave before the death squad struck. Early victims included a Peronist congressional deputy, a leftist professor who was the brother of former President Frondizi, and the Chilean leader Salvador Allende's former military commander, Carlos Prats.

52. For Triple A methods and personnel linked to the Ministry of Social Welfare, see González Janzen, 15–16. Because of these links, Minister of Social Welfare José López Rega was charged in the 1974 murder of the congressional Deputy Rodolfo Ortega Peña (*Pagina Doce*, Apr. 19, 1988). The popular perception of official sponsorship is reflected in the alternate designation of the death squad as "Los Tres A"—which had the double meaning of the group's acronym and a shortened form for the Armed Forces ("Las Tres Armas").

53. See Amnesty International, *Argentina: The Military Juntas*, 7; Villalba Walsh, 119; Duhalde, *El estado terrorista argentino*, 47.

54. See Richard Gillespie, *Soldiers of Perón*, 204, and Amnesty International, *Argentina: The Military Juntas*, 3; Frontalini and Caiati, *El mito de la guerra sucia*, 58, and Andersen, *Dossier secreto*, on the disparity between armed forces and guerrilla combatants. Frontalini claims it was 5,000 to 500, while Andersen presents new evidence that the ERP fielded a maximum of only 120 guerrillas—and usually fewer than one hundred.

55. See Bousquet, 36; Cavarozzi, *Autoritarismo y democracia, 1955–1983*, 57; and Frontalini and Caiati, *El mito de la guerra sucia*, 74.

56. Comisión Nacional sobre la Desaparición de Personas, *Nunca más*, 55; Verbitsky, *La posguerra sucia*, 145–50; also see "La guerra sucia empezó en 1975," *El Periodista*, Jan. 31–Feb. 6, 1986, for a more comprehensive treatment of clandestine repression before the coup.

57. Richard Gillespie, *Soldiers of Perón*, 235; Duhalde, 146.

58. The prisoners involved were generally socialist, communist, anarchist, or labor activists who had been officially imprisoned. It was a Liga lawyer who popularized the use of habeas corpus as a defense for political prisoners, and Liga attorneys persisted despite tremendous personal risks—including being jailed, tortured, and (later) disappeared along with their clients. See Villalba Walsh, 107–8. A Liga lawyer interviewed had been jailed eight times, under a variety of governments, for periods of up to six years (interview, Apr. 6, 1988).

59. Rodriguez Molas, *Historia de la tortura*, 193.

60. Interview with a former member of a committee, Sept. 28, 1988. Other precursors of human rights activity during this era include the 1961 publication of newspaper advertisements by the wife of a prominent detainee, and protests at the funerals of priests killed by the Triple A during the early 1970's (see Rodriguez Molas, *Historia de la tortura*, 202; González Janzen, 114).

61. The Centro de Estudios Legales y Sociales's archives house a report by

the Forum condemning prison abuses of the early 1970's, including the Trelew massacre. The affiliated Asociación Gremial de Abogados had 400 members in 1973; see Richard Gillespie, *Soldiers of Peron*, 69.

62. Perón, who had alternately favored various social forces while consolidating his power, turned definitively against the left on May Day 1974, when he ordered the Montonero guerrillas out of the Plaza de Mayo during a May Day rally. In the provinces, a right-wing faction overthrew the elected (leftist Peronist) governor of Cordoba province after the governor had fired the repressive police chief—and Perón backed the right-wing usurpers. On these incidents, see Corradi, *Fitful Republic*, 100; Richard Gillespie, *Soldiers of Perón*; and González Jansen, 113.

63. For a detailed account, see Verbitsky, *Ezeiza*. Crassweller cites attendance figures at somewhere between one and a half million and four million, with a "consensus estimate of two hundred dead and more than a thousand injured" (*Perón and the Enigmas of Argentina*, 357–58).

64. Vázquez, *PRN la ultima*, 18.

65. Rock, *Argentina, 1516–1987*, 365–66; a typical austerity measure was a 160 percent devaluation of Argentine currency; also see Monteón, 25. Inflation figures can be found in William Smith, *Authoritarianism*, 230.

66. Andersen's *Dossier secreto* provides systematic and detailed refutation of the Dirty War argument. For a general rejection of equating guerrilla and state terror, see Cavarozzi in A. Bruno, M. Cavarozzi and V. Palermo, eds., *Los derechos humanos en la democracia*. Waisman notes that no real revolutionary threat existed during the 1970's because the state apparatus was still intact, labor was still Peronist, and the left pursued a guerrilla rather than a political/organizational strategy (*Reversal of Development*, 279).

67. Frontalini and Caiati, *El mito de la guerra sucia*, 63. "At the height of their power, with their political and organizational structures practically intact, the insurgent forces didn't exceed 2,000 people, of which only 20 percent were armed (deduced from the composition of the cells) . . . the Armed Forces and security forces accounted for a quantity of approximately 200,000 troops" (ibid., 72).

68. See Rock, *Argentina, 1516–1987*, 376; Richard Gillespie, *Soldiers of Peron*; Amnesty International, *Argentina: The Military Juntas*, 56.

69. A study based on newspaper reports of the period shows that in 1973–74, 91.8 percent of those listed as guerrillas were detained rather than killed, while almost one-third of base activists were killed or injured rather than captured. See Marín, *Los hechos armados*, 147. A disproportionate number of Montonero leaders were warned or offered exile, while detaining people in family homes and workplaces obviously increased confrontations with more open activists rather than underground guerrillas.

70. See Asamblea Permanente por los Derechos Humanos, "Informe realizado por la APDH," which addresses this issue focusing on data from Tucumán, the area of greatest armed conflict. A typical relationship between deaths from subversion (including civilian casualties of urban terrorism and death squad victims) and state terror is 1:14 (ibid., table 2). In Tucumán, with less

urban terrorism and more armed conflict, the relationship rises to 1:25. Also see Duhalde, 89, and Comisión Nacional sobre la Desaparición de Personas, *Nunca más* (1986), 220–21, which note the suspiciously high proportion of prisoners killed while being transferred—with no prisoners injured and no casualties among security forces.

71. Particularly influential incidents were the 1969 Cordobazo and 1971 Viborazo, economically inspired protests that turned into riots, involving both students and workers. See Rock, "Survival of Peronism," 211–15.

72. See O'Donnell, *El estado burocrático-autoritario*, 464, 467.

73. See William Smith, *Authoritarianism*, 218; O'Donnell, *El estado burocrático-autoritario*, 476–78.

74. Richard Gillespie, *Soldiers of Perón*, 120.

75. This analysis is offered by Marcelo Cavarozzi in "Argentine Political Cycles," 42. This perception, and its link to preexisting intellectual currents, can be seen in the following text offered at a 1977 political training session attended by the military high command: "Populism, classism, and socialism are three examples of ideologies whose infiltration into Argentine nationalism distorts and confuses. . . . Populism is radically subversive. . . . As the Church teaches . . . power and political sovereignty come from God. . . . The consent of the governed is not even necessary. . . . The legitimacy of a government is not rooted in elections . . . Legitimacy or justification is obedience to the goal, which is to serve the Common Good" (Vázquez, *PRN la ultima*, 83–87).

76. A direct example of international learning in this regard is provided by the experience of an Abuela (grandmother) who begged a high-ranking officer to transfer her disappeared daughter to official, acknowledged imprisonment "at the disposal of the Executive." The officer replied: "In Uruguay, I saw that the Tupumaros [guerrillas] got stronger in prison, and even began to convince the guards. So here we don't imprison people" (from the television broadcast "¡Nunca más!" in July 1984). Similarly, an officer told CELS activist Augusto Conte, pleading for a trial for his disappeared son, "By the third execution, international reaction would make us stop" (Verbitsky, *La posguerra sucia*, 82).

77. Between 1950 and 1978, Argentina—a nation of dubious strategic significance—had received $250 million in U.S. military aid and trained over 4,000 officers at the U.S. Army School of the Americas in Panama. See Schoultz, *Human Rights and U.S. Policy Towards Latin America*, 232. Specifically, several of the leaders of the dictatorship had trained in the United States. In turn, the Proceso included a role for Argentina as a U.S. surrogate in Latin America, training traditional U.S. clients in covert methodologies not acknowledged by the U.S. government: Argentina provided paramilitary training to the Nicaraguan Contras, Hondurans, Guatemalans, and Salvadorans. See Dabat and Lorenzano, 80–82; also see *Clarín*, June 20, 1988.

78. See Bousquet, 36, on U.S. policymakers' oblique warning to the Argentine military "not to create another Chile"; this interpretation was also stressed by Asamblea leaders (interview, Aug. 10, 1987). One of the more outspoken advocates of state terror, General Ramón Camps, disagreed with this strategy but admitted that "no one told the truth so as not to affect international eco-

nomic aid" (interview with Camps, Jan. 1983, cited in Rock, *Argentina, 1516–1987*, 385).

79. Kissinger is said merely to have warned that problems should be solved before the U.S. Congress reconvened in 1977. Details appear in a story by the U.S. journalist and long-time Argentine correspondent Martin Edwin Andersen in *El Periodista*, Oct. 23–28, 1987, which also appeared in *The Nation*, Oct. 24, 1987.

80. See Andersen, *Dossier secreto*.

81. On this point, see William Smith, *Authoritarianism*, 231–33. Smith traces the repression more to foundational than to counterrevolutionary strategy, echoing the critique of the "Dirty War" argument presented above. Corradi distinguishes the Proceso as "a dictatorship *sine die* with developmental goals" in contrast to the bureaucratic-authoritarian Onganía regime, "a dictatorship *sine die* with negative reconstructionist objectives" ("Mode of Destruction," 64). Vázquez cites a series of political programs discussed or adopted by the military, which reflect a spectrum from neopopulism to tutelary phased transition to totalitarian mobilization and "reeducation" of civil society (*PRN la ultima*, passim). One index of the level of corruption during the Proceso was the discovery during 1982 IMF negotiations that there was no record of what had been done with $10 billion of Argentina's external debt, which then totaled $40 billion. See William Smith, "Reflections on the Political Economy of Authoritarian Rule," 64.

82. The classic demobilization definition of bureaucratic-authoritarianism is found in O'Donnell, *Modernization and Bureaucratic-Authoritarianism*, 54, who also discusses the redefinition of popular mobilization as subversion (72).

83. Corradi, "Mode of Destruction," 65.

84. "Acta fijando el propósito y los objetivos basicos para el Proceso de Reorganización Nacional," *Boletín Oficial*, Mar. 29, 1976, reprinted in Vázquez, *PRN la ultima*, 216.

85. The acts of the Proceso and other basic documents are reprinted in Vázquez, *PRN la ultima*, 213; also see Organization of American States, *Report*, 15–18, 220–24. In a move fraught with future significance, one of the military's first acts was a law subjecting all security forces exclusively to military justice (Duhalde, 103).

86. In the past, the Army had always dominated military governments. One indication of both the level of military control and the feudalization of power is the assignment of a television station to each service (Vázquez, *PRN la ultima*, 159).

87. For succinct expressions of the Argentine doctrine, see Fuerzas Armadas Argentinas, *Marxismo y subversion*, and Luciano Benjamin Menéndez, "Terrorismo o tercera guerra mundial?" *La Nación*, Dec. 3, 1980, reprinted in Montenegro, *Así piensa . . . Luciano Benjamin Menéndez*. It is curious that a regime supposedly engaged in a Third World War against communism maintained its largest trading relationship with the Soviet Union, and exchanged military missions with the communist superpower. See Vázquez, *PRN la ultima*, 136; Frontalini and Caiati, *El mito de la guerra sucia*, 47–49.

200 ~ Notes to Pages 34–35

88. This point is stressed in Rouquié, "Hegemonía militar," esp. 356. A collection of essays on the influence of the national security doctrine on the Proceso is Lozada et al., *Inseguridad y desnacionalización*. The role of the national security doctrine in sponsoring a role for the armed forces as "restorers of equilibrium" as it corresponds to adjustment crises of dependent capitalism, as well as some contradictions between the doctrine and traditional military nationalism, are treated more briefly in Lázara, *Poder militar*, 36–50.

89. There is increasing evidence that in many cases the military did invent or exaggerate the guerrilla threat. "Of the nearly 700 assassinations attributed to the guerrillas during a ten-year period, about a quarter were the result of unrelated common crimes, intraservice military rivalries, and accidents" (Andersen, *Dossier secreto*, 13). Faced with an impending strike in September 1976 in Cordoba, soldiers printed strike leaflets signed "Montoneros" (the largest guerrilla group), thus providing justification for total war on the workers (Comisión Nacional sobre la Desaparición de Personas, *Nunca más* [1986], 371–72).

90. See Comisión Nacional sobre la Desaparición de Personas, *Nunca más* (1986), 333.

91. This Latin version of *Kinder, Kirche, und Küche* was also found (to a somewhat lesser extent) in Brazil and Chile. See Alvarez, *Engendering Democracy in Brazil*.

92. See William Smith, *Authoritarianism*, 235, for a summary of the program, and 236–42 for an account of the phases of its implementation and modification.

93. On the growth of finance capital and capital flight, see Peralta-Ramos in Peralta-Ramos and Waisman, eds., 50–60; also see Dabat and Lorenzano, 28–34. A supporting statistic indicates that between 1972 and 1982, annual growth averaged less than 1 percent, but the financial sector grew more than 5 percent a year (Lázara, *Poder militar*, 319).

94. Between 1975 and 1981, industrial production declined 17 percent (William Smith, *Authoritarianism*, 253). On how local industrialists were hurt by the military's economic policies, see Rouquié, "Hegemonía militar," 48; Pion-Berlin, *Ideology of State Terror*, 120–21.

95. First, the size of the industrial working class fell 26 percent between 1976 and 1981 (Waisman, "Argentina: Autarkic Industrialization," 82). About half of all workers moved to the tertiary sector, and the remaining industrial workers lost hours, wages, benefits, and purchasing power (Villareal, "Changes in Argentine Society," 80–85). In 1976 alone, real wages fell almost 50 percent (Rock, *Argentina, 1516–1987*, 368). Furthermore, from 1975 to 1980, salaried workers' share of the national income declined from nearly one-half to one-third. See Poneman, 5.

96. William Smith, *Authoritarianism*, 259.

97. See Pion-Berlin and Lopez, "Of Victims and Executioners," 63–86.

98. Pion-Berlin, *Ideology of State Terror*, 98. Generally, national security ideologies contribute to state terror a geopolitical focus and assessment of threat, an organic model in which the regime is equivalent to the state and state security a paramount concern, a framework of war that grants a mandate to employ

violence in the service of the dominant ideology and economic development model, and a conviction that terror represents "economy of force." See George Lopez, "National Security Ideology as an Impetus to State Violence and State Terror," 80–90.

99. Frontalini and Caiati, *El mito de la guerra sucia*, 28–29.

100. A comparative study by Pion-Berlin found a general correlation between orthodox stabilization programs and government repression of organized labor ("Political Repression and Economic Doctrines," 49).

101. Schoultz, 11. O'Donnell also stresses the "crucial importance of government coercion for bureaucratic authoritarian 'success' in excluding and deactivating the popular sector" (*Modernization and Bureaucratic-Authoritarianism*, 100).

102. General José Antonio Vaquero in *La Prensa*, May 24, 1978 (cited in Frontalini and Caiati, *El mito de la guerra sucia*, 19).

103. Frontalini and Caiati, *El mito de la guerra sucia*, 32–33.

104. The most extensive documentation of human rights violations may be found in Comisión Nacional sobre la Desaparición de Personas, *Nunca más*. Other representative accounts include Amnesty International, *Report of an Amnesty International Mission to Argentina, 6–15 November 1976*, and Organization of American States, *Report*.

105. See Figure 1; Asamblea Permanente por los Derechos Humanos, *Informe*; Dabat and Lorenzano, 149.

106. Mitchell et al., "State Terrorism," 4–5.

107. For example, after the coup, many members of the Triple A death squad were incorporated into the task forces and/or military intelligence operations (González Janzen, 20).

108. Comisión Nacional sobre la Desaparición de Personas, *Nunca más* (1986), 12–15.

109. For example, on August 22, 1976, the corpses of 30 persons alleged to have died in an armed confrontation were found handcuffed and blindfolded at Fátima (Amnesty International, *Argentina: The Military Juntas*, 26).

110. Poneman, 36.

111. Comisión Nacional sobre la Desaparición de Personas, *Nunca más* (1986), 52.

112. On torture, see ibid., 20–51. For a brief summary, see Amnesty International, *The "Disappeared" of Argentina*, 37.

113. See Comisión Nacional sobre la Desaparición de Personas, *Nunca más* (1986), 404, for 157 such cases. A well-known case with similar features involved the former senator Hipólito Solari Yrigoyen, who was originally detained by uniformed military officers, released in a faked armed confrontation owing to international pressure, and subsequently again picked up by police, brutally beaten, and held for another year. See Gabetta, *Todos somos subversivos*, 209.

114. The existence and content of central orders was established at the trials of the juntas; see *El diario del juicio*; also see on Naval Commander Massera's personal participation in task force activities, Comisión Nacional sobre la Desaparición de Personas, *Nunca más* (1986), 122. The command structure of the

repression is documented most extensively in Mittelbach, *Informe sobre desaparecedores*. Amnesty International has summarized trials testimony that, the prosecutor argued, showed "that the different branches of the armed forces exchanged both information and prisoners, loaned each other facilities and had officers visiting one another's secret prison camps" (*Argentina: The Military Juntas*, 38).

115. General Ramón Camps, a "true believer," writes that the war against subversion was directed by President Videla and conducted by regular forces (*El caso Timerman—Punto Final*, 40). Furthermore, while a handful of military and police officers were prosecuted for "excesses" during the Proceso, these always involved personal gain rather than the routine methodology of the repression—abduction, torture, and murder (Comisión Nacional sobre la Desaparición de Personas, *Nunca más* [1986], 10).

116. Trials testimony of Carlos Muñoz, Official Copy 76-6189, and Victor Melchor Basterra, Official Copy 6030-6031—this witness describes the destruction of such records in October 1983. Also see Amnesty International, *Argentina: The Military Juntas*, 28. Further details on the command structure and existence of documentation are provided in testimony by General Carlos Suarez Mason following his extradition from the United States to Argentina; see *Pagina Doce*, May 8, 1988. A persistent account of Admiral Massera, a junta member, presenting documentation of disappearances to a French official in Paris (in an attempt to mitigate French pressure on the Argentine government) is cited in Veiga, *Las organizaciones de derechos humanos*, 80–81.

117. Duhalde, 95; for the incident concerning the recalcitrant officer, see Comisión Nacional sobre la Desaparición de Personas, *Nunca más* (1986), 243–44.

118. For example, the subdirector of the Naval Mechanics School—which housed one of the largest detention centers—was prosecuted for perjury after testifying that he was not aware of the presence of any detainees, although his office was responsible for feeding them (*El Periodista*, Apr. 26–May 2, 1985).

119. Comisión Nacional sobre la Desaparición de Personas, *Nunca más* (1986), 64. Some guards engaged in "personalistic" sadism toward victims (especially rape and beatings), but they did not generally engage in systematic mistreatment of detainees, and on occasion guards tried to mitigate conditions within the camps.

120. This later served as a source of conflict within the military over the responsibility for repression. This point is confirmed in interviews with military officers; see Waisbord, 165.

121. Moncalvillo and Fernandez, *La renovación fundacional*, 29–33.

122. On looting of the property of the disappeared, see Comisión Nacional sobre la Desaparición de Personas, *Nunca más* (1986), 272–83; in some cases, it appears that the looting of property was the main motive for the selection of a particular victim. On the appropriation of children born to detainees, see Nosiglia, *Botín de guerra*.

123. The 1986 translation of the report of the Comisión Nacional sobre la Desaparición de Personas concludes: "We can state categorically . . . that they

did not pursue only the members of political organizations who carried out acts of terrorism. Among the victims are thousands who never had any links with such activity but were nevertheless subjected to horrific torture because they opposed the military dictatorship, took part in union or student activities, were well-known intellectuals who questioned state terrorism, or simply because they were relatives, friends, or names included in the address book of someone considered subversive" (*Nunca más*, 448). An internal military document issued in 1978 described the "error rate" in disappearances as "no more than 25 percent" (2,500–7,500 people) (Duhalde, 146).

124. Mitchell et al., "State Terrorism," 4–5.

125. Comisión Nacional sobre la Desaparición de Personas, *Nunca más* (1986), 285; also see 332–37 on the treatment of disabled detainees.

126. According to one analysis, 48 percent of the disappeared were union members, and members of the largest and most powerful unions were disproportionately subject to repression (see Pion-Berlin, *Ideology of State Terror*, 112). Specific incidents illustrate this pattern: the disappearance of the Light and Power union leader Oscar Smith in the midst of a labor dispute, abductions at Acindar—a company directed by Finance Minister Martinez de Hoz (Comisión Nacional sobre la Desaparición de Personas, *Nunca más* (1986), 381–82), and mass disappearances of Ledesma sugar organizers in Tucumán province. The pattern extended to multinational employers: the first three union delegations from Ford Motors Argentina all disappeared, as did the first two delegations from Mercedes Benz Argentina (ibid., 375; Vázquez, *PRN la ultima*, 60).

127. For example, on the persecution of journalists, see Comisión Nacional sobre la Desaparición de Personas, *Nunca más* (1986), 363–64, and Asociación de Periodistas de Buenos Aires, *Con vida los queremos*.

128. About 1,500 Jews disappeared during military rule. For treatments of the sources and incidence of anti-Semitism during the Proceso, see Kaufman; Timerman, *Prisoner Without a Name, Cell Without a Number*; Comisión Nacional Sobre la Desaparición de Personas, *Nunca más* (1986), 67–72, and Andersen, *Dossier secreto*.

129. Official military documents outline a strategy for the persecution of "subversive" members of the clergy (*Pagina Doce*, Sept. 23, 1988). Incidents involving clerics registered by CONADEP include the disappearances of a half dozen parish priests, several Protestant pastors, two French nuns, an Irish priest, and a priest from the United States (both the last two were eventually released), as well as the deaths of two bishops in suspicious accidents widely attributed to the military (Comisión Nacional sobre la Desaparición de Personas, *Nunca más* [1986], 347–55). Also see Mignone, *Iglesia y dictadura*. Victims thus included foreign citizens, including the above members of the clergy, refugees registered with the United Nations, and, in the Hagelin case, the teenage daughter of a Swedish industrialist (see Bennett and Simpson, 126). Most foreign victims of repression were other Latin Americans, especially Uruguayans; at one point, almost 20 Chileans were disappearing every week (Bennett and Simpson, 139–44; see also *Nunca más* [1986], 240, 255).

130. The scope of the repressive apparatus and potential for bureaucratic/

totalitarian administration of repression is seen in the discovery of a Proceso-era blacklist in Cordoba containing the names of 10,000 citizens under investigation, in one city alone (*El Periodista*, Apr. 19–25, 1985). The prosecutor's summary at the trials of the junta includes numerous cases of erroneous organizational identification. See *El diario del juicio*, 250.

131. One of the highest-level and most notorious cases of this type involved the abduction of one of the regime's own diplomats, Elena Holmberg, attributed to her discovery of unorthodox activities in Paris by Admiral Massera, including meetings with exiled Montonero guerrilla leaders. A family friend pursuing the investigation of her death, also a member of the Buenos Aires elite generally supportive of the regime, was himself abducted and murdered (*Buenos Aires Herald*, June 6, 1981; Sept. 9 and 25, 1982).

132. The dictatorship belatedly recognized this effect when it attempted to declare the disappeared dead by law.

133. For a treatment of mass murder in Argentina in a comparative context, see Staub.

Chapter 3

1. On the galvanizing effect of the technique of disappearance, see Echave and Ulla, *Despues de la noche*, and García Delgado and Palermo.

2. Comisión Nacional sobre la Desaparición de Personas, *Nunca más* (1986), 284, 11.

3. Ibid., 321–22.

4. The statutes of the Proceso claimed to supersede the Constitution and suspended some of its features. For general treatments of the role of the judiciary during the dictatorship, see Groisman, *Poder y derecho* and *Corte Suprema*.

5. Mignone, Estlund, and Issacharoff, "Dictatorship on Trial," 121.

6. For a systematic account of the use of habeas corpus under the dictatorship and key rulings, see Barcesat, "Defensa legal." For typical cases, see the *Buenos Aires Herald* column "The Law," Nov. 29, 1980 ("An Equivocal Demand?"), and Mar. 20, 1982 ("Contradictory Court Rulings").

7. The Supreme Court dismissed a case showing judicial complicity in illegal burials (Americas Watch, *Truth and Partial Justice*, 9). On judicial awareness of torture, see "Judges Who Should Be Tried," *Buenos Aires Herald*, Aug. 31, 1985.

8. Familiares de Desaparecidos y Detenidos por Razones Politicas, *Testimonios sobre la represión y la tortura*, no. 2 (Feb. 21, 1984), cited in Frontalini and Caiati, *El mito de la guerra sucia*, 108.

9. Organization of American States, *Report*, 220, lists these cases; for legal documents, see also Carrió, *El caso Timerman*. These cases were exceptional.

10. Interview, Sept. 13, 1988. An extreme example of this phenomenon is an April 1977 ruling in which the Supreme Court disqualified itself, appealing to the Executive to create conditions in which magistrates could exercise their

constitutional responsibility. See Leís, *El movimiento por los derechos humanos*, 80–86.

11. See Pozzi, "Argentina, 1976–82," 111–38, which stresses the distinct roles played by mainstream labor leadership and the dissident "25" group under the dictatorship.

12. At least 27 prominent unionists disappeared during the first four years of the dictatorship; see Bennett and Simpson, 189.

13. Pozzi, *Oposición obrera*, 123.

14. See ibid., 81, on sabotage, and for extensive documentation of strike activity, 70–100. Resistance ranged from strikes on behalf of disappeared or detained co-workers to an incident in which workers refused to give the military the names of union delegates, saying, "As of March 24th [the date of the military coup], there are no more delegates" (77–85). Also see Dabat and Lorenzano, 74, 142.

15. Pozzi, *Oposición obrera*, 124. The speaker, Ricardo Perez, later became the head of the CGT's Human Rights Secretariat during the Alfonsín period (see Chapter 5).

16. The military recognized this attitude in a 1977 secret document: "If the Church does not actively participate, she shows herself in the understanding and acceptance of the basic principles enunciated, without failing to warn about some aspects and certain errors that could affect her support" (Secret Military Document #77, Apr. 1977, cited in Rosales, "La reconciliación," 52).

17. See Mignone, *Iglesia y dictadura*, esp. chs. 1, 5, and 6, for an extensive treatment of the historic role of the Church and its relationship with the military, and 47–48 for an assessment of human rights advocacy by bishops. Also see Bennett and Simpson, 177.

18. Comisión Nacional sobre la Desaparición de Personas, *Nunca más* (1986), 248–51, 338–40.

19. Mignone, *Iglesia y dictadura*, 34.

20. See Organization of American States, *Report*, 125.

21. Brian Smith, "Churches and Human Rights in Latin America," 181.

22. The Abuelas' experience was typical: "We also had recourse to the Catholic Church, and to the Ecclesiastical Hierarchy from the first days of our tragedy. We found closed doors, offensive and sometimes cruel words: 'They are in the hands of people who have paid five million for the babies, so they are in good hands, do not be concerned.' 'We cannot do anything; go away.' 'Pray, you are lacking in faith!' . . . we never recovered a child through the mediation of the Church" (Abuelas de Plaza de Mayo, *Missing Children*, 9).

23. For an overview, see Veiga, *Las organizaciones de derechos humanos*; and see also the pamphlet by Emilio Mignone, *Organizaciones de derechos humanos en Argentina*. A collection of Proceso-era movement documents is reprinted in Leís, *El movimiento por los derechos humanos* A rough chronology of organizational development is given in Figure 2. Since the Asociación de Ex-Detenidos was not active during the Proceso, for obvious reasons, it is not discussed in this chapter.

24. For a different schema of functional divisions, including party-linked

and assistance movements, see García Delgado and Palermo, "El movimiento de los derechos humanos," 416.

25. To give a sense of the volume of legal activity engaged in by these groups, there were 5,487 habeas corpus petitions presented in Buenos Aires alone between 1976 and 1979, and 2,848 cases between 1980 and 1983 (Vázquez, *PRN la ultima*, 64; note that not all cases necessarily involved human rights organizations, but the majority involved the movement at some stage).

26. See Fruhling, 20.

27. For more information on La Liga, see Veiga, 15–26; Villalba Walsh; Liga Argentina por los Derechos del Hombre, *Sepa que es y que hace La Liga*. Interviews with leaders of La Liga, Apr. 6 and Sept. 20, 1988.

28. On the Asamblea, see Veiga, 111–24; Echave, *Después de la noche* (a biography of Graciela Fernandez-Meijide), esp. 73–103; references in reports of international organizations, such as Amnesty International, *Argentina: The Military Juntas*, 5; the Asamblea's journal *Derechos Humanos*; and the pamphlet *¿Que es APDH?* Sources include interviews with APDH representatives, Aug. 10, 1987; June 27 and Aug. 23, 1988.

29. See Centro de Estudios Legales y Sociales, *Boletín*; Veiga, 87–99; Americas Watch, *Human Rights in Argentina* (1983), 6, on CELS legal action; Mignone, *Organizaciones de derechos humanos en Argentina*, 4–5. Sources include interviews with representatives of CELS, Aug. 5, 1987; Aug. 24 and Dec. 12, 1988.

30. On the Madres, see Bousquet; Bennett and Simpson; Fisher, *Mothers of the Disappeared*; Piera Paolo Oria, *De la casa a la Plaza*; Bonafini, *Historias de vida*; and Diago, *Hebe Bonafini*. Sources include interviews with representatives of Las Madres, Aug. 8, 1987; May 3 and Nov. 2, 1988.

31. Bennett and Simpson, 160. The advertisement appeared in October 1977, along with photographs of the disappeared whose very existence was being denied by the government.

32. Madres de Plaza de Mayo, *Boletín Informativo*, Aug. 1980, cited in Leís, 100.

33. See Bousquet, 47. For a larger theoretical treatment of this aspect of the Mothers, see Franco, "Gender, Death, and Resistance."

34. Bousquet, 48.

35. Since 1984, Las Madres have split into two groups, one keeping the name Madres de Plaza de Mayo and the other calling itself the Linea Fundadora (founding line). The former group, under the leadership of Hebe de Bonafini, kept most of the organization's resources and was more critical of the Alfonsín administration.

36. *La Prensa*, May 8, 1978, reprinted in Leis, 90.

37. For more information on the Abuelas, see Veiga, 57–74; Nosiglia; Abuelas de Plaza de Mayo, *Missing Children*. Sources include interviews with representatives of Las Abuelas, Mar. 19, Apr. 18, and Nov. 17, 1988.

38. In this way, Familiares was closer in spirit to pre-Proceso forms of human rights activism.

39. On Familiares, see Familiares de Desaparecidos y Detenidos por Ra-

zones Politicas, *Testimonios de nuestra lucha*; Veiga, 74–87. Sources include interviews with representatives of the Familiares, June 14 and July 14, 1988.

40. *Paz y Justicia* 5/4, no. 47 (Feb. 1977), "Numero especial dedicado a la campaña por los derechos humanos—Cartilla de Orientación."

41. On SERPAJ, see Veiga, 124–35; Servicio Paz y Justicia, *Peace and Justice Service*. Sources include interviews with representatives of SERPAJ, Aug. 7, 1987; July 25, Aug. 8, and Nov. 5, 1988.

42. See Veiga, 99–111; MEDH, *InformeDH, ¿Que es el MEDH?* Sources include interviews with representatives of MEDH, June 17, and July 14, 1988.

43. For example, the Movimiento Judío often linked the experience of state terror to the Holocaust—in some cases, through the life histories of Jewish human rights activists. The movement's views were generally expressed through the journal *Nueva Presencia* (later *Nuestra Presencia*), edited by Herman Schiller. Sources include interviews with representatives of the Moviemiento Judío, Aug. 12, 1987; Dec. 14, 1988.

44. Interview with Emilio Mignone, Aug. 24, 1988.

45. An international regime is generally defined as a nonbinding collection of arrangements and institutions that shape state behavior. "International regimes are defined as principles, norms, rules and decision-making procedures around which actor expectations converge in a given issue-area" (Krasner, *International Regimes*, 1). Donnelly applies this model to the international organizations and mechanisms concerned with human rights in "International Human Rights." Also see Forsythe, *Human Rights and World Politics*, 211.

46. Henderson, "Human Rights and Regimes," 529.

47. Argentina was officially committed to these international institutions, since it was a signatory to the United Nations, Organization of American States, and Geneva conventions. One example of the emergence of a multilateral human rights forum during this period is that the OAS Human Rights Commission went from a 1976 caseload of 139 new cases and 145 pending to a 1980 figure of 2,900 new cases and 4,730 pending (Farer, *Grand Strategy*, 75). The transnational organization Amnesty International opened its Washington, D.C., office in 1976, the year of the Argentine coup (Schoultz, 83).

48. Guest, 169.

49. Linkage to multilateral lending was especially important to Argentina. Prior to the Proceso, Argentina had ceased to qualify for AID funds. Multilateral development banks became more important as direct aid declined; by 1976, Argentina was the fourth-largest borrower in Latin America, and the seventh in the world (Schoultz, 268). PL94-302 specified that U.S. representatives to multilateral development banks must vote against any loan to any government that violated human rights, unless the loan would provide direct benefits to the needy (ibid., 281–82). Some analysts connect this new channel of international sensitivity to the repression itself, claiming that the bureaucratic authoritarian dictatorship displaced the costs of economic restructuring and concomitant repression onto international finance, thus increasing reliance on multilateral lending (Pion-Berlin, *Ideology of State Terror*, 47).

50. Schoultz, 295, 320.

51. For a complete account of U.S. policy and overview of human rights conditionality in aid and lending, see Schoultz; Forsythe, *Human Rights and World Politics*, esp. 141; Berg "Human Rights Sanctions."

52. Amnesty International, *Argentina: The Military Juntas*, 5.

53. Guest, 63, 135, 198–99, 318.

54. The OAS received 5,580 complaints in two weeks, see Organization of American States, *Report*, 6; closing recommendations, 264–66. For reactions among opinion leaders, see coverage in the *Buenos Aires Herald* for elite reactions, esp. "The Law" column, Oct. 8, 1980, and Nov. 15, 1981.

55. Organization of American States, *Report*, 135.

56. Some of the U.S. aid lost was made up from international lending or less scrupulous competitors (see Berg for an argument on the ineffectiveness of sanctions in this case; also see Forsythe, 106). Restrictions on military aid did not prevent a U.S. firm from supplying the dictatorship with one of its "weapons" of choice—a crematorium (Duhalde, 247). Clandestine detention centers were dismantled and detainees concealed prior to inspection visits by OAS and International Red Cross representatives (Comisión Nacional sobre la Desaparición de Personas, *Nunca más* [1986], 75, 130, 160, 190). And the release of Timerman under international pressure also inspired an (unsuccessful) nationalistic military uprising by the hard-liner General Benjamín Menendez (see Timerman, 183; Bousquet, 163).

57. For the debate on the impact of international pressure—mostly U.S. policy—on the Argentine juntas, see Sikkink, Falcoff, Tulchin, and Escudé in *Exporting Democracy*, ed. Lowenthal.

58. Bennett and Simpson, 274.

59. Interview with imprisoned and released CELS leader, Aug. 5, 1987.

60. Guest, 272–73 and n. 36.

61. See Fisher, 73.

62. Interview with SERPAJ representative, July 28, 1988.

63. Guest, 167.

64. Interview with a member of Las Madres, May 3, 1988.

65. Comisión Nacional sobre la Desaparición de Personas, *Nunca más* (1986), 310.

66. See Strassera and Moreno Ocampo, 157–58; interview with an Argentine human rights activist who prepared such lists, July 25, 1988.

67. Fisher, 74.

68. On the kidnapping of Las Madres founders and two French nuns, see Comisión Nacional sobre la Desaparición de Personas, *Nunca más* (1986), 128, and Bousquet, 73–74. The Madres were infiltrated by Navy Captain Alfredo Astiz (whose promotion became a key issue under democracy), purporting to be the relative of a *desaparecido*. The kidnapping, timed to prevent the publication of a paid newspaper announcement in December 1977, took place as the Madres were leaving a church in which they had taken refuge. The ad appeared as planned, and the organization persisted.

69. See Organization of American States, *Report*, 201; Comisión Nacional sobre la Desaparición de Personas, *Nunca más* (1986), 382.

70. Comisión Nacional sobre la Desaparición de Personas, *Nunca más* (1986), 131–32. The manipulation of Thelma Jara de Cabezas of Familiares extended to a prearranged interview, surrounded by plainclothes members of a military task force, with a conservative women's magazine (*Para Tí*). This incident later raised the issue of journalistic complicity with the repression.

71. For example, see Duhalde, 257, on the arrest of 300 Madres following a 1977 petition drive. Also see Strassera and Ocampo, 95–96; the wife of a disappeared union leader was detained during a 1976 Amnesty International visit to prevent her from testifying.

72. Organization of American States, *Report*, 257.

73. See Amnesty International, *Argentina: The Military Juntas*, 4; Bousquet, 20. Ironically, this stimulated the growth of the human rights movement—the Madres first met in this and similar government offices. Similarly, the Abuelas first recognized their common situation while searching for traces of their grandchildren in the offices of juvenile courts.

74. Bousquet, 141–45; Organization of American States, *Report*, 126; Rodriguez Molas, 156; Amnesty International, *Argentina: The Military Juntas*, 5.

75. The challenge to the Ley de Presunción de Fallecimiento was led by Asamblea and Liga lawyers and involved about 700 relatives of the disappeared (interview, La Liga attorney, Sept. 20, 1988; Organization of American States, *Report*, 129).

76. Organization of American States, *Report*, 121, 215–16, 248. These were generally in cases of corruption or personal profiteering that did not involve human rights violations or implicate the repressive apparatus as such.

77. A similar account of shifting stages of military discourse is provided in García Delgado and Palermo, 428–29.

78. Speech on Mar. 31, 1976, reprinted in Cavarozzi, *Autoritarismo y democracia*.

79. See Duhalde, 220, and Rodriguez Molas, 156. "*Los ausentes para siempre*" was one of the first oblique official acknowledgements of the disappeared.

80. *Clarín*, Mar. 18, 1981, reprinted in Comisión Nacional sobre la Desaparición de Personas, *Nunca más* (1986), 444–45; for similar statements, see Bousquet, 174–75.

81. See *La Razon*, Mar. 16, 1982, and *Buenos Aires Herald*, Mar. 26, 1983.

82. *Pagina Doce*, June 25, 1988.

83. Comisión Nacional sobre la Desaparición de Personas, *Nunca más* (1986), 126, 134.

84. Bousquet, 155.

85. See Ferrari, "Historia del deporte Argentino," 150–64; *Pagina Doce*, June 25, 1988 (the tenth anniversary of the World Cup). Human rights critics disagreed over the promotion of a boycott of this event; the majority position of attendance with special support for domestic human rights protest was expressed by Amnesty International with the slogan *Fútbol sí, tortura no* (Amnesty International—Argentina, *Actividades sobre Argentina*).

86. Galtieri, "Celebración del Día del Ejército," 7.

87. Vázquez, *PRN la ultima*, 194–95.

88. See Pion-Berlin, "Military Breakdown and Redemocratization in Argentina." On the loss of military cohesion, also see Fontana, *Fuerzas armadas, partidos politicos y transición.*

89. For general accounts, see Peralta-Ramos in Peralta-Ramos and Waisman; Pion-Berlin, "Fall of Military Rule in Argentina." The total increase in foreign debt between 1976 and 1982 was from $10 billion to $45 billion—80 percent of GDP. See William Smith, *Authoritarianism*, 260, 270. Over half of the debt contracted between 1976 and 1982 was capital flight (Peralta-Ramos, 57–59).

90. Rock, *Argentina, 1516–1987*, 370, 374; William Smith, *Authoritarianism*, 242; Dabat and Lorenzano, 142.

91. William Smith, "Reflections on the Political Economy of Authoritarian Rule," 60.

92. See Dabat and Lorenzano, 70–71; Allende et al., *Informe sobre el Proceso para la reorganización nacional.*

93. Dabat and Lorenzano, 74. The peace component of the slogan was a reference to the repression, and the march was attended by some human rights activists. For the statement on the Church, see ibid., 72.

94. Multipartidaria Nacional, *Antes que sea tarde*. The parties included were the Radicales, Peronists, Partido Intransigente, Christian Democrats, and Movimiento de Integración y Desarrollo. Shortly after this proposal, the group issued a document whose title translates as "Peace has a price, the National Constitution." On this period, also see Fontana, *Fuerzas armadas, partidos politicos y transición.*

95. See Beltrán, "Political Transition in Argentina," 217, for a linkage between the Malvinas and the military's legitimacy crisis; the author is a former instructor at the national military academy.

96. Pion-Berlin, "Fall of Military Rule in Argentina," 222.

97. For accounts of these demonstrations and their connection to the invasion, see Rock, *Argentina, 1516–1987*, 377, and Bennett and Simpson, 326.

98. Dabat and Lorenzano, 76; for an extensive treatment of this theme, see Rozitchner, *Malvinas: De la guerra sucia a la guerra limpia*, esp. 58–59, 95, 97–98. A military spokesman made the link explicit in the context of the crisis in a 1982 statement that the Proceso's historical validity was based on the defeat of subversion, the recovery of the Malvinas, and the creation of conditions for a political opening. See Aliverti, 70.

99. On command structures, see Beltrán. For an overview from within the military itself, see Argentina, Comisíon Rattenbach, *Informe Rattenbach: El drama de Malvinas.*

100. Vázquez, *PRN la ultima*, 149.

101. Dabat and Lorenzano, 107–8.

102. See Americas Watch, *Argentina: Human Rights during the Falklands/Malvinas Crisis.*

103. Waisman, "Argentina: Autarkic Industrialization," 83.

104. Dabat and Lorenzano, 149.

105. Rock, *Argentina, 1516–1987*, 384–85.

106. República Argentina, *Documento final*, esp. 11–13, 15.

107. Dabat and Lorenzano, 155.

108. For the text of the measure, see *La Nación*, Sept. 24, 1983, and "Effects of the 'Amnesty,' " *Buenos Aires Herald*, Sept. 23, 1983. Since the law excluded guerrillas living outside Argentine territory and was limited to actions not yet investigated, the amnesty's apparent evenhandedness was illusory.

109. See *Tiempo Argentino*, Sept. 24, 1983, for a series of reactions.

110. See Barcesat, "Defensa legal de los derechos a la vida y la libertad personal," 160. This prefigured the emergence of judicial autonomy, which played a critical role in human rights reform.

111. The final vote was 51.74 percent for the Radical party and 40.15 percent for the Peronists. See Landi, *Las culturas políticas en numeros*, 11. And see Cavarozzi, "Argentine Political Cycles since 1955," 45–47, on human rights as a Radical campaign issue. Pollsters found that women—a central element in the "Alfonsín coalition"—were especially influenced by the association of the Radicales with peace and the Peronists with a return to political violence. See Canton, *El pueblo legislador*; Mora y Araujo, "Nature of the Alfonsín Coalition"; and Cecilia Kaplan and Susana Perez in *Gente*, no. 3 (special ed., Nov. 3, 1983).

112. Italo Luder's political philosophy of democracy as majority will (rather than a system of guarantees) is expressed in an interview published in López Saavedra, *Apelación a la democracia*, 167–68. Luder, who had served as Isabel Perón's interim president during her leaves of office and as intermittent president of the Senate during the early 1970's, was also resented for his refusal to mitigate Isabel's disastrous policies—or remove her (ibid., 164).

113. Bennett and Simpson, 385–86; Andersen, *Dossier secreto*, "Argentina's Return to Civility."

114. On the influence of the candidates' personal images, especially confidence in Alfonsín's leadership, see Catterberg, *Los argentinos frente a la política*, 102. Catterberg's data also show the importance of fears of Peronism, based on Isabel's administration.

115. On the union-military pact, see *La Nación*, May 3, 1983.

116. Interview with Dr. Emilio de Ipola, Mar. 24, 1988. For a similar interpretation, see Portantiero, "La transición entre la confrontación y el acuerdo," 278. For a more general discussion of the nature of citizenship in Latin America, see O'Donnell, "Tensions in the Bureaucratic Authoritarian State and the Question of Democracy."

Chapter 4

1. The Nuremberg trials do not parallel those in Argentina, since they were imposed by occupying foreign powers, and the 1975 trials of the Greek military junta were for illegitimate seizure of power rather than for human rights violations per se. The U.S. trials of military officers for human rights violations at

My Lai were in some ways similar, but they did not involve violations against American citizens, former rulers as defendants, or a transition of regime type—and took place entirely in military courts. The post-Nuremberg domestic denazification trials in Germany do show some parallels to the Argentine experience.

2. Democratizing nations such as Peru and the Philippines continue to experience severe human rights violations in the context of civil insurgencies. Neighboring Brazil has not tried its military officers and reports continuing police abuse and restriction of civil and political rights.

3. The Familiares newsletter *Decimos* 9, no. 4 (Aug. 1985): 2.

4. Raúl Alfonsín, "Mensaje a la Asamblea Legislativa—Presidente de la nación," Dec. 10, 1983, reprinted in Sancinetti, 155–70.

5. Familiares declaration of principles, *Decimos* 9, no. 2 (May 1985), originally proclaimed at an April 26th demonstration. Amplification of the principles reads: "TRUTH that we still demand, to know what happened to each of our detained/disappeared. As long as we don't receive an answer, there will not be peace or tranquility in thousands of Argentine homes. FREEDOM for all the political prisoners who remain in Argentine prisons and guarantees for those who have suffered long years of exile, who see their freedom threatened by the opening of state cases with which [the state] attempts to create a 'counterweight' to the trials brought by the victims of state terror. JUSTICE for all those guilty of detentions, disappearances, torture, and murders, the only guarantee that these crimes will not be repeated in this country or in the world. There will be no justice if open or hidden amnesties are dictated, if there is no punishment for the guilty and [if there is no] immediate and total dismantling of the repressive apparatus." For a general discussion of these themes, see Lázara, *Poder militar*.

6. Note the parallel (which has been discussed by some religious human rights activists) to Genesis, where God asks Cain "Where is your brother?" and the demand for information forces Cain to acknowledge his accountability. See Rodolfo Mattarollo, "¿Dónde están?" *Pagina Doce*, May 13, 1988.

7. My translation from the Radical party's taped version of Alfonsín's closing campaign speech, Oct. 27, 1983.

8. All quotations from Alfonsín's closing campaign speech. Another sign of Alfonsín's early recognition of the human rights movement is the government's inclusion (in its own listing of achievements during the first hundred days of the new administration) of the first meeting between the human rights groups and an Argentine president (República Argentina, *Los primeros 100 días*, 5).

9. Presidential advisors who were influential in creating human rights policy include Jaime Malamud Goti, Carlos Nino, and Eduardo Rabossi. Nino and Malamud Goti drafted most of the transition-era "human rights package," and Goti later served as attorney general; Rabossi was the secretary of human rights. Nino, Goti, Ricardo Entelman, and others associated with the Argentine Philosophical Society often stood in opposition to a faction of more traditional Radical party stalwarts represented by Antonio Troccoli, Raúl Borras, and Horacio Jaunarena—ministers of the interior, defense, and (later) defense respectively. In addition to the patterns noted above, many of the advisors on human rights

policy came from an academic background, and academics were represented more heavily in the Alfonsín administration than in most previous Argentine governments, giving the new regime a "best and brightest" quality. On these points, see Ferrari and Herrera, *Los hombres del presidente*, 14–20, 112–13.

10. Several members of the administration did have a personal history of persecution. Senator Hipólito Solari Yrigoyen and Ministry of Education Under Secretary Alfredo Bravo, for example, had both been kidnapped, tortured, and imprisoned for several years by the military. In addition, a young female relative of Alfonsín's was among the disappeared (Asamblea staff identified her as a niece or daughter-in-law, but could not confirm the relationship). However, a contrasting element of the president's background is Alfonsín's attendance at a military academy, which some believe created personal ties to and some sympathy for military officers. For example, Albano Harguindeguy—the Proceso's minister of the interior—was a former schoolmate of the president's; see Giussani, *¿Por qué, Doctor Alfonsín?* 65. For an allegation of improper influence through this connection, see Osvaldo Bayer, "Ahora son todos culpables," *Crisis*, no. 50 (Jan. 1987).

11. Alfonsín sits on the Asamblea's largely honorary Council of Presidents, which has over 120 members and meets once a year. The daily work of the organization is performed by the Executive Board, while most policy decisions are made by the Directive Board. This assessment of Alfonsín's role and the general structure of the organization was shared by several members and confirmed by the Executive Board's co-president, Alfredo Bravo (interview, Aug. 23, 1988).

12. Presidential statements of these themes can be found in Alfonsín's message to the legislature; a July 5, 1985, speech to the military in which Alfonsín characterized all coups as joint civil-military enterprises; a December 1985 speech at Parque Norte (reprinted in Horowicz, ed., *¿Hacia dónde va el Alfonsinismo?*); the speech preceding the introduction of the Punto Final legislation in December 1986 (reprinted in Sancinetti, 233) and an interview response in Giussani, 117. The human rights movement position, and particularly the treatment of the national security doctrine as an international and socioeconomic issue, is detailed in Lozada's *Inseguridad y desnacionalización* and the APDH's *La desaparición*, ch. 1. A treatment of relevant themes in English that shares the general framework of divergent ideological packages but differs on some of their contents is Osiel's "Making of Human Rights Policy in Argentina."

13. Interview with Carlos Nino, July 28, 1987.

14. Interview with member of the Executive Board of the APDH, Aug. 4, 1988.

15. Rock, *Argentina, 1516–1987*, 389 (emphasis added). Also see Giussani, 239, and Boeker, 57.

16. Interview with Alfredo Bravo, Aug. 23, 1988. Bravo cites Alfonsín's remarks at a 1980 youth seminar. Alfonsín repeated the distinction on several occasions, including his opening message to the legislature.

17. An early sign of the difference in Executive and movement interpretations of the Proceso was that the decree mandating the trial of the juntas was

carefully paired with a decree ordering the trial of a group of former guerrilla leaders, to show that both sides in the "Dirty War" were being treated equally.

18. For a discussion of these measures and complete references to statutes, see Alfonsín, "Building Democracy," 123–25. An overview of the Alfonsín administration's early policy initiatives is provided in *Los primeros 100 días de la democracia*.

19. For a summary of previous movement positions and criticism of the CONADEP panel created, see Emilio F. Mignone, "Debe crearse una comisión parlamentaria, ya," *Madres de Plaza de Mayo* 1, no. 4 (Mar. 1985).

20. Data from the human rights movement's Technical Commission appears in Familiares' *Testimonios sobre la represión y la tortura*, 7–8, 9, Sept. 20, 1984.

21. The Oct. 1983 joint communique listing all of the human rights movement's demands appears in Diaz Colodrero and Abella, *Punto Final*, 77–80. For a concise listing, see Madres de Plaza de Mayo, *Boletín Informativo* 2, nos. 18 and 19 (July and Sept. 1984). Also see the interview with Adolfo Perez-Esquivel in Verbitsky, *La posguerra sucia*, 265–85.

22. Socialist legislators had initiated several parliamentary investigations of human rights abuses, the most recent in 1958. See Rodriguez Molas, *Historia de la tortura*, 130–32. The latest bicameral commission, founded by Perón in 1950, had been ultimately and ironically used to investigate and persecute the Liga por los Derechos del Hombre. See Villalba Walsh, 41.

23. Emilio Mignone, whose organization, CELS, did cooperate with CONADEP, nevertheless stresses its limitations vis-à-vis a bicameral legislative commission in terms of the power to subpoena (Mignone, Estlund, and Issacharoff, 125–28).

24. Hugo Piucil (Rio Negro) and Federico Storani (Buenos Aires) are Radical legislators who campaigned on the basis of a bicameral commission but changed their program once in office. Although Cesar Jaroslawsky was an influential legislator (and head of the UCR bloc in the Congress) who generally reflected and promoted official policies, it is unlikely that he was reflecting an official commitment during this incident—but it serves to demonstrate the general atmosphere of anticipated policy (reported in *La Razon*, Dec. 9, 1983). Also see Las Madres' transcription of the interview with Jaroslavsky in *Madres de Plaza de Mayo* 1, no. 1 (Dec. 1984).

25. Diaz Colodrero, 87. These proposals were never debated by the full House.

26. In the province of Rio Negro, a provincial-level executive commission similar to CONADEP was established. It forwarded the results of its investigation to the regional judiciary and catalyzed civil libertarian reforms such as public access to police records. Interview with Hugo Piucil, a former deputy from Rio Negro, Sept. 25, 1988.

27. Interview with Deputy Horacio Ravenna, Aug. 19, 1988. The mechanism for pressuring the Executive has usually been to file a *pedido de informes* (parliamentary request for information and justification) with the provincial Ministry of the Interior. Relevant examples of these challenges initiated by the provincial bicameral commission followed the police shooting of unarmed youths

in the Budge district of Buenos Aires (D/37, May 11, 1987–88) and the creation of a vigilante-style "special citizens' security force" in the municipality of Moron (D/592, 1988–89). A measure of the extent of bipartisan consensus achieved is that the full House has taken up all of the commission's projects, regardless of their party sponsorship.

28. Interview with Jaime Malamud Goti, Aug. 17, 1988. (A hypothetical example of the kind of investigations that would violate this consensus might be in-depth investigations of death squads prior to the coup, since Peronists and Radicales had a tacit agreement not to examine human rights violations committed before 1976 under the civilian government of Isabel Perón.)

29. Interview with Antonio Troccoli, Dec. 13, 1988.

30. Interview with Jaime Malamud Goti, Aug. 17, 1988. Also see interview with Antonio Troccoli in Ferrari, 237.

31. Interview with Eduardo Rabossi, a former CONADEP member and secretary of human rights, Nov. 23, 1988. Human rights activists' emotional capacity to process the horrifying details of repression was a significant resource. CONADEP had very high turnover of nonmovement clerical staff, who could not bear to work with this material, and the commission was eventually forced to institute weekly therapy sessions for all its staff (interview with Hugo Piucil, a former CONADEP member and deputy, Sept. 25, 1988).

32. Interview with Graciela Fernandez-Meijide, Aug. 10, 1988.

33. See *Clarín*, Dec. 24, 1983, for Perez-Esquivel's statement. As a Linea Fundadora (breakaway faction) Madre explained, the Madres' refusal to participate was more symbolic than substantive, since the Madres' cases had already been registered with the Asamblea and would thus be transmitted to CONADEP through the APDH (interview, May 3, 1988).

34. Interview with Hebe de Bonafini, Aug. 7, 1987. Also see "Los desaparecidos no se archivan," *Madres de Plaza de Mayo* 1, no.1 (Dec. 1984).

35. The human rights movement had already identified 200 detention centers; see Asamblea Permanent por los Derechos Humanos, *Consejo de Presidencia*, July 1, 1985, 14. In the CONADEP report, Graciela Fernandez Meijide wrote most of the documentation of individual concentration camps, while Hugo Piucil wrote the section on conscripts and adolescents. The section on missing children was based heavily on the work of the Abuelas.

36. See Comisión Nacional sobre la Desaparición de Personas, *Nunca más* (1986), 431; interview with the local activist who sent a telegram to Ernesto Sabato, the head of CONADEP (Nov. 2, 1988).

37. Comisión Nacional sobre la Desaparición de Personas, *Nunca más* (1986), 434–37.

38. Interview with Deputy Hugo Piucil, Sept. 25, 1988.

39. See Verbitsky, *Civiles y militares*, 90, and Poneman, 89.

40. See Diaz Colodrero, 239; Amnesty International, *Argentina: The Military Juntas*, 9. The 1984 incident in Cordoba was followed by a march of repudiation that drew an estimated 50,000 persons.

41. Under the reform of the military code of justice, the commission should logically have brought cases to the military courts. The decision to bring cases

only to civilian courts was interpreted by some as a display of CONADEP's independence and support for civilian trials (e.g., by the former CONADEP member Eduardo Rabossi, interview, Nov. 23, 1988), but criticized by others as a source of delay and obfuscation (see, e.g., the interview with Luis Zamora in Diaz Colodrero, 85).

42. For the number of cases brought by CONADEP, as well as publishing figures for *Nunca más*, see República Argentina, *La Subsecretaría de Derechos Humanos y la CONADEP*, 4. It is likely that the official distribution of *Nunca más* was enhanced by pressure from Deputy Augusto Conte, a human rights movement legislator (Camera de Diputados File 2724-D-1984).

43. Verbitsky, *Civiles y militares*, 102.

44. *¿Que Pasa?* Oct. 3, 1984.

45. Americas Watch, *Truth and Partial Justice in Argentina*, 22.

46. Interview with Antonio Troccoli, Dec. 13, 1988. This is the stance referred to by the human rights movement as the "doctrine of the two demons," illustrating the divergent analyses of the nature and origins of state terror. A brief critique in English of Troccoli's statement appears in the *Buenos Aires Herald's* column "The Law," July 7, 1984.

47. This incident was followed by a change in the military command. See Americas Watch, *Truth and Partial Justice in Argentina*, 22.

48. For a general discussion of the difficulties in gathering an accurate count of the disappeared, see Brysk, "Politics of Measurement." Activists in working-class neighborhoods report personal knowledge of three to four times the number of cases reported to CONADEP in their districts, and even a former member of the commission estimates that there may have been twice the official figure of 9,000 disappeared. Graciela Fernandez Meijide reports that the commission was able to process only about 30 percent of the material received during its nine-month existence, in Fruhling, ed., *Represión política*, and Asamblea Permanente *por los Derechos Humanos, Consejo de Presidencia*, July 1, 1985, p. 15. Since the commission did not directly investigate the repressive forces and relied on reporting by victims, cases with no witnesses or cases in which whole families disappeared would also not be reported. The human rights movement claims a total figure of 30,000 disappeared.

49. *El Periodista*, Nov. 3–9, 10–16, 1984. Las Madres refused to participate in the march supporting submission of the final report on the basis that the repressor list had been excluded. See "¿Para que sirvío la CONADEP?" *Madres de Plaza de Mayo* 1, no. 1 (Dec. 1984): 6. A brief general critique of the government action appears in the *Buenos Aires Herald* column "The Law," Dec. 12, 1984; and see also ibid., "Priests and Secret Camps," Nov. 10, 1984.

50. Abuelas de Plaza de Mayo, *Informaciones*, no. 14 (June–July 1987). Since the woman was pregnant when kidnapped, the Abuelas took her case. This issue reprints a letter to the president documenting the inquiries pursued by her family since the transition to democracy, on the occasion of the tenth anniversary of her disappearance. Note that early in the work of CONADEP, Ernesto Sabato had speculated that some of the disappeared might still be alive (*Tiempo Argentino*, Dec. 30, 1983).

51. The forensic anthropologist Clyde Snow has established a vast increase in the interment of unidentified bodies in a relatively young age group, and a sudden increase in deaths listed as resulting from gunshot wounds. See Snow and Bihurriet, "Epidemiology of Homicide," and *Página Doce*, June 15, 1988. There is also other evidence of illicit disposal of bodies, such as the appearance of dozens of corpses at particular spots on the banks of the Rio de la Plata. In addition, human rights groups allege massive falsification and/or destruction of records (*Clarín*, Apr. 14, 1984, reported the destruction of 140,000 fingerprints of unidentified corpses in 1981; see also "Courts Drag Feet on NN Graves Probe," *Buenos Aires Herald*, Apr. 29, 1988).

52. For an overview of the exhumations, see Stephen G. Michaud, "Identifying Argentina's Disappeared," *New York Times Magazine*, Dec. 27, 1987. See also the Forensic Anthropology Team's report in Asamblea Permanente por los Derechos Humanos, *La desaparición*.

53. These included the trial of the former military rulers (discussed below), the prosecutions of generals Camps and Suarez-Mason, and the Carlotto and Pereyra missing children cases.

54. Interview with several members of the Forensic Anthropology Team, July 2, 1988; see also "Argentina: Forensic Investigation of Past Human Rights Violations," *The Lancet* 337, no. 8757 (June 29, 1991): 1593. Besides identification of specific individuals, and determination that childbirth had taken place, the team has shown several times that individuals who were listed as killed in shoot-outs were executed at point-blank range. The legal significance of exhumations vis-à-vis statutes of limitations is discussed in Diaz Colodrero, 170.

55. The MEDH shares office space with the Forensic Anthropology team, and support for exhumations is one of the positions that distinguishes the Madres–Linea Fundadora from Las Madres.

56. Interview with Hebe de Bonafini, Aug. 7, 1987; also see Fisher, 128–30, for an extended discussion of Las Madres' opposition to exhumations.

57. Interview with the under secretary of justice, province of Buenos Aires, Aug. 30, 1988.

58. Interviews with Luis Brunatti, minister of government, province of Buenos Aires, Dec. 20, 1988, and Forensic Anthropology team, Nov. 16, 1988. The loan of Brunatti's personal guard was necessary since the Buenos Aires provincial police were implicated in the crimes being investigated, and thus members of the regular police force could not be relied on to provide adequate protection.

59. The official Technical Commission was created on Dec. 1, 1986, by Decree 1526, and recognized by the Supreme Court on Dec. 11, 1986. Interviews with Forensic Anthropology team and interview with Eduardo Rabossi, Nov. 23, 1988. Also see the official view in República Argentina, *La Subsecretaría de Derechos Humanos y la CONADEP*, 17–19. Criticisms are reported in *El Periodista*, Nov. 14–20, 1986, and in an interview with Clyde Snow in ibid., July 24–30, 1987.

Chapter 5

1. On this view of transitions, see Acuña and Smulovitz, ¿*Ni olvido ni perdón?* 4–5. Their treatment, which speaks of many small transitions, also draws on the work of Adam Przeworski.

2. On information as a source of power in the judicial system, see Acuña and Smulovitz, ¿*Ni olvido ni perdón?* 51.

3. Interview with Carlos Nino, July 28, 1987. Alfonsín himself cites a target figure of "around 100" in Giussani, 240. Alfonsín's former advisor Jaime Malamud-Goti justifies this limited trials strategy in moral, legal, and political terms in "Transitional Governments in the Breach."

4. The legal expression of the trial of individuals rather than an institution was the failure to treat the military as an "illicit association" (as had been done with the SS at Nuremberg). Although the juntas were not charged with rebellion by the Alfonsín administration (to avoid any sense that the trials were politically motivated), a private individual did bring a case for sedition against the juntas, which zigzagged through multiple jurisdictions and technical difficulties and was eventually dismissed (Sancinetti, 18–21; Diaz Colodrero, 94–95; see also "Rebellion as a Felony," *Buenos Aires Herald*, "The Law," Apr. 7, 1984). In an interview during the trials, the Radical legislator Moreau stressed that the trials were trials of individuals and not of the armed forces as an institution (*El Periodista*, Oct. 11–17, 1985). In his speech preceding the introduction of the Punto Final law, Alfonsín reiterated that "the imputation of responsibility was [directed at] the state agents involved and not at the institutions" (reprinted in Sancinetti, 236).

5. The military code of justice had previously operated as a self-contained parallel judicial system; the reform of the military code maintained military justice as the first recourse in allegations of civil crimes brought against members of the armed forces, but introduced the possibility of appeal to civilian courts of cases against officers accused of human rights violations between 1976 and 1983. This meant that every human rights prosecution, including the trial of the juntas, started in a military court and ended in a civilian court. Even cases originally brought in civilian courts (because of the plaintiff's distrust of military courts, ignorance of the reform, or as a protest measure by human rights movement lawyers) were eventually returned to military courts as the venue of first resort. The reform of the military code of justice involved significant constitutional issues, pitting a clause that requires that all citizens be subject to their "natural judges" against a clause specifying equal protection and prohibiting special group privileges (see Sancinetti, 12).

6. Mignone, Estlund, and Issacharoff, 142–43. Las Madres staged a 24-hour march in front of the Congreso Nacional as an "outsider" protest of the reform of the military code (*El Tiempo Argentino*, Jan. 4, 1984). The Familiares' newsletter published an early critique of the limited trials strategy, "Juicios: El comienzo, no el final," *Decimos* 9, no. 2 (May 1985).

7. A detailed account of the evolution of this legislation is contained in

Horacio Verbitsky's *Civiles y militares*, 73–81. Also see Americas Watch, *Truth and Partial Justice in Argentina*, 18–19. The original parliamentary debate is in República Argentina, *Diario de sesiones: Diputados*, 6th *reunion*, 4th *sesión extraordinaria*, Jan. 5, 1984, esp. 436, and *Senadores*, 10th *reunión*, 1st *sesión especial extraordinaria*, Jan. 31–Feb. 1, 1984, esp. 339. The human rights movements— especially the *afectados*—were invoked several times during the legislative debate, as were alternative movement-sponsored proposals for a bicameral commission, elimination of military courts, and the declaration of forced disappearance as a crime against humanity. The "atrocious and aberrant" clause put the burden of justification on the accused military officer for any act that could not be shown or plausibly construed to be the result of legitimate military orders, so that routine methodologies of the repression such as rape, torture, and child-stealing could be prosecuted.

    8. Americas Watch, *Truth and Partial Justice in Argentina*, 29.

    9. See Mignone, "Dictatorship on Trial," 138–41, and Verbitsky, *Civiles y militares*, 107.

    10. The official record of the trials of the juntas is *El diario del juicio*, which was released on a weekly basis throughout the trials and was subsequently published as a multivolume record. General accounts appear in Verbitsky, Americas Watch, Amnesty International, and the preface to the English edition of *Nunca más*. A more detailed legal analysis is Sancinetti's *Derechos humanos en la Argentina post-dictatorial*, which goes on to cover the various measures limiting future trials and includes the text of all relevant legislation and presidential addresses. Journalistic reflections on the revelations and significance of the trials are to be found in Moncalvillo et al., *Juicio a la impunidad* and Ciancaglini and Granovsky, *Cronicas del apocalipsis*. Interviews with the prosecutors, along with the prosecution and defense summations and the final sentence, appear in Strassera and Moreno Ocampo, *Será justicia*.

    11. However, the television broadcast did not include sound until the prosecutor's summation. In October, a group of 375 Argentine journalists petitioned without success for the release of daily sound transmissions (*El Periodista*, Oct. 11–17, 1985). Official videotapes of the trials were never shown in full, but were obtained during 1988 by human rights groups, which organized private showings and petitioned for television rebroadcast.

    12. International experts were present, not only as witnesses to the repression, but often to represent claims of foreign governments, since hundreds of foreign citizens also disappeared in Argentina. Fifty countries had filed over 3,000 claims on behalf of 1,652 disappeared persons, some holding dual citizenship (Strassera and Moreno Ocampo, 161). Foreign experts included the forensic anthropologist Clyde Snow; Patricia Derian, a former U.S. State Department official; Tom Farer, a member of the OAS's Interamerican Commission on Human Rights; and Theo van Bowen, former head of the UN Human Rights Commission.

    13. Pablo Diaz, the only survivor of the "Night of the Pencils," was tortured and imprisoned in a clandestine detention center, then transferred to a regular prison, and released after several years; his companions remain "disappeared."

14. On the testimony of union leaders, see Horacio Verbitsky in *El Periodista*, May 3–10, 1985.

15. See Ciancaglini, 98–100, 105–11. The prime witness to her case, a member of the Buenos Aires elite, suffered the disappearance of his brother in 1982 as a consequence of the witness's investigation of the diplomat's death.

16. This occurred in October 1984; see Diaz Colodrero, 243.

17. Verbitsky, *Civiles y militares*, 129–40. Alfonsín took advantage of this mobilization of popular support to announce a series of unpopular economic measures, alienating many participants, who felt that their support for the democratic regime had been manipulated in the service of partisan policies; there was a massive walk-out during the economic portion of Alfonsín's speech (see Diaz Colodrero, 199, for the statement of a disgruntled Radical Youth leader).

18. For various examples, see Strassera and Moreno Ocampo, 42; Americas Watch, *Truth and Partial Justice in Argentina*, 75; "Piden garantias los testigos," *Clarín*, May 8, 1985. Examples include forcing a potential witness to give testimony on a military base, forcing a potential witness to identify an accused repressor face to face (and sometimes leaving the witness alone with the accused), and threatening potential witnesses who were members of the military or police with internal prosecution. In response to the publication of threatening pseudonymous accusations of guerrilla activity against Ex-Detenido witnesses, which included information only available in the concentration camps, the Ex-Detenidos Association filed a formal complaint with the appeals court.

19. Based on interviews with Prosecutor Luis Moreno Ocampo and various members of his staff, Aug. 12, 1987, and Nov. 15, 1988.

20. In the "Dirty War" argument, the defense cited the example of Hiroshima as an instance justifying the indiscriminate use of repression in wartime (Ciancaglini, 204). One attorney bolstered his contention of lack of junta-level coordination by pointing to military defeat in the Malvinas (ibid., 182). The argument that the repression was carried out under orders from a civilian government was undercut both by the fact that this was the same civilian government overthrown by the military, and by the testimony of the civilian president who signed the order to "annihilate" that the decree was clearly framed by existing military and civilian law.

21. One of the precedents cited for this argument was the Eichmann trial. See Moncalvillo, 318, and Sancinetti, 27–29.

22. Ciancaglini, 23–25, 31, 82; Sancinetti, 31.

23. Ciancaglini, 151.

24. Diaz Colodrero, 253. Also see press accounts, Sept. 6, 1985.

25. Full text of the accusation in *El diario del juicio*, esp. 243, 249–50, 325.

26. For a discussion of the general significance of the sentence, see Amnesty International, *Argentina: The Military Juntas*. Sancinetti criticizes the sentence on legal grounds, including the substitution of proportionality among defendants for proportionality in relation to similar crimes in sentencing, and the computation of concurrent rather than consecutive charges for repetitions of the same crime (26, 47–48). A feature of the sentence that would later assume

political significance was the relatively light penalty assigned to the Air Force commanders.

The Air Force was less directly implicated in the repression, and during subsequent military rebellions against democratic governments, it was the least involved and most loyal service.

27. Interview with Jorge Torlasco, Sept. 13, 1988.

28. For one account, see Fontana, "La política militar del gobierno constitucional argentino," 392–96. A different version of a proposed pardon by Alfonsín appears in Acuña and Smulovitz, 40.

29. Rock, *Argentina, 1516–1987*, 401.

30. Americas Watch, *Truth and Partial Justice in Argentina*, 54–56; Verbitsky, *Civiles y militares*, 102.

31. Americas Watch, *Truth and Partial Justice in Argentina*, 26; Verbitsky, *Civiles y militares*, 204.

32. The best-known cases brought by foreign governments were the Swedish inquiry over the disappearance of a Swedish teenager, Dagmar Hagelin, and the French government's case in connection with the disappearance of two French nuns.

33. Americas Watch, *Truth and Partial Justice in Argentina*, 60. The nature, origins, and development of military tension and military uprisings are covered at length in Chapter 6.

34. For an exposition of this point, see Acuña and Smulovitz, 24–25. Alfonsín defends the instructions in his 1986 *Mensaje presidencial*, xxxii–xxxiii.

35. Human rights movement reactions to the instructions and Alfonsín's response are reported in *El Periodista*, May 2–8, 1986. In an example of the kind of "shaming" legitimacy challenge to institutional honor discussed by Prosecutor Ocampo in connection with the Punto Final law, the Ex-Detainees protested both the instructions and the increasing use of statutes of limitation to avoid human rights prosecutions by marching on the Hall of Justice (Tribunales) with signs reading: "Witnesses available" and "Are there any judges left who are willing to see that justice is done?"

36. Interview with Jorge Torlasco, Sept. 13, 1988; Amnesty International, *Argentina: The Military Juntas*, 92; Verbitsky, *Civiles y militares*, 168–69; Americas Watch, *Truth and Partial Justice in Argentina*, 63. For a representative human rights movement view, see MEDH, "Instrucciones al fiscal militar, atentado a la justicia," *InformeDH*, no. 44 (June 1986). The instructions also led the Senate to formally challenge Defense Minister Jaunarena, discussed in *El Periodista*, June 11–17, 1986.

37. Verbitsky, *Civiles y militares*, 271. An open amnesty would have evoked memories of the 1973 Peronist government's amnesty, which freed significant numbers of leftist guerrillas and death squad members (a brief history of political amnesties in Argentina can be found in Sancinetti, 75–76). An open amnesty would also have violated Argentina's international treaty obligations, which are spelled out in Rodolfo Mattarollo, "Crímenes imprescriptibles," *Crisis*, no. 50 (Jan. 1987). The timing of the Punto Final proposal also coincided with the introduction of Uruguay's amnesty law for military officers.

38. Rock, *Argentina, 1516–1987*, 401; Verbitsky, *Civiles y militares*, 287; Diaz

Colodrero, 15. For various human rights movement arguments against Punto Final, see Molina, *Inconstitucionalidad de la ley de Punto Final*; APDH, "Un rechazo fundamentado," *Derechos Humanos* 1, no. 7 (Dec. 1986); and Osvaldo Bayer, "Ahora son todos culpables," *Crisis*, no. 50 (Jan. 1987).

39. Americas Watch, *Truth and Partial Justice in Argentina*, 78; interview with Jorge Torlasco, Sept. 13, 1988.

40. *Clarín*, Dec. 9, 1986; *La Razon*, Dec. 5, 1986.

41. Verbitsky, *Civiles y militares*, 282; interview with Eduardo Rabossi, Apr. 20, 1988; interview with Radical youth official, Sept. 5, 1988. Also see *El Periodista*, Dec. 26 [1986]–Jan. 1, 1987. A particularly telling example of internal opposition is that of the Radical Youth leader Marcelo Lopez Alfonsín, the president's nephew, who characterized the measure as a contradiction of the achievements of human rights policy, ethically misguided, unconstitutional, and destined to undermine faith in democracy (*Nueva Presencia*, Jan. 2, 1987).

42. Verbitsky, *Civiles y militares*, 288; interview with representatives of the Asociación de Ex-Detenidos, July 6, 1988.

43. The popular and progressive Radical legislator Federico Storani, who had initially opposed the measure, graphically characterized this conflict between party discipline and conscience in an interview on the eve of passage of the "due obedience" law: "Look, I lost my moral virginity when I voted for the Punto Final law" (*El Periodista*, June 5–11, 1987).

44. The Senate debate is in República Argentina, *Diario de sesiones: Senadores*, 36th *reunion*, 3d *sesión especial extraordinaria*, Dec. 22, 1986; the reference to the Abuelas is on 4609.

45. Renovador Peronism is a progressive tendency that arose among a new generation within the Peronist party as a response to the traumas of the dictatorship and Peronism's unexpected defeat in the 1983 transition elections. Renovation Peronism emphasizes the social democratic elements of Peronism, downplays the Catholic-derived social conservatism, seeks greater internal democracy within the movement, and explicitly recognizes and supports human rights claims.

46. The House debate is in República Argentina, *Diario de sesiones: Diputados*, 63d *reunion*, 2d *sesión especial extraordinaria*, Dec. 23–24, 1986. A complete tally of the vote is provided in the joint human rights movement informational pamphlet *Ley de Punto Final*, 8–10.

47. For example, a set of human rights groups filed a single brief involving 1,000 alleged repressors in January 1987: see Centro de Estudios Legales y Sociales, *Boletín* 3, no. 9 (June 1987), and Madres de Plaza de Mayo–Linea Fundadora, *Hoja Informativa*, no. 1, which also recounts meetings with Executive and judicial officials lobbying against Punto Final, shows a protesting Madre being removed from the Congress during the debate, and describes an appeal to the Supreme Court after passage of the legislation.

48. Amnesty International, *Argentina: The Military Juntas*, 93.

49. Interviews with Luis Moreno Ocampo, Aug. 12, 1987, and Nov. 15, 1988. I have translated his term *la fuerza de la verdad* as "the force of the facts," but it could also be rendered as "the power of the truth." He also stresses the

challenge experienced by members of the judiciary when faced with the human rights organizations' presentation of their efforts and the failure of the legal system during the Proceso, which at times inspired an impulse to reclaim the lost honor of the judiciary.

50. The subsequent course of these cases is detailed in a joint movement document issued after promulgation of the "due obedience" law, *Culpables para la sociedad, libres por la ley*.

51. Interview with the provincial secretary of human rights for Entre Rios, July 14, 1988.

52. Interview with Renée Epelbaum, May 3, 1988.

53. Although some activists and opposition forces maintain that the Obediencia Debida law was part of a pact to end the rebellion, Alfonsín's early statements and projects support the administration's claim that the principle of due obedience extended in the new legislation was always inherent in Alfonsín's policy of "levels of responsibility." Following statements by the leader of the rebellion that Alfonsín had promised a series of measures, the president made a speech to the Armed Forces in which he asserted that there had been no negotiation and that a due obedience proposal had already been in the works before the rebellion (Apr. 21, 1987, reprinted in Sancinetti, 263). The Radical legislator Leopoldo Moreau also defended the law in terms of previous policy (*El Periodista*, May 15–21, 1987).

54. Prosecutions for rape have been rare; acts of rape were generally associated with exempt acts of torture and murder, and perpetrators are difficult to identify since victims were usually blindfolded, gang rape was common, and many victims were subsequently murdered.

55. Interview with Deputy Leopoldo Moreau, *El Periodista*, May 15–21, 1987.

56. Legislative debate in República Argentina, *Diario de sesiones: Diputados*, 8th *reunion*, 5th *sesión ordinaria*, May 15–16, 1987, and *Senadores*, 13th *reunion*, 7th *sesión ordinaria*, June 4–5, 1987. This time the measure was actually strengthened in the Senate.

57. *El Periodista*, May 22–28, 1987.

58. Interview with CELS representatives, Dec. 12, 1988. The human rights organizations claimed that the Obediencia Debida law violated Argentina's international treaty obligations (especially the International Convention Against Torture). Legal arguments regarding the constitutionality and international legality of this law are reviewed extensively in Sancinetti, and briefly in English in "The Constitutionality Question," *Buenos Aires Herald*, "The Law," June 23, 1987. The federal appeals court of the province of Bahia Blanca did rule the due obedience law unconstitutional, but the Supreme Court validated it. An OAS ruling condemning Argentina's trial limitations was issued in 1992.

59. The joint human rights movement publication *Culpables para la sociedad, libres por la ley* profiles individual cases dropped under the Obediencia Debida law.

60. Interview with CELS representatives, Dec. 12, 1988. A particularly notorious release of this type involved a police physician, Jorge Bergez, who had been convicted of participating in torture sessions.

61. See Americas Watch, *Truth and Partial Justice in Argentina*; Acuña and Smulovitz; *Latin America Weekly Report*, Oct. and Nov. 1989 and Dec. 1990.

62. Fisher, 154.

63. General information on the issue of missing children and the work of the Abuelas can be found in Nosiglia's *Botín de guerra*; Abuelas de Plaza de Mayo, *Missing Children*; Torres Molina, "La problematica especifica de los niños desaparecidos," and UN Human Rights Commission, *Prevention of the Disappearance of Children*.

64. Interview with Ramos Padilla, Nov. 24, 1988.

65. During the 1987 Supreme Court crisis, one justice circulated an internal memorandum that described the child's disappeared biological parents as "sucked up and liquidated [*chupados y liquidados*]," language echoing that of the repressors (see Abuelas, *Informaciones*, no. 15, Aug.–Sept. 1987). The Juliana case was covered exhaustively in the Argentine press between August and September 1988; see esp. *Pagina Doce* and the *Buenos Aires Herald* throughout this period.

66. Andersen, *Dossier Secreto*, "Epilogue."

67. The Abuelas' criticism is expressed by President Isabel de Mariani in an interview in *Pagina Doce*, July 8, 1988. The meeting with Alfonsín is documented in *Pagina Doce*, Nov. 3, 1988.

68. The national genetic data bank was created by Law 23.511; the pensions were provided for in Law 23.466. The Napoli pension proposal was introduced in June 1984, but the compromise legislation was not approved until October 1986; the Asamblea's role was confirmed by the Asamblea Legislative Committee in an interview, June 27, 1988.

69. Political prisoners, in contrast with the disappeared, were usually arrested openly and often charged or tried in some fashion. The fundamental and critical difference is that the dictatorship acknowledged the presence, identity, and location of political prisoners—and thus, most political prisoners survived, while most of the disappeared did not. A complicating factor is that a significant number of political prisoners were originally disappeared and held clandestinely, but subsequently transferred to the regular prison system and acknowledged as political prisoners.

70. See Diaz Colodrero and Abella, 154–69. Case review rather than early release was the preferred strategy, since it not only would have freed the vast majority of prisoners, but also would have helped to reestablish the role of legal guarantees by highlighting their absence in some cases and judicial collaboration in others. On April 18, 1984, a coalition of human rights groups marched to the Villa Devoto prison while 100 Madres protested in front of the Palace of Justice (*La Voz*, Apr. 18, 1984); the first hunger strike took place in May 1984 (*La Voz*, May 11, 1984).

71. Case revision proposals had been presented by the Radical dissident Lucia Alberti, the Christian Democrats, and the Partido Intransigente (Diaz Colodrero and Abella, 163). Alfonsín's advisor Malamud Goti claims that he drafted a legislative proposal to review the cases of political prisoners in the Supreme Court, but that it was rejected because it violated the administration's desire to give an "evenhanded" treatment to the military and the victims of

repression (interview, Aug. 17, 1988). The human rights movement, especially Familiares, then proposed triple-counting of Proceso-era time served, but the final revision involved only double-counting.

72. CELS appealed these cases to the OAS Human Rights Commission (see *Boletín* 4, no. 12 [Apr.–May 1988]). The national Human Rights Secretariat also proposed legislation to review the cases of the remaining political prisoners, which was not passed by the legislature (interview with an official of the national Human Rights Secretariat, Apr. 20, 1988). The official noted that the reopening of the cases by the original judges after 12 years is logistically problematic and not equivalent to review by an appellate body.

73. For documentation of their cases, see Familiares de Desaparecidos y Detenidos por Razones Políticas, *Presos políticos.*

74. Some employers may have been motivated to denounce trade union activists because temporary disappearance was most common among the latter. The most prominent case of alleged employer involvement in a disappearance is the Giorgi case, in which a chemical engineer was abducted from the National Technology Institute with the apparent complicity of his superiors (see "Still Unexplained," *Buenos Aires Herald*, July 27, 1983).

75. "Fallo," *Pagina Doce*, Sept. 3, 1988. Ironically, several former victims (or their relatives) have won civil judgments outside of Argentina, notably in the United States, where the former zone Commander General Suarez Mason was ordered to pay $20 million to victims and their survivors.

76. Interview with CELS representatives, Dec. 12, 1988. A typical case dismissed under the statute of limitations is noted in "No indemnizaran a un ex detenido," *Pagina Doce*, Sept. 17, 1988.

77. See *Latin American Weekly Report*, 92-02 (Jan. 16, 1992); *Latin American Regional Report—Southern Cone*, Feb. 6, 1992; *Latin American Database*, Jan. 22, 1992.

78. See Malamud Goti, 11–12.

79. See Hugo Vezetti, "El Juicio: Un ritual de la memoria colectiva."

80. A retired military officer of democratic convictions characterized the significance of the trials thus: "That impunity with which the commanders customarily operated has run out. There is no more impunity" (interview with Col. Jose Luis Garcia, in Diaz Colodrero, 309). A democratic-era judge, leader of a judicial reform movement, summarized the transition to democracy by saying: "Impunity has disappeared" (interview, Dec. 19, 1988).

81. The author Santiago Kovadloff said: "The trial is founding the Republic. We, through this trial . . . are founding the Republic. Founding civil rights. Founding the autonomy and the independence of Justice" (in Moncalvillo, *Juicio*, 332).

82. See Acuña and Smulovitz, 56, on the combined effect of trials plus pardons and how they differ from amnesties, under which trials never occur.

83. Lucas Orfano of Familiares in Diaz Colodrero and Abella, 148. This point is made more abstractly by Carlos Altamirano: "Preventing the centers of torture, debasement, and extermination from reappearing in our country depends on a national collective will. And the reflection and debate over this

public trial will perhaps contribute more to that will than the number of criminals that justice succeeds in condemning" ("Sobre el juicio a las juntas militares").

Chapter 6

1. Alfonsín's remark to this effect, which I have made the epigraph to Chapter 6, is quoted in Giussani, 240.

2. Molino, "Democratic Establishments," 54–55. In his framework, Argentina would be a protected democracy (the most open form of tutelary democracy). Many analysts of civil-military relations classify Argentina more optimistically—for example, as "partial democratic control" in Fitch and Fontana, "Military Policy and Democratic Consolidation in Latin America."

3. Lázara, *Poder militar*, 324.

4. Alfonsín's speech to an Armed Forces dinner, July 5, 1985, quoted in Montserrat "Inspiraciones de la actual política de defensa en la Argentina," 17. This speech is considered a critical enunciation of key concepts in military policy.

5. One reflection on the corporate logic of the military, Miguens's *Honor militar*, discusses the conflict between military honor, based on loyalty to and the prestige of the "estate," and the personal conscience of the citizen, based on moral equality and individual responsibility (see esp. 16–18).

6. Perelli, "Legacies of Transitions to Democracy in Argentina and Uruguay," discusses this strategy in terms of the principles underlying this logic and the missing elements in Argentine civil-military relations.

7. See Waisman, "Legitimation of Democracy," 104.

8. This analysis of administration beliefs is echoed in Leís, 67. In subsequent self-criticism, Jaime Malamud Goti, a presidential advisor, summarized the failures of government human rights policy vis-à-vis the military: "We didn't act swiftly enough." He chose as an example the failure to break up military neighborhoods. Interview, Aug. 17, 1988.

9. See República Argentina, *Tres años ganados*; Alcántara Sáez and Floria, 18.

10. From 1985 onward, every edition of the Madres' newsletter *Madres de Plaza de Mayo* carried a regular feature called "Gallery of Repressors" with a detailed history of human rights charges against current military personnel. Another indication of the emphasis on the identity of transition actors was the movement's call for the replacement of Proceso-era judges.

11. See Rial, "Armed Forces and the Question of Democracy," 17; Stepan, ch. 7.

12. The classic sources on the history and nature of the Argentine military are Potash, *Army and Politics in Argentina*; Rouquié, *Poder militar*, esp. ch. 9; and Fontana, *Fuerzas Armadas*. See also Lázara, *Poder militar*, an academic history in terms of the development of the national security doctrine, written by a member of the Congreso Nacional and APDH vice president.

13. For examples of this norm, which cuts across military factions and is consistent over time, see the military documents compiled in Verbitsky, *Medio siglo de proclamas militares*. During the proclamation of the 1943 GOU coup (the coup involving Perón), the military referred to itself as "The Armed Forces, faithful and jealous guardians of the honor and traditions of the nation. . . . the Army, which is the people" (ibid., 47). The 1966 Onganía coup, animated by a very different ideology and a generation later, expressed a similar sentiment: "Today, as in all the decisive stages of our history, the Armed Forces, interpreting the highest common good, assumes the responsibility for assuring national union and making possible the general welfare" (ibid., 100).

14. General Luciano Benjamín Menéndez, "Las intervenciones militares en la vida política nacional," *Revista Militar*, no. 707 (Jan.–Mar. 1982).

15. The term *estado de derecho* means both constitutional government and the rule of law, with implications of both due process and the institutionalization of democratic procedures.

16. Giussani, 123.

17. See the comments of Brigadier Horacio Crespo, in José Thiago Cintra, ed., *Seguridad nacional y relaciones internacionales*, 35.

18. See Lázara, *Poder militar*, 48, 50, 54–55.

19. On this aspect of military identity, see Waisbord, "Politics and Identity in the Argentine Army." One interviewee said, "We won the war against the communist subversion militarily, and the generals lost it ideologically" (ibid., 166).

20. "Martinian" refers to General José de San Martín, one of Argentina's founding patriots and a hero of Latin American independence. San Martín linked independence with the establishment of constitutional democracy and is seen as a model of the use of military force for nationalist liberation. An essay on this theme, "San Martín y la obediencia debida," can be found in Giussani, 218–20.

21. This identification of factions within the military is based on that made by Lopez, *El último levantamiento*, 111–18; also see Moneta in Thiago Contra, 34, and Lázara, *Poder militar*. The distinction between *ejercito nacional* and *ejercito constitucional* is in Alcántara Sáez and Floria, 67.

22. Norden, "Democratic Consolidation and Military Professionalism," 157, 165.

23. See Stepan, ch. 6.

24. See López, *El último levantamiento*, 170; Lázara, *Poder militar*, 344; MEDH, "¿Que hacer con los militares?" *InformeDH*, no. 52 (June 1987).

25. On military professionalism trading off a higher threshold of intervention for more comprehensive rule, see O'Donnell, *Modernization and Bureaucratic Authoritarianism*, 165. On the self-managed nature of military reform in Argentina, and consequent increase in the military's political role, see Lopez, "La reforma debida," *Unidos* 4, no. 9 (Apr. 1986). Since the Proceso represented an alliance between liberal internationalist and right nationalist military elements, the predominant factional dynamic of reform was that right-wing revolt was followed by professional concessions to the "liberals."

26. These and other reforms are discussed in Varas, "Democratization and Military Reform in Argentina"; Zagorski, "Civil-Military Relations and Argentine Democracy"; Rock, *Argentina, 1516–1987*, 395–96; Poneman, 86; Verbitsky, *La posguerra sucia*, 69; Lopez, *El último levantamiento*; and various publications of the Fundación Arturo Ilia. The statistic on levels of conscription is from a Defense Ministry source, interview, Oct. 5, 1988.

27. During the Proceso, one form of disappearance was the kidnapping of drafted youths. *El Periodista*, May 23–29, 1986, reports mistreatment and torture of conscripts during training exercises and documents the death of around 100 conscripts between 1983 and 1985. Further allegations of severe mistreatment of conscripts can be found in *Pagina Doce*, Apr. 24, 1988. In part as a response to these phenomena, several deputies introduced legislation to exempt the relatives of persons who had disappeared from military service (to date, not passed by either house of the legislature).

28. Criticisms of structural military reform are from Ernesto López, *El último levantamiento*, ch. 7; and interviews with the military scholar (and retired captain) Luis Tibiletti, Aug. 11, 1987; the former Defense Ministry advisor Martinez Noguera, Sept. 12, 1988; and representatives of CEMIDA, the Association of Democratic Military Officers, Apr. 12, 1988. The Defense Ministry official Angel Tello confirmed that redeployment efforts have been piecemeal and mostly achieved through selective reinforcement rather than reassignment (interview, Oct. 5, 1988). Also see Beltrán, 224.

29. For a representative administration position on the reform of strategic doctrine, see the Defense Ministry official Angel Tello's *Algunas reflexiones sobre teoría, doctrina, e hipótesis de conflicto*.

30. Interview with CELS representatives, Aug. 24, 1988.

31. *La Nación*, Aug. 18, 1986; some analysts point to the mere fact that the military was invited to comment on the legislation as a sign of continued corporatist influence.

32. Information on the new defense law is derived from Montserrat, 18–19, and the International Conference on Military Reform, especially the presentations by Deputy Conrado Storani (*hijo*) and Senator Antonio Berhongaray of the Senate Defense Committee. Also see works by López and Fontana, as well as the Giadone pamphlet *Hipótesis de guerra* and Rattenbach et al., *Fuerzas armadas argentinas*. An example of a practical change implied by the elimination of internal intervention as a hypothesis of conflict would be a concentration on heavier weapons systems suited for external war rather than light weaponry.

33. *La Nación*, Mar. 13, 20, 1989.

34. Julio Carretto, *La ideología y la nueva guerra*, esp. see 9, 102, 107, 115–17; 78–82; 46, 120; 32, 49; 52–60, 47.

35. Interview with Martinez Noguera, a former Defense Ministry education advisor, Sept. 12, 1988. The commission rejected the promotion of any explicit discussion of human rights in military curricula, since this might well serve as an opportunity for nationalist "revindication" of the Dirty War. The universities of Belgrano and La Plata have both signed exchange compacts with the Navy in which officers attend civilian classes but constitute the majority of

students within the "integrated" classes. (Not only does this form of educational integration defeat the purpose of the reform, but civilian students at the institutions affected have reported informal ideological pressure by military students on both civilian students and instructors, thus militarizing civilian education.)

36. Since the "due obedience" law suspended some trials under appeal, at times the promotion lists even included officers already convicted of human rights violations. Again, the Centro de Estudios Legales y Sociales played a particularly strong role in lobbying, through the provision of information to relevant senators (interview withs CELS representatives, Aug. 24, 1988).

37. See *Madres de Plaza de Mayo* 1, no. 3 (Feb. 1985): 9.

38. Verbitsky, *Civiles y militares*, 54; Centro de Estudios Legales y Sociales, *Boletín* 1, no. 4 [1985?]: 5.

39. Verbitsky, *Civiles y militares*, 78. According to Verbitsky, the Radical involved was an advisor to Senator LaFerriere, and the officer promoted was General Dasso (interview with Horacio Verbitsky, Nov. 21, 1988).

40. See Grecco and Gonzales, *¡Felices Pascuas!* 28.

41. For a general treatment of the Astiz case, see Fontana, "La política militar del gobierno constitucional argentino"; on international condemnation, see *Pagina Doce*, Feb. 25, 1988.

42. Interviews with the leadership of CEMIDA, Nov. 10, 1987, and Apr. 12, 1988, and CEMIDA conference on the new defense law and military reform, July 25, 1988.

43. Interviews with the leadership of CEMIDA, Nov. 10, 1987, and Apr. 12, 1988, and CEMIDA conference on the new defense law and military reform, July 25, 1988.

44. Although they did not reach the level of national uprisings, Horacio Verbitsky considers the following to be politically significant military incidents: the "unplanned maneuvers" during the 1984 CONADEP broadcast of the television program "¡Nunca más!"; the 1985 Cordoba bombing attempt during Alfonsín's visit; another 1985 incident in Alsina; threats by Hector Ríos Ereñu (then chief of staff) during 1986; incidents in Polvorines during Sept.–Oct. 1987; unusual military activity in Cordoba every time significant human rights trials were attempted in that province; and Navy threats every time the Astiz case came to trial (interview, Nov. 21, 1988). Grecco and Gonzales (25) cite another incident in June 1984 involving General Mansilla and a refusal to deliver junior officers charged with human rights violations to justice. Beltrán (222–23) also discusses 1984 incidents in Cordoba.

45. For example, Norden (174) cites an unpublished military study indicating that loss of prestige was the most important issue for most military officers.

46. This discussion of the role of military factions is based on distinctions in Ernesto López, *El último levantamiento*, 111–18; Lázara, *Poder militar*, 340–45.

47. The sequence of human rights trials and associated legislation is detailed extensively in Chapter 5. The Punto Final legislation, an attempt to limit human rights prosecutions by setting an artificial deadline, resulted unexpectedly in hundreds of new prosecutions because of human rights movement

pressure and judicial activism. On military reactions to Punto Final, see Fontana, "La política militar del gobierno constitucional argentino," 407–15.

48. Grecco and Gonzales, 62.

49. Interview, Aug. 11, 1987.

50. Rico himself had no particular role in the Proceso-era repression, and he was not subject to trial.

51. See Ernesto López, *El último levantamiento*, 71–78. The details of the rebellion and its resolution are also covered in the *New York Times* and *Washington Post*, Apr. 17–22, 1987.

52. The rebels thus became known as the *carapintadas* (war-paint wearers). Janowitz, *Military Institutions and Coercion in the Developing Nations*, 117, describes the military skill structure as composed of heroic leaders, military managers, and military technologists—with modernization and reform increasing the proportion of managers and improving opportunities for transfers to civilian activity. During Argentina's military rebellions, a key symbolic theme was the affirmation of the heroic leadership role. This represented a partial reversal of the human rights movement's political theater, which had discredited the military's claim to heroic leadership.

53. See Grecco and Gonzales, ¡*Felices Pascuas!* 239. The rebels' use of the metaphor of a general strike underlines the parallel between the military's role and the corporatist organization of the labor movement, as well as the legitimacy of corporatist claims in Argentine political discourse.

54. See Grecco and Gonzales, 182. This was considered a critical step because previous military coups had always been abetted by the support of disgruntled civilian outgroups.

55. Americas Watch gives a figure of "almost 50,000" civilian demonstrators outside the Campo de Mayo military base (*Truth and Partial Justice in Argentina*, 68).

56. Alfonsín's speech to the nation, in Sancinetti, 254.

57. A chant by Radical supporters cited in Grecco and Gonzalez, 68, shows the level of macho confrontation involved:

> No queremos más golpes, no queremos más patotas
> Porque tenemos un Presidente, un Presidente con pelotas.

> We don't want any more coups, we don't want any more thugs
> Because we have a president, a president with balls.

58. Sancinetti, 261.

59. See Grecco and Gonzales, 123, 143, 170.

60. See Ernesto Lopez, *El último levantamiento*, 83, 87.

61. The most loyal service was the Air Force: some sources claim that the Air Force would have been willing to attack the rebels if negotiations had failed, while others contend that the Air Force refused to intervene in what was seen as an internal Army problem (for the first view, see Grecco and Gonzales, 208–16; for the second, Verbitsky, *Civiles y militares*, 364). In a further illustration of the distinction between military loyalty and democratic orientation, the loyal

general who offered to put down the uprising, Ernesto Alais, had commanded the regiment that received the most denunciations for human rights violations during operations against guerrillas in Tucumán during 1976 (Verbitsky, *La posguerra sucia*, 259).

62. The president's meeting with Rico was in and of itself an indicator of a collapse of authority for many military officers; "the commander in chief of the armed forces or any military superior should never 'talk' to a subordinate" (Waisbord, 160).

63. Grecco and Gonzales, 130–31.

64. For various accounts, see Verbitsky, *Civiles y militares*, 366, Ernesto López, *El último levantamiento*, 88, Grecco and Gonzales, 222–31.

65. Caridi was not one of the candidates suggested by Rico, but he was clearly a loyal rather than democratic officer. During the Proceso, Caridi had been active in the repression, and human rights groups objected to his promotion. His appointment is further evidence of factional conflict within the military, based on subsidiary visions of military interests within a common antidemocratic framework.

66. Ernesto Lopez, *El último levantamiento*, 109–10, 123–25, 128–30.

67. Ibid., 126–27; *San Francisco Chronicle*, Sept. 28 and 29, 1987.

68. A list of the rebellious regiments is provided in Ernesto López, *El último levantamiento*, 141. On Rico's loss of support, see ibid., 145; the due obedience legislation of June 1987 had limited human rights prosecutions to a handful of serving officers. For an analysis of the rebellion by service, rank, and functional branch, see *El Periodista*, Feb. 19–25, 1988, 4–6.

69. The unfolding details of this incident are chronicled in *Clarín*, Mar. 6, 1988, p. 4, *Pagina Doce* and *Buenos Aires Herald*, June 16 and 17, 1988, and *Pagina Doce*, June 28 and 30, 1988. Although the airport was only held for a few hours, the group of rebels involved apparently planned to kidnap the Air Force commander, promote the replacement of Alfonsín by his vice president and advance the command of Colonel Mohamed Alí Seineldín (who led the next uprising). At their trial, the airport rebels argued—as Rico had in the Semana Santa rebellion—that their actions were an extreme form of protest, comparable to a general strike.

70. For statements by party leaders across the spectrum, see *Clarín*, Jan. 16, 1988, p. 7.

71. See *Clarín*, Feb. 28 and Mar. 3, 1988; *Pagina Doce*, Mar. 9 and Apr. 24, 1988; *Buenos Aires Herald*, May 16, June 14 and 24, July 16, 22, and 30, 1988; *Pagina Doce*, July 14, 16, 20, 23, and 29, 1988.

72. *Pagina Doce*, Apr. 26, 1988.

73. The military's request was framed in terms of a salary scale corresponding to that of the judiciary; this illustrates the struggle for institutional legitimacy reinforcing the struggle for resources—particularly since the judiciary had been the most legitimate institution and the institution most willing to resist military pressure. The increase received was around 30 percent, which exceeded both inflation and the guidelines for public officials by 6–11 percent. See *Pagina Doce*, Mar. 26 and Aug. 25, 1988; *Buenos Aires Herald*, Aug. 25, 1988.

74. Rico followers arrested in connection with a series of bombings in April were financially linked to military intelligence services and connected with death threats to human rights organizations, and arms caches were also discovered (*Buenos Aires Herald* and *Pagina Doce*, Apr. 20 and 21, 1988, and *La Nación*, Apr. 25, 1988). In June, a group of blackmailers linked to Rico were arrested for extortion (*Buenos Aires Herald*, June 25, 1988).

75. *Pagina Doce*, Sept. 1, 2, 6, 13, 17, and 21, 1988; *Buenos Aires Herald*, Sept. 6, 7, 14, 15, 17, and 21, 1988. While temporarily effective in disciplining the rebels, this move perpetuated the autonomy of the military's parallel legal system.

76. *Pagina Doce* and *Buenos Aires Herald*, Oct. 5, 6, 7, 8, 9, and 12, 1988; *Clarín*, Oct. 10, 1988.

77. *Pagina Doce* and *Buenos Aires Herald*, Nov. 18, 19, and 21, 1988.

78. The Coast Guard had never been involved in military unrest.

79. The following treatment of the Villa Martelli uprising is based on the author's field notes, incorporating coverage from *Pagina Doce*, the *Buenos Aires Herald*, *Clarín*, and state television broadcasts, Dec. 2–7, 1988, as well as eyewitness accounts. For a brief summary in English, see *Latin America Regional Report—Southern Cone*, Dec. 22, 1988.

80. See *Latin America Weekly Report*, July 6, 1989; *Latin America Regional Report*, Feb. 2 and Aug. 3, 1989; Acuña and Smulovitz, 34.

81. *Buenos Aires Herald*, Dec. 13, 1988.

82. In October 1990, the new president, Carlos Menem, issued pardons that suspended all human rights trials. Included in the pardons were 174 officers who had participated in the military rebellions under Alfonsín. On December 3, 1990, President Menem faced another military rebellion headed by Seineldín, which included the seizure of military headquarters across from the Presidential Palace. Loyal forces put down the rebellion, killing at least a dozen and injuring several hundred (including civilians). The apparent catalyst was the scheduled release of a military modernization plan. See *Latin America Weekly Report*, Oct. 19, 1989, and Dec. 13 and 20, 1990; *Latin America Regional Reports—Southern Cone*, Dec. 27, 1990.

83. There have been dozens of incidents of kidnapping and torture of political activists; a few are listed in *El Periodista*, July 17–23, 1987, p. 5; *Pagina Doce*, Aug. 5, 1987, and Mar. 29 and May 12, 1988.

84. See Poneman, 145. Although the number of individuals involved is impossible to verify, one indication of the potential size of this labor force is the fact that just one of the many institutions involved in the repression—the Buenos Aires Federal Police—had hired around 7,000 new agents in the wake of the 1976 military coup (Pozzi, *Oposición obrera*, 51–54). For a satirical treatment of a new economic plan based on the "work of the unemployed," see Verbitsky, *La posguerra sucia*, 132–35.

85. One illustration of the ties between these sectors is the case of Alerta Nacional, a neo-Nazi group arrested for a series of bombings during March and April 1988. The vice president of Alerta Nacional was a former police officer, and the group was originally called Crislam—a bizarre ultranationalist

Catholic-Islamic fundamentalist doctrine shared by Colonel Mohamed Ali Seineldín, the leader of the Villa Martelli military uprising. However, Alerta Nacional also referred to itself as a Peronist group, and was only repudiated by
the party in 1988. Some ties are also reported to a right-wing Peronist intelligence official linked to the CGT head Saul Ubaldini. For an overview, see *El
Periodista*, Apr. 15–21, 1988.

86. See Rojas, *Violaciones de los derechos humanos bajo el gobierno constitucional*.
Also see periodic Madres newsletters' tallies, such as "Un atentado por día,"
Madres de Plaza de Mayo 1, no. 1 (Dec. 1984).

87. Also see *El Periodista*, Sept. 29–Oct. 5, 1984.

88. A general listing for both years can be found in *El Periodista*, May 3–9,
1985. The 1984 bombings included attacks on members of CONADEP, the
head of the appeals court judging the former military rulers, the television
station broadcasting the "¡Nunca más!" television program, a Communist party
member who had been active in human rights, and an association of democratic
military officers. The 1985 bombings and state of siege are detailed in *El Periodista*, Nov. 15–21, 1985.

89. See *El Periodista*, July 3–9, 1987; the journal counted 40 attacks in a 60-
day period.

90. See *Pagina Doce* and *Buenos Aires Herald*, Mar. 30 and 31 and Apr. 2, 3,
8, 9, and 10, 1988, and *La Nación*, Apr. 4, 1988.

91. See *La Nación*, Dec. 15, 1988, for the study by the Centro para la Nueva
Mayoria, a center-right think tank. In South America, only Columbia and Peru
lead Argentina in (documented) political violence.

92. The organizational relationships are explained in Rattenbach et al.,
Fuerzas armadas argentinas, 155–56.

93. Interview, Oct. 5, 1988.

94. *El Periodista*, Dec. 6–12, 1985, and Feb. 28–Mar. 6, 1986. In the latter, it
is noted that almost 80 percent of the members of Army Intelligence—theoretically dedicated to external military intelligence—were posted in Buenos Aires.

95. Interview with Facundo Suarez, *El Periodista*, July 31–Aug. 6, 1987.

96. *El Periodista*, June 19–25, 1987.

97. See *Latin American Weekly Report*, Jan. 25, 1990; *Latin American Regional
Reports—Southern Cone*, Feb. 8, 1990.

98. *Pagina Doce*, Oct. 22 and 23, 1988; interview with Roberto Manuel Pena,
former head of SIDE (civilian state intelligence), in *El Periodista*, Aug. 9–15,
1985.

99. Interview, Apr. 1988.

100. *Pagina Doce*, Aug. 26, 1988.

101. *Buenos Aires Herald* and *Pagina Doce*, June 12 and 15, 1988.

102. The violent strike took place on September 9, 1988, and was covered
in the Argentine press on September 10, 1988. A man pictured breaking win-
dows in a police photo was identified as Osvaldo "Paqui" Forese by a Uru-
guayan lawyer who had been tortured by him (*Buenos Aires Herald*, Sept. 30,
1988).

103. According to Sivak's widow, Marta Sivak, the kidnappers later told

234 ≈ Notes to Pages 105–10

Sivak's family that the kidnapping was "half work, half business." Interview, Nov. 25, 1988.

104. See *El Periodista*, May 18–22, 1986, and Nov. 13–19, 1987; the latter issue alleges a connection between the kidnappers and Nazi groups.

105. The defense minister under whom the extortion attempt occurred had died in the interim.

106. Interview with Marta Sivak, Nov. 25, 1988; Marta Oyhanarte (Sivak), *Tu ausencia, tu presencia*. Other extortionary kidnappings cited as probably the "work of the unemployed" are the Pescarmona, Meller, and Fusito cases.

Chapter 7

1. See Stepan, *Rethinking Military Politics*, ch. 1.

2. The original 1986 CELS study, available from CELS, was presented to the national and provincial secretaries of the interior. For an updated study that frames the phenomenon of police violence in a social context, see Centro de Estudios Legales y Sociales, *La violencia policial*.

3. The most serious allegations of improper police behavior in the course of crowd control concern the 1988 "Black Friday" CGT general strike and the May 1989 food riots.

4. For an instance of the latter, see *Pagina Doce*, Oct. 7, 1988.

5. Interview with Judge Eugenio Zaffaroni, Nov. 17, 1988.

6. Interview with Ministry of the Interior official, Sept. 30, 1988. The proposed reforms transfer the investigative function from first-instance judges to prosecutors and assign judges faculties to guarantee the rights of suspects, while placing the police investigation under the supervision of the prosecutor. In 1988, the reform had passed in committee and was being considered in the House.

7. Interview with a Ministry of the Interior advisor on police reform, Dec. 21, 1988. The courses that have a civil rights component are Constitutional Law, Penal Law, and Penal Procedures. One problem with these reforms is that they only affect commissioned police officers; police "subofficials" (roughly, non-commissioned officers) undergo a much briefer training, with less of a legal component, but often have the same power on the street as their putatively better-trained and more sensitive superiors.

8. Interview with Judge Eugenio Zaffaroni, Nov. 17, 1988.

9. The beating and kidnapping of a witness in the Budge case is reported in the *Buenos Aires Herald*, July 26, 1987; various threats and beatings of witnesses in the San Francisco de Solano case are in *Pagina Doce* and the *Buenos Aires Herald*, June 8, 9, 12, 18, and 19, 1988, and *Clarín*, June 14 and 15, 1988. In both Budge and San Francisco de Solano, several of the victims were politically active—although in all cases the deaths are attributed by police to a confrontation following prosecution of a common crime.

10. Interview with Deputy Marco DiCaprio, Aug. 30, 1988.

11. Interview with an official of the Buenos Aires provincial Ministry of the Interior, Dec. 20, 1988.

12. The Budge case and the formation of the neighborhood defense committee, as well as subsequent persecution, are detailed in Ubertalli.

13. Interviews with SERPAJ representatives, Tucumán, Nov. 5, 1988. For a national summary of incidents of police abuse during the early years of the Alfonsín administration, see "Cronología de la violencia uniformada," *Madres de Plaza de Mayo*, 2, no. 28 (Mar. 1987); for some later incidents, see *Madres de Plaza de Mayo* 4, no. 42 (June 1988).

14. *Pagina Doce* and *Buenos Aires Herald*, May 3, 4, and 5, 1988.

15. *Pagina Doce*, Oct. 5, 1988.

16. *Pagina Doce*, Sept. 2, 1988; Aug. 20, 1988.

17. *Pagina Doce*, Sept. 18, 1988.

18. See *Latin American Regional Reports—Southern Cone*, 6 Aug. 1992; *Latin American Database*, Jan. 22 and 26, 1992.

19. *Latin American Database*, Aug. 4, 1992.

20. Laurence Whitehead identifies prison conditions as a litmus test for democratic consolidation ("The Consolidation of Fragile Democracies," 87).

21. Interview with SASID representative, Oct. 3, 1988. Also see Elias Neuman, "Encierro carcelario." On general prison conditions, see *Madres de Plaza de Mayo* 2, no. 18 (May 1986).

22. See *El Periodista*, Nov. 1–7, 1985, which claims 30 mutinies during the early years of the administration; on prison mutinies with claims of abuse, see *Pagina Doce*, Oct. 6, 1988 (Santiago del Estero), and Dec. 20, 1988 (Caseros).

23. *El Periodista*, Nov. 1–7, 1985.

24. See Comisión Especial de la Subsecretaría de Derechos Humanos, *Carceles argentinas: ¿Suplicio o reeducación?* This report mentions the role of the human rights organizations in forming the commission, in response to being called upon during prison mutinies. It especially criticizes punitive searches of visitors and prison hygiene, and illustrates the problem of preventative detention with a case in which an inmate had served eleven years without a trial.

25. Interview with the provincial minister of the interior, Dec. 20, 1988.

26. *Pagina Doce*, Oct. 7, 1988.

27. *Pagina Doce*, Oct. 28, 1988.

28. Several other legislators during the first post-transition Congress drew heavily on human rights issues (the Radicales Hipólito Solari Yrigoyen, Hugo Piucil, and Lucia Alberti; the four members of the Partido Intransigente bloc, the Movimiento Popular Neuqueño; and, in the 1985 and 1987 legislatures, many Renovador Peronists, especially the Partido Justicialista's Roberto Digon), but Conte's is the clearest case of human rights movement representation. Conte's campaign slogan was "Human rights to Congress!" At one point, newly registered human rights activists composed around one-third of the Christian Democrats' membership; a party official referred to the sudden influx of new members as "the Foreign Legion" (interview, Nov. 22, 1988). Conte and a key staffer were from CELS, a legislative aide was concurrently SERPAJ human

rights coordinator, and the *afectados* (Madres, Abuelas, and Familiares) were also well-represented.

29. His platform is described in Verbitsky, *La posguerra sucia*, 81–82, 87–88; it is also drawn here from an interview with Conte's former legislative aide, Sept. 30, 1988.

30. Conte led the floor fight against Punto Final, modified the pensions for the relatives of disappeared persons, and introduced several proposals regarding political prisoners that shaped the final legislation. He sat on the Constitutional Affairs and Penal Legislation committees; on the former, about 80 percent of his proposals were considered in committee. This influence was exercised during a fraction of his term, since ill health forced him to take a leave during most of 1984 and then to resign in 1987 (interview, Nov. 22, 1988). Following Conte's resignation, many of his projects were taken up by his ally Deputy Raúl Rabanaque of the Partido Intransigente (interview, Dec. 7, 1988).

31. In 1985, a coalition of small leftist parties tried to duplicate the Conte phenomenon by running a group of activists with links to the human rights movement together on one slate, without success. Simon Lázara, co-president of the APDH, was elected to Congress in 1987 on a platform that stressed human rights but was tied to a special electoral arrangement with the ruling Radicales.

32. Interview with Horacio Verbitsky, Nov. 21, 1988. Verbitsky documented numerous instances of military lobbying in his weekly newspaper columns in *Pagina Doce*. During the interview, he recalled an incident following the Semana Santa military uprising in which the Radical deputy who chaired the House Defense Committee attempted to dismiss the "military liaisons" appointed by the Joint Chiefs of Staff (who served as lobbyists for military interests). The committee held a large retirement party for the military liaisons and their staff on a Tuesday—and on Wednesday they returned to work, backed by the Ministry of Defense.

33. For an overall discussion of the Alfonsín administration's human rights legislation, see Garzon Valdez et al., 202. Most of the legislation was written by Alfonsín's advisors Carlos Nino and Jaime Malamud Goti. Goti had met with human rights movement representatives, and he considered the proposal to designate forced disappearance as a crime under Argentine law but rejected the idea for "prudential reasons" (interview, Aug. 17, 1988).

34. *La Nación*, Nov. 2, 1983.

35. Interview with a representative of Las Abuelas, Nov. 17, 1988.

36. Expositions of the treatment of forced disappearance in Argentine law, the need for legislation, and the text of the proposal are in the Asamblea's *La desaparición*; see esp. the essays by the jurists Baigún, González Gartland, and Barcesat. A petition for the proposal circulated by the human rights organizations gathered almost 200,000 signatures (Verbitsky, *La posguerra sucia*, 102).

37. For a systematic analysis of Latin American legal systems in terms of the protection of human rights, with special emphasis on Argentina, see Zaffaroni, *Sistemas penales y derechos humanos*.

38. The legislation granting women equal rights is known as "Patria Potes-

tad Compartida" and was a part of the Radical campaign platform. Thus far, the blatant conflict between the antidiscrimination law and the Argentine Constitution's requirement that the president be a Catholic has not been discussed.

39. Interview with a representative of CELS, Dec. 12, 1988.

40. The figure on the incidence of preventative detention is from Deputy Marco DiCaprio, who served on the Penal Justice Committee of the Camera de Diputados (interview, Aug. 30, 1988); Judge Eugenio Zaffaroni confirmed the estimate of 60 percent and characterized preventative detention as a de facto sentence (interview, Nov. 17, 1988).

41. See the proceedings of the Asamblea Permanente por los Derechos Humanos, *Mesa redonda: Edictos policiales*. The figure on the frequency of "contraventional" offenses is given by the Radical Senate advisor and attorney Luis Diaz (ibid., 5).

42. An analysis of the undermining of the structure of the legal system during the Proceso is Groisman's *Poder y derecho*.

43. See *Clarín*, Mar. 2, 16, and 22, May 31, July 6, Aug. 23, and Sept. 4, 13, 27, and 30, 1984.

44. Interview with Judge Julio Virgolini, Dec. 20, 1988. For a general review, see "Los jueces suben a escena," *El Periodista*, Apr. 29–May 5, 1988. Upon retirement, Ramos Padilla became a Radical party activist, while Zaffaroni has worked closely with Peronist organizations.

45. Interview with Jorge Torlasco, Sept. 13, 1988.

46. Interview, Nov. 24, 1988. Here I have translated *la fuerza de la verdad* as "the force of the facts" because of the context of the statement; when *la fuerza de la verdad* was previously cited by Prosecutor Luis Moreno Ocampo in a different context, it was rendered as "the power of the truth."

47. Interview with Julio Virgolini, Dec. 20, 1988.

48. Interview with Luis Brunatti, Dec. 20, 1988.

49. See *Buenos Aires Herald*, "Law Reforms Mulled," June 22, 1988.

50. A particular irony of her case is that she was accused of participation in a 1974 kidnapping that did not yet fall under the statute of limitations, while the men who kidnapped her in 1978 were already immune from prosecution. She was released in late 1988.

51. The case exercised a "chilling effect" on these activists, such as limiting their right to travel. See *Pagina Doce*, Sept. 27, 1988, and the *Buenos Aires Herald*, Sept. 28, 1988.

52. The Familiares newsletter *Decimos* 9, no. 2 (May 1985): 8.

53. *Pagina Doce*, Dec. 15, 1988.

54. The only other permanent state institution to deal with human rights policy is the Foreign Ministry Human Rights Secretariat. At one point, a coordinating Commission on Missing Children existed under the Ministry of Social Action, but it stopped functioning sometime before 1988. Similarly, a transition-era Executive Committee on the Return of Argentine Exiles seems to have been dissolved.

55. The Subsecretariat of Human Rights has been retained under the succeeding Menem administration. It was initially headed by a minor party (Chris-

tian Democrat) human rights activist, Guillermo Frugoni Rey, who subsequently resigned in protest over Menem's human rights policies.

56. Interviews with Subsecretariat of Human Rights staff, Apr. 1988.

57. Interview with Department of Prevention, Human Rights Subsecretariat, Apr. 13, 1988.

58. Interviews with Eduardo Rabossi, Apr. 20 and Nov. 23, 1988. Dr. Rabossi justified the classification of the CONADEP records by pointing out that open files would also be accessible to former repressors, and that the human rights organizations can no longer use the files to bring new legal actions in any case. When the Menem administration subsequently released Argentina's records on Nazi war criminals, human rights activists renewed their campaign for the opening of the CONADEP archives—without results as of December 1992.

59. Interview with Eduardo Rabossi, Apr. 20, 1988.

60. Interviews with Eduardo Rabossi; in 1985, the subsecretary did review the Edictos Policiales (under which police chiefs may arrest any person for 24 hours in order to "verify their records") at the request of the Ministry of the Interior—and decided that their usefulness outweighed the potential for abuse.

61. The subsecretary, Eduardo Rabossi, is a philosophy professor who had served on CONADEP but had no other previous experience in human rights, law, or administration. Several human rights activists interviewed stated their belief that Dr. Rabossi was appointed precisely because of his lack of practical background in this field, in order to assure that the subsecretariat would take a passive role in policy formulation. For more general criticism of the institution, see Fernandez Meijide in Fruhling, 71–72.

62. Interviews with former staff members of the Subsecretariat of Human Rights, Apr. 1988.

63. Interviews with Entre Rios's subsecretary of human rights, July 14, 1988.

64. Their proposal has been published as CGT / Servicio Paz y Justicia, *Reforma constitucional.*

65. Interview with the Liga attorney and law professor Eduardo Barcesat, Sept. 20, 1988; also see his contribution to the APDH volume, *La desaparición.*

66. In a speech during the Semana Santa crisis, Alfonsín appealed to the nation for support, saying, "We are no longer an international pariah" (Sancinetti, 255).

67. Interview with Foreign Ministry Human Rights Secretariat staff, Oct. 5, 1988. However, there are treaties that have been signed but that are not in force because of lack of ratifying legislation. For example, the Convention on Torture was signed but not ratified before the passage of the due obedience law, which appears to violate the treaty; the Convention was ratified by the Argentine Senate on June 3, 1988.

68. If this measure were implemented, it would make states accountable for forced disappearance perpetrated by agents of the state—and the burden of proof would rest with the state. The proposal would subject state agents accused of perpetrating forced disappearance to universal extradition and forbid amnesties or pardons for this class of crimes. The proposal and arguments for

its adoption are included in APDH's *La desaparición*. In October 1988 the Argentine human rights movement convened an international conference at the University of Buenos Aires to discuss and promote this measure. As of 1992, the measure was being treated by the full OAS.

69. See United Nations, Human Rights Commision, *Prevention of the Disappearance of Children*, Aug. 10, 1988.

70. For general accounts of the attack, see the *New York Times* and *La Nación*, Jan. 24–Feb. 5, 1989, and *Latin America Regional Reports—Southern Cone*, 9 Mar. 1989.

71. See James Neilson, "Ha vuelto la normalidad," *Pagina Doce*, Jan. 27, 1989, and CONADEP Chair Ernesto Sabato's response to attacks in the same issue.

72. *Latin America Regional Report, Southern Cone*, Mar. 9, 1989.

73. Text of radio interview with Alfonsín, *La Nación*, Feb. 6, 1989.

74. See Amnesty International, *Argentina: The Attack of the Third Infantry Regiment Barracks at La Tablada*. These allegations are also reported in *La Nación*, Feb. 6 and Mar. 9, 1989; *El Porteño* 8, no. 87 (Mar. 1989), special edition, "Contra el silencio"; *Clarín*, Feb. 24, 1989; *La Prensa*, Feb. 23, 1989; and the joint press release of the Ex-Detenidos, Madres (both Lineas), Familiares, Liga, Movimiento Judio, and SERPAJ, Feb. 22, 1989, which confirms that human rights movement observers verified physical indications of torture of prisoners. Shortly before his death, Federal Police Chief Juan Pirker criticized the military for failing to use tear gas and other nondeadly measures.

75. Joint human rights movement press release cited in n. 74; *Sur*, June 12, 1989; Asociación de Ex-Detenidos, "¿Porqué asumimos la defensa juridica de los presos de La Tablada?" May 8, 1989.

76. *Pagina Doce*, Feb. 17, 1989. The attorney general's statement reflects a disturbing sacrifice of civil liberties to efficacy. While it may sometimes frustrate the punishment of crime, the linkage between the validity and legitimacy of evidence gathering and the judicial assignment of penalty is, of course, one of the fundamental principles of civil liberties.

77. *La Nación*, Jan. 30 and Feb. 13, 1989.

78. *La Voz del Interior*, Aug. 8, 1989.

79. Las Madres refused to condemn the attack because they claimed that government accounts did not reliably describe what occurred, the attackers may have been sincerely attempting to prevent a coup d'état, and the use of the attack to discredit the human rights movement was more significant than the attack itself.

80. CELS, "A la opinión pública," *Clarín*, Feb. 28, 1989.

81. *Pagina Doce*, Feb. 17, 1989.

82. APDH press release, Feb. 23, 1989.

83. Roberto Herrscher, "Reflections on Human Rights," *Buenos Aires Herald*, Feb. 23, 1989.

84. Personal communications to the author; *Pagina Doce*, Apr. 19, 1989.

85. *Pagina Doce*, Feb. 17, 1989.

86. *Clarín*, Feb. 28, 1989; *Pagina Doce*, Feb. 28, 1989.

87. *Pagina Doce*, Feb. 22, 1989.

Chapter 8

1. This definition is more traditional than the framework cited in Chapter 7, and would include both Stepan's civil society and elements of his political society. See Stepan, *Rethinking Military Politics*.

2. For an examination of the corresponding question of how Argentine civil society provided one of the bases for the establishment of authoritarianism, see O'Donnell, "Democracia en la Argentina, micro y macro."

3. For a summary of Alfonsín administration economic policies and conditions, see William Smith, *Authoritarianism and the Crisis of the Argentine Political Economy*, ch. 10.

4. Lack of participatory success and perceptions of goal distortion are treated as sources of political disillusionment (with some specific reference to the human rights agenda) in the context of a wider discussion of transition and demobilization in Echegaray and Raimondo, *Desencanto político*, 96–99.

5. Interview, Apr. 6, 1988.

6. See Leís, 53–54. If anything, the association benefited the left at the expense of the human rights movement.

7. Interview, May 3, 1988.　　　　8. Interview, July 28, 1987.

9. Interview, June 14, 1988.　　　　10. Interview, Aug. 10, 1988.

11. Garretón, *Reconstruir la política*, 35.

12. See Perelli, "Legacies of Transitions," 42–43.

13. Cavarozzi, "Argentine Political Cycles since 1955," 19–20; O'Donnell, *¿Y a mi, que me importa?* 30. O'Donnell explicitly contrasts the repression of civil society in Argentina with the situation in Chile; he also describes a wider occlusion of the accessible public sphere, as the political arena is filled by corporations at the expense of general mediators such as political parties (20).

14. Leís, 24–28. Leís cites the movement's attitude to the Malvinas adventure as an early indicator of this autonomous logic: while the electoral left accepted the nationalist *raison d'état* of the war and temporarily suspended its opposition to military rule, the human rights movement linked legitimate national principles to its own legitimacy challenge with the slogan "The Malvinas are Argentine—and so are the disappeared."

15. All of these themes are treated in Spitta, "Experiencias cotidianas." Also see dos Santos and Garcia Delgado, "Democracia en cuestión," 68–70. These authors argue that this orientation is inherently incompatible with a democratic social order. For the claim that inflation and speculative practices undermine democracy, see Peralta-Ramos in Peralta-Ramos and Waisman, 40, and Portantiero's concept of an "inflationary culture" (linked to political disillusionment), discussed in Echegaray and Raimondo, 61. Mainwaring summarizes "the need of all sectors of society to abide by democratic rules of the game, even when doing so involves some short-term sacrifices. These themes are relative novelties

in Argentine political society. Since 1930, Argentina has been characterized by a golpista political culture" ("Authoritarianism and Democracy," 415).

16. Mainwaring and Viola, "New Social Movements, Political Culture and Democracy," 24, cites factionalism and "the tendency to privilege short-term self-interest at the expense of long-term social concerns"; the institutionaliza-tion of violence appears in Peralta-Ramos and Waisman, xii; all of these themes are also treated in Cavarozzi, "Argentina's Political Cycles." All of the above are sometimes argued to be determinants as well as results of authoritarianism.

17. For some discussion of the human rights movement recovering the ethi-cal limits of the political, see Flisfisch, "Derechos humanos, política y poder," 106.

18. Landi, *El discurso sobre lo posible*, 27. An ironic recognition of this source of change comes from the military jailers of the publisher Jacobo Timerman, partisans of a militantly anticommunist ideology, who objected to Timerman's printing of poems by Soviet dissidents on the grounds that they glorified *the principle of dissidence* (Timerman, *Prisoner Without a Name, Cell Without a Number*, 57).

19. Landi, *El discurso sobre lo posible*, 30–32. Symptoms of the unresolved role of the past in political discourse include: a public school version of Argen-tine history that stops in the 1920's (the first military coup took place in 1930), the destruction of historical documents and archives, the issuance of 27 politi-cal amnesties since Argentine independence, and the robbery of "objects of memory"—specifically, corpses of political figures.

20. See Dahl, *Polyarchy*, esp. ch. 3, on historical sequences of democratiza-tion. On incomplete contestation in Argentina, see Chapter 2 above.

21. In Argentine Spanish, human rights are often referred to as "rights and guarantees" (*derechos y garantias*); the literal term *derechos humanos* is also used.

22. Eder, "New Social Movements," 886, introduces a model of protest as collective learning.

23. "In totalitarian countries all places of detention ruled by the police are made to be veritable holes of oblivion into which people stumble by accident and without leaving behind them such ordinary traces of former existence as a body and a grave" (Arendt, *Origins of Totalitarianism*, 434).

24. *Clarín*, Oct. 25, 1983. Adding to the sense of a lost generation of citizens, the supplement lists special categories for disappeared adolescents who would have been old enough to vote at the time of the transition, and missing children who will never vote under their true identity.

25. See Daniel Llano of MEDH in Villela, 28; interview with Abuelas rep-resentative, Mar. 19, 1988.

26. Jelin, "Los movimientos sociales en la Argentina," in Jelin, ed., *Los nue-vos movimientos sociales*, esp. 24.

27. For a broad review of Proceso-inspired changing interpretations of the Argentine past in drama, film and fiction, see Halperin Donghi, "Argentina's Unmastered Past."

28. A pointed collection of apologist articles published by the mass-circula-

tion Argentine press during the Proceso is contained in Varela-Cid, ed., *Los sofistas y la prensa canalla.* Many of these selections emphasize the military contention that accusations of human rights violations derived from an international "anti-Argentine campaign."

29. See nos. 45, 55, 92, 104, and 109 of *Humor.* One indication of the popularity of this coverage is popular response to the military seizure of the January 1983 edition; supporters raised funds to cover the entire cost of forgone sales from the missing issue.

30. *Buenos Aires Herald,* Mar. 17, 1984.

31. See *Unidos* 4, nos. 10, 14, 15.

32. Information provided by the Instituto Nacional del Cine, Buenos Aires. Review cited from Lopez, ed., *Catálogo del nuevo cine argentino, 1984–1986.*

33. Serious films exclude titles such as *Los gatos,* in which "the sexual orgies take the characters to limits it will be difficult to return from" (López, ed., *Catalogo del nuevo cine argentino, 1984–1986,* 94).

34. "¡Nunca más!" ratings figures provided by the survey firm Mercados y Tendencias; information on *La noche de los lapices* in *Pagina Doce,* Oct. 7, 1988.

35. However, the impact of this is somewhat blunted by Timerman's current role as a Radical supporter; his show has been extremely supportive of government positions (see *Pagina Doce,* Nov. 8 and 11, 1988). Nevertheless, in 1988, when Timerman interviewed Prosecutor Luis Moreno Ocampo on a legislative problem in Congress, Ocampo used the program as a forum to urge Argentines to "call your representative"—an unprecedented form of citizen activism in Argentina (Ocampo even provided the phone numbers of the individuals in question).

36. *Pagina Doce,* Dec. 16, 1988.

37. *Pagina Doce,* Dec. 8, 22, and 28, 1988. Media organizations included the Argentine Actors' Association, Documentary Filmmakers Association, Argentine Directors Group, Film Union, and Film Industry Association.

38. Data from the Argentine polling firm SOCMERC show the salience of human rights as a first-ranked source of concern, varying between 1 and 3 percent (contrasting with 52 percent for inflation); also see Catterberg, *Los Argentinos frente a la política,* 44. Similarly, Landi registers only 8 percent who identify human rights movements as "organizations that best defend the interests of persons like yourself"; but 31 percent feel that human rights organizations are helping to solve the problems of the country (as compared to 21 percent for unions). See Landi, *Las culturas políticas en numeros.*

39. Sources: SOCMERC; Gallup Argentina; Landi.

40. *El Porteño,* Dec. 1987.

41. General trials support figures from SOCMERC; support for levels of responsibility from Landi, *Cultura política.* (In 1984, SOCMERC obtained a similar response of 71 percent support for "energetic" rather than exemplary trials of the military, which is similar to a more specific result obtained by an anonymous source in 1987.)

42. General figures from SOCMERC and Gallup Argentina. It should be noted that both these sources also show support for government handling of

Semana Santa. The comments on the significance of the due obedience law are from a poll conducted by *El Porteño*, July 1987.

43. As a historical baseline for support for democracy, see the early poll cited by Guillermo O'Donnell in which 60 percent agree that "there are too many platforms and political programs; what we need is a strong man to lead us" (*Modernization and Bureaucratic Authoritarianism*, 149). Also see Susan Tiano, "Authoritarianism and Political Culture."

44. Gallup Argentina, Nov. 1988.

45. Landi, *Cultura política*, 55, 57. For contrasting data showing that economic performance is rated as an important component of democracy, see Catterberg, 144.

46. See Catterberg, *Argentina Confronts Politics*.

47. See García Delgado and Palermo, 417.

48. Quilmes Human Rights Commission internal document, "Informe sobre Derechos Humanos" (mimeograph, June 29, 1988), and interview with members, Aug. 1988.

49. Servicio de Asistencia Integral al Detenido, "¿Qúe es el SASID?"

50. Interview with a representative of SASID, Sept. 25, 1988.

51. Servicio de Asistencia Integral al Detenido, "Sepa como defenderse," which includes the statement: "If for reasons of *fuerza mayor* you cannot avoid signing a document, always put . . . 'I appeal' before your signature. If you have suffered maltreatment by security forces . . . also write 'I want a doctor.' "

52. Servicio de Asistencia Integral al Detenido, "¿Qué es el preso social?"

53. Interview with a representative of SASID, Sept. 25, 1988.

54. Interview with members of the Fundación para la Memoria, Sept. 7, 1988.

55. See Shifter, "Institutionalizing Human Rights in Chile and Argentina."

56. *Pagina Doce*, Aug. 9, 1988; *Buenos Aires Herald*, Aug. 31, 1988. Interview with a participating human rights lawyer, Aug. 18, 1988, who cited the testimony of witnesses as the turning point in eliciting the condemnation.

57. *Pagina Doce*, Nov. 17, 1988.

58. *Pagina Doce*, Nov. 4, 1988.

59. *Pagina Doce*, Nov. 22, 1988; *Buenos Aires Herald*, Nov. 27, 1988.

60. Interview, Aug. 14, 1988.

61. For an illustration of Proceso-era attitudes, see Aliverti, *El archivo de la decada*, 59.

62. *La Razon*, May 10, 1985.

63. At the 1987 Pedagogical Congress, for example, around 120 of 300 delegates were from the Church—and 19 of Buenos Aires's 22 representatives (interview, Sept. 22, 1988).

64. It is unclear whether this was because of bureaucratic inertia, lack of resources, desire to avoid controversy, or some combination of the three.

65. See *Pagina Doce*, Nov. 29, 1988.

66. Montes's *¿Que es esto de la democracia?* includes a section on coups, concluding: "It is not easy to return to living in a democracy. Authoritarian governments make people forget how to participate. We are all accustomed to receive

244 ≈ Notes to Pages 134–38

orders and to give orders, not to receive opinions and to give opinions. We
forget how to discuss. And, in a democracy, discussion is very important" (12).
In Montes's *Los derechos de todos*, the disappeared are discussed explicitly,
an illustration shows protesting Madres asking for justice and respect for all
life, and young readers are assured that even bad people and criminals have
rights.

67. Interview with Program Director Roxana Morduchowitz, Mar. 31, 1988;
Tenemos la palabra 5, no. 15 (May–June 1988). The director is a practicing journalist who had worked closely with Jacobo Timerman. The radio discussion of
democracy included the following: "Democracy doesn't only mean voting, but
democracy must be lived—and to live in democracy, one must participate and
respect one another. . . . if one is opposed to what is happening in the country,
you cannot go to Government House and throw out the president. One must
respect the laws and persons. And if someone doesn't like how a president
elected by the majority is governing, in the next elections [he or she can] vote
for another candidate."

68. Interview with Emilio Mignone, Aug. 24, 1988; Mignone, *Educación
cívica*.

69. See Castagno, 34–36.

70. *Pagina Doce*, Sept. 18, 1988; *Buenos Aires Herald*, Sept. 19, 1988. The
commemoration proposal was introduced by Horacio Ravenna, a member of
the APDH, provincial deputy, former official of the Foreign Office Human
Rights Secretariat, and informal human rights liaison to President Alfonsín.

71. See *El Periodista*, Apr. 5–11, 1985. The Lomas de Zamora program was
established by a rector with ties to the Liga, MEDH, and APDH—and the
program has suffered administratively since his departure. Various human
rights organizations have provided materials and/or lecturers for the human
rights courses.

72. Interview with Eduardo Barcesat, Sept. 20, 1988; also see Castagno.

73. Interview with a professor of education at the University of Buenos
Aires, Sept. 22, 1988.

74. *Pagina Doce*, Sept. 24, 1988.

75. *Pagina Doce*, Nov. 19, 1988.

Chapter 9

1. On the latter point, see Offe, "Reflections on the Institutional Self-Transformation of Movement Politics."

2. See Dalton and Kuechler, eds., *Challenging the Political Order*, 297.

3. On the general pattern of surge and decline of popular mobilization in
transitions to democracy, see Schmitter, O'Donnell, and Whitehead, eds., 55–
56.

4. "The military regime fell because consent to it collapsed, as a consequence of the defeat in the Malvinas-Falklands War with Britain, the economic
catastrophe, and the massive violation of human rights; but the institutional

infrastructure of authoritarianism and corporatism was not broken" (Waisman, "Legitimation of Democracy," 97). Also see Landi, *El discurso sobre lo posible*, 45.

5. "Given a political system of weak parties dominated by caudillos, movimientos, corrientes, corporaciones, and tendencias, all of whom (in a reversal of Clausewitz's famous dictum) view political competition as the pursuit of war by other means, it is natural that Argentine politics should be periodically subject to overt military intervention" (Buchanan, "Exorcising Collective Ghosts," 185). And see, too, Cavarozzi, "Argentina's Political Cycles," 22, who specifically claims that Peronism demoted both party and parliamentary channels of representation vis-à-vis corporations. Also see Portantiero in Nun and Portantiero, 283–85.

6. See Waisman, "Legitimation of Democracy," 102. On parties and movements, see Boschi, *On Social Movements and Democratization*.

7. For example, the March 1988 newsletter is headlined WHITEWASHING THE ARMED FORCES TO GUARANTEE THE SELL-OUT TO IMPERIALISM: THE HOLY ALLIANCE IS STRENGTHENED and features a montage of President Alfonsín, Armed Forces Commander Caridi, and a U.S. flag whose stripes are composed of vipers (*Madres de Plaza de Mayo* 4, no. 39 (Mar. 1988). Another recent edition devoted one-third of its 24 pages to a Madres trip to Cuba, headlined THIS IS THE UTOPIA OUR CHILDREN DREAMED OF—at best, a controversial proposition for civil libertarians, nonmovement allies, and those *afectados* who protested the dictatorship's labeling of their children as revolutionaries (ibid., no. 47 (Nov. 1988).

8. As a Linea Fundadora Madre explained one difference, "This government is our enemy in so far as it doesn't meet our needs, but it is not the same government that disappeared our children" (interview, May 3, 1988). Personal and sociological factors also played a role in the split; for example, the main branch drew more working-class members, while the Linea Fundadora was populated more by women of middle-class background.

9. Interview with Asamblea dissidents, Dec. 20, 1988; also see *Buenos Aires Herald* and *Pagina Doce*, July 30, 1988.

10. Palermo, *Movimientos sociales y partidos políticos* .

11. Earlier violations of human rights under Radical stewardship include the massacres of striking workers during the Semana Trágica and in the Patagonia Rebelde incident. See Chapter 2 for details.

12. Veiga, *Las organizaciones de derechos humanos*, 82.

13. See *La Republica*, esp. May 1981, Feb. 1982, and May 1983.

14. The Human Rights Commission was initiated when the La Plata Radical activist and lawyer Carlos Raimundi was elected the president of the national Radical Youth in 1985 (interview with member of the UCR Human Rights Commission, Sept. 5, 1988). La Plata is the only city in which Radical activists had disappeared in large numbers.

15. Several kindred organizations, such as the Radical think tank Fundación Karakachoff, display La Plata and Asamblea influence. The president of the Fundación was the president of the La Plata UCR and a member of the Asamblea's Consejo General (interview, Sept. 13, 1988). Radical activists cited

the Asamblea's multiparty composition and "evenhanded" approach to government policy as a basis for their participation.

16. Details of this incident are treated in Chapter 3.

17. The above measures are discussed in Unión Civica Radical, Juventud Radical, "Comunicado interno"; and Unión Cívica Radical, Juventud Radical, Comisión de Derechos Humanos, "Documento final de conclusiones"; "Instrucciones al fiscal militar"; and "Ley de Obediencia Debida."

18. Interview with a member of the UCR Human Rights Commission, Sept. 5, 1988; Unión Civica Radical, Juventud Radical, Comisión de Derechos Humanos, "Propuesta de creación de comités de defensa de la democracia." The citizen committees proposed by the UCR commission are primarily educational, with some emergency management planning,whereas the human rights movement has stressed a more active role for nonviolent civil resistance.

19. An example of Radical alienation from the human rights movement is Alfonsín's labeling of the Madres as "not in the national interest." See Verbitsky, *Civiles y militares*, 114, and the response in *Madres de Plaza de Mayo* 1, no. 2 (Jan. 1985). Exceptions include the congressional deputies Lucia Alberti and Federico Storani and the provincial deputy Horacio Ravenna. Discussions of conflict with the UCR can be found in interviews with Alberti, in *El Periodista*, Jan. 2–8, 1987, and Storani, in *Pagina Doce*, Sept. 30, 1988.

20. During the 1988 presidential primaries, when no human rights issues were present and polls showed these issues to be of extremely low salience, Radical campaign material stressed the party's role as the restorer of democracy and defender of human rights. See paid political announcements in *Pagina Doce*, June 26 and 30, 1988. Another example of this phenomenon is the Radical party's support of the Abuelas' (legally correct) demand for the return of a 10-year old missing child to her biological family (the Juliana case, discussed above); popular sentiment was strongly against "breaking up the [illicit adoptive] family."

21. Alfonsín's internal wing of the party, the Movimiento Renovación y Cambio, called for the freedom of political prisoners and an end to torture as early as 1972 (see Ferrari and Herrera, 158). Alfonsín himself mentioned human rights as a "leading national problem" and called for tolerance for the human rights organizations in a 1978 interview at the height of the repression (see López Saavedra, *Testigos del "proceso" militar*, 10–26).

22. Unión Cívica Radical, Juventud Radical, "Comunicado interno."

23. Ferrari and Herrera, 235.

24. Interview with Antonio Troccoli, Dec. 13, 1988.

25. For details, see Chapter 2.

26. Comisión Nacional sobre la Desaparición de Personas, *Nunca más* (1986), 448, lists 30.2 percent of the documented disappeared as blue-collar workers.

27. Renovador Peronism is a progressive tendency that arose among a new generation within the Peronist party as a response to the traumas of the dictatorship and Peronism's unexpected defeat in the 1983 transition elections. Renovador (Renovation) Peronism emphasizes the social democratic elements of

Peronism, downplays the Catholic-derived social conservatism, seeks greater internal democracy within the movement, and explicitly recognizes and supports human rights claims.

28. Interview, secretary of the Peronist Human Rights Commission (Buenos Aires) and aides, Aug. 17, 1988. Activists stressed that the secretariat was founded *before* the trials of the juntas, emphasizing the continuing nature of their commitment.

29. Interview, secretary of the Peronist Human Rights Commission (Buenos Aires) and aides, Aug. 17, 1988. Since the Peronist *unidad basica* is a heavily utilized center for neighborhood mobilization and the provision of services, the introduction of a human rights secretary at this level represents a significant reform. However, attempts to verify the precise nature of the operation of base-level human rights secretariats suggest that the reform may correspond more to a doctrinal goal than a concrete experience.

30. Interview, secretary of the Peronist Human Rights Commission (Buenos Aires) and aides, Aug. 17, 1988.

31. See Partido Justicialista, Secretaría de Derechos Humanos, *Los derechos humanos y el Peronismo.* And see, too, Partido Justicialista, Movimiento Renovador, *Los contenidos de la esperanza,* 21, where the Radical film *La república perdida* is singled out for criticism, with the Peronist reading of recent Argentine history as popular struggle versus repression and demobilization of popular sectors being substituted for the Radical interpretation of it as a conflict of democracy versus authoritarianism.

32. I am grateful to the Argentine sociologist Oscar Landi for this insight.

33. See Verbitsky, *Civiles y militares,* 43. The slogan contrasts markedly with Perón's own doctrine, "For the enemy, not even justice."

34. This incident is referred to in Dabat and Lorenzano, 155.

35. "Anti-imperialism . . . apart from personalities and symbols, has been historically the only unifying theme with which the mass of Peronists could identify" (Richard Gillespie, *Soldiers of Peron,* 17).

36. *Jotapé* also asserted that the only deprivation of rights ever experienced under Peronism was that "three opposition activists were killed by the police (in the middle of the most profound revolution the country has known in its history), in that some demonstrations were put down, and in that a few members of the Argentine aristocracy, such as Silvina Ocampo, were detained for a few hours" (*Jotapé,* Sept. 1988, pp. 12–13, 24).

37. *La Nación,* May 2, 1989, p. 5.

38. *Pagina Doce,* August 13, 1988.

39. Interview with Peronist party human rights secretary, Aug. 17, 1988.

40. Interview with Peronist human rights activist, Aug. 1988.

41. Interview with an aide to legislators of the Partido Intransigente and former member of the PI Human Rights Commission, Dec. 7, 1988.

42. Ibid.

43. Ibid. See also Partido Intransigente documents, including the official Partido Intransigente, *Síntesis de los proyectos presentados por el bloque entre di-*

ciembre de 1985 y marzo de 1988. And see, too, *Pagina Doce*, Mar. 19, May 14, June 21, and Dec. 10, 1988; *Buenos Aires Herald*, Nov. 20, 1988. Several of these publications treat the eventual electoral alliance with Peronism.

44. By 1989, this figure had receded to around 6 percent, as the Argentine political system consolidated around the two major parties.

45. See *Pagina Doce*, Mar. 20, 1988.

46. Interview, Sept. 1, 1988.

47. *Pagina Doce*, Oct. 22, 1988, and *Buenos Aires Herald*, Dec. 34, 1988; interview with Maria Julia Alsogaray, *El Periodista*, June 7–13th, 1985. Alvaro Alsogaray once called U.S. President John F. Kennedy a "disguised socialist."

48. *Buenos Aires Herald*, Aug. 21, 1988; *La Nación*, May 18, 1988.

49. Interview, Sept. 1, 1988. Among other things, the subject claimed that participants in human rights demonstrations were paid to attend and that some of the disappeared were hiding in Nicaragua.

50. The notable exceptions to this trend are the economic elites: the landowners' association (Sociedad Rural) and manufacturers' group (UIA).

51. For the history of labor responses to the repression, see Chapter 2. A representative incident is the testimony of two union leaders at the trials of the military juntas who "could not remember" the disappearances of any union members. Also see Pozzi, *Oposición obrera a la dictadura (1976–1982).*

52. Interviews with a member of the FOETRA Human Rights Commission and CGT Human Rights Secretariat, Apr. 8, 1988; May 16, 1988.

53. Interview with CGT Human Rights Secretariat, Sept. 30, 1988.

54. Memorializing disappeared members has become an important activity for many unions: several have commemorative plaques or ceremonies—in a related example, the Judicial Workers' Association of Buenos Aires sponsored a photo exhibit entitled "Derecho a la Vida, Derecho a la Niñez, Derecho a la Ancianidad, por la Mujer, por Nuestros 30 Mil Desaparecidos." Both the journalists' and bank workers' unions have published memorial volumes to their disappeared comrades, including captioned photos reminiscent of those displayed by the family-based human rights movement, titles evoking human rights movement slogans, and a reinterpretation of the history of the repression. See Asociación de Periodistas de Buenos Aires, *Con vida los queremos*, and Comisión Gremial Interna de la Caja Nacional de Ahorro y Seguro, *Están con nosotros.*

55. Interview, Apr. 8, 1988. An example of member complaints is the early 1988 case of three female union delegates who were kidnapped, beaten, and threatened in separate incidents within a short period and in a similar location. The CGT filed a formal complaint with the government human rights secretary, sent telegrams to the Ministry of Interior, circulated a petition, and called a march. The incidents have not been repeated following the CGT's reaction.

56. I believe this meeting to be fairly typical of the CGT commission; I was invited to attend rather spontaneously, and was only formally introduced to those present at the beginning of the meeting.

57. For further documentation on these and related CGT human rights activities, see *Pagina Doce*, Mar. 9, 1988 (constitutional reform); ibid., June 3, July 7, and Aug. 6, 1988 (political prisoners); ibid., Aug. 31, 1988 (missing

children); and ibid.,, Oct. 6, 1988 (paid political announcement by press workers' union protesting police pressure on camera operators at public events).

58. Meeting of the CGT Human Rights Secretary Directive Council, May 1988.

59. Interview, Apr. 8, 1988.

60. Interview with Ricardo Perez, *Pagina Doce*, Nov. 23, 1988.

61. *Pagina Doce*, Dec. 21, 1988. This statement followed the Villa Martelli military uprising and attendant military pressures.

62. See *Pagina Doce*, Dec. 10, 1988 for the latest example.

63. *Pagina Doce*, Dec. 14, 1988.

64. Interview with a representative of FOETRA Human Rights Secretariat, Apr. 8, 1988.

65. For a discussion of the historical evolution of Church doctrine and nationalism, see Rosales.

66. Conferencia Episcopal Argentina, *Democracia, responsibilidad y esperanza*, 3–4.

67. For extensive documentation, see Mignone's *Iglesia y dictadura*; also Ezcurra's *Iglesia y transición democrática*, 65–100; and Waisman, "Argentina: Autarkic Industrialization and Illegitimacy," 92. The Church has not hesitated to engage in political activity to implement its own vision of the common good. A prominent instance of Church activism (in opposition to government policy) under democracy was a campaign of intense lobbying, organized demonstrations, and threats of excommunication against legislators in conjunction with Argentina's 1985 divorce law.

68. See Comisión Nacional sobre la Desaparición de Personas, *Nunca más* (1986), 248–52; *Madres de Plaza de Mayo* 1, no. 1 (Dec. 1984), for brief reviews.

69. See Camps, *El caso Timerman—Punto Final.*. For a complementary account of the activities of Archbishop Plaza, see *Madres de Plaza de Mayo* 2, no. 29 (Apr. 1987), back cover.

70. Conferencia Episcopal Argentina, *La Iglesia y los derechos humanos*.

71. Interview with an aide to a bishop active in human rights, Nov. 1988.

72. Conferencia Episcopal Argentina, *Democracia, responsibilidad y esperanza*, 7.

73. *La Razon*, May 2, 1987.

74. *Pagina Doce*, Dec. 7, 1988. A week later, following military pressures for an amnesty, Cardinal Raúl Primatesta emphasized the subtle spiritual differences between "reconciliation," "amnesty," and "pacification," and included a reference to human rights—following the results of a Church opinion poll that showed widespread concern with the Church's attitude (*Pagina Doce*, Dec. 15, 1988).

75. *Buenos Aires Herald*, July 27, 1988.

76. See Rosales, 44.

77. For a brief account, see "A Silenced Voice?" *Buenos Aires Herald*, Aug. 7, 1988. The Angelelli case was officially discussed by the Church for the first time in the second episcopal plenary of 1988 (see *Pagina Doce*, Oct. 25, 1988). Four bishops defended Angelelli's memory and right to an interest in social doctrine

against UCD accusations of communism (*Buenos Aires Herald*, Aug. 22, 1988). Angelelli's successor criticized the progress of judicial investigations and the application of the Obediencia Debida law to some of those implicated (*Buenos Aires Herald*, June 13, 1988).

78. See *Pagina Doce*, Nov. 18, 23, 25, 27, 29, and 30, and Dec. 2, 9, and 11, 1988; *Buenos Aires Herald*, Nov. 23 and 28, and Dec. 14, 1988.

79. Interview with the vicar of Quilmes and assistant to Bishop Jorge Novak, Nov. 23, 1988. Incidents in Quilmes include the unexplained police shooting of base-level activists in San Francisco de Solano and escalating confrontations between growing numbers of squatters and police. For the memorial service for the French nuns, see *El Periodista*, Dec. 18–24, 1987.

80. *El Periodista*, Dec. 26, 1986–Jan. 1, 1987.

81. The Movimiento Popular Neuqueño was the party that introduced the "atrocious and aberrant" clause into the trials legislation when it was debated in Congress, widening the scope for prosecutions of the military (see Chapter 5).

82. Interview with parish priest of Tilcara, Oct. 30, 1988.

83. See *Pagina Doce*, Oct. 4, 1988; interview with the parish priest of Tilcara; Tilcara Church newsletter *El Chasqui*, June 1988; Padre Eloy Roy, *El Pañuelo Blanco de la Virgen de Tilcara* (Aug. 1988); and correspondence from Padre Eloy Roy to Bishop Raúl Casado, Sept. 21, 1988.

Chapter 10

1. *New York Times*, Sept. 10 and Oct. 8, 1989; *Latin American Weekly Report*, Jan. 10, 1991; *Latin American Regional Report—Southern Cone*, Feb. 7, 1991.

2. See Weschler, *A Miracle, a Universe*, 241–46.

3. Discussed in Palermo's introduction to A. Bruno, M. Cavarozzi, and V. Palermo, eds., 8. The phrase *la deuda interna* deliberately evokes the term for Argentina's foreign debt—usually referred to as *la deuda externa*.

4. See Landi, "La transición política argentina y la cuestión de los derechos humanos," 40, and Morande, "Debate," 75, in Villela, ed.

5. The remark, which occurred during a September 1985 trip to Europe, is recorded in Veiga, 49; Ferrari and Herrera, 22, and Fernandez, *La claudicación de Alfonsín*, 43.

6. Interview, Aug. 10, 1987. Also see Fruhling, "La defensa de los derechos humanos en el Cono Sur."

7. Fontana, "La politica militar del gobierno constitucional argentino," 376–77.

8. Mainwaring, "Urban Popular Movements," 132.

9. The classic source of the definition of democracy as contestation and participation is Dahl, *Polyarchy*. See Karl, "Dilemmas of Democratization in Latin America," 2, for this expanded definition.

10. "These social movements have contributed to the erosion of military rule, and they may play a role as bearers of a more democratic political culture" (Mainwaring and Viola, 17). Also see Evers's extensive discussion of new social

movement identity as a new form of politics, specifically an assertion of human dignity through identity, autonomy and emancipation (Evers, "Identity," 56).

11. See Navarro; Femenia, 9–18; Schirmer, "Those Who Die for Life Cannot Be Called Dead."

12. See Alvarez, *Engendering Democracy in Brazil*, on the distinction between feminine and feminist movements.

13. Interview with a representative of Familiares, June 14, 1988.

14. Boschi, 8, who also questions the implicit assumption that participation is inherently democratizing and shifts attention to the movement's links with the state (12).

15. Fisher, 156.

16. Interview, Northern Argentina, Nov. 1988.

17. Lefort, 172.

18. Garreton labels the recomposition of civil society as one of the meanings of democracy, and links democratic consolidation to an autonomous relationship between the state and society, in *Reconstruir la política*, 35, 53–54. Similarly, Baloyra defines a democratic regime as one constrained by autonomous intermediary institutions, in *Comparing New Democracies*, 11. Lefort expands Hannah Arendt's concept of the "right to have rights" (40–41).

19. The following dialogue illustrates this democratizing effect of the movement. At the 1988 annual human rights movement March of Resistance, less than a week after the Villa Martelli military uprising, which involved several civilian deaths and dozens of casualties, frustrated militants in the crowd transformed a customary rallying cry in a violent direction: "El pueblo unido jamas será vencido" ("The people united will never be defeated") became "El pueblo armado jamas será atrasado" ("The people in arms will never be set back"). Hebe de Bonafini, leader of Las Madres, interrupted her assertive prepared speech to respond: "We are not armed—our arms are our struggle, justice, and memory." (March of Resistance, Buenos Aires, Dec. 9, 1988, attended by the author.)

20. Landi "La transición política argentina y la cuestión de los derechos humanos," 40.

21. Catterberg, *Los argentinos frente a la política*, ch. 4, esp. 63–66, 71. Along these lines, further caution is required in linking individual attitudes to system outcomes. For example, popular support for civil libertarian principles is notoriously weak in fully consolidated democracies such as the United States.

22. Landi, "La transición política argentina y la cuestión de los derechos humanos," 80.

23. Lefort, 16. This theorist also focuses on the indeterminacy of democratic processes.

24. Interview, Apr. 8, 1988.

25. Giussani, *Los días de Alfonsín*, 9. One telling illustration is Evita Perón's statement, "He who does not feel himself to be a Peronist, cannot feel himself an Argentine" (Crassweller, 214).

26. For example, Adam Przeworski's procedural definition: "Democracy is only a system for processing conflicts without killing one another" (*Democracy*

and the Market, 95). Lorenzo Meyer points out that purely institutional definitions of democracy are likely to be the least satisfying to the most committed democrats in Latin America ("Democracy from Three Latin American Perspectives," 31).

27. Howard and Donnelly, "Human Dignity, Human Rights and Political Regimes," 806.

28. Leaders of the human rights movement even labeled the Alfonsín regime, "a constitutional government still in transition to democracy" (interviews on Aug. 5 and 10, 1987, with leaders of civil libertarian organizations in the human rights movement).

29. At a press conference during the 1987 Semana Santa uprising, Alfonsín defended a limited procedural definition: Question—"Could this massive support [*mobilización*] be the kick-off for consensus [*convergencia*]?" Answer—"I think that we have already achieved consensus [*ya estamos en convergencia*], since you know that the basis of political democracy is periodic elections. Here we have conflicts that are the result of the rules of the game" (Grecco and Gonzalez, 137).

30. The issue of the inherited political prisoners illustrates this conflict: substantive justice demanded their release, procedural justice demanded their retrial, and the defense of civilian rule required a private arrangement that would not involve the military or a reexamination of Proceso institutions.

31. Interview with a representative of Las Abuelas, Apr. 18, 1988.

32. The spirit of this challenge is captured by Villela's question: "Can a model of democracy be established separated from the substantive content of human rights, a development model and the democratic legitimacy of the actors involved?" (Villela, ed., 16). Landi is even more direct in evaluating Alfonsín's approach, stating that Alfonsín's discourse is based on a return to the rules— but never deals with the basis of legitimacy that makes rules effective and ignores the identity of the actors (in Villela, 80).

33. On both traditional left critiques of democracy for failure to provide substantive equality and the newer call for democratic institutions combined with a democratic ethos and identity, see Barros, "The Left and Democracy."

34. Although the human rights movement argument encompassed several dimensions, one concern based on actor identities was simply repressor recidivism. For example, a task force member named Etchekolatz who was released by reason of Obediencia Debida was later implicated in both the bombing of a judge's home and the January 1988 takeover of Jorge Newberry airport associated with the Monte Caseros military uprising. And when Menem pardoned 277 military officers for human rights violations and uprisings in 1989, 174 went on to participate in the December 1990 mutiny (*Pagina 12*, Dec. 4, 1990).

35. For example, see the analysis of Radical strategy in the 1987 midterm elections by Edgardo Catterberg—a pollster long associated with the UCR—as "broadcasting the image that it was the only party able to assure the deepening of the democratic transition" (Catterberg, *Los argentinos frente a la política*, 118). Alfonsín himself labeled the UCR "the instrument of democracy" in his 1985 Parque Norte speech (in Horowicz, ed., *¿Hacia dondé va el Alfonsinismo?* 103–

5). Also see Cavarozzi, "Patterns of Elite Negotiation," in Higley and Gunther, eds., *Elites and Democratic Consolidation*, 228.

36. Also see (Renovador Peronist) Landi's statement, "But Alfonsín is not democracy, he is the politician who best captured the demand for democracy" (in Villela, ed., 59).

37. Mainwaring, "Urban Popular Movements," 153.

38. The Argentine human rights movement is predominantly composed of persons 50–70 years old, the generation of parents of the disappeared. Some organizations now have a second cohort of college- and secondary-school-age supporters. But the movement draws many fewer activists aged 30–50—the generation possessing the greatest political resources, and also the generation of the disappeared.

39. See *Latin American Weekly Report*, Jan. 10 and 17, and Feb. 28, 1991.

40. The protests involved police corruption and incompetence as well as abuse of power. See *New York Times*, Jan. 19, 1990.

41. This dimension of institutionalization of human rights is stressed by the Liga lawyer Eduardo Barcesat, who specifies access to the right, permanence of the right, and immunity from arbitrary state action in exercise of the right (Conference on Human Rights, University of Lomas de Zamora, Sept. 20, 1988).

42. On the pardon, see *New York Times*, Oct. 9, 1989; *San Francisco Chronicle*, Sept. 25, 1989. Also see Aryeh Neier's Op-Ed piece, "Menem's Pardons and Purges," *New York Times*, Oct. 2, 1990.

43. *San Francisco Chronicle*, Jan. 9, 1990.

44. See Major Ernesto Barreiro's op-ed piece "If Menem Falters in Argentina . . . ," *New York Times*, Mar. 23, 1990. Barreiro, indicted for human rights violations during the Proceso, was one of the leaders of the 1987 Semana Santa military rebellion. Also see more general expressions of military unrest in "Argentina's Military Chiefs Warn of Anarchy," *New York Times*, Jan. 2, 1990.

45. This is an extension of the observation by Guillermo O'Donnell that the mobilization of civil society during transitions to democracy both incites hardliners and raises the costs of a coup ("Transitions to Democracy: Some Navigation Instruments," 72).

46. Juan Linz and Alfred Stepan conclude that "political perception of desired alternatives has a greater impact on the survival of democratic regimes than economic and social problems per se" ("Political Crafting of Democratic Consolidation or Destruction," 46).

47. See Boeker, 11.

48. Catterberg, *Los argentinos frente a la política*, 147–48, expresses the administration position and ties it to work on democratization by Dankwart Rustow (democratic routines), Juan Linz (stability and economic growth), and Albert Hirschman (democracy as patience). Also see Mols, "La Argentina: El difícil camino hacia la normalidad democratica," and Zuleta Alvarez, "El concepto de la democracia argentina en el contexto latinoamericano," both in Garzón Valdés et al., eds.

49. Succinct statements of the movement position can be found in Bruno,

Cavarozzi, and Palermo, 64, 91. The latter statement, by Deputy Augusto Conte, includes the assessment: "I believe that we already have a basis to conclude that the more or less easy attitude of conciliation will not allow us to set up a minimally solid system of political and juridical relations. So that it seems to me that this path is mistaken, and one of the most fitting stages [of the transition] and precious time has been wasted."

50. Varas, "Democratization and Military Reform in Argentina," in Augusto Varas, ed., 58. Also see Vacs, "Authoritarian Breakdown and Redemocratization in Argentina," in Malloy and Seligson, eds., 34. For a contrasting view, see Fitch and Fontana, "Military Policy and Democratic Consolidation in Latin America."

51. For a comprehensive discussion of the role of pacts in transitions, see O'Donnell and Schmitter, ch. 4. Also see Karl, "Dilemmas of Democratization in Latin America," and DiPalma, *To Craft Democracies*.

52. On administration policy, see an early interview with the Radical Senator Antonio Berhongaray (later head of the Senate Defense Commission), in which he ties military retirements to judicial condemnation (*El Porteño*, Sept. 1984, p. 9). In 1988, Antonio Troccoli, former minister of interior, confirmed, "We couldn't dissolve the Army or police, all we could do is prosecute them when they appeared [as human rights violators]" (interview, Dec. 13, 1988).

53. Sidney Tarrow depicts this relationship for social movements in general: "Reform is seldom the object of people who dare, but reform is unlikely without their struggle" (*Struggle, Politics and Reform*, 103).

54. In general, NGOs have played a critical role in sparking U.N. human rights activity, see Forsythe, *Internationalization of Human Rights*, 72–73.

55. As of this writing, the proposal is still wending its way through the OAS structure, albeit in weakened form. The original proposal was sponsored by both the Latin America–wide group of relatives of the disappeared, FEDEFAM, and the Argentine Initiative Group for an International Convention Against the Disappearance of Persons. On the Commission, see Forsythe, *Internationalization*, 101.

56. Forsythe, *Internationalization*, 78.

57. For example, see *Encuentro Regional contra la Impunidad*.

58. See *La Voz del Interior*, Aug. 24, 1989.

59. *New York Times*, July 4, 1989.

60. See *New York Times*, Sept. 11, 1991, on Soviet Georgia. In South Africa the women's organization Black Sash has joined with various family organizations (such as the Detainees Parents Support Committee). Many of these groups appear in the documentary "Madres de Plaza de Mayo."

61. Interview, Apr. 18, 1988.

62. *New York Times*, July 5, 1987.

63. See "Long-Suffering Uganda Finding Internal Peace," *San Francisco Chronicle*, Oct. 4, 1989.

Selected Bibliography

This bibliography is divided into three sections: Books, Articles, and Essays; Periodicals; and Publications by Argentine Human Rights Organizations.

Books, Articles, and Essays

Abella, Monica. *Punto Final: Amnistia o voluntad popular*. Buenos Aires: Puntosur Editores, 1987.

Acuña, Carlos, and Catalina Smulovitz. *¿Ni olvido ni perdón? Derechos humanos y tensiones civico-militares en la transición argentina*. Buenos Aires: CEDES, 1991.

Alcántara Sáez, Manuel, and Carlos Floria. *Democracia, transición y crísis en Argentina*. Costa Rica: Instituto Interamericano de Derechos Humanos, 1990.

Alfonsín, Raul R. *Mensaje presidencial del Dr. Raul Alfonsín a la Honorable Asamblea Legislativa*. Congreso Nacional, 104th session, May 1, 1986.

———. "Building Democracy." *Yale Journal of International Law* 12, no. 1 (Winter 1987): 121–33.

Aliverti, Eduardo. *El archivo de la decada/2: La dictadura*. Buenos Aires: Quatro Editores, 1987.

Allende, José Antonio, et al. *Informe sobre el Proceso para la reorganización nacional*. Buenos Aires: Agencia Periodistica CID, prepared, 1979, released, 1981.

Altamirano, Carlos. "Sobre el juicio a los juntas militares." *Punto de Vista* 7, no. 24 (Aug.–Sept. 1985): 1–2.

Alvarez, Sonia. *Engendering Democracy in Brazil*. Princeton: Princeton University Press, 1990.

Alvarez, Sonia, and Arturo Escobar. "Theoretical and Political Horizons of Change in Latin American Social Movements." In *The Making of Social Movements in Latin America*, ed. Arturo Escobar and Sonia Alvarez, 317–29. Boulder, Colo.: Westview Press, 1992.

Americas Watch. *Argentina: Human Rights During the Falklands/Malvinas Crisis.* New York: Americas Watch, 1982.

———. *Human Rights in Argentina: A Report from CELS in Buenos Aires.* New York: Americas Watch, 1983.

———. *The State Department Misinforms: A Study of Accounting for the Disappeared in Argentina.* New York: Americas Watch, 1983.

———. *Truth and Partial Justice in Argentina.* New York: Americas Watch, 1987.

Amnesty International. *Report of an Amnesty International Mission to Argentina, 6–15 November 1976.* London: Amnesty International Publications, 1977.

———. *The "Disappeared" of Argentina.* London: Amnesty International, 1980.

———. *Argentina: The Military Juntas and Human Rights—Report of the Trial of the Former Junta Members.* London: Amnesty International, 1987.

———. *Argentina: The Attack of the Third Infantry Regiment Barracks at La Tablada: Investigations into Allegations of Torture, "Disappearances" and Extrajudicial Executions.* London, 1990.

Amnesty International—Argentina. *Actividades sobre Argentina, 1972–1987.* Buenos Aires: Amnesty International, n.d.

Andersen, Martin. *Dossier secreto.* Boulder, Colo.: Westview Press, 1993.

Ansaldi, Waldo. *La ética de la democracia.* Buenos Aires: Consejo Latinoamericano de Ciencias Sociales, 1986.

Arendt, Hannah. *The Origins of Totalitarianism.* New York: Meridian, 1958.

———. *The Human Condition.* Chicago: University of Chicago Press, 1958.

———. "Communicative Power." In *Power,* ed. Steven Lukes. Oxford: Basil Blackwell; New York: New York University Press, 1986.

Argentina. Comisíon Rattenbach. *Informe Rattenbach: El drama de Malvinas.* Buenos Aires: Ediciones Espartaco, 1988.

Asociación de Periodistas de Buenos Aires. *Con vida los queremos.* Buenos Aires: Asociación de Periodistas de Buenos Aires, 1987.

Asociación Patriotica Argentina. *La Argentina y sus derechos humanos.* Buenos Aires: Asociación Patriotica Argentina, 1978.

Astiz, Carlos. "The Argentine Armed Forces: Their Role and Political Involvement." *Western Political Quarterly* 22, no. 4 (1969): 862–78.

Avellaneda, Andres. *Censura, autoritarismo y cultura: Argentina, 1960–1983.* Buenos Aires: Centro Editor de América Latina, 1986.

Axelrod, Robert. *The Evolution of Cooperation.* New York: Basic Books, 1984.

Bachrach, Peter, and Morton Baratz. "Two Faces of Power." *American Political Science Review* 56, no. 4 (Dec. 1962): 947–53.

———. "Decisions and Non-Decisions: An Analytical Framework." *American Political Science Review* 57, no. 3 (Sept. 1963): 632–43.

Baloyra, Enrique, ed. *Comparing New Democracies: Transition and Consolidation in Mediterranean Europe and the Southern Cone.* Boulder, Colo.: Westview Press, 1987.

Barberis, Daniel, et al. *Los derechos humanos en el "otro país."* Buenos Aires: Puntosur, 1987.

Barcesat, Eduardo S. "Defensa legal de los derechos a la vida y la libertad personal en el regimen militar argentina." In *Represión política y defensa de los derechos humanos*, ed. Hugo Fruhling. Santiago, Chile: Academia de Humanismo, 1986.

Barker, Rodney. *Political Legitimacy and the State*. Oxford: Clarendon Press, 1990.

Barros, Robert. "The Left and Democracy: Recent Debates in Latin America." *Telos*, no. 68 (Summer 1986): 49–70.

Bayer, Osvaldo. *La Patagonia rebelde*. Buenos Aires: Nueva Imagen, 1980.

————. "Ahora son todos culpables." *Crisis*, no. 50 (Jan. 1987): 56–58.

Beltrán, Virgilio. "Political Transition in Argentina: 1982 to 1985." *Armed Forces Quarterly* 13, no. 2 (Winter 1987): 215–34.

Bennett, Jana, and John Simpson. *The Disappeared and the Mothers of the Plaza*. New York: St.Martin's Press, 1985.

Berg, Gracia. "Human Rights Sanctions as Leverage: Argentina, a Case Study." *Journal of Legislation* 7 (1980): 93–112.

Bermeo, Nancy. "Redemocratization and Transition Elections." *Comparative Politics* 19, no. 2 (Jan. 1987): 213–31.

————. "Democracy and the Lessons of Dictatorship." *Comparative Politics* 24, no. 3 (Apr. 1992): 273–91.

Blanksten, George. *Perón's Argentina*. Chicago: University of Chicago Press, 1953.

Boeker, Paul. *Lost Illusions: Latin America's Struggle for Democracy, as Recounted by Its Leaders*. La Jolla, Calif.: Institute of the Americas, 1990.

Bonafini, Hebe de. *Historias de vida*. Buenos Aires: Fraterna / del Nuevo Extremo, 1985.

Bonasso, Miguel. *Recuerdo de la muerte*. Mexico: Ediciones Era, 1984.

Borrini, Alberto. *Como se hace un presidente*. Buenos Aires: El Cronista Comercial, 1984.

Boschi, Renato. *On Social Movements and Democratization*. Palo Alto: Stanford-Berkeley Joint Center for Latin American Studies, 1984.

Bousquet, Jean-Pierre. *Las locas de la Plaza de Mayo*. Buenos Aires: El Cid, 1983.

Bright, Charles, and Susan Harding, eds. *State-Making and Social Movements*. Ann Arbor: University of Michigan Press, 1984.

Bruno, A., M. Cavarozzi, and V. Palermo, eds. *Los derechos humanos en la democracia*. Buenos Aires: Centro Editor De América Latina, 1985.

Brysk, Alison. "From Above and Below: Social Movements, Human Rights and the International System in Argentina." *Comparative Political Studies* 26, no. 3 October (1993): 259–85.

————. "The Politics of Measurement: Counting the Disappeared in Argentina." In *Human Rights and Developing Countries*, ed. David Louis Cingranelli. Greenwich, Conn.: JAI Press, 1994.

Buchanan, Paul. "Exorcising Collective Ghosts: Recent Argentine Writings on Politics, Economics, Social Movements and Popular Culture." *Latin American Research Review* 25, no. 2 (1990): 177–203.

Camarasa, Jorge. *El juicio: Proceso al horror*. Buenos Aires: Sudamericana Planeta, 1985.

Camps, Ramón. *El caso Timerman—Punto Final*. Buenos Aires: Tribuna Abierta, 1982.

———. "Los desaparecidos están muertos," *El Bimestre Político y Economico*, no. 7 (1983):. 62–65.

Canton, Dario. *El pueblo legislador: Las elecciones de 1983*. Buenos Aires: Centro de Investigaciones en Ciencias Sociales, 1986.

Cardoso, Oscar R. *Malvinas: La trama secreta*. Buenos Aires: Editorial Planeta, 1983.

Carnoy, Martin. *The State and Political Theory*. Princeton: Princeton University Press, 1984.

Carretto, Julio. *La ideología y la nueva guerra*. Buenos Aires: Circulo Militar, 1987.

Carrío, Genaro. *El caso Timerman*. Buenos Aires: Editorial de la Universidad de Buenos Aires, 1987.

Castagno, Antonio. *Los derechos humanos en la Argentina: Problematica de su docencia*. Buenos Aires: Editorial de Belgrano, 1988.

Catterberg, Edgardo. *Argentina Confronts Politics: Political Culture and Public Opinion in the Argentine Transition to Democracy*. Boulder, Colo.: Lynne Rienner, 1991.

———. *Los argentinos frente a la política: Cultura política y opinión pública en la transición a la democracia*. Buenos Aires: Editorial Planeta, 1989.

Cavarozzi, Marcelo. *Autoritarismo y democracia, 1955–1983*. Buenos Aires: Centro Editor de América Latina, 1983.

———. "Argentina's Political Cycles since 1955." In *Transitions to Democracy*, ed. Philippe Schmitter, Guillermo O'Donnell, and Lawrence Whitehead. Baltimore: Johns Hopkins University Press, 1986.

———. "Derechos humanos y cultura política: Blandos y maximalistas." In *Los derechos humanos en la democracia*, ed. A. Bruno, M. Cavarozzi, V. Palermo, 15–18. Buenos Aires: Centro Editor de América Latina, 1985.

———. *Peronism and Radicalism: Argentina's Transition in Perspective*. Latin American Program of the Woodrow Wilson International Center for Scholars Working Paper no. 170. Washington, D.C.: Woodrow Wilson International Center for Scholars, 1986.

———. "Patterns of Elite Negotiation and Confrontation in Argentina and Chile." In *Elites and Democratic Consolidation in Latin America and Southern Europe*, ed. John Higley and Richard Gunther, 208–36. Cambridge: Cambridge University Press, 1992.

Chaney, Elsa. *Supermadre: Women in Politics in Latin America*. Austin: University of Texas Press, 1979.

Chodorow, Nancy. *The Reproduction of Mothering: Psychoanalysis and the Sociology of Gender*. Berkeley and Los Angeles: University of California Press, 1978.

Ciancaglini, Sergio, and Martin Granovsky. *Crónicas del apocalipsis*. Buenos Aires: Contrapunto, 1986.

Claude, Richard P. *Comparative Human Rights*. Baltimore: Johns Hopkins University Press, 1976.

Cobb, Roger W., and Charles D. Elder. *Participation in American Politics: The Dynamics of Agenda-Building*. Boston: Allyn & Bacon, 1972.

Cohen, Jean. "Strategy or Identity: New Theoretical Paradigms and Contemporary Social Movements." *Social Research* 52, no. 4 (Winter 1985): 663–717.

Colombo, Ariel, and Vicente Palermo. *Participacion política y pluralismo en la Argentina contemporanea.* Buenos Aires: Centro Editor de América Latina, 1985.

Comisión Argentina por los Derechos Humanos. *Argentina: Proceso al genocidio.* Madrid: Elias Querejeta, 1977.

Comisión Gremial Interna de la Caja Nacional de Ahorro y Seguro. *Están con nosotros: Trabajadores de la caja por un futuro con memoria.* Buenos Aires: Comisión Gremial Interna de la Caja Nacional de Ahorro y Seguro, 1987.

Comisión Nacional sobre la Desaparición de Personas. *Anexos CONADEP.* Buenos Aires: Editorial de la Universidad de Buenos Aires, 1985.

———. *Nunca más.* Buenos Aires: Editorial Universitaria de Buenos Aires, 1984.

———. *Nunca más: The Report of the Argentine National Commission on the Disappeared,* ed. Ronald Dworkin. New York: Index on Censorship / Farrar, Straus & Giroux, 1986.

Conferencia Episcopal Argentina. *Democracia, responsibilidad y esperanza.* Buenos Aires: Conferencia Episcopal Argentina, 1984.

Connolly, William. *Legitimacy and the State.* New York: New York University, 1984.

Corradi, Juan. "The Mode of Destruction: Terror in Argentina." *Telos,* no. 54 (Winter 1982–83): 61–76.

———. *The Fitful Republic: Economy, Society, and Politics in Argentina.* Boulder, Colo.: Westview Press, 1985.

———. "The Culture of Fear in Civil Society." In *From Military Rule to Liberal Democracy in Argentina,* ed. Monica Peralta-Ramos and Carlos H. Waisman, 113–129. Boulder, Colo.: Westview Press, 1987.

Corradi, Juan, Patricia Weiss Fagen, and Manuel Antonio Garretón, eds. *Fear at the Edge: State Terror and Resistance in Latin America.* Berkeley and Los Angeles: University of California Press, 1992.

Cortés Conde, Roberto. "Some Notes on the Industrial Development of Argentina and Canada in the 1920's." In *Argentina, Australia and Canada: Studies In Comparative Development, 1870–1965,* ed. D. C. M. Platt and Guido DiTella. Oxford: Macmillan, 1975.

Crahan, Margaret E. "National Security Ideology and Human Rights." In *Human Rights and Basic Needs in the Americas,* ed. Margaret Crahan. Washington, D.C.: Georgetown University Press, 1982.

Crassweller, Robert. *Perón and the Enigmas of Argentina.* New York: Norton, 1987.

Dabat, Alejandro, and Luis Lorenzano. *Argentina: The Malvinas and the End of Military Rule.* London: Verso, 1984.

Dahl, Robert. *Polyarchy.* New Haven: Yale University Press, 1971.

Dalton, Russell J., and Manfred Kuechler, eds. *Challenging the Political Order: New Social and Political Movements in Western Democracies.* New York: Oxford University Press, 1990.

Dassin, Joan. "The Culture of Fear Project Report." *ITEMS: Social Science Research Council* 40, no. 1 (Mar. 1986).

Davies, James C. "Toward a Theory of Revolution." *American Sociological Review* 27, no. 1 (Feb. 1962): 5–18.

De La Cruz, Rafael. "Nuevos movimientos sociales en Venezuela." In *Los movimientos populares en América Latina*, ed. Daniel Camacho and Rafael Menjívar. Mexico: Siglo Veintiuno Editores, 1989.

DeNardo, James. *Power in Numbers: The Political Strategy of Protest and Rebellion.* Princeton: Princeton University Press, 1985.

Derlega, V., and J. Grzelk, eds. *Cooperation and Helping Behavior.* New York: Academic Press, 1981.

Diago, Alejandro. *Hebe Bonafini: Memoria y esperanza.* Buenos Aires: Ediciones Dialectica, 1988.

Diamand, Marcelo. "Overcoming Argentina's Stop-and-Go Economic Cycles." In *Latin American Political Economy*, ed. Jonathan Hartlyn and Samuel Morley, 129–64. Boulder, Colo.: Westview Press, 1986.

Diamond, Larry, Juan J. Linz, and Seymour Martin Lipset, eds. *Latin America.* Vol. 4 of *Democracy in Developing Countries.* Boulder: Lynne Riemer, 1989.

Diaz Alejandro, Carlos. *Essays on the Economic History of the Argentine Republic.* New Haven: Yale University Press, 1970.

Diaz Colodrero, Jose, and Monica Abella. *Punto Final: Amnistía o voluntad popular.* Buenos Aires: Puntosur, 1987.

DiPalma, Giuseppe. *To Craft Democracies: An Essay on Democratic Transitions.* Mexico City: Siglo Veintiuno Editores, 1989.

DiTella, Guido. *Perón-Perón, 1973–76.* Buenos Aires: Sudamericana, 1983.

DiTella, Guido, and Rudiger Dornbusch, eds. *The Political Economy of Argentina, 1946–83.* Oxford: Macmillan, 1989.

DiTella, Torcuato. *Evolución del sistema de partidos políticos en Argentina, Brasil y Peru, 1960–1985.* Cuadernos Simon Rodriguez. Buenos Aires: Editorial Biblos, 1986.

DiTella, Torcuato, and Tulio Halperin Donghi. *Los fragmentos del poder.* Buenos Aires: Jorge Alvarez, 1969.

Dominguez, Carlos Horacio. *La nueva guerra y el nuevo derecho.* 2 vols. Buenos Aires: Circulo Militar, 1980.

Donnelly, Jack. *The Concept of Human Rights.* New York: St. Martin's Press, 1985.

———. "International Human Rights: A Regime Analysis." *International Organization* 40, no. 3 (Summer 1986): 599–642.

———. *Universal Human Rights in Theory and in Practice.* Ithaca, N.Y.: Cornell University Press, 1989.

Dos Santos, Mario, and Daniel Garcia Delgado. "Democracia en cuestión y redefinición de la política," *Critica y Utopia*, no. 8 (1982): 53–77.

Downs, Anthony. "Up and Down with Ecology: The Issue-Attention Cycle," *The Public Interest* 28 (Summer 1972): 38–50.

Drescher, Seymour, David Sabean, and Allan Sharlin, eds. *Political Symbolism in Modern Europe.* New Brunswick, N.J.: Transaction Books, 1982.

Duhalde, Eduardo. *El estado terrorista argentino.* Buenos Aires: El Caballito, 1983.

Dworkin, Ronald. *Taking Rights Seriously*. Cambridge, Mass.: Harvard University Press, 1977.

Echave, Hugo, and Noemí Ulla. *Despues de la noche: Diálogos con Graciela Fernandez-Meijide*. Buenos Aires: Contrapunto, 1986.

Echegaray, Fabian, and Ezequiel Raimondo. *Desencanto político, transición y democracia*. Buenos Aires: Centro Editor de América Latina, 1987.

Eckstein, Susan, ed. *Power and Popular Protest: Latin American Social Movements*. Berkeley and Los Angeles: University of California Press, 1989.

Edelman, Murray. *The Symbolic Uses of Politics*. Urbana: University of Illinois Press, 1964.

Eder, Klaus. "New Social Movements: Moral Crusades, Political Pressure Groups, or Social Movements?" *Social Research* 52, no. 4 (Winter 1985): 869–90.

Eisenstadt, S. N., ed. *Max Weber: On Charisma and Institution Building*. Chicago: University of Chicago Press, 1968.

Elshtain, Jean. *Public Man, Private Woman: Women in Social and Political Thought*. Princeton: Princeton University Press, 1981.

———. "Antigone's Daughters." *Democracy*, no. 2 (Apr. 1982): 46–60.

———. *Women and War*. New York: Basic Books, 1987.

Encuentro regional contra la impunidad. Santiago, Chile, 1987.

Escobar, Arturo, and Sonia E. Alvarez. "Introduction: Theory and Protest in Latin America Today." In *The Making of Social Movements in Latin America*, ed. Arturo Escobar and Sonia Alvarez, 1–15. Boulder, Colo.: Westview Press, 1992.

Escudé, Carlos. "Derechos humanos y soberanía política." *Criterio* 56/1917 (Jan. 1984): 7–18.

———. "Argentina: The Costs of Contradiction." In *Exporting Democracy: The United States and Latin America*, ed. Abraham F. Lowenthal, 125–61. Baltimore: Johns Hopkins University Press, 1991.

Evers, T. "Identity: The Hidden Side of New Social Movements in Latin America." In *New Social Movements and the State in Latin America*, ed. D. Slater. Amsterdam: CEDLA, 1985.

Eyerman, Ron. "Modernity and Social Movements." In *Social Change and Modernity*, ed. Hans Haferkamp and Neil J. Smelser, 37–54. Berkeley and Los Angeles: University of California Press, 1992.

Ezcurra, Ana Maria. *Iglesia y transición democratica: Ofensiva del neoconservadurismo católico en América Latina*. Buenos Aires: Puntosur Editores, 1988.

Falcoff, Mark. "The Timerman Case." In *Human Rights and U.S. Human Rights Policy*, ed. Howard Wiarda. Washington: American Enterprise Institute, 1982.

Farer, Tom. "The OAS: Righting Human Rights." *Harvard International Review* 8 (Dec. 1985): 13–15.

———. *The Grand Strategy of the United States in Latin America*. New Brunswick: Transaction Books, 1988.

Feijóo, María del Carmen. "The Challenge of Constructing Civilian Peace: Women and Democracy in Argentina." In *The Women's Movement in Latin America: Feminism and the Transition to Democracy*, ed. Jane Jacquette, 72–94. Boston: Unwin Hyman, 1989.

Feijóo, María del Carmen, and Monica Gogna. "Las mujeres en la transición a la democracia." In *Los nuevos movimientos sociales*, ed. Elizabeth Jelin, 41–82. Buenos Aires: Centro Editor de América Latina, 1985.

Feldman, Steven D. "Stories as Cultural Creativity: On the Relation between Symbolism and Politics in Organizational Change." *Human Relations* 43, no. 9 (1990): 809–28.

Femenia, Nora. "Argentina's Mothers of the Plaza." *Feminist Studies* 13 (Spring 1987): 9–18.

Fernandez, Gabriel. *La claudicación de Alfonsín: Derechos Humanos–Militares–Economia–Sindicatos, 1983–1987*. Buenos Aires: Ediciones Dialectica, 1987.

Fernandez Meijide, Graciela. "Historia de los organismos de derechos humanos en Argentina y su rol en la democracia." In *Represíon política y defensa de los derechos humanos*. ed. Hugo Fruhling, 70–75. Santiago, Chile: Academia de Humanismo, 1986.

Ferrari, Alberto. "Historia del deporte argentino y la dictadura militar." In *El archivo de la decada/2—La dictadura*, ed. Eduardo Aliverti, 145–51. Buenos Aires: Quatro Editores, 1987.

Ferrari, Alberto, and Francisco Herrera. *Los hombres del presidente*. Buenos Aires: Ediciones Tarso, 1987.

Fisher, Jo. *Mothers of the Disappeared*. Boston: South End Press, 1989.

Fitch, J. Samuel. "Armies and Politics in Latin America, 1975–85." In *Human Rights and Basic Needs in the Americas*, ed. Margaret Crahan. Washington: Georgetown University Press, 1982.

Fitch, J. Samuel, and Andres Fontana. "Military Policy and Democratic Consolidation in Latin America." Paper presented to the 16th International Congress of the Latin American Studies Association, Washington, D.C., Apr. 4–6, 1991.

Flisfich, Angel. "Derechos humanos, política y poder." In *La ética de la democracia*, ed. Waldo Ansaldi. Buenos Aires: Consejo Latinoamericano de Ciencias Sociales, 1986.

Fontana, Andres. *Fuerzas armadas, partidos políticos y transición a la democracia en la Argentina*. Buenos Aires: Centro de Estudios del Estado y Sociedad, 1984.

———. "La política militar del gobierno constitucional argentino." In *Ensayos sobre la transición democratica en la Argentina*, ed. Jose Nun and Juan Carlos Portantiero, 375–418. Buenos Aires: Puntosur, 1987.

Foro de Estudios sobre la Administración de Justicia. *Definitivamente nunca más: la otra cara del informe de la CONADEP*. Buenos Aires: Foro de Estudios sobre la Administración de Justicia, 1985.

Forsythe, David. *Human Rights and World Politics*. Lincoln: University of Nebraska Press, 1983.

———. *The Internationalization of Human Rights*. Lexington, Mass.: D. C. Heath, 1991.

Foucault, Michel. *Discipline and Punish*. New York: Vintage Books, 1979.

———. *Power/Knowledge*. New York: Pantheon Books, 1980.

Franco, Jean. "Gender, Death and Resistance: Facing the Ethical Vacuum." In *Fear at the Edge: State Terror and Resistance in Latin America*, ed. Juan Corradi,

Patricia Weiss Fagen, and Manuel Antonio Garretón, 104–18. Berkeley and Los Angeles: University of California Press, 1992.

Freire, Paolo. *Pedagogy of the Oppressed.* New York: Continuum, 1970.

Frontalini, Daniel, and Maria Cristina Caiati. *El mito de la guerra sucia.* Buenos Aires: Centro de Estudios Legales y Sociales, 1984.

Fruhling, Hugo. "La Defensa de los derechos humanos en el Cono Sur: Dilemas y perspectivos hacía el futuro." In *Represión política y defensa de los derechos humanos,* ed. Hugo Fruhling, 18–32. Santiago, Chile: Academia de Humanismo, 1986.

Fuerzas Armadas Argentinas. *Marxismo y subversión.* Buenos Aires: Estado Mayor General del Ejercito, 1980.

Fundación Arturo Illia. *Lineamientos para una reforma militar.* Buenos Aires: Fundación Arturo Illia, 1988.

———. *Organización del sistema militar.* Buenos Aires: Fundación Arturo Illia, 1988.

Gabetta, Carlos. *Todos somos subversivos.* Buenos Aires: Editorial Bruguera Argentina, 1983.

Galtieri, Leopoldo. "Celebración del Día del Ejercito." *Revista del Circulo Militar,* no. 702 (1979–80): 4–11.

Gamson, William. *The Strategy of Social Protest.* Homewood, Ill.: Dorsey Press, 1975.

Gamson, William, Bruce Fireman, and Steven Rytina. *Encounter with Unjust Authority.* Homewood, Ill.: Dorsey Press, 1982.

García, Cesar Reinaldo, and Apolinar Edgardo Garcia. *Instrucción cívica.* Buenos Aires: Sainte Claire Editora S.R.L., 1985.

García Delgado, Daniel R., and Vincent Palermo. "El movimiento de los derechos humanos en la transición a la democracia en Argentina." In *Los Movimientos Populares en America Latina,* ed. Daniel Camacho and Rafael Menjivar, 415–38. Mexico City: Universidad de las Naciones Unidas, 1989.

Garretón, Manuel. *Dictaduras y democratización.* Santiago, Chile: Facultad Latinoamericano de Ciencias Sociales, 1984.

———. *Reconstruir la política.* Santiago, Chile: Editorial Andante, 1987.

Garzón Valdés, Ernesto, Manfred Mols, and Arnold Spitta, eds. *La nueva democracia argentina, 1983–86.* Buenos Aires: Editorial Sudamericana, 1988.

Genta, Jordan. *Acerca de la libertad de enseñar y de la enseñanza de la libertad.* Buenos Aires: Dictio, 1976.

George, Alexander. "The Operational Code: A Neglected Approach to the Study of Political Leaders and Decision Making." *International Studies Quarterly* 13, no. 2 (June 1969): 190–222.

Gewirth, Alan. *Human Rights: Essays on Justification and Applications.* Chicago: University of Chicago Press, 1982.

Giadone, Dante. *Las reformas de la Constitución y la reforma militar.* Buenos Aires: Fundación Arturo Illia, 1987.

———. *Las hipótesis de conflicto y de guerra.* Buenos Aires: Fundación Arturo Illia, 1988.

Gibbons, Michael T., ed. *Interpreting Politics.* Oxford: Basil Blackwell, 1987.

Giddens, Anthony. *Central Problems in Social Theory*. Berkeley and Los Angeles: University of California Press, 1979.

Gillespie, Charles. "From Authoritarian Crises to Democratic Transitions." *Latin American Research Review* 22, no. 3 (Winter 1987–88): 165–84.

Gillespie, Richard. *Soldiers of Perón: Argentina's Montoneros*. Oxford: Clarendon Press, 1982.

Giussani, Pablo. *Los días de Alfonsín*. Buenos Aires: Legasa, 1986.

———. *¿Por que, Doctor Alfonsín?* Buenos Aires: Sudamericana, 1987.

Gomez, José Maria. "Derechos humanos, política y autoritarismo en el Cono Sur." In *La ética de la democracia*, ed. Waldo Ansaldi. Buenos Aires: Consejo Latinoamericano de Ciencias Sociales, 1986.

González Janzen, Ignacio. *La Triple A*. Buenos Aires: Editorial Contrapunto, 1986.

González Bombal, Maria Ines, and Maria Sondereguer. *Derechos humanos y democracia*. Buenos Aires: Centro de Estudios del Estado y Sociedad Working Paper, 1986.

Gramsci, Antonio. *Selections from the Prison Notebooks*. New York: International Publishers, 1971.

Granovetter, Mark. "The Strength of Weak Ties." *American Journal of Sociology* 78, no. 6 (May 1973): 1360–80.

———. "Threshold Models of Collective Behavior." *American Journal of Sociology* 83, no. 6 (May 1978): 1420–43.

Grecco, Jorge , and Gustavo González. *¡Felices Pascuas! Los hechos ineditos de la rebelión militar*. Buenos Aires: Sudamericana Planeta, 1988.

Groisman, Enrique. *Poder y derecho en el "proceso de reorganización nacional."* Buenos Aires: CISEA, 1983.

———. *La Corte Suprema de Justicia durante la dictadura, 1976–1983*. Buenos Aires: CISEA, 1984.

Guest, Iain. *Behind the Disappearances*. Philadelphia: University of Pennsylvania Press, 1990.

Gurr, Ted. *Why Men Rebel*. Princeton: Princeton University Press, 1970.

Habermas, Jürgen. *Legitimation Crisis*. Boston: Beacon Press, 1975.

Halperin Donghi, Tulio. *Argentina en el callejón*. Montevideo: Editorial Arcos, 1964.

———. "Argentina's Unmastered Past." *Latin American Research Review* 23, no. 2 (1988): 2–25.

Hamilton, Alexander, James Madison, and John Jay. *The Federalist Papers*. 1787–88. Ed. Clinton Rossiter. New York: Signet, 1961.

Hare, A. Paul, and Herbert H. Blumberg, eds. *Dramaturgical Analysis of Social Interaction*. New York: Praeger, 1988.

Harff, Barbara. *Genocide and Human Rights: International Legal and Political Issues*. University of Denver Graduate School of International Studies Monograph Series in World Affairs, vol. 20, bk. 3. Denver: University of Denver Graduate School of International Studies, 1984.

Hartsock, Nancy. *Money, Sex and Power: Towards a Feminist Historical Materialism*. Boston: Northeastern University Press, 1983.

Hegedus, Zsuzsa. "Social Movements and Social Change in Self-Creative Society: New Civil Movements and Social Change in the International Arena." In *Globalization, Knowledge, and Society,* ed. Martin Albrow and Elizabeth King, 263–80. London: Sage, 1990.

Held, David. *Models of Democracy.* Stanford: Stanford University Press, 1987.

Henderson, Conway. "Human Rights and Regimes: A Bibliographic Essay." *Human Rights Quarterly* 10 (Nov. 1988): 525–43.

Hennelly, Alfred T., and John P. Langan. *Human Rights in the Americas: The Struggle for Consensus.* Washington, D.C.: Georgetown University Press, 1982.

Higley, John, and Richard Gunther. *Elites and Democratic Consolidation in Latin America and Southern Europe.* New York: Cambridge University Press, 1992.

Hirschmann, Albert. *Exit, Voice and Loyalty.* Cambridge, Mass.: Harvard University Press, 1970.

Hodges, Donald. *Argentina, 1943–76: The National Revolution and Resistance.* Albuquerque: University of New Mexico Press, 1976.

Horowicz, Alejandro, ed. *¿Hacia dónde va el Alfonsinismo?* Buenos Aires: Catalogos Editora, 1986.

Horowitz, Irving. *Taking Lives: Genocide and State Power.* New Brunswick: Transaction Books, 1980.

Howard, Rhoda, and Jack Donnelly. "Human Dignity, Human Rights and Political Regimes." *American Political Science Review* 80, no. 3 (Sept. 1986): 801–17.

Huber Stephens, Evelyne. "Democracy in Latin America: Recent Developments in Comparative Historical Perspective." *Latin American Research Review* 25, no. 2 (1990): 157–76.

Huberts, Leo. "The Influence of Social Movements on Government Policy." In *Organizing for Change: Social Movement Organizations in Europe and the United States,* ed. Bert Klandermans, 395–426. Greenwich, Conn.: JAI Press, 1989.

Huntington, Samuel. *Political Order in Changing Societies.* New Haven: Yale University Press, 1968.

Imaz, José Luis de. *Los que mandan* [Those Who Rule]. 1964. Translated by Carlos Astiz with Mary F. McCarthy. Albany: State University of New York Press, 1970.

International Commission of Jurists. "Attacks on the Independence of Judges and Lawyers in Argentina." *International Commission of Jurists Bulletin* 1 (Feb. 1978).

Ipola, Emilio, M. Ines Gonzalez Bombal, and Oscar Landi. *El discurso político: Lenguages y acontecimientos.* Buenos Aires: Hachette, 1987.

Janeway, Elizabeth. *Powers of the Weak.* New York: Knopf, 1980.

Janowitz, Morris. *Military Institutions and Coercion in the Developing Nations.* Chicago: University of Chicago Press, 1977.

Jelin, Elizabeth, ed. *Los nuevos movimientos sociales.* Buenos Aires: Centro Editor de América Latina, 1985.

———. *Ausencias y espacios: Actores sociales en la transición democratica.* Buenos Aires: Centro de Estudios del Estado y Sociedad Working Paper, 1987.

266 ≈ Selected Bibliography

————, ed. *Women and Social Change in Latin America.* Translated by Ann Zammit and Marilyn Thomson. London: Zed, 1990.
Kaminsky, Gregorio. "Vigilar, sospechar y denunciar." *Controversia,* no. 4 (Feb. 1980): 30.
Karl, Terry. "Dilemmas of Democratization in Latin America." *Comparative Politics* 23, no. 1 (Oct. 1990): 1–21.
Kaufman, Edy. "Jewish Victims of Repression in Argentina under Military Rule (1976–1983)." *Holocaust and Genocide Studies* 4, no. 4 (1989): 479–99.
Keane, John. *Civil Society and the State.* New York: Verso Press, 1988.
Kelman, Herbert C., and V. Lee Hamilton. *Crimes of Obedience.* New Haven: Yale University Press, 1989.
Kirkpatrick, Jeane. *Leader and Vanguard in Mass Society: A Study of Peronist Argentina.* Cambridge, Mass.: MIT Press, 1971.
Klandermans, Bert, Hanspeter Kriesi, and Sidney Tarrow, eds. *From Structure to Action: Comparing Social Movement Research across Cultures.* International Social Movement Research, vol. 1. Greenwich, Conn.: JAI Press, 1988.
Klandermans, Bert, ed. *Organizing for Change: Social Movement Organizations in Europe and the United States.* International Social Movement Research, vol. 2. Greenwich, Conn.: JAI Press, 1989.
Krasner, Stephen D., ed. *International Regimes.* Ithaca, N.Y.: Cornell University Press, 1983.
Kriesi, Hanspeter. "The Interdependence of Structure and Action: Some Reflections on the State of the Art." In *From Structure to Action: Comparing Social Movement Research across Cultures,* ed. Bert Klandermans, Hanspeter Kriesi, and Sidney Tarrow. Greenwich, Conn.: JAI Press, 1988.
Kuper, Leo. *The Prevention of Genocide.* New Haven: Yale University Press, 1985.
Laclau, Ernst. "New Social Movements and the Plurality of the Social." In *New Social Movements and the State in Latin America,* ed. D. Slater. Amsterdam: CEDLA, 1985.
Laitin, David. "Capitalism and Hegemony: Yorubaland and the International System." *International Organization* 36, no. 4 (Autumn 1982): 687–713.
Lamas, Raúl. *Los torturadores: Crimenes y tormentos en las carceles argentinas.* Buenos Aires: Editorial Lamas, 1956.
Landi, Oscar. *El discurso sobre lo posible: (La democracia y el realismo político).* Buenos Aires: Centro de Estudios del Estado y Sociedad, 1985.
————. "La transición política argentina y la cuestión de los derechos humanos." In *Los derechos humanos como política,* ed. Hugo Villela. Santiago: Ediciones Amerinda, 1985.
————. *Las culturas políticas en numeros: Argentina en democracia.* Madrid: Editorial Centro de Investigación Sociologica de Madrid, forthcoming.
————. *Reconstrucciones: Las nuevas formas de la cultura política.* Buenos Aires: Puntosur Editores, 1988.
Langan, John. "Defining Human Rights." In *Human Rights in the Americas: The Struggle for Consensus,* ed. Alfred T. Hennelly and John P. Langan. Washington, D.C.: Georgetown University Press, 1982.
Latin American Studies Association. *La represión en Argentina, 1973–74.* Mexico City: Universidad Nacional Autonoma de Mexico, 1978.

Lázara, Simón. *Poder militar: Origen, apogeo y transición*. Buenos Aires: Editorial Legasa, 1988.

Lechner, Norbert. *Los derechos humanos como categoria política*. FLACSO Working Paper no. 201. Santiago, Chile: Faculdad Latinoamericano de Ciencias Sociales, 1983.

Lefort, Claude. *Democracy and Political Theory*. Cambridge: Basil Blackwell, 1988.

Leís, Hector Ricardo. *El movimiento por los derechos humanos y la política argentina*. Buenos Aires: Centro Editor de América Latina, 1989.

Leuco, Alfredo, and José Antonio Diaz. *Los herederos de Alfonsín*. Buenos Aires: Sudamericana Planeta, 1984.

Levine, Daniel. "Religion and Politics in Comparative and Historical Perspective." *Comparative Politics* 19, no. 1 (Oct. 1986): 95–122.

El libro del diario del juicio. Buenos Aires: Perfil, 1985.

Linz, Juan. "Totalitarian and Authoritarian Regimes." In *Handbook of Political Science*, ed. F. Greenstein and N. Polsby, 175–411. Reading, Mass.: Addison-Wesley, 1975.

Linz, Juan J., and Alfred Stepan. *The Breakdown of Democratic Regimes: Latin America*. Baltimore: Johns Hopkins University Press, 1978.

Lipsky, Michael. "Protest as a Political Resource." *American Political Science Review* 62, no. 4 (Dec. 1968): 1144–59.

Little, Walter. "The Popular Origins of Peronism." In *Argentina in the Twentieth Century*, ed. David Rock, 162–78. Pittsburgh: University of Pittsburgh Press, 1975.

Lofland, John, and Michael Fink. *Symbolic Sit-Ins*. Washington: University Press of America, 1982.

López, Daniel, ed. *Catalogo del nuevo cine argentino, 1984–1986*. Buenos Aires: INCINE, 1986.

López, Ernesto. "La Reforma Debida." *Unidos* 4, no. 9 (Apr. 1986): 100–106.

———. *El último levantamiento*. Buenos Aires: Legasa, 1988.

López, George. "National Security Ideology as an Impetus to State Violence and State Terror." In *Government Violence and Repression: An Agenda for Research*, ed. Michael Stohl and George López. New York: Greenwood Press, 1986.

López Saavedra, Emiliana. *Apelación a la democracia*. Buenos Aires: Editorial Redacción, 1983.

———. *Testigos del "proceso" militar*. Buenos Aires: Centro Editor de América Latina, 1984.

Lowenthal, Abraham F. *Armies and Politics in Latin America*. New York: Holmes & Meier, 1976.

———, ed. *Exporting Democracy: The United States and Latin America*. Baltimore: Johns Hopkins University Press, 1991.

Lowi, Theodore. *The Politics of Disorder*. New York: Basic Books, 1971.

Lozada, Salvador Maria, et al. *Inseguridad y desnacionalización: La "doctrina" de la seguridad nacional*. Buenos Aires: Ediciones Derechos del Hombre, 1985.

Lukes, Steven. *Power: A Radical View*. London: Macmillan, 1974.

Madsen, Douglas. "Political Self-Efficacy Tested." *American Political Science Review* 81, no. 2 (June 1987): 571–81.

Madsen, Douglas, and Peter G. Snow. "Recruitment Contrasts in a Divided Charismatic Movement." *American Political Science Review* 81, no. 1 (Mar. 1987): 233–38.

Mainwaring, Scott. "Authoritarianism and Democracy in Argentina." *Journal of Interamerican Studies and World Affairs* 26, no. 3 (Aug. 1984): 415–31.

————. "Urban Popular Movements, Identity, and Democratization in Brazil." *Comparative Political Studies* 20, no. 2 (July 1987): 131–59.

Mainwaring, Scott, and Eduardo Viola. "New Social Movements, Political Culture and Democracy: Brazil and Argentina in the 1980s." *Telos*, no. 61 (Fall 1984): 17–52.

Malamud-Goti, Jaime. "Transitional Governments in the Breach: Why Punish State Criminals?" *Human Rights Quarterly* 12 (Feb. 1990): 1–16.

Malloy, James M., and Mitchell A. Seligson. *Authoritarians and Democrats: Regime Transition in Latin America*. Pittsburgh: University of Pittsburgh Press, 1987.

Marín, Juan Carlos. *Los hechos armados, un ejercicio posible*. Buenos Aires: CICSO, 1984.

Martínez, Tomás Eloy. *La novela de Perón*. Buenos Aires: Editorial Legasa, 1987.

Marwell, Gerald, and Pamela Oliver. "Collective Action Theory." In *Research in Social Movements, Conflicts and Change*, vol. 7. Greenwich, Conn.: JAI Press, 1984.

Mason, T. David. "Non-Elite Response to State-Sanctioned Terror." Paper presented at the Annual Meeting of the American Political Science Association, Washington, D.C., August 1986.

Mattarollo, Rodolfo. "Crímenes imprescriptibles." *Crisis*, no. 50 (Jan. 1987): 61.

McAdam, Doug. *Political Process and Black Insurgency, 1930–1970*. Chicago: University of Chicago Press, 1982.

Melucci, Alberto. "The Symbolic Challenge of Contemporary Movements." *Social Research* 52, no. 4 (Winter 1985): 789–817.

————. *Nomads of the Present: Social Movements and Individual Needs in Contemporary Society*. Edited by John Keane and Paul Meier. London: Hutchinson Radius, 1989.

Meyer, Lorenzo. "Democracy from Three Latin American Perspectives." In *Democracy in the Americas: Stopping the Pendulum*, ed. Robert Pastor, 28–45. New York: Holmes & Meier, 1989.

Mignone, Emilio F. *Educación cívica*. Buenos Aires: Ediciones Colihue, 1986.

————. *Iglesia y dictadura*. Buenos Aires: Ediciones del Pensamiento Nacional, 1986.

————. *Organizaciones de derechos humanos en la Argentina*. Buenos Aires: Centro de Estudios Legales y Sociales, n.d.

Mignone, Emilio F., Cynthia L. Estlund, and Samuel Issacharoff. "Dictatorship on Trial: Prosecution of Human Rights Violations in Argentina." *Yale Journal of International Law* 10, no. 1 (Fall 1984).

Miguens, Jose Enrique. *Honor militar, conciencia moral y violencia terrorista*. Buenos Aires: Sudamericana/Planeta, 1986.

Mirelman, Victor. "The Semana Trágica of 1919 and the Jews of Argentina." *Jewish Social Studies* 37 (Jan. 1975): 61–73.

Mitchell, Christopher, Michael Stohl, David Carleton, and George A. López. "State Terrorism: Issues of Concept and Measurement." In *Government Violence and Repression: An Agenda for Research*, ed. Michael Stohl and George López. New York: Greenwood Press, 1986.

Mitchell, Neil, Rhoda Howard, and Jack Donnelly. "Liberalism, Human Rights and Human Dignity." *American Political Science Review* 81, no. 3 (Sept. 1987): 921–27.

Mittelbach, Federico. *Informe sobre desaparecedores*. Buenos Aires: Ediciones de la Urraca, 1986.

Molino, Leonardo. "Democratic Establishments." In *Comparing New Democracies*, ed. Enrique Baloyra, 53–78. Boulder, Colo.: Westview Press, 1987.

Mols, Manfred. "La Argentina: El difícil camino hacia la normalidad democrática." In *La nueva democracia argentina, 1983–1986*. ed. Ernesto Garzón Valdés, Manfred Mols, and Arnold Spitta. Buenos Aires: Editorial Sudamericana, 1988.

Moncalvillo, Mona, Alberto Fernandez, and Manuel Martin. *Juicio a la impunidad*. Buenos Aires: Ediciones Tarso, 1985.

Moncalvillo, Mona, and Alberto Fernandez. *La renovación fundacional*. Buenos Aires, 1986.

Moneta, Carlos. "Doctrinas de Seguridad y Proceso Político." In *Seguridad nacional y relaciones internacionales: Argentina*. ed. José Thiago Cintra, 33–35. Mexico: Centro Latinoamericano de Estudios Estratégicos, 1987.

Montealegre, Hernan. "Security of the State and Human Rights." In *Human Rights in the Americas: The Struggle for Consensus*, ed. Alfred T. Hennelly and John P. Langan. Washington, D.C.: Georgetown University Press, 1982.

Montenegro, Nestor. *Así piensa. . . Luciano Benjamin Menéndez*. Buenos Aires: Nemont Ediciones, 1981.

Monteón, Michael. "Can Argentina's Democracy Survive Economic Disaster?" In *From Military Rule to Liberal Democracy in Argentina*, ed. Monica Peralta-Ramos and Carlos H. Waisman, 21–38. Boulder, Colo.: Westview Press, 1987.

Montes, Graciela. *¿Qué es esto de la democracia?* Buenos Aires: Libros del Quirquincho, 1986.

———. *Los derechos de todos*. Buenos Aires: Libros del Quirquincho, 1986.

Montovio, Ismael. *Derechos humanos y terrorismo*. Buenos Aires: Ediciones De-Palma, 1980.

Montserrat, Marcelo. "Inspiraciones de la actual política de defensa en la Argentina." In *Seguridad nacional y relaciones internacionales: Argentina*, ed. José Thiago Cintra, 17–26. Buenos Aires: Centro de Latinoamericano de Estudios Estratégicos, 1987.

Moore, Barrington. *Social Origins of Dictatorship and Democracy*. Boston: Beacon Press, 1966.

———. *Injustice: Social Bases of Obedience and Revolt*. White Plains, N.Y.: M. E. Sharpe, 1979.

Morande, Pedro. "Comment." In *Los derechos humanos como política*, ed. Hugo Villela, 75–80. Santiago, Chile: Ediciones Amerinda, 1985.

Mora y Araujo, Manuel. "The Nature of the Alfonsín Coalition." In *Elections and Democratization in Latin America*, ed. Paul W. Drake and Eduardo Silva, 175–88. San Diego: UCSD, 1986.

Mount, Ferdinand. *The Theatre of Politics*. New York: Schocken Books, 1973.

Multipartidaria Nacional. *Antes que sea tarde: Propuesta y llamamiento al país*. Buenos Aires: El Cid Editor, 1981.

Munck, Gerardo. "Identity and Ambiguity in Democratic Struggles." In *Popular Movements and Political Change in Mexico*, ed. Ann Craig and Joe Foweraker, 23–42. Boulder, Colo.: Lynne Rienner, 1990.

Nash, June, and Helen Icken Safa, eds. *Sex and Class in Latin America*. New York: Bergin, 1980.

Navarro, Maryssa. "The Personal Is Political: Las Madres de Plaza de Mayo." In *Power and Popular Protest*, ed. Susan Eckstein, 241–58. Berkeley and Los Angeles: University of California Press, 1989.

Neuman, Elias. "Encierro carcelario." In *Los derechos humanos en el "otro país,"* ed. Daniel Barberis, 185–216. Buenos Aires: Puntosur, 1987.

Nickel, James W. *Making Sense of Human Rights*. Berkeley and Los Angeles: University of California Press, 1987.

Norden, Deborah. "Democratic Consolidation and Military Professionalism: Argentina in the 1980's." *Journal of Interamerican Studies and World Affairs* 32, no. 3 (Fall 1990): 151–76.

Nosiglia, Julio. *Botín de guerra*. Buenos Aires: Abuelas de Plaza de Mayo, 1985.

Nun, José, and Juan Carlos Portantiero. *Ensayos sobre la transición democrática en la Argentina*. Buenos Aires: Puntosur, 1987.

Oberschall, Anthony. *Social Conflict and Social Movements*. New York: Prentice-Hall, 1973.

O'Brien, Philip, and Paul Cammack. *Generals in Retreat: The Crisis of Military Rule in Latin America*. Manchester: Manchester University Press, 1985.

O'Donnell, Guillermo. *Modernization and Bureaucratic-Authoritarianism*. Berkeley: Institute of International Studies, 1973.

———. "Reflections on Patterns of Change in Bureaucratic Authoritarianism." *Latin American Research Review* 13, no. 1 (1978): 3–38.

———. "State and Alliances in Argentina: 1955–76." *Journal of Development Studies* 15, no. 1 (1978): 3–33.

———. "Tensions in the Bureaucratic-Authoritarian State and the Question of Democracy." In *The New Authoritarianism in Latin America*, ed. David Collier, 285–318. Princeton: Princeton University Press, 1979.

———. *El estado burocrático-autoritario, 1966–1973*. Buenos Aires: Editorial Belgrano, 1982.

———. *¿Y a mi, que me importa?: Notas sobre sociabilidad y política en Argentina y Brasil*. Buenos Aires: Centro de Estudios del Estado y Sociedad, 1984.

———. "Democracia en la Argentina: Micro y macro." In *Proceso, crisis y transición democrática*, ed. Oscar Oszlak, 13–30. Buenos Aires: Centro Editor de América Latina, 1987.

O'Donnell, Guillermo, and Philippe Schmitter. *Transitions from Authoritarian*

Rule: Tentative Conclusions about Uncertain Democracies. Baltimore: Johns Hopkins University Press, 1986.

Offe, Claus. "New Social Movements: Challenging the Boundaries of Institutional Politics." *Social Research* 52, no. 4 (Winter 1985): 817–69.

————. "Reflections on the Institutional Self-Transformation of Movement Politics: A Tentative Stage Model." In *Challenging the Political Order: New Social and Political Movements in Western Democracies,* ed. Russell J. Dalton and Manfred Kuechler, 232–50. New York: Oxford University Press, 1990.

Ollier, Matilde Maria. *El fenómeno insureccional y la cultura política, 1969–73.* Buenos Aires: Centro Editor de América Latina, 1986.

Olson, Mancur. *The Logic of Collective Action.* Cambridge, Mass.: Harvard University Press, 1965.

Organization of American States. Interamerican Commission on Human Rights. *Report on the Situation of Human Rights in Argentina.* Washington, D.C.: Organization of American States, 1980.

Oria, Piera Paola. *De la casa a la Plaza.* Buenos Aires: Editorial Nueva América, 1987.

Osiel, Mark. "The Making of Human Rights Policy in Argentina: The Impact of Ideas and Interests on a Legal Conflict." *Journal of Latin American Studies* 18, pt. 1 (May 1986): 135–78.

Oszlak, Oscar, ed. *"Proceso", crisis y transición democratica.* Buenos Aires: Centro Editor de América Latina, 1984.

Page, Joseph. *Perón: A Biography.* New York: Random House, 1983.

Palermo, Vicente. *Movimientos sociales y partidos políticos: Aspectos de la cuestión en la democracia emergente en la Argentina.* Buenos Aires: Centro de Estudios del Estado y Sociedad, 1986.

Paoletti, Alipio. *Como los Nazis, como en Vietnam: Los campos de concentración en la Argentina.* Buenos Aires: Editorial Contrapunto, 1987.

Parsons, Talcott. *Max Weber: The Theory of Social and Economic Organization.* New York: Free Press, 1947.

Partido Intransigente. *Síntesis de los proyectos presentados por el bloque entre diciembre de 1985 y marzo de 1988.*

Partido Justicialista. Movimiento Renovador. *Los contenidos de la esperanza.* Buenos Aires: Peronismo Renovador, 1988.

————. Secretaría de Derechos Humanos. *Los derechos humanos y el Peronismo.* Buenos Aires: Partido Justicialista, n.d.

Peralta-Ramos, Monica. "The Structural Basis of Coercion." In *From Military Rule to Liberal Democracy in Argentina,* ed. Monica Peralta-Ramos and Carlos H. Waisman, 38–68. Boulder, Colo.: Westview Press, 1987.

Peralta-Ramos, Monica, and Carlos H. Waisman, eds. *From Military Rule to Liberal Democracy in Argentina.* Boulder, Colo.: Westview Press, 1987.

Perelli, Carina. "The Legacies of Transitions to Democracy in Argentina and Uruguay." In *The Military and Democracy: The Future of Civil-Military Relations in Latin America,* ed. Louis Goodman, Johanna S. R. Mendelson, and Juan Rial, 39–54. Lexington, Mass.: D. C. Heath, 1990.

Pescatello, Anne, ed. *Female and Male in Latin America*. Pittsburgh: University of Pittsburgh Press, 1973.

Pineiro, Armando Alonso. *Cronica de la subversión en la Argentina*. Buenos Aires: Ediciones Depalma, 1980.

Pion-Berlin, David. "Political Repression and Economic Doctrines: The Case of Argentina." *Comparative Political Studies* 16, no. 1 (Apr. 1983): 37–66.

———. "The Fall of Military Rule in Argentina, 1976–83." *Journal of Interamerican Studies and World Affairs* 27, no. 2 (Summer 1985): 55–76.

———. "Military Breakdown and Redemocratization in Argentina." In *Liberalization and Redemocratization in Latin America*, ed. George López and Michael Stohl. New York: Greenwood Press, 1987.

———. *The Ideology of State Terror: Economic Doctrine and Political Repression in Argentina and Peru*. Boulder, Colo.: Lynne Riemer, 1989.

Pion-Berlin, David, and George López. "Of Victims and Executioners: Argentine State Terror, 1975–1979." *International Studies Quarterly* 35, no. 1 (March 1991): 63–87.

Piven, Frances Fox, and Richard Cloward. *Poor People's Movements: Why They Succeed, How They Fail*. New York: Vintage Books, 1979.

Pizzorno, Alesandro. "Political Exchange and Collective Identity in Industrial Conflict." In *The Resurgence of Class Conflict in Western Europe since 1968*, vol. 2, ed. Colin Crouch. New York: Holmes & Meier, 1978.

Platt, D. C. M., and Guido Di Tella. *Argentina, Australia and Canada: Studies in Comparative Development, 1870–1965*. Oxford: Macmillan, 1985.

Poneman, Daniel. *Argentina: Democracy on Trial*. New York: Paragon, 1987.

Popkin, Samuel. *The Rational Peasant*. Berkeley and Los Angeles: University of California Press, 1979.

Portantiero, Juan Carlos. "La transicíon entre la confrontacíon y el acuerdo." In *Ensayos sobre la transicíon democratica en la Argentina*, ed. José Nun and Juan Carlos Portantiero, 257–94. Buenos Aires: Puntosur Editores, 1987.

Potash, Robert A. *The Army and Politics in Argentina, 1945–62: Perón to Frondizi*. Stanford: Stanford University Press, 1980.

Potter, Anne. "The Failure of Democracy in Argentina, 1916–1930: An Institutional Perspective." *Journal of Latin American Studies* 13, no. 1 (May 1981): 83–109.

Pozzi, Pablo A. "Argentina 1976–1982: Labour Leadership and Military Government." *Journal of Latin American Studies* 20 (May 1988): 111–38.

———. *Oposición obrera a la dictadura, 1976–1982*. Buenos Aires: Editorial Contrapunto, 1988.

Przeworski, Adam. "Some Problems in the Study of the Transition to Democracy." In *Transitions to Democracy*, ed. Philippe Schmitter, Guillermo O'Donnell, and Laurence Whitehead. Baltimore: Johns Hopkins University Press, 1986.

———. *Democracy and the Market*. New York: Cambridge University Press, 1991.

Ranis, Peter. "The Dilemmas of Democratization in Argentina." *Current History* 85, no. 507 (Jan. 1986): 29–33.

Rattenbach, Col. A. B., et al. *Fuerzas armadas argentinas: El cambio necesario.* Buenos Aires: Editorial Galerna, 1987.

Remmer, Karen. "Redemocratization and the Impact of Authoritarian Rule in Latin America." *Comparative Politics* 17, no. 3 (Apr. 1985): 253–75.

República Argentina. *Diario de sesiones: Senadores/Diputados.* 1983–89.

———. *El derecho a la libertad.* Buenos Aires: Ejercito Argentino, 1980.

———. *Observaciones y comentarios críticos del gobierno argentino al informe de la CIDH sobre la situación de los derechos humanos en la Argentina.* Buenos Aires, 1980.

———. *Documento final de la junta militar sobre la guerra contra la subversión y el terrorismo.* Buenos Aires: Registro Oficial, 1983.

———. *Los primeros 100 días de la democracia.* Buenos Aires: Secretaría de Información Pública, 1984.

———. *Tres años ganados: Balance de gestión del gobierno democrático desde el 10 de diciembre de 1983 hasta diciembre de 1986.* Buenos Aires: Secretaría de Cultura de la Nación, 1987.

———. *La Subsecretaría de Derechos Humanos y la CONADEP: Informe sobre las tareas realizadas.* Buenos Aires: Ministerio del Interior, 1987.

———. *Ejercito Argentino, Marxismo, y subversión.* Buenos Aires: Estado Mayor General del Ejercito, n.d.

Rial, Juan. "The Armed Forces and the Question of Democracy in Latin America." In *The Military and Democracy: The Future of Civil-Military Relations in Latin America*, ed. Louis Goodman, Johanna S. R. Mendelson, and Juan Rial, 277–95. Lexington, Mass.: D. C. Heath, 1990.

Rochon, Thomas R. *Mobilizing for Peace: The Antinuclear Movement in Western Europe.* Princeton: Princeton University Press, 1988.

Rock, David. "Lucha civil en la Argentina: La semana trágica de enero de 1919." *Desarrollo economico* 11, no. 42 (July 1971): 165–215.

———. *Politics in Argentina, 1890–1930: The Rise and Fall of Radicalism.* London: Cambridge University Press, 1975.

———. "Radical Populism and the Conservative Elite, 1912–1930." In *Argentina in the Twentieth Century*, ed. David Rock, 66–87. Pittsburgh: University of Pittsburgh Press, 1975.

———. "The Survival and Restoration of Peronism." In *Argentina in the Twentieth Century*, ed. David Rock, 179–221. Pittsburgh: University of Pittsburgh Press, 1975.

———. *Argentina, 1516–1987.* Berkeley and Los Angeles: University of California Press, 1987.

———. "Political Movements in Argentina." In *From Military Rule to Liberal Democracy in Argentina*, ed. Monica Peralta-Ramos and Carlos H. Waisman, 3–19. Boulder, Colo.: Westview Press, 1987.

Rock, David, ed. *Argentina in the Twentieth Century.* Pittsburgh: University of Pittsburgh Press, 1975.

Rodriguez Molas, Ricardo. *Historia de la tortura y el orden represivo en la Argentina.* Buenos Aires: Editorial de la Universidad de Buenos Aires, 1987.

Rojas, Federico E. *Violaciones de los derechos humanos bajo el gobierno constitucional.* Buenos Aires: Privately printed, 1987.

Rosales, Juan. "La reconciliación (o cómo convertir la 'guerra sucia' en 'guerra santa')." In *El complot militar: Un país en obediencia debida.* Buenos Aires: Ediciones Dialectica, 1987.

Rosenberg, Shawn. *Reason, Ideology, and Politics.* Durham, N.C.: Duke University Press, 1988.

Rosenthal, Naomi, and Michael Schwartz. "Spontaneity and Democracy in Social Movements." In *From Structure to Action: Comparing Social Movement Research across Cultures,* ed. Bert Klandermans, Hanspeter Kriesi, and Sidney Tarrow. Greenwich, Conn.: JAI Press, 1988.

Rossi, Phillip. "Moral Community, Imagination and Human Rights." In *Human Rights in the Americas: The Struggle for Consensus,* ed. Alfred T. Hennelly and John P. Langan. Washington, D.C.: Georgetown University Press, 1982.

Rouquié, Alain. "Hegemonía militar, estado y dominación social." In *Argentina hoy,* ed. Alain Rouquié. Mexico City: Siglo Veintiuno, 1982.

————. *Poder militar y sociedad política en la Argentina, 1943–1973.* Translated by Arturo Iglesias Echegaray. Buenos Aires: Emecé, 1982.

Roy, Eloy. "El Pañuelo Blanco de la Virgen de Tilcara." Tilcara, Argentina, 1988.

Rozitchner, Leon. *Malvinas: De la guerra sucia a la guerra limpia.* Buenos Aires: Centro Editor de América Latina, 1984.

Sancinetti, Marcelo. *Derechos humanos en la Argentina post-dictatorial.* Buenos Aires: Lerner Editores, 1988.

Scharr, John. *Legitimacy in the Modern State.* New Brunswick, N.J.: Transaction Books, 1981.

Schirmer, Jennifer. "'Those Who Die for Life Cannot Be Called Dead': Women and Human Rights Protest in Latin America." *Harvard Human Rights Yearbook,* vol. 1 (Spring 1988): 41–77.

Schoultz, Lars. *Human Rights and U.S. Policy Towards Latin America.* Princeton: Princeton University Press, 1981.

Schmitter, Philippe, Guillermo O'Donnell, and Laurence Whitehead, eds. *Transitions from Authoritarian Rule.* Baltimore: Johns Hopkins University Press, 1986.

Scobie, James R. *Buenos Aires: Plaza to Suburb, 1870–1910.* New York: Oxford University Press, 1974.

Scott, James. *Weapons of the Weak: Everyday Forms of Peasant Resistance.* New Haven: Yale University Press, 1985.

————. *Domination and the Arts of Resistance: Hidden Transcripts.* New Haven: Yale University Press, 1990.

Shifter, Michael. "Institutionalizing Human Rights in Chile and Argentina: If Not Now, When?" Paper presented at the 17th International Congress of the Latin American Studies Association, Los Angeles, Sept. 1992.

Showstack Sassoon, Anne. *Gramsci's Politics.* Minneapolis: University of Minnesota Press, 1987.

Sikkink, Kathryn. "The Effectiveness of U.S. Human Rights Policy: The Case of Argentina and Guatemala." Paper presented at the 16th International Congress of the Latin American Studies Association, Washington, D.C., April 1991.

Sikkink, Kathryn, and Lisa L. Martin. "U.S. Policy and Human Rights in Argentina and Guatemala, 1973–1980." In *Double-Edged Diplomacy: International Bargaining and Domestic Politics*, ed. Peter Evans, Harold K. Jacobson, and Robert D. Putnam, 330–62. Berkeley and Los Angeles: University of California Press, 1993.

[Sivak] Oyhanarte, Marta. *Tu ausencia, tu presencia*. Buenos Aires: Editorial Contexto, 1987.

Skocpol, Theda. *States and Social Revolutions*. Cambridge: Cambridge University Press, 1979.

Slater, D. "Social Movements and a Recasting of the Political." In *New Social Movements and the State in Latin America*, ed. D. Slater, 1–25. Amsterdam: CEDLA, 1985.

Smelser, Neil. *Theory of Collective Behavior*. New York: Free Press, 1963.

Smith, Brian. "Churches and Human Rights in Latin America." In *Churches and Politics in Latin America*, ed. Daniel Levine, 155–94. Beverly Hills, Calif.: Sage, 1979.

———. *The Church and Politics in Chile*. Princeton: Princeton University Press, 1982.

Smith, Peter H. *Argentina and the Failure of Democracy: Conflict among Political Elites*. Madison: University of Wisconsin Press, 1974.

Smith, William. "Reflections on the Political Economy of Authoritarian Rule and Capitalist Reorganization in Contemporary Argentina." In *Generals in Retreat: The Crisis of Military Rule in Latin America*, ed. Philip O'Brien and Paul Cammack, 37–88. Manchester: Manchester University Press, 1985.

———. *Authoritarianism and the Crisis of the Argentine Political Economy*. Stanford: Stanford University Press, 1989.

Snow, Clyde C., and Maria Julia Bihurriet. "An Epidemiology of Homicide: *Ningún nombre* Burials in the Province of Buenos Aires from 1970 to 1984." In *Human Rights and Statistics*, ed. Thomas B. Jabine and Richard P. Claude, 328–63. Philadelphia: University of Pennsylvania Press, 1992.

Snow, David P., and Robert D. Benford. "Ideology, Frame Resonance and Participant Mobilization." In *From Structure to Action: Comparing Social Movement Research across Cultures*, ed. Bert Klandermans, Hanspeter Kriesi, and Sidney Tarrow, 197–217. Greenwich, Conn.: JAI Press, 1988.

Snow, Peter. *Political Forces in Argentina*. Boston: Allyn & Bacon, 1971.

Solberg, Carl. *Immigration and Nationalism: Argentina and Chile, 1890–1914*. Austin: University of Texas Press, 1970.

———. "Land Tenure and Land Settlement: Policy and Patterns in the Canadian Prairies and the Argentine Pampas, 1880–1930." In *Argentina, Australia and Canada: Studies in Comparative Development, 1870–1965*, ed. D. C. M. Platt and Guido DiTella, 53–75. Oxford: Macmillan Press, 1985.

———. *The Prairies and the Pampas*. Stanford: Stanford University Press, 1987.

Sondreguer, Maria. "El movimiento de derechos humanos en la Argentina." In

Los nuevos movimientos sociales, ed. Elizabeth Jelin, 7–35. Buenos Aires: Centro Editor de América Latina, 1985.

Spitta, Arnold. "Experiencias cotidianas en la primera etapa de la recuperada democracia acerca de algunos elementos de la cultura política argentina." In *La nueva democracia argentina, 1983–1986*. ed. Ernesto Garzón Valdés, Manfred Mols, and Arnold Spitta. Buenos Aires: Editorial Sudamericana, 1988.

Staub, Ervin. *The Roots of Evil: The Origins of Genocide and Other Group Violence.* New York: Cambridge University Press, 1989.

Stepan, Alfred. *Rethinking Military Politics: Brazil and the Southern Cone.* Princeton: Princeton University Press, 1988.

Stohl, Michael, and George López, eds. *The State as Terrorist: The Dynamics of Government Violence and Repression.* New York: Greenwood Press, 1984.

———. *Government Violence and Repression.* New York: Greenwood Press, 1986.

Stohl, Michael. "Outside of a Small Circle of Friends: States, Genocide, Mass Killing and the Role of Bystanders." *Journal of Peace Research* 24, no. 2 (June 1987): 151–66.

Strassera, Julio C., and Luis Moreno Ocampo. *Será justicia: Entrevistas.* Buenos Aires: Distal, 1986.

Tarrow, Sidney. *Struggling to Reform: Social Movements and Policy Change During Cycles of Protest.* Western Societies Occasional Papers, no. 15. Ithaca, N.Y.: Cornell University, 1984.

———. "National Politics and Collective Action: Recent Theory and Research in Western Europe and the U.S." In *Annual Review of Sociology*, vol. 14, ed. W. Richard Scott and Judith Blake, 421–40. Palo Alto: Annual Reviews, 1988.

———. *Struggle, Politics, and Reform: Collective Action, Social Movements, and Cycles of Protest.* Western Societies Occasional Papers, no. 21. Ithaca, N.Y.: Cornell University, 1989.

Taussig, Michael. "Culture of Terror—Space of Death." *Comparative Studies in Society and History* 26, no. 3 (July 1984): 467–97.

Tello, Angel. *Algunas reflexiones sobre teoría, doctrina e hipótesis de conflicto.* Buenos Aires: Fundación Sergio Karakachoff, 1987.

Terán, Oscar. "El discurso del orden." *Cuadernos de marcha* 1, no. 2 (July–Aug. 1979): 49–54.

Thiago Cintra, José, ed. *Seguridad nacional y relaciones internacionales: Argentina.* Buenos Aires: Centro Latinoamericano de Estudios Estratégicos, 1987.

Tiano, Susan. "Authoritarianism and Political Culture in Argentina and Chile in the Mid-1960's." *Latin American Research Review* 21, no. 1 (1986): 73–98.

Tilly, Charles. *The Formation of Nation States in Western Europe.* Princeton: Princeton University Press, 1975.

———. *From Mobilization to Revolution.* Reading, Mass.: Addison-Wesley, 1978.

———. "Models and Realities of Collective Action." *Social Research* 52, no. 4 (Winter 1985): 717–47.

———. "European Violence and Collective Action since 1700." *Social Research* 53, no. 1 (Spring 1986): 159–84.

Timerman, Jacobo. *Prisoner Without a Name, Cell Without a Number.* Translated by Toby Talbot. New York: Random House, 1981.

Torres Molina, Ramón. *Inconstitucionalidad de la ley de Punto Final.* Buenos Aires: Abuelas de Plaza de Mayo, n.d.

————. "La problemática específica de los niños desaparecidos." In *La Desaparición: crimen contra la humanidad.* ed. Patricia Tappata de Valdez, 137–48. Buenos Aires: APDH, 1987.

Touraine, Alain. "An Introduction to the Study of Social Movements." *Social Research* 52, no. 4 (Winter 1985): 749–89.

Treng, Ana. "Argentina: Women of the Plaza de Mayo." *NACLA Report on the Americas* 15, no. 3 (May–June 1981): 48.

Troncoso, Oscar. *El Proceso de reorganización nacional.* Buenos Aires: Centro Editor de América Latina, 1984.

Tulchin, Joseph. *Argentina and the United States: A Conflicted Relationship.* Boston: Twayne, 1990.

Turner, Frederick, and José Enrique Miguens. *Juan Perón and the Reshaping of Argentina.* Pittsburgh: University of Pittsburgh Press, 1983.

Turner, Ralph. "Determinants of Social Movement Strategies." In *Human Nature and Collective Behavior*, ed. Tamotsu Shibutani, 145–64. Englewood Cliffs, N.J.: Prentice-Hall, 1970.

Turner, Victor. *Dramas, Fields, and Metaphors: Symbolic Action in Human Society.* Ithaca, N.Y.: Cornell University Press, 1974.

Tweedy, John, Jr. "The Argentine 'Dirty War' Trials: The First Latin American Nuremberg?" *Guild Practitioner* 44 (Winter 1987): 15–32.

Ubertalli, Jorge Luis. *¡Al suelo señores . . . !: La matanza de Ingeniero Budge.* Buenos Aires: Puntosur, 1987.

Unión Cívica Radical. Juventud Radical. "Comunicado interno." Mar del Plata Aug. 1986.

Unión Cívica Radical. Juventud Radical. Comisión de Derechos Humanos. First national meeting. "Documento final de conclusiones." Mina Clavero, Oct. 1986.

————. "Las instrucciones al fiscal militar." Mimeograph. Buenos Aires, n.d.

————. "La Ley de Obediencia Debida." Mimeograph. Buenos Aires, n.d.

————. "Propuesta de creación de comités de defensa de la democracia." Buenos Aires: UCR, n.d.

United Nations. Human Rights Commission. *Prevention of the Disappearance of Children.* E/CN.4/Sub.2/1988/19.

Vacs, Aldo. "Authoritarian Breakdown and Redemocratization in Argentina." In *Authoritarians and Democrats: Regime Transition in Latin America*, ed. James M. Malloy and Mitchell A. Seligson, 15–42. Pittsburgh: University of Pittsburgh Press, 1987

Varas, Augusto. "Democratization and Military Reform in Argentina." In *Democracy under Siege*, ed. Augusto Varas, 50–65. New York: Greenwood Press–SSRC, 1989.

Varela-Cid, Eduardo, ed. *Los sofistas y la prensa canalla.* Buenos Aires: El Cid, 1984.

Vázquez, Enrique. *PRN (Proceso) la última—origen, apogeo y caída de la dictadura militar.* Buenos Aires: Editorial de la Universidad de Buenos Aires, 1985.

Veiga, Raúl. *Las organizaciones de derechos humanos.* Buenos Aires: Centro Editor de América Latina, 1985.

Vélez-Ibañez, Carlos. *Rituals of Marginality: Politics, Process, and Culture Change in Urban Central Mexico, 1969–1974.* Berkeley and Los Angeles: University of California Press, 1983.

Veliz, Claudio. *The Politics of Conformity in Latin America.* London: Oxford University Press, 1967.

Verbitsky, Horacio. *Ezeiza.* Buenos Aires: Editorial Contrapunto, 1985.

————. *La posguerra sucia: Un análisis de la transición.* Buenos Aires: Editorial Legasa, 1985.

————. *Civiles y militares: memoria secreta de la transición.* Buenos Aires: Editorial Contrapunto, 1987.

————. *Medio siglo de proclamas militares.* Buenos Aires: Editora 12, 1987.

Vezetti, Hugo. "El juicio: Un ritual de la memoria colectiva." *Punto de Vista* 7, no. 24 (Aug.–Sept. 1985): 3–5.

Villalba Walsh, Alfredo. *Tiempos de ira, tiempos de esperanza.* Buenos Aires: Rafael Cedeno Editor, 1984.

Villareal, Juan. "Changes in Argentine Society: The Heritage of the Dictatorship." In *From Military Rule to Liberal Democracy in Argentina,* ed. Monica Peralta-Ramos and Carlos H. Waisman, 69–89. Boulder, Colo.: Westview Press, 1987.

Villela, Hugo, ed. *Los derechos humanos como política.* Santiago, Chile: Ediciones Amerinda, 1985.

Waisbord, Silvio. "Politics and Identity in the Argentine Army: Cleavages and the Generational Factor." *Latin American Research Review* 26, no. 2 (1991): 157–70.

Waisman, Carlos. "The Legitimation of Democracy under Adverse Conditions: The Case of Argentina." In *From Military Rule to Liberal Democracy in Argentina,* ed. Monica Peralta-Ramos and Carlos H. Waisman, 97–110. Boulder, Colo.: Westview Press, 1987.

————. *Reversal of Development in Argentina: Postwar Counterrevolutionary Policies and Their Structural Consequences.* Princeton: Princeton University Press, 1987.

————. "Argentina: Autarkic Industrialization and Illegitimacy." In *Democracy in Developing Countries: Latin America,* ed. Larry Diamond, Juan Linz, and Seymour Martin Lipset, 59–110. Boulder, Colo.: Lynne Riemer, 1989.

Waterman, Harvey. "Reasons and Reason: Collective Political Activity." *World Politics* 33, no. 4 (July 1981): 554–89.

Webb, K., et al. "Etiology and Outcomes of Protest: New European Perspectives." *American Behavioral Scientist* 26, no. 3 (1983): 311–31.

Weber, Max. *Theory of Social and Economic Organization.* Glencoe, Ill.: Free Press, 1964.

Weschler, Lawrence. *A Miracle, a Universe: Settling Accounts with Torturers.* New York: Pantheon, 1990.

Whitehead, Lawrence. "The Consolidation of Fragile Democracies: A Discussion With Illustrations." In *Democracy in the Americas: Stopping the Pendulum,* ed. Robert Pastor, 78–95. New York: Holmes & Meier, 1989.

————. "International Aspects of Democratization." In *Transitions to Democracy*, ed. Philippe Schmitter, Guillermo O'Donnell, and Lawrence Whitehead, 3–46. Baltimore: Johns Hopkins University Press, 1986.

Wiarda, Howard. *Politics and Society in Latin America: The Distinct Tradition*. Boston: University of Massachusetts Press, 1982.

Wilson, James Q. *Political Organizations*. New York: Basic Books, 1973.

Wynia, Gary. *Argentina in the Post-War Era: Politics and Economic Policy-Making in a Divided Society*. Albuquerque: University of New Mexico Press, 1978.

Zaffaroni, Eugenio. *Sistemas penales y derechos humanos en América Latina: Instituto Interamericano de Derechos Humanos (1982–1986)*. Buenos Aires: Ediciones Depalma, 1986.

Zagorski, Paul. "Civil-Military Relations and Argentine Democracy." *Armed Forces and Society* 14, no. 3 (Spring 1988): 407–32.

Zuleta Alvarez, Enrique. "El concepto de la democracia argentina en el contexto latinoamericano." In *La nueva democracia argentina, 1983–1986*, ed. Ernesto Garzón Valdés, Manfred Mols, and Arnold Spitta. Buenos Aires: Editorial Sudamericana, 1988.

Periodicals

Buenos Aires Herald.
La Causa Peronista (Buenos Aires).
El Chasqui (Tilcara, Argentina).
Christian Science Monitor.
El Ciudadano [UCR], (Buenos Aires).
Clarín (Buenos Aires).
Gente (Buenos Aires).
Humor (Buenos Aires).
Jotapé [Juventud Peronista], (Buenos Aires).
Lancet (London).
Latin American Database (Albuquerque, N.M.)
Latin America Regional Report—Southern Cone.
Latin America Weekly Report.
La Nación (Buenos Aires).
New York Times.
Página Doce (Buenos Aires).
El Periodista (Buenos Aires).
El Porteño (Buenos Aires).
La Prensa (Buenos Aires).
¿Que Pasa?
La Razón (Buenos Aires).
La República: Vocero de la Democracia Argentina en el Exilio—Organo Oficial de Exiliados del Radicalismo Argentino (Paris).
Revista del Circulo Militar (Buenos Aires).
San Diego Union.

San Francisco Chronicle.
Sur (Buenos Aires).
Tenemos la Palabra (Buenos Aires).
Tiempo Argentino (Buenos Aires).
Tributo [FAMUS—Familiares de los Muertos por la Subversión], (Buenos Aires).
Unidos [Peronismo Renovador], (Buenos Aires).
La Voz (Buenos Aires).
La Voz del Interior (Córdoba).
Washington Post.

Publications by Argentine Human Rights Organizations

1. Abuelas de Plaza de Mayo

Informaciones (newsletter). Buenos Aires.
Missing Children Who Disappeared in Argentina, 1976–1983. Translated by Ricardo Couch. Buenos Aires: Abuelas de Plaza de Mayo, n.d.
Torres Molina, Ramón. *Inconstitucionalidad de la ley de Punto Final.* Buenos Aires: Abuelas de Plaza de Mayo, n.d.

2. Asamblea Permanente por los Derechos Humanos

Derechos Humanos (newsletter). Buenos Aires.
Familiares de Detenidos y Desaparecidos. *Exigimos JUSTICIA porque queremos la PAZ: La familia víctima de la represión.* Neuquén, Argentina: APDH (Delegacíon Neuquén) and Comisión de Familiares de Detenidos y Desaparecidos del Neuquén, 1982.
Consejo de Presidencia. Buenos Aires: APDH, 1985.
Mesa redonda: Edictos policiales y libertades. Buenos Aires: APDH, 1985.
La desaparición: Crimen contra la humanidad. Edited by Patricia Tappata de Valdez. Buenos Aires: APDH, 1987.
"Informe realizado por la APDH con la colaboración de la Comisión de Asuntos Sociales dirigida por la Sra. Graciela Fernandez Meijide." Buenos Aires: APDH, 1987.
¿Qué es APDH? Buenos Aires: APDH, n.d.

3. Asociación de Ex-Detenidos-Desaparecidos

Porque asumimos la defensa jurídica de los presos de La Tablada. Buenos Aires: Asociación de Ex-Detenidos-Desaparecidos, 1989.
Acto de presentación. Buenos Aires: Asociación de Ex-Detenidos-Desaparecidos, n.d.

4. Centro de Estudios Legales y Sociales

Boletín (newsletter). Buenos Aires.
Terrorismo de estado: 692 responsables. Buenos Aires: Centro de Estudios Legales y Sociales, 1986.
La violencia policial. Buenos Aires: Centro de Estudios Legales y Sociales, forthcoming.

5. Familiares de Desaparecidos y Detenidos por Razones Políticas

Decimos (newsletter). Buenos Aires.
Presos políticos en la República Argentina, 1988. Buenos Aires: Familiares de Los Desaparecidos y Detenidos por Razones Políticas, 1988.
Testimonios de nuestra lucha. Buenos Aires: Familiares de Los Desaparecidos y Detenidos por Razones Políticas, 1988.
Testimonios sobre la represión y la tortura. Buenos Aires.

6. Liga Argentina por los Derechos del Hombre

Sepa que es y que hace La Liga. Buenos Aires: Liga Argentina por los Derechos del Hombre, 1984.

7. Madres de Plaza de Mayo

Boletín Informativo (newsletter). Buenos Aires, –1985.
Madres de Plaza de Mayo (newsletter). Buenos Aires, 1985–.

8. Madres de Plaza de Mayo–Linea Fundadora

Hoja Informativa (newsletter). Buenos Aires, 1984–.

9. Movimiento Ecuménico por los Derechos Humanos

InformeDH (newsletter). Buenos Aires.
¿Qué es el MEDH? Buenos Aires: Movimiento Ecuménico por los Derechos Humanos, 1984.
El derecho a ser joven. Buenos Aires: Movimiento Ecuménico por los Derechos Humanos, 1986.

10. Movimiento Judío por los Derechos Humanos

Nuestra Presencia / Nueva Presencia (newsletter). Buenos Aires.

11. Servicio Paz y Justicia

Paz y Justicia (newsletter). Buenos Aires.
Confederación General de Trabajadores / Servicio Paz y Justicia. *Reforma constitucional y protagonismo popular.* Buenos Aires: CGT / SERPAJ, 1988.
The Peace and Justice Service in Latin America. Buenos Aires: Servicio Paz y Justicia, n.d.

12. Other

Abuelas, Asamblea, Asociación de Ex-Detenidos-Desaparecidos, CELS, Familiares, La Liga, Madres–Linea Fundadora, MEDH, SERPAJ. *Culpables para la sociedad, libres por la ley.* Buenos Aires: Centro de Estudios Legales y Sociales, 1987.

Abuelas, Asamblea, CELS, Familiares, La Liga, Madres–Linea Fundadora, MEDH, Movimiento Judío, SERPAJ. *Ley de Punto Final.* Buenos Aires, 1987.

Comisión Especial de la Subsecretaría de Derechos Humanos. *Carceles argentinas: ¿Suplicio o reeducación?* Buenos Aires: APDH, 1986.

Mignone, Emilio. *Organizaciones de derechos humanos en la Argentina.* Buenos Aires: Centro de Estudios Legales y Sociales, n.d.

Quilmes Human Rights Commission. "Informe sobre derechos humanos." Mimeographed. Buenos Aires, 1988.

Servicio de Asistencia Integral al Detenido. "Sepa como defenderse." Mimeograph. Buenos Aires: SASID, n.d.

———. "¿Qué es el preso social?" Mimeograph. Buenos Aires: SASID, n.d.

———. "¿Qúe es el SASID?" Mimeograph. Buenos Aires: SASID, n.d.

Index

In this index an "f" after a number indicates a separate reference on the next page, and an "ff" indicates separate references on the next two pages. A continuous discussion over two or more pages is indicated by a span of page numbers, e.g., "57–59." *Passim* is used for a cluster of references in close but not consecutive sequence.

abduction, *see* kidnapping
Abuelas de Plaza de Mayo, 43, 47–49, 53–55, 72, 78–85 *passim*, 113, 118, 124, 152, 160, 175
afectados, 45f, 56, 70, 73, 78, 91, 117, 131, 142, 145, 210, 227, 236
Agosti, Brig. Orlando, 79
agriculture, 24f, 27, 35, 58, 184
air force, 60, 79, 93, 101, 105, 212, 221f
Alerta Nacional, 104, 143, 223f
Alfonsín, Raul, 19f, 61–73, 75–104 *passim*, 117–19, 139, 141, 155, 162–67
All for the Fatherland Movement, 118–19
Allis-Chalmers, 54
Alsogaray, Alvaro, 145, 239
Alvear, Marcelo T., 29
American Association for the Advancement of Science, 72
Amin, Idi, 168, 171
amnesty, 33, 47, 61f, 67f, 75, 80f, 100, 144, 149f, 167
Amnesty International, 31, 56, 111, 129, 170, 187
Angelelli, Bishop Enrique, 150, 240f
Angeloz, Eduardo, 144

anti-Semitism, *see* Jews
"aparición con vida," 16, 125
APDH, *see* Asamblea Permanente
Appeals Court, 76–81 *passim*, 99, 211, 214, 224
Aragon, Raul, 69
Aramburu, Genl. Pedro, 27, 30
Argentina Information and Service Center, 53
Argentine Church, *see* Catholic Church
Argentine League for the Rights of Man, 29, 175
armed forces, *see* military
army, 30f, 56, 59, 67, 71, 83, 93, 99–103, 105, 140. *See also* military
Asamblea Permanente, 7, 45–47, 54–56, 66–71, 109–11, 124–25, 139–41, 144–46, 175
Astiz, Lt. Alfredo, 60, 97, 115, 199, 220
"atrocious and aberrant acts," 76, 83
Attorney General, 120, 203, 230
authoritarianism, 1–3, 13, 18–28 *passim*, 32–34, 39, 56, 107, 124–26, 141, 154, 156–57, 165

Ejercito Revolucionario del Pueblo, *see*
ERP
El exilio de Gardel, 128f
El Periodista, 72, 128
El Salvador, 170–71
elections, 28–29, 36, 61f, 77, 90, 112, 118,
126, 134, 142, 162f, 165
elite, 25, 27f, 59, 71, 102, 123, 145, 182,
184, 186, 195, 199, 211, 244
Entre Rios, 69, 71, 82, 84, 111, 115, 117,
132, 214, 229
Epelbaum, Renee, 55, 82, 214
ERP, 30, 32, 119, 187
ESMA, *see* Naval Mechanics School
estado de derecho, *see* democratic
institutions
estado de excepción, *see* state of siege
Ethical Tribunal, 131, 133
Europe, 8–9, 24, 52, 55, 168, 170f, 176,
179, 184, 241
Ex-Detainees, 70, 73, 78, 81, 115, 124,
175
Executive branch, 28, 65–69 *passim*, 80–
87 *passim*, 92, 94, 96, 112–13, 115–16,
164, 167
exhumations, 72f, 114, 125, 155, 208
Export-Import Bank, 54
exilio de Gardel, *see El exilio de Gardel*
Ezeiza airport, 32, 188

Fabricaciones Militares, *see military*
factionalism, 126, 232
Falklands War, *see* Malvinas
Familiares, 43–49 *passim*, 54, 56, 68, 78,
124f, 160, 175
Febres, Héctor, 132
FEDEFAM (Latin American Federation
of Families of the Disappeared) 147,
170
Federal Appeals Court, 76f, 80, 99, 214
Federal Police, 31, 105, 109, 112, 223, 230
feminism, 35, 49, 54, 159, 176, 178f. *See
also* women
Fernandez Meijide, Graciela, 45, 69, 70–
71, 78, 135
Final Document, 61
Ford Argentina, 86
Ford Foundation, 52, 55
foreign aid, 51–53, 170

foreign debt, 59, 141, 201, 241. *See also*
economy
Foreign Ministry, 55, 66, 118
foreign policy, 165
Forensic Anthropology Team, 73, 170,
208
Forum for Human Rights, 31
France, 36, 52, 53–56, 97, 151, 193f, 199,
212, 241
Frondizi, Arturo, 139, 186f
Fundación Para La Memoria, 132, 234

Gallery of Repressors, 131, 217
Galtieri, Leopoldo, 59, 79, 201
Gattinoni, Bishop Carlos, 69, 78
Geneva, 47, 52, 198
Germany, 168, 171, 203
government, *see specific branches and offices*
Gran Bourg, 110
Grandmothers of the Plaza de Mayo, *see*
Abuelas
grants, 52, 182, 191
Green List for a Democratic Judiciary,
114
guerrillas, 15, 29–40 *passim*, 56, 59, 61,
66, 77, 84, 95, 100, 115–22 *passim*, 156,
165. *See also* ERP; Montoneros

habeas corpus, 43, 50
Hagelin, Dagmar, 97, 115, 128, 194, 212
Harris, Tex, 55
Hesayne, Bishop Miguel, 127, 151
Holland, 55
Holmberg, Elena, 195
Holocaust, 132, 184, 198. *See also* Jews
Holy Week, *see* Semana Santa
Honor Code, 97
House, *see* Congress
human rights: reform, 3, 6, 63, 67, 74,
88, 98, 104–8 *passim*, 112–16 *passim*,
120–23 *passim*, 155, 166–68; principles
of, 7, 13–15, 46, 64–66, 109, 113, 122,
124, 162–63. *See also* disappeared;
murder; rape; torture
Humor, 127, 233

Iglesias, Herminio, 61
Illia, Arturo, 28f
immigration, 24, 118, 184

Library of Congress Cataloguing-in-Publication Data

Brysk, Alison, 1960–
    The politics of human rights in Argentina: protest, change,
and democratization / Alison Brysk
        p.   cm.
    Includes bibliographical references and index.
    ISBN 0-8047-2275-7 (alk. paper)
    1. Human rights—Argentina.   2. Civil rights—Argentina.
3. Political persecution—Argentina.   4. Argentina—Politics
and government—1955–   .   I. Title.
JC599.A7B79   1994
323'.0982—dc20   93-34802
                                                    CIP

⊗ This book is printed on acid-free paper.